IDENTITY
CRISES

IDENTITY CRISES

A Social Critique of Postmodernity

ROBERT G. DUNN

University of Minnesota Press
Minneapolis
London

Published by the University of Minnesota Press
111 Third Avenue South, Suite 290
Minneapolis, MN 55401-2520
http://www.upress.umn.edu

Library of Congress Cataloging-in-Publication Data

Dunn, Robert G.
    Identity crises : a social critique of postmodernity / Robert G. Dunn.
       p.   cm.
    Includes bibliographical references and index.
    ISBN 0-8166-3072-0 (hardcover : alk. paper).—ISBN 0-8166-3073-9
(pbk. : alk. paper)
    1. Postmodernism—Social aspects. I. Title.
HM73.D795   1998
300'.1—dc21   97-39564

In memory of my family

Contents

Acknowledgments \ ix

Introduction \ 1

1 **Regrounding Theory** The Social Relations of Identity and Difference \ 17

2 **Modernity and Postmodernity** Transformations in Identity Formation \ 51

3 **On the Transition from Modernity to Postmodernity** Transformations in Culture \ 81

4 **Explaining the Destabilization of Identity** Postmodernization, Commodification, and the Leveling of Cultural Hierarchy \ 107

5 **Identity, Politics, and the Dual Logic of Postmodernity** Fragmentation and Pluralization \ 143

6 **Redeeming the Subject** Poststructuralism, Meadian Social Pragmatism, and the Turn to Intersubjectivity \ 175

Conclusion Postmodernity and Its Theoretical Consequences \ 221

Notes \ 231

Bibliography \ 259

Index \ 281

Acknowledgments

The writing of a theoretical work, especially on a topic as layered and complex as identity and postmodernity, is necessarily indebted to people and past experiences too numerous to mention. While their influences might not be plainly evident, those professors from whom I learned my theory and culture as a student—Ernest Becker, Reinhard Bendix, Herbert Blumer, Peter Etzkorn, Leo Lowenthal, Philippe Nonet, Philip Selznick, and Neil Smelser—deserve special mention for the ways that they shaped my thinking, interests, and concerns. Over the years, Todd Gitlin has helped me to appreciate the importance of culture and the mass media and ways of thinking about them interpretively and politically.

I have also incurred a debt of gratitude to a number of people who have directly contributed in various ways to the successful completion of this book. Troy Duster and David Wellman provided advice and encouragement after reading an early statement of my plans. Elliott Currie not only read parts of the manuscript but, as an enduring friend and intellectual companion, has been a model of clarity and constructive thinking about social, political, and personal issues and their interlinkages. What I have written has benefited from the valuable and supportive comments of Barbara Epstein, Barry O'Connell, Brian Rich, Steven Seidman, and Kenneth Tucker, all of whom read pieces of the manuscript at various stages of its evolution. I also want to express special thanks to Norman Denzin and Douglas Kellner, who read a preliminary draft in its entirety, and especially to George Lipsitz, whose detailed and informed commentary and strong support for the project helped it into print.

I have benefited from many years of wide-ranging conversations with my friends David Fogarty and Terry Kandal, both of whom helped educate me about the material and political foundations of social life. I also wish to express my gratitude to Juan Gonzales, Eric Gordy, Karl Kreplin, Paul Lopes, Michael Messner, Roy King, and David Simon for their friendship, support, and many moments of intellectual and interpersonal pleasure during the years this book was coming into being. The thinking and ideas around which the book took form reflect many engaging, rigorous, and encouraging conversations with Jon Cruz and, most of all, Ron Lembo, whose knowledge, perceptions, and insights have powerfully shaped my own understandings of theory, culture, and commodity society.

To my editor at University of Minnesota Press, Micah Kleit, my gracious thanks for his abiding enthusiasm. Finally, my thanks to Michael Belfer for research assistance and to California State University at Hayward, whose funding of a Small Grant Award (1993–94) and relief from teaching duties through an RSCA Grant (1994) made it possible to finish the book.

Introduction

The postwar era in the West, especially the United States, has been witness to a complex series of intellectual, social, cultural, and political changes suggestive of major transformations, of epochal endings and beginnings, and of new perceptions and sensibilities widely characterized by the overworked term "postmodern." Despite the troublesome ambiguities of the word, the daunting task of identifying and possibly reconciling inconsistent and contradictory usages of "postmodern" is less urgent than discerning the concept's underlying thematics. While the term, its uses, and much of what it has come to represent have provoked a variety of responses, it is rare to find systematic and impartial accountings of the broad historical and institutional circumstances of its ascendance. Toward this goal, I propose in this book to situate the intellectual currency of "the postmodern" within the larger landscape of social and cultural change shaping this movement over the past several decades.

While planning originally to settle my own accounts with postmodernism through a systematic mapping and critique of its various discourses, I soon came to realize that we learn less from maps than material landmarks. Over time, my own readings made it increasingly clear that at the center of this intellectual movement was a vital but rather circumscribed preoccupation with the problem of identity. If nothing else, the mere recurrence of the term "identity" in recent academic and political discourses seemed to be a sign of something deeper at work that these discourses had insufficiently articulated. It became further apparent that questions of identity had import beyond the particular movements of the Left with which they had become associated in recent decades but had also increasingly come to define the politics of the Right. Besides being a major theme in left academic theory, questions of identity in the past twenty-five years have assumed central importance in a range of struggles and debates across the political spectrum in the United States and elsewhere. In reflecting on the postmodern controversy, it became further evident that *the concept of the postmodern itself was an attempt to articulate a growing sense of the problematization of identity as a generalized condition of life in postwar Western society.*

"Postmodernism" and "Postmodernity"

In linking the postmodern to questions of identity, historical and social context seemed to me to assume crucial importance. This, in turn, seemed to lead to a basic distinction between two interrelated aspects of the postmodern. Whereas the term "postmodernism" has occupied an influential place in academic discourse as a designation of a series of theoretical and epistemological claims or positions, some writers have employed the term "postmodernity" to refer to a series of sociohistorical developments. Accordingly, I have taken the term "postmodernism" to refer to a set of epistemological, theoretical, and political *responses* to *postmodernity,* which I define as a historically and structurally specific set of cultural conditions. I regard postmodernism as a loose array of philosophical and theoretical attitudes, a mode of inquiry and representation, and a movement, style, and mood that *reflect* and *parallel* fundamental changes in the cultural condition of Western societies, most notably the United States. However, without completely dismissing the claims of postmodernists who advocate new epistemologies and political positions, I argue that, to the extent that questions of identity are at the core of postmodern concerns, the problem of identity and identity formation needs to be addressed in a much broader, deeper, and more direct manner. Namely, I propose looking at problems of identity from within the context of *a theory of postmodernity as an objective sociohistorical condition rooted in material and technological change and corresponding transformations in the production and consumption of culture.* Additionally, while some see postmodernism as just a fashionable academic movement based in the life experiences of left university faculty, or a manifestation of postsixties political exhaustion and pessimism, I believe postmodernism needs to be understood as a theoretically suggestive yet ultimately inadequate response to the failures of the European Enlightenment. However, unlike many postmodernists, who with some justification regard the demise of the modern philosophical subject as an inevitable consequence of the rise of new collective identities, transformations in culture, and new ways of *thinking* about identity, I see a more generalized and structurally based *destabilization* of identity. I regard this destabilization as tied to economic and technological transformation in the realms of cultural production and, especially, consumption, a condition to which we have yet to formulate adequate theoretical and political responses.

Identity, Identification, and Difference

In *The Making of Political Identities*, Ernesto Laclau (1994) makes an important distinction between *identity* and *identification*. Whereas the former term designates an object of discovery or recognition, implying an originary *essence* defining the person, the latter term refers to a process of identity *construction* based on a Freudian-derived notion of "radical lack." Social and cultural change has engendered identity crises in both senses. Belief in a substantial identity determined by birth or inner life experience has been seriously eroded in twentieth-century philosophical and social thought. At the same time, sources and means of *identification* in the form of agencies external to the individual have proliferated beyond our wildest imaginations. How are we to become persons, to construct our own identities among the seemingly limitless possibilities and intrusions of contemporary life (Melucci 1996)? In a chaotic and unsettled world, how are we to fill the "lack"? Behind these questions remain unresolved issues associated with the very distinction Laclau draws. On the one hand, despite persistent attacks on "essentialisms," given the legacies of biology, birth, culture, and history, there are reasons to pause at arguments against substantialist notions of identity. On the other hand, the concept of identification raises critical questions about identity-forming processes, such as whether identities are self-constructed or externally imposed, an issue that in turn poses fundamental questions about the social and cultural relations of power.

Intersecting the tension between essentialist and constructivist conceptions of identity formation are questions of difference. How are we to define "difference," and what is the relationship between identity and difference? More centrally, why have identity and difference become such major concerns in contemporary theoretical discourse? While *identity* means sameness, with implications of continuity and repetition, *difference* means the opposite of sameness, or otherness and discontinuity. Exploring the relationship between "identity" and "difference" in her book *Identification Papers*, Diana Fuss (1995) elaborates the distinction between identity and identification, arguing that processes of identification set in motion a complicated dynamic that brings a sense of identity into being while simultaneously calling that identity into question. Identification always keeps identity at a distance, making it problematic. Importantly, Fuss points out that identification always does its work *relationally*. As "the detour through the other that defines a self," identification operates in a field of social relations, "as the play of *difference* and *similitude* in self-other relations" (Fuss 1995: 2; emphasis added). Thus, while a case might be made for preserving (strategically or otherwise) substantialist notions of identity, what we call "identity" is perhaps better thought of as the more persistently recurring elements of multiple and situationally contingent *processes of identification*. The concept of identification, then, shows how identity is constituted in and through yet problematized by difference—thus the impossibility of theorizing one without the other.

In this book, I attempt to address these questions against the grain of what I take to be the prevailing modes of thought in cultural studies and related academic fields. While acknowledging their contributions, I propose an alternative to an epistemology and politics of group-based identity and difference, arguing for a shift of focus toward the historically situated structural conditions in which identities form. Accordingly, I believe issues of identity ought to be approached not just in terms of group histories and oppressions but in relation to broad changes in the sociohistorical circumstances of social individuals.

Identity Crises, Politics, and Academic Theory

Viewed historically, the crisis of Western subjectivity at the center of postmodern thought consists of numerous interrelated identity crises. Politically speaking, the Eurocentric subject has been eclipsed by historical trends disrupting colonial and imperial relationships between Europe, the United States, and the "Third World," evident especially in the new social and cultural movements, changing patterns of immigration, and newly emerging patterns of global trade and telecommunications. Reflective of this crisis is a widespread reckoning with the historically subjugated identities of race, class, ethnicity, gender, sexuality, and other subordinated social categories and groupings. The invocation of otherness in postmodern discourse reflects, and serves to intensify, an upheaval in historically defined relations between dominants and subordinates in Western society, and their corresponding modes of representation. The modernist encodings of patriarchy, white supremacy, class privilege, heterosexuality, the domination of nature, and cultural elitism have been major targets of the new social movements, an expression of the politicization of identity and culture in many Western countries. However, alongside and interacting with these collective identity crises, *changes in the structural and institutional conditions of advanced capitalist society have generated strains on personal and social identity.* The much-commented-on fragmentation of society and culture caused by commodification and technological change casts a shadow over beliefs in a unified and coherent ego or self. The triumph of commodity society threatens inherited modern conceptions of the individual, casting doubt on previously accepted notions of personal and social identity. I argue, then, that despite recent attention to Eurocentrism and its patterns of racial, gender, and other forms of domination, broader, more diffuse but fundamental crises of personal and social identity and meaning have been occurring in the commodified structures of highly developed capitalist societies.

Certainly, our conversations about identity have had other origins. There are many possible ways to tell the story of the complex relationship between the emergence of postmodernism and the construction of identity as a problem for a Left increasingly preoccupied with group-based politics. The new social movements of the sixties and seventies provided the impetus for a politicization of identity by challenging the white, male, heterosexual, and middle-class-dominated hierarchies of modern Western society. The discourses of difference that eventually grew from these movements came to inform a version of post-modernism that emphasized the particularity and contingency of the social, cultural, and historical locations of knowing and speaking subjects. Feminism led the way by deconstructing modern patriarchy, an order that subordinated women in fixed gender roles. The movements of people of color and gays and lesbians further contributed to a politicization of identity focused on the oppression of groups whose particular histories, cultural heritages, and rights had been silenced in the universalizing social practices and official history of the West. An activist and progressive version of postmodernism can thus be seen as emerging in the wake of the particularistic and inclusionary impulses of what came to be known as "identity politics." But this postmodernism, focusing on the epistemological play of particularity in the construction of gender, race, and sexuality, developed mainly from a critique of the essentialism that came to be seen as inherent in identity politics, and emerged more fully in theoretical arguments about the constructed relations of difference. While finally seen by many theoreticians as incompatible with identity politics, postmodernism nonetheless appropriated for its own purposes the deconstructive thrust of the identity movements, creating a broad sense of crisis in Western thought and culture through its articulation of the themes of difference and otherness. As such, postmodern theory in the United States has become a signifier of the identity crises inherent in the critical challenges to European, hierarchically based modes of authority, inquiry, and knowledge precipitated by identity politics.

While the identity movements provided the impetus for a critique of the political and moral subject of modernity, academic postmodernism, largely through the influence of French poststructuralism, eventually came to define itself through claims of the demise of the subject of modern Enlightenment philosophy. In this context the crisis of modern subjectivity was articulated more explicitly as an epistemological crisis. This crisis was increasingly traced to the writings of the anti-Enlightenment philosophers Friedrich Nietzsche and Martin Heidegger and endorsed in the works of such prominent postmodern theorists as Jacques Derrida, Michel Foucault, Jean-François Lyotard, and Richard Rorty. Despite their many differences, as postmodern philosophers these authors attempted to "decenter" the subject in the contingencies, particularities, and relativizations of discursive constructions, thereby attacking modern notions of a rationally centered ego. Especially in its poststructuralist versions, this type of postmodernism has attempted to replace the epistemologically sovereign subject of the Enlightenment with a subject constituted in the "always already present" effects of discourse and power.

In hindsight, however, the celebrated Nietzschean crisis of truth could be seen as anticipating, and recent poststructuralist formulations about the instability of culture as reflecting, a materially based sociohistorical crisis of the subject. By privileging discursive relations, poststructuralism posits as a world of textual instability what could be read as a decline of reason and a withering of unitary identity in a *society* fragmented by technologically based processes of signification, consumption, and power. The instabilities and incommensurabilities of language in poststructuralist theory can be seen as a theoretically mediated reflection of a real fragmentation and destabilization of social and cultural relations, and therefore modern forms of identity, resulting from economic and technological change in advanced capitalist societies. In its emphases on instability and heterogeneity, postmodernism more generally resonates a series of transformations in identity and identity-forming processes in society itself that have worked to throw the nature and boundaries of the subject into question.

The intellectual displacement of themes of disunity and instability from sociohistorical context to textuality and culture (from "context" to "text") is partly attributable to the circumstances of postmodernism's beginnings. Originating in the humanities, postmodernism reflects many of its traditions, perspectives, and methods. Despite occasional overtures to interdisciplinary approaches, postmodernists have with few exceptions advocated literary and ethnographic methods as the appropriate and strategically most effective means of practicing theory and research in all fields of knowledge. Curiously, the interdisciplinary implications of many postmodern formulations seem inconsistent with postmodern biases against Enlightenment philosophy, much of which is foundational to the natural and social sciences. Furthermore, many postmodern thinkers—and this is evident especially in the field of cultural studies—have failed to acknowledge similarities or connections between the new approaches and knowledges they espouse and ideas and methods long advocated or debated in the social sciences (consider, for example, parallels between standpoint epistemology and the sociology of knowledge).

Aside from the disciplinary reasons behind the textual and cultural turns in academic theory and the corresponding limitations of postmodern thought, it is worth mentioning yet another set of factors. The social relations of the post-modern movement perhaps shed additional light on the often disembodied ways the issues of subjectivity and identity have been valorized. While in no way reducible to social position or status, the theoretical and political agendas of postmodernists need to be read against their own relationship to the changing roles and identities surrounding consumption, class, gender, race, and sexuality as these are experienced in their particular social contexts. Specifically, how problems of identity and difference get constructed can be partly accounted for by the conditions of intellectual production in the social and political environ-ments of professional academics themselves.

In summary, on the premise that most varieties of postmodernism can be read as a reified reflection of and rejoinder to an underlying state of cultural dismemberment in society itself, I propose shifting the grounds of discourse about identity to an analysis of postmodernity as a cultural condition. A socio-historical account would resituate postmodern discourses and politics in funda-mental structural changes in society and culture. Such a move, I argue, casts a different light on the postmodern problem of identity and difference by relocat-ing it within a more encompassing perspective, one that grounds theory in material social and cultural transformations. While I begin and end with select features of postmodern thought, returning later in the book to the theoretical problem of the subject, my major concern is to formulate a diagnostic definition of the postmodern condition that enables us to think about the problematiza-tion of identity in historically and socially grounded ways.

Social Relations, Cultural Transformation, and Theory: An Overview

The crisis of subjectivity defining the postmodern condition calls for a mode of analysis that situates the problem of identity and difference in the realities of social and cultural disintegration and change. While postmodernists and post-structuralists have captured a strong sense of cultural fragmentation and the as-cendant powers of discourse, they have typically fallen short of understanding these phenomena as manifestations of lived cultural conditions or connecting them in any meaningful way, as Fuss would suggest, to the dynamics of social re-lations and interacting selves. The discursively reductionist tendencies in post-structuralism specifically are both cause and consequence of a relative (although not complete) neglect of the wider social and institutional fields in which dis-cursive or cultural instability operates.

In contrast, I attempt to treat the destabilization of identity and culture as a product of changes in the conditions of material and social existence and within a framework of individual experience and need. I start from the premise that identity and difference are better understood through an analysis of the post-modern condition rather than through the epistemological and political discourses and arguments of postmodernists and poststructuralists. In framing my position, I begin with a critique of identity politics and a discussion of the problems associated with this perspective and subsequent postmodernist and poststructuralist emphases on difference. I propose what I call a "social relational" approach that grounds the concepts of identity and difference in a social field. Having framed identity socially, I proceed to explore the transition from modernity to postmodernity, the accompanying transformations of culture brought about by the postmodernization of advanced capitalist society, and the consequent destabilization of identity resulting from the commodification and globalization of culture. I then address the overall shape of postmodernity and its ideological and cultural landscape, employing the notions of fragmentation and pluralization to diagnose and theorize the problems of cultural politics. Finally, I return to questions of theory by exploring the convergent and divergent claims of poststructuralism and Meadian social pragmatism and their implications for theoretical renewal under postmodern conditions.

Chapter 1 begins with a discussion of identity politics, tracing its sources to changes in postwar U.S. society. I characterize identity politics as a modern form of politics and a bridge between modern and postmodern perspectives. I argue that identity politics founders on the problem of difference. I propose an approach based on the writings of George Herbert Mead that addresses the problem of identity and difference from within a self-other framework that recognizes both the structural and processual determinants of identity within a field of social relations. This approach serves as the context for developing a social foundation for a theoretical construction of the problematization of identity in the postmodern era.

While recognizing the political and intellectual contexts in which identity has arisen as a topic of debate, I argue in this chapter that prevailing discourses, by taking identity as a production of strictly cultural and political processes, have neglected the problematization of identity and identity formation at the level of the self and in relation to institutional and structural transformations in advanced capitalist society. In effect, the prevailing focus on gender, race, ethnicity, and sexuality as privileged objects of discourse has often culturalized and politicized identity at the expense of other issues associated with identity formation.

Additionally, a social relational approach challenges the unquestioned constructionism at the forefront of contemporary discussions of identity, enabling us to raise issues obscured by a strongly antiessentialist stance. The contemporary rhetoric and uses of constructionism beg fundamental questions about the nature, form, and scope of identity formation. Reformulating the problem of identity and difference in terms of social relations and the self restores an important balance between discursive and social theories of construction while making it possible to recognize a complex and necessary tension between constructionist and essentialist readings of identity. The approach I propose attempts to nullify the constructionism/essentialism distinction as we have known it by reposing basic questions about social process and social structure and their interrelationship in the context of identity formation.

Specifically, my analysis presupposes important distinctions between cultural identity, on the one hand, and social and personal identity, on the other. While the former locates identity and identification processes in shared collective, historical experience, as constituted in forms of representation, the latter situates identity in the institutional contexts of the individual. Since social relations pervade the formation of cultural meanings and identities, questions of cultural identity are inseparable from their social context. Social relations, therefore, need to be distinguished from discursive relations and problematized as part of the changing structural and cultural conditions of society as a whole. The elevation of culture to a conceptually dominant position in contemporary theory has frequently obfuscated the underlying social and material processes shaping cultural production and consumption. In addressing the conditions of culture, I attempt to contextualize it structurally, considering how it undergoes change and destabilization through the effects of commodification and technology.

By shifting the discussion of identity to a material and social context, I am proposing to reinstate the modern concept of the "individual," with its inherent connection and opposition to "society," as a methodological strategy for conceptualizing postmodern identity crises. A theorization of the problem of identity in postmodernity presupposes a model of the individual tied to its predecessor, modernity. By reasserting a concept of the individual, it becomes possible to broaden current thinking about identity beyond collective entities such as the group and community to institutionalized structures to which the individual often has a more direct functional relationship. Whereas in modern society these included the family, church, and workplace, in postmodern society a shift has occurred toward the means of consumption and technological reproduction as major sites of identity formation. Moreover, by reinvoking the individual it becomes possible to relocate identity in processes of self-definition. Understanding how identity is constructed is therefore no longer solely a matter of the influences of history, culture, geography, and power but depends also on choices and constraints immediately available to individuals who as actors negotiate their lives within a broad field of social meanings and actions and within a range of institutional settings.

Finally, understanding the nature and formation of identity in advanced society, and its problematization in the face of technological and economic change, depends increasingly on the concept of personal identity. The conditions of postmodern society hasten the subsumption of cultural and social definitions of self under the goals of personal fulfillment, growth, and development. In a highly individualized and privatized society, the self becomes relatively detached from collective structures and traditions and more directly rooted in individual need and desire. The self stands at a remove from society, as aspirations, ideals, and myths acquire greater personal specificity through privatization and consumption. The stage at which the search for identity collapses into the construction of narrowly personal meaning poses the problem of how the social self survives in a society and culture that, while promising new forms of community, have become ominously fragmented and attenuated, and correspondingly narcissistic.

In chapter 2, identity is taken up in a historically developmental perspective. Insight into the problematization of identity in our time depends on a set of arguments about the direction of societal change, namely, the transition from modernity to postmodernity. These arguments reject claims of a "break" between modernity and postmodernity by establishing continuities between the two, pointing to the emergence of a set of conditions within modern society that contribute to postmodern changes in the formation of subjectivity and social relations. Identity is seen as a problem of modernity, whose history is inseparable from the rise of individualism and the disintegration of traditional society following the sweeping changes of modernization, in particular the separation of public and private life. Through the creation of a private sphere, modern society posed the problem of knowing oneself in ways that foreshadowed postmodern identity problems. Identity is also seen as more problematic under modernity than many postmodern writings imply. In considering the problems of modern identity, attention is focused on the fate of community, historically the major means of identity formation.

While continuities can be drawn between the predicaments of identity in the two historical types, however, the postmodern period is distinguished by fundamental changes in the bases and processes of identity formation. In this respect, traditional institutions have been threatened by new sites of consumption and entertainment and new means and forms of identification provided by mass media and other reproductive technologies. An overarching world of images and information now creates almost infinite possibilities for identifications extending far beyond concrete personal and group relations. This new environment has extended the locus of identity formation beyond the self-other relation to technologically controlled modes of signification. As a result of a globalized, simulated, and artificially constructed world of communications, the construction of identity has become increasingly externalized and instrumental in nature. The impact of a consumerist mass culture is seen as posing both opportunities and dangers for self-identity. While privatized forms of consumption offer new freedoms and means of individualized self-creation, trends toward the externalization of identification processes threaten not only a coherent sense of personal identity but the very boundaries of self as constituted by modernity through the distinction between individual and society. As a manifestation of the commodity form, the technologies of consumption and mass communication, as exemplified by television, have the potential for fragmenting the self within a vast world of visual and auditory stimuli. Yet while commodification threatens community and social relations generally, new kinds of community, however attenuated, emerge within consumer culture, offering new but limited possibilities of self-formation and identification.

Chapter 3 turns to the broader context of cultural transformation, examining the transition from modernity to postmodernity in terms of changes in the nature, structure, and condition of culture. The leading theme here, as throughout much of the discussion of postmodernity, is fragmentation through the commodification of culture. Whereas modern society can be characterized as fragmented through the differentiation of social roles and social functions within an urban landscape, postmodernity can be defined as the fragmentation of symbolic experience through new means of signification and technological reproduction within a landscape defined by mass media and mass consumption. This is suggestive not merely of a *change* in identity-forming processes but of a *problematization* of identity through a dissolution of self-unity and meaning accompanied by a crisis of reality itself.

The technological transformation of culture can be understood in relation to two processes at work in the transition from modernity to postmodernity. First, our relationship to culture undergoes dramatic change as a direct consequence of technological innovation. This occurs in the form of a compression of time and space and a reversal of modernity's privileging of time *over* space by new spatializations of culture made possible by its visualization through a world of images. Second, and relatedly, society undergoes massive aestheticization as part of a process of "de-differentiation" of the separate cultural spheres of reason, ethics, and aesthetics, and a loss of autonomy of the cultural sphere from the rest of society. This tendency involves an extensive interpenetration of capital and culture in which the aesthetic dimension is reintegrated into production and consumption, harnessed by the commodity form for purposes of capital accumulation. These tendencies are accompanied by a generalized shift toward consumption as the dominant cultural pattern. Here, the consumer increasingly assumes the role of producer, a paradoxical twist in the commodification of culture reflective of the incipient populism of postmodern culture. The aestheticization of society, finally, can be considered from the standpoint of Jean Baudrillard's claims (1983a) that technologies of cultural reproduction have created a "simulacrum" or "hyperreality" that replaces "reality" as it is normally defined.

The postmodern transformation of culture undermines unitary conceptions of identity in numerous ways. The modern self is problematized by a privatized mode of consumption, the fragmentation of symbolic experience, and a present-oriented culture in which conventional notions of self-formation through socialization are undermined by absorption of the self in images. At the same time, the reorientation of culture toward the consumer introduces new, potentially democratic possibilities.

Such possibilities are the topic of chapter 4, which explores the relationship between postmodernization and the decline of cultural hierarchy. Modernity monitored a set of exclusionary boundaries whose legitimacy has been thrown into question by the impact of postwar economic and technological development and the new social movements. Persistent patterns of social exclusion notwithstanding, the logic of capitalist development during this period has weakened many formal and structural barriers to democratic cultural relations, setting in motion a process of cultural democratization disruptive of hierarchical structures of identity.

In this sense, the incipient decline of modernity can be accounted for by a number of institutional shifts in capitalist social and cultural relations. These shifts are attributable to specific developments in economic organization, technology, and forms of cultural and political participation. First, innovative economic practices, based in what David Harvey (1989) has called a regime of "flexible accumulation," have disrupted modern status hierarchies and class relations through an enlargement of a consumer economy increasingly destructive of cultural distinctions. An eclectic and adaptable consumerism has weakened class identities and loyalties in favor of more ephemeral identifications with corporate-based images of leisure, pleasure, and celebrity, in which a regime of regulated and institutionalized "taste" is replaced by a system of commercially mediated and highly fluid "lifestyle." From this vantage point, the condition of postmodernity is inseparable from the rise of post-Fordist economics, whose major impact has been to create a highly differentiated and fluctuating marketplace of goods and images. Second, commercial media have intensified these trends by replicating and strengthening consumption relations through various technological strategies facilitating a recycling of cultural images. As a commodity form, mass media reproduce the consumptive mode through simulation, whose logic is to further destabilize inherited social and cultural hierarchies. In the functionally autonomous world of the media, the subject is cast adrift in an eclectic world of images characterized by a dissociation of class and other collective identifications. Third, in a series of changes involving migration, transnational capital, communications technologies, and cultural exportation, new processes of economic and cultural globalization have been destabilizing identity in the West and throughout the world. Finally, the reconfiguration of political discourse by the new social movements represents yet another set of forces working to dismantle hierarchical cultural conceptions and notions of self predicated on modern conceptions of identity and authority relations. These developments have worked in combination to undermine forms of collective identity embedded in modern social and political arrangements and to create a multitude of democratizing tendencies in the realm of culture. In these ways, postmodernization has set in motion numerous inclusionary trends, forcing difference from the cultural margins to the center.

In an attempt to further clarify the overall shape of postmodernity, as well as multiple and inconsistent uses of the term "postmodern," chapter 5 discusses two separate and antagonistic but overlapping processual logics contained in the themes of heterogeneity and democratization characterizing the postmodern condition. Tendencies toward fragmentation and simulation generate the widely commented-on crises of meaning and reality attributable to commodification and the effects of media-based technologies of reproduction problematizing subjectivity in everyday life. However, the dismantling of broad patterns of social and cultural hierarchy by social movements and globalizing trends represents an opposing tendency toward pluralization, a destabilizing but formative process consisting of the construction and assertion of a range of new identities, meanings, and communities as against the commodification of culture and the consensual frameworks of modern society. These interrelated but opposing currents of postmodernity are manifest, respectively, in what I call "commercial" and "political" postmodernism. Whereas the former is shaped by the forces of commodification, the latter refers to the formation of a new realm of cultural politics.

The frequent conflation of this distinction stems from the observable trends toward democratization and eclecticism in mass culture and the valorization of "particularity" and "difference" in postmodern theory. These trends tend to obscure the inherently contradictory relationship between processes of fragmentation and pluralization. While the fragmentations of consumption and technology reflect the workings of the consumer marketplace, movements that politicize culture and identity involve group formation and collective struggles for change. Commercial culture works to create a democracy of consumerism that enlists difference in the interest of the market, while cultural politics works to articulate difference in the name of group identity, in both politically progressive and reactionary directions. These opposing tendencies stand in a dialectical relationship, mutually influencing each other in complex and unpredictable ways.

Furthermore, the distinction I am proposing provides access to a much deeper phenomenon in postmodern culture. Spanning the contrast between the commercial and political forms of postmodernity is a *revivalist culture* seeking to retrieve a sense of authenticity, often through a reassertion of tradition and the historical past. Precipitating a loss of place and meaning, mass culture motivates a search for personal moorings through an attachment to diverse groups, communities, value systems, and cultural traditions. Thus, while destabilizing identity, postmodernity simultaneously produces movements of restabilization and reconstruction. In these movements, an attempt is made to recuperate the past as a source of authentic meanings and identities, a development having complex and ideologically ambiguous consequences. While the cultural politics of gender, racial, sexual, and other identities frequently draw on historical heritages to mount challenges to the social repressions of modernity, pushing the pluralizing process in a progressive direction, various conservative movements represent a backward-looking quest for stability through the appropriation of tradition and authority. In the disjointed and eclectic political culture of the nineties, many movements, of course, could be read as embodying both progressive *and* reactionary elements. The search for meaning and identity thus crosses conventional ideological lines, disrupting predictable patterns of culture along with liberal consensus politics. As a basic feature of postmodernity in the United States, symptoms of loss and regeneration get expressed in an often volatile identity politics extending from left to right, reflecting a broad and deepening sense of personal crisis associated with the effects of unsettling change and a collapse of modern belief systems.

Finally, in chapter 6 I reconnect my analysis of the problematization of identity in postmodernity to the theoretical themes of social relationality and the self outlined in chapter 1. In searching for a redeemable theoretical response to the postmodern condition—a processual, emergent theory of social relations and the self that speaks to the condition of postmodernity—I critique poststructuralism for neglecting the connections between discursive and social practices. I propose a reconsideration of Meadian social pragmatism and the writings of V. N. Voloshinov as constituents of an alternative theoretical paradigm addressing the social foundations of language and consciousness. I attempt to demonstrate convergences between Meadian philosophy and poststructuralism (an antimetaphysical stance, a belief in the provisionality and contingency of knowledge, a view of the subject as constituted in multiplicity and disunity) as well as divergences, as represented by Mead's naturalized social conception of the pragmatic and generative capacities of mind, language, and the self.

While representing a number of developments resistant to easy summarization, poststructuralism, it could be said, generally addresses the decenteredness and fluidity of the subject implied by a fragmented mass culture and the proliferation of group identities associated with the interventions of cultural politics. This approach, as exemplified particularly by certain aspects of the work of Jacques Derrida, Michel Foucault, and Judith Butler, translates these conditions into linguistic and discursive heterogeneity, locating potentialities of resistance in the productiveness and gaps of discursive practices. Poststructuralism thus draws attention to the multiple and unstable character of meaning and identity while at the same time refusing notions of a subject that preexists signification. However, by dissolving the subject in the workings of discourse and power, poststructuralism detaches notions of identity and difference from the social processes in which they are rooted. Instead, most poststructuralist formulations tend to *replicate the logic of signification within the commodity form,* implicitly reifying the salient features of mass culture. Serving as a metaphor for mass culture, as John Mowitt (1992) has suggested, the "text" replaces the subject, obscuring the generative and formative possibilities of the interactive processes shaping and shaped by a self in a field of social relations. The disunities and instabilities textually valorized by poststructuralism thus re-create in a disembodied form the crises of identity and difference in postmodern culture while failing to address their underlying causes and how relations of identity and difference might be reconstituted or transformed within a realm of social action.

The writings of Mead, especially his *Mind, Self, and Society* (1934) and *The Philosophy of the Present* (1932), bear an intriguing resemblance to aspects of poststructuralism but redress the limitations of this approach by focusing on the social production and functions of language while insisting on the centrality of the social self in the interpretive production of meaning. Mead's pragmatic conceptions of the self-other relationship, of the inseparability of self from environment—understood as a problem-solving situation—and of the temporal and emergent qualities of communication and social action complement the poststructuralist attempt to situate the subject in a context of discursive relations marked by fluidity and instability. While rejecting Cartesian dualism, however, Mead nonetheless retains a *functional* concept of a socially constituted consciousness, which he sees as a precondition for a reflexive self. Mead further posits the inseparability of discursivity from what he calls "sociality" and in this fashion links subjectivity to an irreducibly practical relationship of social *intersubjectivity.* In these ways, Mead's pragmatism overlaps with poststructuralist textualism and indeterminacy while retaining the idea of mind as a socially con-stituted form of reflexive consciousness.

A theory of identity in postmodern society must address the simultaneously fragmented and pluralized conditions creating the tensions and dilemmas of identity and difference. The themes of interpretation, becoming, and multiplic-ity common to poststructuralist writings and Meadian philosophy capture the sense of contingency pervading the postmodern condition. In its emphasis on the inherently emergent character of social life and the self-reflexive subject, Meadian pragmatism implicitly recognizes the provisional nature of identity and the constitution of identity in difference. Contrary to poststructuralism, how-ever, Meadian thought provides conceptions of the subject that incorporate these themes into a socially grounded, naturalistic, and empirically oriented framework of analysis.

My goal in this study is to outline a diagnostic foundation for a reconstruc-tion of social theory by laying out the sociohistorical ground of the postmodern condition. But this task can only be accomplished through a rehabilitation of the idea of a *social* subject shaped by but reflexively engaging this condition. By recognizing language and discourse as social products and therefore as having a social form and structure, thinkers like Mead and Voloshinov thematize the poststructuralist emphasis on multiplicity and difference within a context of social interaction and group life while still acknowledging the significance of language in social processes. Significantly, however, both thinkers recognize the impossibility of explaining the workings and effects of language and discourse *except* in social context. Finally, I argue that a focus on social relations has im-portant political consequences. Social relations and social selves are necessary foundations of communication and action, of community, culture, and politics. Textual reductionism and the reification of mass culture are shortcomings for which poststructuralism can be redeemed by a social pragmatist account that grounds symbolic processes in the social relations of the problem-solving acts of individuals and the reflexive capacities of social selves.

1
Regrounding Theory
The Social Relations of Identity and Difference

During the past twenty-five years the theme of identity has come to dominate a variety of theoretical and political discussions on the Left in the United States. Significantly, while usually presumed to be a phenomenon specific to the Left, the issue of identity has assumed a central role in popular forms of political struggle across the ideological spectrum, including the Right. This development is both suggestive of a sea change in the character of contemporary politics, and, relatedly, symptomatic of increased anxiety over the fate of personal, social, and cultural life in a society undergoing accelerating crisis and change. The politicization of identity in the United States and the West more generally can be seen as an effect of dramatic transformations in the culture of advanced society after World War II, transformations that intensified during and following the turmoil of the sixties. More contemporaneously, the reorientation of politics toward issues of identity reflects a growing mood of uncertainty arising from economic insecurity, social and cultural change, worsening inequality, a perception of moral decay, and a sense of threatened social disintegration. These domestic fears can in turn be viewed more broadly as stemming from new global realities in a transfigured, shrinking, non–Cold War world in which older identifications, and specifically modern conceptions of national and cultural identity, are being seriously challenged.

Despite an abundance of concern about identity, however, hardly any serious analytical attention has been given to the underlying social and historical causes of the identity crises of our time, both collective and personal, or the broader structural conditions of social change behind these crises. The relative absence of such perspectives in recent theoretical discussions is in part a manifestation of the pervasive influence of postmodern and poststructuralist discourses in academic theory. These discourses have tended to construct identity issues along predominantly culturalist lines and narrowly in terms of issues that have arisen in the context of the new social movements. Generally speaking, analytical and historical conceptions of identity have been largely ignored in favor of more politically focused treatments.

Given its origins in the new movements, beginning in the late sixties, the Left's preoccupation with identity has centered controversially on what has come to be known as *identity politics,* a term characterizing those movements in which membership in oppressed and marginalized groups provides the basis of a common identity for the making of political claims. The debates about identity politics, however, have often obscured the larger social and cultural transformations behind the rise of these movements and, more importantly, the broader destabilization of identity resulting from institutional and technological change in the West. As a result, the politicization of identity has seldom been theorized symptomatically in relation to the wider social changes to which it is a response. Identity politics, however consequential, are but an aspect of a larger set of changes taking place in the structure, culture, and geopolitical situation of the United States and other Western societies. Slow to comprehend the problem of identity beyond its immediate collective manifestations on the Left in the United States, academic theorists have largely overlooked the broad and complex impact of these changes in institutional life and the personal and cultural contexts of the individual.

Given these concerns, I propose shifting the discussion of identity from the political terrain toward (1) an analytical approach that draws on well-established conceptions of social relations and the social self, and (2) an exploration of the underlying historical and institutional changes behind the construction of identity and difference as political issues. Discussions of identity have been severely limited by lack of attention to the ways it is formed within a field of social relations and the social processes governing interacting selves. Moreover, identity politics broadly understood is a product of deeper historical circumstances preceding and surrounding the debates and social movements through which it has come to be defined. I argue for extending discussions of identity and difference from political preoccupations with culture and power to the wider context of the conditions of postmodernity. This enables a critique of these developments that provides new grounds for theoretical debate. I attempt to outline these new grounds within a framework that emphasizes social and historical conditions of identity formation.

This involves two separate but interrelated tasks. First, I explore the social origins of identity politics and attempt to sort through the neglected meanings and implications of identity's politicization in the postwar period. Second, through a critique of identity politics, I trace the shift to the notion of difference, arguing for a repositioning of questions of identity and difference in what I call a "social relational" approach. This approach both refigures how we think about identity and its relation to difference along social relational lines and forces a much needed rethinking of the constructionist posture pervading contemporary academic theory. I also propose, as part of a strategy for developing a more comprehensive understanding of postmodernity, a conceptual shift from prevailing cultural and political approaches that view identity in terms of collective or group phenomena toward a theoretical focus on the effects of structural and cultural change on the identities of social individuals. Finally, in addition to arguing for recognition of the larger institutional sources of identity destabilization in contemporary society, I argue for a return to more grounded and theoretically fertile conceptions of social and personal identity contained in the ideas of "symbolic interaction" and the "social self" found in the writings of George Herbert Mead.

The Origins and Significance of Identity Politics

While usually considered a postsixties development in the United States, identity politics has been a significant part of modern political and social life for centuries (Calhoun 1994). Group based identities have always been central to traditions of representation in the United States and have served historically as a basis for the exercise of individual and collective rights. The nineteenth century gave rise to innumerable social movements in which identity was the crucial factor, such as the early women's movement, workers' movements, ethnic and nationalist movements, and Utopian communal movements. Nor are the more recent political impulses to convert the self into an object of political discourse and struggle new to a society historically infused with ideas of individualism and democracy. In fact, drawing attention to the needs of self and group as a means of social and political reform is indigenously and inescapably "American." In this sense, identity politics in the late twentieth century is a continuation of long-standing political traditions.

This is not to deny that the rise of identity politics registers an important transformation in our consciousness and valuation of identity and its relationship to political practice. Indeed, the naming of identity as a problem did not occur until the early years of the postwar period when rapid change, the growth of new subcultures, and pressures to assimilate into mainstream society made who/what we were a major preoccupation within both intellectual and popular culture. During this period, the thematizing of identity as a problem of personal adjustment and life meaning was prominent in the writings of Erik Erikson (1980), who attempted to integrate social and historical conceptions of identity formation into psychoanalysis. However, although identity had acquired some social scientific and literary importance during the fifties as a thematic expression of the problems of personal pathology, life adjustment, and existential rebellion, it was not until the outbreak of collective protest during the sixties that it became a focus of political struggle.

An examination of postwar society provides important insights into the social and cultural changes behind the politicization of identity in an era of new social movements in the United States. However, one of the difficulties facing a historical accounting is that the politicization of identity was an important aspect of a *variety* of struggles during the sixties and seventies, each of which, while appearing to be part of a larger movement of change, had its own goals and agendas. In addition, the ways in which each of these struggles took up concerns for identity, and the extent and consequences of these concerns, varied from one struggle to the next. More importantly, I suggest, it is necessary to regard identity politics as a key element in a *variety* of kinds of organized protest, often transcending the ideological differences of Left and Right and involving more generally questions of how people view themselves and their places in society and politics. This is often overlooked in the case of identity politics in the university, whether involving the canon wars, admissions policies, or other battles over equity and representation in a "multicultural" society. But the rise of white ethnicity, religious fundamentalism, antiabortionism, antidesegregationism, and other conservative ideologies and movements associated with the New Right in the United States are manifestations of the same basic trend toward the politicization of identity, a fact usually overlooked in discussions that assume identity politics to be an exclusively left-wing phenomenon (Calhoun 1994). The spread of identity politics, then, is symptomatic of major changes in culture and politics on a broad scale. Inscribed in a wide assortment of political agendas and practices from Left to Right, identity politics, moreover, reveals itself to be an ambiguous and ideologically conflicted phenomenon.

To venture a more comprehensive definition, "identity politics" refers to a strategy whereby individuals define themselves through identification with or membership in groups or categories regarded as the source of distinct feelings and experiences of marginalization and subordination. Such a strategy is premised on suppositions of a singular identity established predominantly through a set of ascribed characteristics, including both "natural" (physical, biological) traits and cultural heritages. Possession of an identity established by these criteria becomes a means for distinguishing oneself from the rest of society and a ground for moral and political claims against the state, involving individual and group challenges to what are perceived as oppressive social, cultural, and political practices. Importantly, identity formulated by means of group identification is understood as foundational. As Ilene Philipson (1991) has pointed out, "According to many of its proponents, such identity is seen as immutable, discrete, and clearly delineated. The boundaries of identity set the in-group apart from the rest of society, therefore making their determination a critical, if not the critical ingredient in defining identity" (51). Implicit in such a view, Philipson observes, is the paramount importance of questions of inclusion and exclusion, since identity is premised on membership in "a clearly demarcated group." Accordingly, identity politics involves a preoccupation with group membership, the determination of group boundaries being a necessary condition for definitions of the self.

Most discussions have recognized that the processes by which identity gets defined in terms of groups or categories consciously or unconsciously presuppose a hierarchical system of power. Questions of identity are presumed to be inseparable from considerations of power relations and oppression more generally, and identity claims made in the name of the group often are intended to expose and redress these relations in favor of greater equality and justice (Wilmsen and McAllister 1996; I. Young 1990). Membership in a dominated or oppressed group, therefore, becomes a basis for legitimacy claims and grounds for exercising one's moral and political rights (E. Willis 1991: 59; I. Young 1990).

The civil rights movement was decisive in opening the door to a politics focused on the problem of exclusion, raising for the first time in the postwar era questions about who was excluded from the political process and on what grounds. Drawing attention to exclusionary practices politicized identity in a number of ways. First, it demonstrated a selective denial of equal rights on the basis of categorical and group-based criteria, such as being black or female. Second, it raised issues of cultural representation by showing that members of excluded groups were stereotypically constructed by the mass media and other culturally hegemonic apparatuses. Third, by protesting their exclusion from the political process, participants in these movements confronted questions of self-perception and definition as well as questions about how such self-definitions might be validated or transformed through personal and collective struggle.

Although the crucible of identity politics, the new social movements were themselves an outward manifestation of deeper tendencies in postwar U.S. society. Among a multitude of economic, social, and cultural changes, perhaps most fundamental was a decline in the importance of social class as a basis of identification and organized action. Following an intense period of union activity immediately following the war, the fifties saw a gradual decrease in the politics of class as a consequence of affluence, suburbanization, social mobility, consumerism, and higher educational levels, all of which conspired to create an increasingly nebulous class system. The decline of class politics was paralleled by the emergence during the sixties of political struggles over nonclass issues, for example, civil rights and antiwar sentiments. By the end of the decade, class identities had been increasingly displaced by concerns for race, followed in the seventies by gender and ethnicity as major categories of identity, and later in the decade by struggles over sexual orientation. These and other collective identifications thus became important new signifiers of inequality and marginalization within movements of protest.[1]

Not that older notions of class conflict disappeared entirely. However, although an implicit model of class struggle still informed much of movement politics, issues of deprivation and oppression were redefined along new lines. Indicative of the shift from production to consumption in the economy, protest now focused less on the material relations of production than on consumption-related issues of social, political, and cultural representation and power. The issue of exploitation was gradually subsumed under the problem of exclusion, and questions of class power were supplanted by emphases on *other* forms of power.

But the obscuring of class identities and the emerging obstacles to the expression of class interests cannot by themselves explain the explosion of new identity-based movements. The disarticulation of class in U.S. society was merely part of a broader set of changes that created the conditions for a politics of the self, of which identity politics was an indirect outgrowth. The same forces that eroded class politics gave rise to a conformist mass culture based on what Philipson (1991) has called an "ideology of sameness," a prescription for negating diversity and difference in the name of "Americanism" (52). This ideology's refusal to recognize cultural difference engendered feelings of alienation and a search for an "authentic self" based on people's unique "histories and experiences" (52–53). In this view, identity politics has deep roots in a rejection of anonymity and a pursuit of authenticity through the mythology of a "real self" based in an "ideological community."[2]

As Philipson notes, however, organized identity politics did not acquire a definite shape until the breakdown of a leftist community toward the end of the sixties, a transition marked by a repudiation of the notions of individuality central to this community in favor of more fixed identifications with the collective heritages of race, ethnicity, and gender.[3] Indeed, Ellen Willis (1991) has argued that identity politics was in some sense a reaction against the refusal of the counterculture and the early New Left to accept fixed identities. The collapse of the Left brought feelings of powerlessness to change society, resulting in the displacement of movement identifications by cultural identifications founded in a shared history and sense of group belonging. What began as a politics of authenticity and individuality in the sixties, variously inflected by different movements, in the early seventies eventually turned into a politics of cultural identity that defined the individual exclusively in terms of historically and ancestrally derived criteria of group membership.

While the decline of class and the political dynamics and misfortunes of the sixties movements offer a partial explanation for the rise of identity politics, the deeper roots of this phenomenon can also be located more broadly in the impact of commodity society and its multiple social consequences. Postwar conformist ideologies were built largely on an expanding culture of consumerism, which propagated the homogenizing tendencies precipitating rebellion against affluent white middle-class society. To a large extent, this became a period during which Americanism was equated with consumerism. The social role of consumer was inherently assimilationist, especially for those at the ethnic and economic margins, necessitating a dissolution of old identities in favor of a prescribed middle-class standard of living. To the degree that consumption became a means of "mainstreaming" people of assorted backgrounds into middle-class culture, the politics of self and identity became a strategy of resistance, a means of countering the pressures to assimilate through the assertion of distinct social and cultural differences.

The relationship between consumption culture and identity politics, and identity formation generally, did not follow a straight line but was complex and dialectical. To begin, consumption in its own way helped forge new identities during the fifties and sixties. Youth and women, for instance, came to see themselves as separate groups with their own specific needs and aspirations as defined by new consumption patterns propagated by industry-based media images aimed at the creation of new consumer markets.[4] Here was a case of the shaping of identities through advertising and marketing strategies. But while it was contributing to the formation of new collective identities, consumer culture was simultaneously encouraging new forms of individuality promising liberation from both traditional and conventional roles, enabling the pursuit of personal tastes and pleasures independently of collective identifications. In this sense, consumer culture was fundamentally privatizing. In yet other ways, however, consumerism worked to produce conformity, especially in its fifties version, creating a culture of suburban abundance that it attempted to impose on an otherwise diverse and divided society. Meanwhile, consumerism had the unintended consequence of raising expectations among oppressed groups who had little hope of ever achieving middle-class prosperity under prevailing social arrangements. For the marginalized, and especially the racially segregated during and after the sixties movements for racial justice, consumerism became a catalyst for despair and anger toward the system. As a norm for measuring social success, consumption became a symbolic focus of rebellion, as reflected in the looting of consumer goods during the black urban riots of the late sixties. For many white youth, although consumer styles provided innovative forms of identification, consumerist values created feelings of estrangement from self and others, motivating a search for personal experience and meaning in opposition to mass culture and its confining middle-class expectations. Simultaneously, however, consumerism provided youth with "a rich source of potentially subversive cultural resources" (Lee 1993: 107) *threatening* middle-class society. For those feeling disenfranchised by their race or gender, the rewards of consumption increased desires to change a system of inequality from which they had been largely excluded.

In these and other ways, consumerism led to a questioning of identity precisely at a time when such questioning was being forsworn by the purveyors of the great American celebration. In addition, however, the search for identity through membership in a group or culture can be understood as a response to the ethos of individualism in a highly mobile and materialistic society. For members of racial and ethnic groups deprived of political power and the rewards of middle-class life, identifications with one's own group or culture can serve to compensate feelings of rejection and failure in a society that pressures its members to compete for success. While this may have been historically true in the United States, the homogenizing and depersonalizing trends specific to the postwar era intensified needs for group solidarity. Moreover, in a culture that stresses individual achievement, failure to attain recognition and prosperity generates feelings of self-blame. Identity politics offers a political understanding of this failure, attributing it to the systematic subordination and oppression of certain groups in favor of others. As Philipson (1991) remarks, identity politics affords a means of avoiding self-blame by explaining failure in terms of discrimination based on factors (such as race or gender) over which the individual has no control. By addressing the particular anxieties and insecurities of the excluded, identity politics provides a powerful means of legitimating the self in the face of a highly competitive culture. This is still of considerable import at a time in U.S. history when state-sanctioned programs of desegregation and affirmative action have inspired groups victimized by discrimination to seek higher levels of educational and economic achievement while many structural and ideological barriers to equality remain stubbornly in place.

Along with these specific developments, the problematization of identity is to a large extent inseparable from the growth of mass society during this era, specifically the erosion of social structure. Feelings of anonymity, impersonality, and powerlessness have been attributed to the breakdown of communal structures and the atomization of social relations accompanying the demise of traditional society and the rise of mass communications and the nation-state. The impact of these changes was strongly felt during a time of rapid expansion of the mass media, suburbanization, and the standardization of daily life through mass consumption.[5]

Finally, the postwar decades additionally suffered the ravages of the paranoid style of Cold War politics, a condition that intensified the need to question and legitimate identity. Questions such as Who am I?, What am I?, and Where do I belong? assumed paramount importance, especially for those whose identities had been subjugated and obscured.[6]

As this brief account suggests, the decades preceding the rise of identity politics in the United States contained the seeds of personal and collective identity crises, especially for members of marginalized groups. On another level, however, postwar U.S. society has also exhibited developmental tendencies of a global as well as domestic nature. Stuart Hall has attributed a generalized destabilization of identity in Western society to major intellectual, social, and political developments characterizing the late twentieth century. It should be no surprise that the question of identity has returned, as Hall (1991) puts it, "with a particular kind of force" (9), since talk about identity is to be expected in a world of accelerating and unpredictable change. As he states, the logic of our discourses about identity "assumes a stable subject," which gives us a sense of security and continuity in a changing world, a kind of "ultimate guarantee" (10). Hall, too, sees the presumptions of a "true" or "authentic" self in the ways we have tended to think and talk about identity as a source of fixity and certitude. While this characterization of identity is meant as a description of how the concept has operated in our conventional discourses, it further serves as a historical explanation for the rise of identity politics. As the ultimate ground of our being, our fundamental sense of place in the world, identity assumes compelling force whenever it seems the world might be falling apart. As Barbara Epstein (1991b: 28) has remarked, as a response to "insecurity and instability" identity politics "provides a basis for building communities in a chaotic environment."

Taking an even wider and longer view, Hall asserts that identity has been seriously "disrupted" in our time by intellectual developments undermining the West's mythology of its own certitude, as based on the assumption of a unified, knowing subject. The major theoretical "decenterings of identity" beginning with Marx's theory of the alienation of labor and continuing in the psychological writings of Sigmund Freud and the linguistic analyses of Ferdinand de Saussure have forever cast doubt on beliefs in a stable and secure identity from which to think and act. These theoretical doubts form a backdrop to the fragmentation of collective identities resulting from modernity's own historical developments. As a consequence of these changes, along with the shift in consciousness away from class to other identities, as Hall argues, people now experience and understand their relationship to all their basic identities—class, gender, race, and sexuality—in more complex and uncertain ways than before. Even national identities have come under siege as a consequence of disturbances associated with a new wave of globalization. In all these respects, identity has been problematized by means of a general "relativization of the Western world" (Hall 1991: 12) or, put differently, a weakening of European-based beliefs and values. In this account, identity has been problematized by sweeping intellectual and cultural changes.

What is still missing from this overview, however, is a sociological understanding of the dramatic shifts in the culture and social relations of the advanced countries of the West caused by economic and technological change. What the accounts discussed thus far neglect is the extent to which the problematization of older categories of identity is a consequence of the *structural* changes transforming Western societies and, specifically, the effects of these changes on everyday cultural experience and the self. Destabilization has been occurring not only in collective and cultural identities but in a range of conventional *social* identities comprising the fabric of everyday life. This includes the social roles of family, workplace, and other institutions affected by changing relations of production and consumption. Reading the postwar situation from this perspective, we see that the appeal of identity politics can also be understood as a response to growing uncertainties accompanying the transformation of routine institutional settings. This is particularly the case insofar as these changes have upset entrenched relations of power and privilege affecting identities of race, ethnicity, class, and gender. While this is most apparent in the realm of consumption, where status boundaries have been increasingly blurred, in the sphere of production the changing structures of work and labor markets have also upset older hierarchies, for example, through labor immigration and affirmative action policies. A sense of crisis in collective identities thus stems not only from cultural and intellectual developments but is integrally related to disruptions in institutionalized social arrangements.

In sum, identity politics represents a response to a generalized condition of destabilization associated with a multiplicity of historical changes. This response has had mixed results. While furthering the interests of disadvantaged groups, the largely group-based discourses of identity and cultural politics are ill equipped to articulate adequately the broad and complex set of institutional changes problematizing identity throughout the range of domestic and global relations. For both better and worse, identity politics has often become a substitute for historical and social theorizing and strategizing, a throwback to more limited categorical claims of group entitlements combined with efforts to reconstruct identities through new kinds of political discourses and struggles. Furthermore, the particular forms that the politicization of identity has taken, both left and right, have left much to be desired for those interested in transforming society and politics. While attempting to extend the pluralism and individualism inherent in liberal democracy to the disenfranchised, certain strains of identity politics have in practice rejected modern liberalism in favor of group solidarities. Moreover, identity politics has remained burdened with the tensions inherent in Western pluralist politics. Both the strength and irony of identity politics consist of its having launched an attack on politics-as-usual while simultaneously drawing on *established* conventions of representative democracy. Put differently, refusing the assimilationist cultural agenda, advocates of identity politics nonetheless have demanded participation in mainstream institutions, seeking recognition within the prevailing social norms. In the process, identity politics has reproduced the conceptual and real contradictions of political liberalism between, for example, conformity and individuality, equality and freedom. In this sense, identity politics has simply reinforced existing political relations without challenging the underlying assumptions of the modern liberal state.

Overall, identity politics has served multiple but ideologically ambiguous purposes. On the one hand, it has been a continuation of historical struggles for equality and justice (I. Young 1990). On the other hand, by striving to revive the underlying cultural and moral foundations of political and social life, it has addressed the alienation, insecurities, and contradictions of the ascendant mass culture and affluence of postwar society. But while creating a form of resistance to the conformity and exclusionism of mainstream society, identity politics has itself engendered conformism and conservatism, attempting to "work" the system to the advantage of oppressed groups instead of questioning established structures of power.[7] In this respect, identity politics has served as a questionable legacy to the struggles of the New Left and the new movements it engendered.

Aporias of Identity Politics: The Problem of Difference

A postmodern political sensibility was implicit in the attacks on hierarchical social values and power relations waged by the new social movements and the challenge to hegemonically constructed identities characterizing movement activism in the sixties and seventies. Despite its inclusionary impulses, however, identity politics depends on essentialist definitions of the self, the maintenance of existing group boundaries, and a belief in the moral foundations of action, rendering it ultimately incompatible with postmodern thought. Crucially, identity politics fails to address or resolve the problem of difference, a definitive theme of postmodern theory. Exhibiting strong pluralist impulses and a purist insistence on the connection between politics and the self, identity politics occupies a compellingly radical moment in the theory and practice of democracy. Nonetheless, and in ways that reveal inherent difficulties in the postmodernist response to this same issue, this form of politics ultimately falters on the problem of difference.

The intellectual decenterings to which Hall has appealed mark the theoretical origins of the recent preoccupations with difference and otherness, the figures of antagonism toward "unitary" modern philosophy derived from Enlightenment thought. The politics of the sixties was immersed in the discovery and valorization of cultural difference, which thereafter received widespread theoretical reinforcement through the reading not only of thinkers like Freud and Saussure but also Theodor Adorno, Derrida, and Gilles Deleuze (Aronowitz 1992). Generally speaking, the postmodern thematizing of "otherness" has been an important dimension of the identity movements and has implicitly informed the antiassimilationist character of identity politics. Ironically, however, while the ideologies of these movements have argued for difference, the very logic of identity politics has led inevitably to the reinstatement of sameness and a redrawing of exclusionary lines.

Premised on but suppressing difference, identity politics is thus founded on a contradiction. Asserting difference in its stance against cultural assimilation, identity politics is obliged to homogenize the group for the sake of solidarity and the implementation of its moral and political demands. The concept of difference therefore comes into play in the relationships among groups and in relation to the larger social and cultural context in which the politics of a single group are enacted. It is abolished, however, in relation to the group or category on which processes of self-definition underlying identity politics depend. In this sense, insofar as it is a manifestation of political fragmentation, identity politics can be seen as part of the postmodern *condition,* but as a form of politics it stands in fundamental contradiction to postmodernism. Through its reliance on unitary, fixed, and essentialist conceptions, the politics of identity remains tied to a modernist model of liberal politics and selfhood, drawing its sustenance from the traditional discourses of political liberalism (Brown 1993). In contrast, postmodernism posits identity as constructed by means of discourse or representation and therefore by nature as heterogeneous, shifting, and tenuous as signification itself. The dependency of identity politics on ethical and moral foundations thus runs afoul of the postmodern theme of contingency (Rosenthal 1992), which in its more extreme forms leads to a relativism making every social location an equally valid ground of knowledge.

The postmodern moment in identity politics emerges in its appeals to difference and the grounding of its moral claims in the recognition and advocacy of the silenced "other." With respect to its appeal to difference, two strategies have emerged. First, difference has been celebrated for its own sake, a salient tendency in the academy and to a lesser extent in the gay and lesbian movements, but apparent more generally in the ethos of multiculturalism.[8] Second, difference has been given a ranking. Here, again paradoxically, identity politics generates new hierarchies of exclusion, an evaluative ordering of the moral claims of various groups on a scale of oppression (Aronowitz 1992). While the first strategy reflects a postmodern stance, however, the second veers back toward a modernist foundational moral and political framework from within which to calculate and judge degrees of subordination. Neither of these strategies resolves the fundamental dilemmas of difference.

Unfortunately, despite a growing rejection of identity politics in favor of a politics of difference, a postmodern move intended to avoid essentializing and stabilizing conceptions, difference has remained inadequately theorized. In most postmodern writings difference has become another essentialism and universal, whether through inclusionary or exclusionary strategies. As Christina Crosby (1992) comments, "difference" has become a substitute for "identity," reproducing the sameness and circularity inherent in the latter term. This is reflected in an "empiricist historicism which is the flip side of the idealism scorned and disavowed by feminisms" (136). Identity and difference, then, *both* become categories of simple recognition, description, and reparation rather than theoretical and strategic problems to be formulated and deployed in the interest of radically reconstructing society and politics.[9]

The problem of difference, in addition to undermining the putative goals of identity politics, poses stubborn difficulties for an overall strategy for uniting multiple groupings in a common movement for change. The well-known solution to this predicament, and to the consequent splintering of the Left in the United States, has been the proposed formation of alliances based on a model of coalition politics. This approach gives voice to different identities while moving beyond the boundaries of singularly based identity movements. The question remains, however, if identity is the irreducible ground of politics, how are we to forestall the disintegration of politics into mere competition among interest groups? How is a politics of the self to survive a potentially infinite regress of separate identities/selves and therefore political claims? At the same time, how is it possible to move beyond the mere invocation and recognition of difference to an articulation of the interests of particular subjectivities within a more universalist perspective of collective change? How can difference be approached as a problem and a process to be grasped theoretically and politically in the context of new identity formations? While it may be true that such questions can be answered only in practice, there still remains a need to understand the logic of difference analytically. This entails theoretical examination of the relational *dynamics* of difference underlying the social and cultural construction of identity.

A Social Relational Approach to Identity and Difference

The idea of difference is central to theoretical arguments that view identity not as a pregiven entity bound by the fixed attributes of a group but as constituted in some type of *processes* (I. Young 1990). The unstable character of identity and its dependence on relations of difference present an idea whose origins can be traced to familiar theoretical traditions, most notably Marxism, psychoanalysis, feminism, and deconstruction. Bulwarks against reification, aspects of these traditions lend support to the notion that identity is constructed and therefore processual and dynamic in nature. The central question raised by these theoretical perspectives is how we are to understand "process" and, crucially, its relationship to "structure." While this remains an imposing analytical problem (Giddens 1979), in terms of theorizing identity some tentative answers to this question can be sought in an idea to which all these theoretical traditions are commonly committed. This is the idea of *relationality*, or the principle that the identity of an entity is conditioned by and to be located in its relations with other entities, both internal and external. Viewed relationally, the concept of process enables us in principle to understand how structure is produced, sustained, and changed. The idea of relationality further enables us to avoid singular, unilinear, and unified conceptions of process and to recognize the multiple and often disjunctive effects of structures. A relational perspective is thus fundamental to understanding the meaning of *process* and to addressing the companion concepts of identity and difference.

In rather competing ways, then, these major theories have already established relational modes of analysis from which it is possible to establish some general premises for thinking about identity and difference. First, and most generally, identity and difference cannot be grasped as an either-or opposition but stand to each other in a both-and relationship. In other words, it is conceptually impossible to think identity without simultaneously thinking difference (Hall 1991; Melucci 1996), whether this involves class relations, intrapsychic conflicts, gender relations, discursive structures, or other relations. As argued in structuralist semiotics, identity needs to be understood as always part of a system of "relations of difference." This is another way of saying, as Diana Fuss (1989) remarks, that we are to locate "differences *within* identity" (103; emphasis in original), that identity must be regarded as potentially internally divided by the very differences that constitute it. Second, and central to my purpose, the concept of relationality enables us to articulate and establish the social bases of identity and difference.[10] The "social" is constituted in relations among persons who interact, belong to groups and communities, and function within institutions. The social is thus located in the interrelationships among different identities and comprises the site at which these differences become structured and defined. Individual persons develop a social character as part of the process of asserting, forming, or acquiring identities, and thus the social enters into the construction of identity and difference in a fundamental way. Third, and most important, if "relationality" leads naturally to a concept of *social* relationality, this immediately focuses attention on the relationship between self and other. Involving both inner and outer worlds, this relation is fundamental to the ways in which identifications get made (Melucci 1996). As selves, we inhabit inner worlds of experience, meaning, and intentionality that, however divided by difference, define our subjectivity as individuals. As members of society, we live and act in outer worlds of relations with others characterized by external social structures of difference. In principle, despite ever shifting imbalances that ultimately privilege the weight of society and culture, the inner relations of self and the outer relations of others are mutually determining, so that identity is formed *within the differences* making up the self-other relation. Given this kind of formulation, it can be argued that self processes and social processes and their interrelationship constitute a basic framework for theorizing the dynamics of identity and difference within a social context.

The rudimentary elements of a processual conception of identity were originally introduced through the psychoanalytic concept of identification (Laclau 1994). This concept implies a lack or split within the personality requiring a filling or completion. According to Freud, identification was the mechanism of self-development by which the child was to find "unity" or "wholeness" as an individual (Zaretsky 1994; Calhoun 1994: 15). In actuality, the conceptual emphasis on a whole and integrated self came to prevail only in later psychoanalytic writings, most notably those of Erik Erikson, who spoke of "identity" rather than "identification" (Zaretsky 1994) as "one's selfsameness and continuity in time" (Erikson 1980: 22). Identity, then, was based on an assimilation and integration of earlier identifications. The principle of difference, however, remained persistently embedded in Freud's own mature formulations, whereas the neo-Freudian stress on unity served to suppress Freud's insights into the inherently unstable character of the self resulting from the fissures and discords of the psyche. For Freud, wholeness was only an ideal that presupposed the overcoming of a multiply conflicted self burdened by the ultimately irreconcilable demands of id and superego. By implication, following Freud, identity had to be thought of as anything but singular and fixed but, rather, as in a state of being continually *made* in the developmental struggle of self-growth and mastery.[11]

Although a self-other view clearly inhered in Freud's structural model of intrapsychic conflict among id, ego, and superego, Freud himself neglected the social dimensions implicit in this model. Recognizing that relations of self to other were in a sense the very center of Freud's concept of identification, object relations theorists later developed a social perspective within psychoanalysis and emphasized the assimilation of the infant's experiences of others into a relationally constituted ego (Epstein 1991; Greenberg and Mitchell 1983; Guntrip 1971). Contextualizing identity even more broadly, Erikson saw it emerging in the interaction between self-development as an internal process and social participation, involving the internalization of culture and the acquisition of statuses and roles (Gleason 1983). For Erikson, the individual could only become what culture and history would allow, and identity formed in a dialectical interplay between personality and culture (Levin 1992).

While falling short of a fully developed picture of self and other in social terms, these later Freudian developments should make it apparent that conceptualizing identity and difference in terms of the self-other relationship avoids the pitfalls of theorizing them exclusively in either psychological or sociological terms, as an attribute of either the individual on the one hand, or the group, social structure, or culture on the other. It further avoids dichotomies between asserting or choosing an identity and acquiring one by external imposition or constraint. In this sense, the self-other relation has always borne the implication of both freedom *and* constraint. This was evident in Marx's classic notions of the social relations of class and historical praxis, where making history was an activity always weighted by inherited circumstances and is implicit in the Freudian theme of the contradictions between conscious and unconscious mental life.

Yet these influential traditions failed to develop a systematic conceptual understanding of the social nature and dynamics of the self-other relationship. This task, though still unfinished, was to fall to the lesser-known tradition of symbolic interactionism, a legacy of the social pragmatist philosophy of George Herbert Mead (1934).[12] At the core of symbolic interactionism is a conception of the "social self" that, according to Mead, has a double nature. The self is constituted socially, through interaction with others and the normative influences by means of which the community controls the behavior of its members. The self, in other words, in some literal sense *includes* "the other." But what makes the self a self is the individual's ability to make an *object* of the self, that is, the reflexive capacity of self-consciousness. The self thus functions as both subject *and* object. In Mead's view, the social environment is continually changing as individuals, groups, and communities adapt to evolving conditions of life and mutually adjust to each others' behaviors within a collective framework of problem solving. The implication of this picture of ongoing social activity is a self that is fluid, exhibiting social continuity through normative patterning while simultaneously existing in a state of multiplicity and flux through situational adaptation. While outside his own nomenclature, Mead would have understood identity emerging in this flux, in the dialectical and formative interplay between social influences and the reflexive responses of the self. To be sure, much is missing from the Meadian version of the self, in particular any account of the divisive and conflictual features of identity formation prominent in the theories of Marx and Freud, as well as a consideration of the workings of power in identification processes. Nevertheless, Mead's naturalistic social psychology brings important focus to the centrality of self processes and the formative character of social relations in the emergence of identity. Importantly, it accomplishes this by conceptualizing the self-other relation as part of a larger process of social interaction within a community, involving both multiple others and an acting self.

The current, loosely postmodern orthodoxy that identity is "constructed," the "effects of complicated discursive practices" (Fuss 1989: 2), is derivative of the poststructuralist claim that identity, and all of culture and social life, is constituted in (or like) representations or "texts." The invocation of difference from this position is meant to reveal the intrinsically fluid and shifting character of identity, its chronic instability in the face of semiotic plenitude and dispersal. However, to the extent that identity *is* destabilized by difference, the argument that this is exclusively attributable to the multiplicities and instabilities of discursive systems and practices does not go far enough. As Mead implied, difference is also deeply implicated in identity at the level of the social processes constituting the self. Relations of difference, therefore, need to be conceptualized not only discursively but also socially. Indeed, language and discourse are unequivocally social in nature: signification presupposes a social ground of meaning, just as social processes themselves are constituted discursively, shaped by interpretive meaning construction.[13] In these terms, difference, understood as the generative factor in identity formation, needs to be thought of as structured socially as well as discursively, produced simultaneously by the dynamics of language *and* social interaction.[14]

The tendency to deprivilege or neglect the social processes of identity formation in favor of discursive effects is fairly widespread in contemporary theory. For instance, in a critique of the dependency of identity politics on the prevailing ideology of individualism, Joan Scott (1992) rightly comments on the importance of putting a political conception of identity in historical context. By historicizing the question of identity, she argues, we call into question the autonomy of any particular identity by recognizing different identities as products of discrimination, thereby introducing the possibility of instability and change in identity. Whereas identity politics conceives of differences as individual in nature and groups as categories or "distinct entities," in fact groups must be thought of "relationally," as "interconnected structures or systems" (17). Scott, however, seems to understand these structures or systems discursively rather than socially, as based in linguistic meanings and relations as opposed to social interactions. While correctly asserting that identities are constructed relationally, she fails to recognize the social nature of the "enunciation of difference that constitutes hierarchies and asymmetries of power" (12). This kind of analysis fails to acknowledge explicitly that historical practices of discrimination are carried out by members of one *group* against those of *another*, in socially organized institutional contexts where dominants and subordinates produce and reproduce relations of power and privilege in socially defined ways.

By insisting on a relational rather than a categorical conception of identity, Scott ipso facto draws attention to the social production of identity and difference. And, in recognizing these as socially produced, it becomes apparent that the divide between biologically or otherwise determined "essentialist" accounts and "constructivist" theories of identity and difference is of less consequence than the question of the social structures and processes behind the ways that identity is perceived and defined. Thus, being black or white, male or female, becomes a matter of the production and reproduction of identities and differences *within social structures* by means of *processes* of social interaction. This involves but is not limited to the capacity of groups, classes, and whole nations to define or construct others' identities in accordance with the interests of those in power and to act in ways that reinforce and normalize these definitions. A theory of identity and difference must therefore be located between the discursive and social logics of self and group relations. The form and shape that identification processes take are ultimately determined by these relations and the larger institutional contexts in which they operate and take shape.

The emphasis that poststructuralism and cultural studies have placed on relations and processes of representation is a reflection of the enlarged powers of representation in a culture saturated by media and continually expanding forms of signification. An awareness of the sheer extent to which social and political hierarchy is created and maintained through the cultural relations of power has been the underlying animating force of cultural studies. Poststructuralism has supplied a theoretical basis for theorizing the *destabilizing* influences that inhere in a culture increasingly dispersed and fragmented by media technologies, rapid change, and the representational demands of historically marginalized groups newly asserting themselves. The theoretical gains of a preoccupation with representation, however, have often been bought at the expense of an adequate understanding of the social fields producing representation in the first place and through which representation operates, and a viable conception of agency on which the effects of representation depend. Identity formation and relations of difference have been articulated too strongly in terms of representational processes and too weakly as the product of group and institutional structures and processes and the material interests shaping them. Fortunately, many of the tools for accomplishing the task of analyzing identity and difference socially are already to be found in established social theories, including but not limited to symbolic interactionism. It is of some significance that notions of identity and difference themselves have always been implicit in many of the major concepts of modern social theory, although these themes have seldom if ever been explicitly theorized or linked to cultural representation in any systematic way.[15]

With these arguments in mind, an outline of a social theory of identity and difference, I suggest, would be based on the following claims. First, the widely accepted postmodern refusal of biology needs to be rejected on the grounds that theorizations of identity and difference can ill afford to ignore the real-world effects of the biological and physical givens of natural difference, for example, skin color and sexually reproductive functions. In this regard, contrary to the influential injunction giving precedence to culture over biology, the recently privileged categories of race, gender, and sexuality need to be seen in terms of both biology *and* culture, as referring to relations based on both natural *and* social difference. While biology should not be essentialized, neither should it be denied as a consequential factor in the social and cultural construction of identity and difference (see below). This calls for a conception of difference that recognizes the complex and multiple interrelationships among social structures, the structures and workings of cultural discourses, and the irreducible facts of biological nature and variability. Questions of identity thus are not reducible to any of these dimensions singly but dependent on their complex combinations.[16]

Second, and simultaneously, as the vehicle of identity formation the self must be understood as a social self, as constituted in a set of social interactions structured as self-other relations. Social relations form the overall framework shaping the intersection of culture, society, and biology in the self. This includes both internal processes of socialization and external processes of social control. However, in keeping with a Meadian conception of self, while socialization and social control imply determinacy, a processual as opposed to exclusively structural understanding of these mechanisms leaves the question of social determination perpetually tentative and open.[17] Such an understanding provides the possibility of regarding identity and difference as moments in ongoing processes of self and social definition and interaction. The logic of difference, therefore, operates between nature and its social and cultural constructions, as part of a definitional process governing self-other relations at all levels of society.

A relational conception of identity and difference overcomes many of the blind alleys of identity politics by introducing a mode of thinking based on the socially constituted and changeful nature of identity, leading to what might be called a "politics of difference" (I. Young 1990; Hall 1991). While it is important to guard against automatic antiessentialism, it is just as important to recognize the intergroup nature of identity construction, specifically the interactive character of processes of group definition. Separatist or "tribalist" conceptions that fix identity in the traits of a single group obscure ways that group identity is socially produced in interactions *among* groups (I. Young 1990). To invoke singularity in talking about identities is to suppress the relational character of these identities as they have been formed historically in group and institutional relations and as they promise/threaten to change in the future. This implies specifically that while marginalized identities may have their source largely in the hegemonic definitions of those in power, the marginalized also possess the potential to challenge these definitions. Moreover, notions of singularity ignore the interrelationship between self-definitions of the marginalized and the ways the powerful perceive and define themselves (see below).

To summarize, identity and difference are not directly given by culture, the group, or biology but are complexly constructed through the *interpenetrations* of these separate forces in a definitional field of social relations. A theory of identity and difference would thus need to take into account how identity is multiply constituted in the differences of both culture and nature. But mainly, how these forces operate in the definitional field must be grasped at the level of the social structures and processes in and through which identity and difference are concretized and experienced by human actors.

The framework I am proposing here should not be viewed as replacing approaches emphasizing culture and power but, rather, as reconceptualizing culture and power in terms of their underlying social processes and as reintroducing a conception of agency. Most versions of poststructuralism and many approaches in cultural studies downplay or eliminate the processual and formative elements of social life inherent in individual and group interaction and the internal deliberations of the self. Those who bind it in the "text" tend to forget that culture is socially generated and meaningful to its participants. The close linking of power to cultural representation, while an important theoretical advance, similarly poses certain problems. Following Foucault (1980), power has been conceptualized in a way that tends to distance it from immediate social contexts in favor of larger cultural and historical formations. Foucault's monumental work has made important contributions to our understanding of the ways power is constituted in the institutions of culture. He has also deepened our grasp of how power, while institutionalized in knowledge formations, can be thought of as circulating throughout society, thereby providing a basis for a micropolitics of resistance. Foucault's particular formulations, however, have created numerous difficulties. In his conception, power seems to be everywhere and available to everyone, making it extremely vague sociologically. While giving implicit recognition to the social and institutional character of power, Foucault paid insufficient attention to the actual *structural relations* and *material foundations* of power as they manifested themselves in the dynamics of domination and subordination. Furthermore, by concentrating on a "discursive" and "productive" conception of power and thus shifting attention to its cultural and historical embodiments, as illustrated by his theory of disciplinary knowledge, Foucault was unable to provide a more direct and immediate picture of the social dynamics and effects of power as they manifested themselves in the lives of social individuals. In contrast, a social relational theorization of identity and difference that built on Foucault's insights would attend more explicitly to the social structural inequalities of culture and power, while recognizing that these inequalities are produced and reproduced by dynamic social processes and social agents and are thus historically mutable.

Social Relationality and the Tasks of Constructionism

Contemporary theorists, and especially postmodernists, have relied heavily on constructionist notions of identity, criticizing essentialist modes of thought frequently found in identity politics. Defined by Diana Fuss (1989) as "a belief in true essence—that which is most irreducible, unchanging, and therefore constitutive of a given person or thing" (2), essentialism has been widely repudiated by poststructuralist- and deconstructionist-influenced thinkers, who see the subject as "constructed" by both discursive and social practices. Whereas essentialists see differences as naturally given, as a manifestation of interior essences or substances waiting to be discovered or named, constructionists focus on the "*production* and *organization* of differences" by "processes of social determination" (Fuss 1989: 2–3; emphasis in original). For constructionists, differences are embedded in the historically specific workings of cultural and social processes and therefore not "natural" (thus necessary) but, rather, provisional and contingent, and thus susceptible to change.

Constructionism by other labels has been axiomatic if only implied in the social sciences for many years, especially in the tradition of symbolic interactionism. Constructionism has also been the dominant tendency in most feminist theorizing since its inception. However, constructionism seems to have been thoroughly reinvented by the poststructuralists, for whom it has often acquired the character of a slogan and been wielded as a weapon in tendentious challenges to essentialist, biologically based notions of identity.[18] Given the social and discursive nature of subjectivity and the self, it is clear that constructionism is a valid principle in theorizations of identity and difference. Yet polemical invocations of constructionism have reduced it to a simplistic formula, rendering it increasingly problematic as a method of analysis.

This can be illustrated in a number of ways. First, those who employ constructionism seldom define and theorize it adequately, so that its many possible meanings never get enunciated. For example, on the assumption that "everything" is constructed, important distinctions seldom get made among different *dimensions* and *sources* of the construction of identity and difference. There seem to be at least two separate but overlapping difficulties here. The first is a problem of the unit of analysis. Assuming the construction of a self or identity, what is the agent of construction? Social structure, social relations, culture, history, or something else, and which aspects of each? All such determinations play different roles and represent different processes in identity formation and relations of difference. The second problem pertains to temporal frame. Whether constructionism has deterministic or indeterministic implications depends on whether it involves accounts of the past, involving childhood socialization, the effects of which are more invariant, or accounts of adult experience, which presupposes the predicates of consciousness and choice, implying more deconstructive possibilities. The underlying unaddressed problem is thus the actual effects of various social and cultural processes on identity formation and difference and how these effects occur or might be destabilized.

Second, constructionism *as a position* has been privileged almost with immunity, acquiring the character of an ideology. In actuality, the line between constructionism and essentialism is problematic. As Fuss argues, constructionism is in unacknowledged ways duplicitous with essentialism, mistakenly deployed against it in what has become a spurious assertion of two falsely opposed positions. For instance, constructionism can be seen as allied with theoretical notions of difference insofar as this concept implies that identity is multiple and even fluid. Thus, in an effort to avoid unified, and therefore presumably essentialist, conceptions of identity, constructionists have come to rely on pluralistic grammatical forms. However, in the process of pluralizing what are actually generalizing or "collectivizing" statements, for example, referring to *women* rather than *woman,* one reverts to essentialism by setting up yet another unity, in this case the collectivity "women" (Fuss 1989: 4). We could find innumerable examples of Fuss's observation that linguistic statements, and by implication theoretical conceptions (for example, "difference"), intended to capture and convey heterogeneity succumb to essentialism despite themselves. As Fuss argues, whereas essentialist thinking sorts things into different "species or kinds," constructionist thinking must necessarily assign names to things, however arbitrarily, through language (and by implication, thought), thereby establishing and fixing categories by linguistic means. The difference between these two operations is simply one of locating "real essences" as opposed to "nominal essences" (Fuss 1989: 4–5). This brings to light an important distinction between essentialism as a belief in a natural state or condition that imparts identity to a person, and essentialism as a fixing or unifying operation without presumptions as to what might be "natural" or "originary." As Fuss implies, the latter form of essentialism would seem to be a necessary condition of any type of conceptual thought, or at minimum a necessary condition for the use of language.

Third, the constructionist characterization of social and cultural life often has been grossly overstated. Some poststructuralists attempt to claim that difference has no foundation in nature whatsoever, thereby eliminating the possibility of essence entirely. For example, Judith Butler has taken the position that sex and sexuality themselves need to be regarded as social constructions in the strict sense that our very concepts of "natural" differences among individuals are themselves constructed. Thus, "the gendered body . . . has no ontological status apart from the various acts which constitute its reality" (Butler 1990a: 336); and "this production of sex *as* the prediscursive ought to be understood as the effect of the apparatus of cultural construction designated by *gender*" (Butler 1990b: 7; emphasis in original). This type of pure constructionism is difficult to reconcile with the facts of biological difference, for example, the childbearing capacity (and experience) of females as opposed to males, or the physical differences of race and age, *however* these differences might in practice be socially, culturally, and politically constructed representationally and institutionally. Constructionists thus often overlook the ontological reality of the physical world of objects, denying the very possibility of a prediscursive realm. Some constructionists seem to suffer the hubris of an idealism that denies the physical world its own material reality.

A fourth criticism of constructionism points to a problem it often shares with essentialism. While the constructionist approach appears to support notions of change—if identities and relations are constructed, they can in principle be deconstructed—there is nothing inherent in constructionist theory that makes it an ally of social or political renewal. On the contrary, it could be argued that the constructionist approach simply adds to biological determinisms its own social determinisms based on essentialist notions of society and culture. The stronger versions of constructionism have implied that the effects of early socialization and social structure are so powerful as to fix patterns of identity permanently (the temporal factor). This has the ironic consequence of essentializing identity with social science concepts whose original purpose was to eliminate naturalizing biological accounts of behavior (Calhoun 1994; Fuss 1989). By failing to clarify and theorize the problem of determination, constructionism itself becomes entrapped in the dilemma of freedom and constraint powerfully thematized by Marx and still haunting social scientific and political thought (Epstein 1987). If constructionism is understood in processual terms, social interaction and self-reflexivity come into play as formative effects in the production of identity in a way that implies conscious agency and potentialities for change. If, in contrast, constructionism is taken as a structural conception to mean the internalization of knowledge or learning laden with existing social beliefs and norms, or the effects of institutional regulation and control, its implications are inescapably deterministic, implying a fixity of identity.[19]

The abstract appeal of the distinction notwithstanding, the contrast between essentialism and constructionism in practice seems unacceptably blurred, if not ultimately unsupportable. Essentialisms are quite vulnerable to change insofar as they are "constructed" historically and culturally, and constructionism seems to be laden with "essentialized" conceptions of structure and normative order (Fuss 1989).

As these arguments suggest, while the attacks on essentialism have been largely justified, the constructionist position creates numerous difficulties of its own. Its occasional excesses and pretenses aside, constructionism remains a complicated and ambiguous strategy for theorizing identity. By itself, the abstract proposition that identity and difference are constructed begs too many questions about the nature, processes, and consequences of construction.

While having served a useful purpose in discussions of gender, race, and sexuality, the debate over essentialism and constructionism now appears to have become irrelevant for either a theory or a politics of identity and difference (Epstein 1987). A helpful distinction for heuristic purposes, both essentialism and constructionism contribute insights to our understanding of identity. While identity develops through processes of social, cultural, and political construction, these processes do not (and cannot) eliminate the differences of nature, which set boundaries and limits on our social and cultural repertoires. Moreover, processes of construction are often simultaneously essentializing processes, to the extent that social and cultural determinations lead to stable identities and social practices and to experiences of an enduring and authentic self. Insofar as it can be both strongly felt as something substantial and internal to the self, and experienced as consisting of multiple, fragmentary, and shifting positions, identity can only be apprehended fully from both positions. As Calhoun (1994) has put the matter, "To essentialist reason we *add* constructionism and to this dualism we add the possibilities of *both* deconstructing and claiming identities" (19, emphasis in original).

Finally, while constructionism has been deployed as the politically and theoretically "correct" position, its unquestioned epistemological hegemony is contradicted by the persistence of real world essentialist identities. As Calhoun (1994: 14) remarks, many such identities "continue to be invoked and often deeply felt." Identities such as woman, Jew, disabled, mother, and Arab remain commonplace, suggesting that identity formation is still very much grounded in fixed, unitary, and even biological notions of the self. The tendency of many constructionists to negate singular or solidified identities by regarding them as wholly imposed by multiple determinations is often inconsistent with the ways that people actually see, feel about, or identify themselves. These inconsistencies, furthermore, raise strategic questions for subordinate groups regarding the political consequences of automatically dropping essentialist notions of, say, gender or race, insofar as such a move would decollectivize such categories.[20]

The more fundamental and important question we should be asking about political matters of identity and difference is at the core of the social relational paradigm: to what extent is identity formation a self-made process as opposed to a hegemonic cultural and historical process manifested in the definitions of others, imposed and controlled from outside and above? As we have seen, the theoretical trends have been toward an emphasis on processes of cultural and political and to a lesser extent social determinations, as constituted in the discursive acts of powerful others. Since social relations are structured unequally, identity and difference can never be theorized entirely apart from questions of inequality and power. Certainly, the politics of identity has rightly focused attention on the role of structures of domination and subordination in the production of marginalized identities. Contrary to identity politics' preoccupation with the victim, however, it is just as important, as Cornel West has reminded us, to talk about "identity-from-above" as well as "identity-from-below" (West 1992). Whiteness, maleness, and heterosexuality, he asserts, are just as much a part of the discourses of race, gender, and sexuality as blackness, femaleness, and homosexuality (see also Messner 1996). Understanding the power relations and discursive practices that structure identity formation, and the hegemonic but often unexamined conceptions of privilege and normalcy inscribed therein, requires an examination of the identities of dominants as well as subordinates. Conceptions that dominants have of themselves are deeply implicated in the construction of subaltern identities; dominant identities are shaped by the notions of otherness on which they depend (Said 1978; Hall 1991). Thus, the construction of whiteness (Frankenberg 1993), while seldom addressed, inheres in the construction of blackness, maleness in femaleness, and so on. In the argument of William Connolly (1991), identity not only requires difference but "converts difference into otherness in order to secure its own self-certainty" (46). For Connolly, the dependence of self-identity on the construction of otherness is a major source of evil, a process in which power plays an important part. Accordingly, identity construction is inseparable from the relations and enactments of power determining the definitional processes transforming various kinds of difference into an *opposition* between identity and otherness.

However, while identity constructions reflect and serve inequality and power, they must be seen also as manifestations of institutional processes that are in certain respects relatively autonomous of the discourses of power. The family, the shopping mall, the school, the church, the mass media, the workplace, and other institutions are sites of social practices and technologies that produce and reproduce prevailing structures of identity partially through the *functional operation* of these institutions and technologies as well as the *uses* that are made of them by social actors. Thus it is important to examine the formation of identity and difference in terms of the functional workings of institutions, which are dependent on the reproduction of the very subjectivities that constitute and sustain them, for instance, the gender identities supporting the bourgeois nuclear family or the lifestyle identities of consumer capitalism. But we further need to consider how the meanings and purposes of these institutions can be subverted by those who use and remake them in normatively unintended or transgressive ways.[21]

In addition, power relations are relations of structured interdependence, and as part of a socially and culturally constructed system of unequal and potentially contested differences, these relations are inherently unstable. As Connolly (1991) argues, dominant identities are "vulnerable" to challenges from those who would "counter, resist, overturn, or subvert definitions applied to them" (66). Put differently, the power of others to define is limited by the potentially disruptive possibilities of social interaction as initiated or forced by reflexive and rebellious selves. While inequalities of power and privilege might be crucial factors in the determination of identity, self-definitions are ultimately a product of the interactions between dominants and subordinates, self and other, and carry the complex, variable, and unpredictable markings of these interactions. As Alberto Melucci (1996) comments, identity always contains "an unresolved and unresolvable tension," a "gap," between self-definitions and how others define us (32). Even among the marginalized, then, the effects of power in defining subordinate identities are conditioned on the internal symbolic and social capacities of the self to renegotiate identities through processes of communal group life (Mead 1934; Blumer 1969).[22] This might be taken as a symbolic interactionist rereading of Foucault's claim that power produces resistance. Yet in this interpretation there is nothing inherent in the nature of power that guarantees resistance, and resistance (when it occurs) is understood as a socially produced and formative process involving social actors.

As these considerations indicate, a social relational approach enables us to transcend the false dichotomy that has been created between essentialism and constructionism by recognizing identity and difference as products of a variety of social processes shaping the self and self-other relations. Individuals see themselves as they think others see them (Cooley 1902; Mead 1934), and this always involves relations of power. But at the same time, individuals reflect on these socially induced self-conceptions according to their own needs, desires, and interests as selves and members of groups. A relational conception of identity formation, then, would take constructionism as describing *interactional* processes working both on the self and its relations to others. These processes are shaped by the larger institutional forces of social structure and culture but in turn impart to them formative properties rooted in the generative powers of interaction and the creative potentialities of the self. In this respect, constructionism needs to be understood as designating a complex set of processes involving a social self that is both structural and processual in nature, reproductive of past cultural and historical constructions, and therefore power, but renegotiating and repositioning these in relation to a practical present and anticipated future, envisioned not only imaginatively but through social action.

On the Tensions between Universalism and Particularism

A social relational approach to identity and difference casts a different light on an issue that parallels the tension between essentialism and constructionism and that in a sense constitutes another version of the same debate. The postmodern denunciation of universalizing thought, believed to be the defining feature of Enlightenment philosophy, is articulated suggestively with the separatist tendency in identity politics toward an enunciation of the particular. Critics of a modernist leaning, and defenders of left politics, however, have attacked the fragmentation and relativism inherent in the trend toward particularistic forms of identity thinking (for example, Gitlin 1994), seeing in this a disturbing Balkanization of politics and theory. While postmodernists and many proponents of identity politics have regarded universalistic modes of thinking as a form of domination, as inherently totalizing and therefore oppressive, others have seen the repudiation of universalism as regressive, divisive, and potentially dangerous. Postmodernists have invoked the principle of particularity as an epistemological strategy, a means of knowing based on recognition of the particular social location of the knower as a determinant or condition of what is known.[23] Proponents of identity politics, however, appeal to particularity as a moral and political strategy, often revoking universalistic modes of thought as one might choose good over evil.

But just as antiessentialists resort to various forms of essentializing, antiuniversalists frequently practice their own version of universalizing. This is done not only through the assertion of general statements but, as we have seen, through the deployment of new universals such as difference. Just as it is impossible not to think in categorical and therefore essentializing terms, it is unlikely that any theory or political practice can dispense with universalistic principles. The posing of a disjunction between the universal and the particular as a mutually exclusive relation therefore replicates the mistake that constructionists make in rejecting essentialist conceptions.

Ernesto Laclau (1992) has compellingly demonstrated the inseparability of the universal and the particular in his argument that particularism by itself leads to complete relativism as well as to inevitable clashes among competing groups. Not only is pure particularism self-defeating, he argues, but in fact "there is no particularism which does not appeal to . . . [universalistic] . . . principles in the construction of its own identity" (87). We have observed that in claiming rights for subjugated groups, identity politics appeals to universal ideas such as equality and justice that it necessarily and safely presumes are shared by the surrounding political community. To the extent that identity politics is predicated on the production or claiming of particular identities in the face of their foreclosure or suppression by others, it must resort to a set of universal rights whose exercise has been partial and whose democratic extension has been thwarted by racism, sexism, and so on.

Furthermore, just as identity and difference presuppose each other, Laclau rightly argues that any particular identity presupposes all the other identities from which it differentiates itself as well as "the total ground which constitutes the differences *as* differences" (88; emphasis in original).[24] The impossibility of differentiating an identity without distinguishing it from a context, Laclau states, suggests that the assertion of a particular identity simultaneously requires the assertion of its context. Particular identities, then, are inseparable from the larger contexts that define them and dependent on appeals to universalistic principles by which the fulfillment of these identities is to be measured. The containment of the universal in the particular in this sense accounts for the inevitably modern stance assumed by identity politics in its search for redemption. More to the point, any given identity acquires its significance within a universal through its *relation to* and *differentiation from* other identities.

While largely hidden and suppressed, something of the same logic haunts postmodernism generally in its attempts to privilege particularity over universalizing or generalizing modes of thought. In its arguments for particularism or disunified subjectivity, postmodern theory necessarily contradicts itself, since such arguments must take the form of general assertions and the positing of general principles, in this case particularity. Furthermore, the reduction of knowledge to particularisms catches postmodernism in a hopelessly relativistic trap. If knowledge can only be particular, as Nietzsche tried to insist, there is no reason to accept or deny any given assertions or claims over any others, Nietzsche's included (Booth 1985; Dews 1987). Postmodernism in practice, then, fails to avoid the insurmountable contradictions involved in renouncing universalistic conceptions (Eagleton 1996). Such renouncements must be made by a coherent subject that argues for the rightness of its own claims. Moreover, such claims necessarily presuppose their own epistemological grounds of legitimation. Thus, to the extent they are required to engage in logical argumentation and epistemological positioning in the antifoundationalist war on Enlightenment philosophy, postmodernists must revert to this philosophy's own foundational assumptions.

Postmodernists argue that their critique of universalism is directed against the contents of universalisms in Western thought, the "master narratives" (Lyotard 1984) of modernity that support totalizing and exclusionary modes of knowledge or belief. This critique purportedly has been made in the name of exposing the particularisms (male, white, Western, heterosexual) behind the universalistic claims of science and democracy. Yet the main question is the extent to which ideas, concepts, or whole bodies of thought and knowledge, however universalistically framed, are capable of claiming validity independently of their social origins (Harding 1991). In other words, the discounting of universalisms for their particular *content* (for example, Eurocentric or masculinist worldviews) hardly amounts to a discrediting of universalism as a general practice, as illustrated by continued widespread support even among postmodernists for such ideals as freedom, equality, and justice. The case against universalism would thus seem to depend on the universalisms, or modes of universalizing, in question, specifically the extent to which their invocation disguises and legitimates privileged and exclusionary interests.

Conclusion: Social Analysis and the Category of the "Individual"

The politicization of identity emerging from the earlier politics of the self and the movements of the sixties and seventies has produced a large volume of theoretical writing and commentary on identity and culture. More recent writings have turned increasingly to a postmodern emphasis on the fluid and contingent character of identity by self-consciously adopting certain poststructuralist themes derived from the works of Derrida, Foucault, and Jacques Lacan, authors who at the extreme imply the abolition of identity altogether through a valorization of difference and otherness. Most of these writings have constructed identity in cultural and political terms, attempting to establish close links between cultural, social, and political representation and the workings of power. These post-Marxist and postideological approaches to identity claim to have replaced earlier materialist paradigms such as Marxism and psychoanalysis by demonstrating the centrality of signification processes and the fundamentally discursive nature of social and political life.

Although the privileging of the cultural domain constitutes an important historical and theoretical corrective to previous materialist perspectives, the collapse of identity into discursive power relations is a form of cultural reductionism that simply inverts the earlier problems of materialism into the equally unacceptable difficulties of idealism. In addition, to the extent that the shift from identity to difference simply creates another universalizing stance, the task of theorizing identity analytically as a *problem* of difference gets lost in rhetorical discourse about the "other." By limiting our understanding of the problem of difference to textual paradigms, much of cultural studies has sidelined the real and potential contributions of systematic social analysis. While their main postulates reflect a real-world crisis of subjectivity and identity, textual models have ignored the *sociohistorical origins and character* of this crisis by their failure to ground the problems of identity and difference in social relations and institutions.[25]

I have suggested that the destabilization and politicization of identity are rooted in numerous social and cultural transformations in postwar mass society. These include economic, technological, and social changes generating needs for group identifications and a search for identity and meaning in the realm of collective experience (Klapp 1969). From this vantage point, identity politics, while comprising a historically important political formation, is symptomatic of deeper social and cultural transformations in U.S. society. To gain a sense of the wider historical significance of identity politics and its failure to address and resolve questions of difference, it is imperative to examine the social processes underlying both the problem of identity and difference and its cultural and political constructions. I have further argued that understanding identity and identity formation requires a processual as well as a structural conception of social relations. This requires a shift from exclusively discursive and cultural conceptions toward group and institutional frameworks as well as a refocusing of identity and difference on the operations of a social self constructed and shaped by the dynamics of group and institutional life.

The shortcomings of textual or discursive approaches to identity are inseparable from the widespread and often dogmatic repudiation of humanist models of ego-centered consciousness. The weaknesses of actually existing humanist models of the "subject" notwithstanding, the refusal of concepts like individual or person necessitated by the poststructuralist rejection of (or inattention to) concepts of consciousness precludes the possibility of understanding identity in the context of lived experience or of grasping the dynamics of its social formation and enactment.[26] The absence of a concept of self in poststructuralist writings portends an inability to comprehend ways in which identities are constituted socially in difference and reproduced, fragmented, or subverted over time in various daily life settings. Lacking notions of self-reflexivity, self-process, or self-consciousness, as well as a conception of social relations, poststructuralism resorts to explaining the constitution and disunities of identity by reference to the structures, disjunctions, and gaps of discourse and power.

In response to narrowly discursive approaches, I have proposed reconstituting the problem of identity along social relational lines. This calls for important distinctions between cultural identity on the one hand, and social and personal identity on the other. While cultural identity implies membership in or identification with a collective entity—a cultural heritage, an ethnic community, a nation—social and personal identity are constituted in the relationship between "individual" and "society." Whereas *social identity* can be thought of as referring to the process of defining the self through social roles and relationships, *personal identity* refers to how self-definition is shaped by the larger social world of recognition and experience in which self-development occurs (Hewitt 1989). While cultural constructions of identity designate the collective or group experiences and meanings of individuals *as members of,* say, racial, gender, ethnic, or sexual categories, notions of social and personal identity shift the analytical frame to a generic individual as constituted by social structures and institutions. This frame draws attention to contemporary social and cultural forces shaping and disrupting identity as part of a general process *sweeping across* particular social categories and collective identifications.

The rehabilitation of the concept of individual partially reinstates a modern paradigm in which individual is paired with society in a relationship that is both productive and antagonistic. This strategy enables a reconceptualization of the crises of identity in contemporary society that is both comprehensive and historically grounded. The universalizing dangers of this strategy are obvious. The individual was the sociological creation of modern markets and forms of political representation that presupposed persons as equivalent units (Macpherson 1962, 1973). An ironic effect of creating individuals was, of course, to repress difference (Calhoun 1994: preface). This was true historically, insofar as modern economic and political actors typically were white male property owners of the educated classes, but it remains true today to the extent that the category of individual implicitly collapses social, economic, cultural, and other differences into a single social universal.

The risks of negating difference, however, have always been intrinsic to the illumination of broad social and historical processes. By displacing particularistic categories of identity, the individual, despite its universalizing character, facilitates analysis of social and cultural processes shaping large trends and movements of a historical nature. First, recuperating the idea of the individual makes it possible to move from collective forms of identification to the institutional sites of identity formation and to the treatment of difference in an institutional context. I argue that institutional sites and structures are as or more central to identification processes, and the problem of difference, than collective identifications based on shared cultural and historical experiences. This is true whether we have in mind modern forms of affiliation such as the family, workplace, school, or church, or postmodern sites of identification connected to new modes of consumption and technological reproduction. Moreover, while the politicization of identity has been facilitated by identification with collective entities, as I have argued this can be accounted for by a set of conditions and needs propagated by structural transformations in postwar capitalist society.

The category individual also creates the possibility of reinstating processes of self-definition in our theoretical accounts. Only partially formed by the determinations of culture, history, power, and geography, identity must also be theorized from a standpoint that assumes the search for self-identities on the part of relatively autonomous social actors seeking to incorporate their social experiences in a variety of ways and settings. Individuals as actors negotiate meanings and self-identities within a broad social field on which larger social and cultural forces place both limiting constraints and creative possibilities.

Finally, a word on a chronic issue in social theory and a recurring theme in this chapter and those to follow. The languishing problem of determinism versus freedom has been perhaps unintentionally revitalized as a result of the postmodern attack on modern notions of subjectivity. As Terry Eagleton (1996) has argued, there is a sense in which the "subject" of postmodernism is paradoxically both "free" and "determined." Culturalist accounts are quite deterministic: behaviors and beliefs are shaped or conditioned by diffuse forces, namely, power, desire, and discourse. But these systems are seen by postmodernists as "multiple and conflicting," decentering the self and thus "lending the subject a lack of fixed identity" easily mistakable for emancipation or freedom. While inescapably determined by various cultural reductions, the postmodern subject is simultaneously and as a direct consequence "strangely free-floating, continent, aleatory" (Eagleton 1996: 89). As Eagleton notes, this picture omits that humans *are* determined but in ways that allow for a degree of *self-determination,* a very different matter from cultural fragmentation and dispersal of the self. As he rightly concludes from this, theoretical oppositions between the conditioned and the autonomous are therefore ultimately false.

But the cloudy issue of determinism has also been reinvoked as a result of the widely unquestioned acceptance of constructionism as the sole strategic means of thinking and talking about identity and difference. As I have suggested, deconstructive approaches that insist on identity's fluidity and tenuousness make questionable assumptions about the consequences of cultural discourses on identity formation. Constructionist ideology, while seeming to assume the fictiveness, contingency, and therefore instability of identity, has evaded specific issues as to whether or not, and to what extent, identities are determined or fixed in ways upholding existing social and cultural arrangements, thus avoiding the question of constructionism's own potential conservatism. Therefore, the question of determination—without illusions as to its final solubility—requires extensive social analysis of processes and mechanisms of identification and identity formation. To be sure, a theoretical arsenal already exists for this purpose. On the one hand, conventional structural conceptions of society and culture, Marxist or otherwise, continue to serve as important explanatory bases of constructed identity. On the other hand, interpretive and voluntarist models provide suggestive insights into the nature of agency and the possible sources of freedom of action. Its neglect of power, culture, and structure notwithstanding, symbolic interactionism—the original but still incomplete theory of social and discursive construction—offers a processual conception of group and institutional life that recognizes the constitution of identity and agency in a social self. The framework I am proposing thus attempts to recognize both the constraints *and* formative potentials of culture, social structure, social process, and the self.

The articulation and negotiation of difference remain the fundamental theoretical and political problems of our time. The type of analysis I am proposing attempts to specify the larger parameters of this problem in the structural and cultural changes lying *behind* the politics of identity and difference, changes conveniently categorized under the rubric of postmodernity. This "larger" picture bridges the gap between cultural inquiry and social analysis by grounding the problem of identity and difference in sociohistorical change, social structure, and social process. Such an approach generates insights into how identity-forming processes have been changing as a result of domestic and global transformation. This approach, finally, challenges us to think of difference in new and deeper ways, specifically questioning how it is both strategically and inadvertently generated and repressed within the institutional workings of particular societies, especially within Western capitalism.

2
Modernity and Postmodernity
Transformations in Identity Formation

The turn to a theory and politics of difference following the critique of identity politics presupposed notions of a "postmodern" condition decentering and destabilizing identity. In fact, the long discussion of identity issues has come to be framed by a growing distinction between the modern and the postmodern, defined as opposing epistemological standpoints, successive historical periods in the development of the West, or divergent sociocultural conditions. This distinction marks an assortment of alleged changes in social, cultural, and intellectual life during the twentieth century, with implications for identity formation and modes of theorizing subjectivity. A sociohistorical account of identity and difference, therefore, needs to face questions about a transition from the modern to the postmodern and attempt to isolate those changes through which a definition of each might be constructed. However, whereas the debate about the modern and the postmodern has been waged largely through questions of epistemology and, to a lesser degree, typology and periodization, I propose formulating the distinction around evolving meanings of identity in the modern era and, more important, the *shifting bases* of identity formation marking the postmodern condition.

Analyzing the sources and nature of identity destabilization in the postmodern world—seen alternately as a threat and a cause célèbre—calls for a historical reprise providing an inventory of changing conceptions of the ways identity has been constituted and problematized. Just as the postmodern cannot be formulated without recourse to the concept of the modern, the problematization of identity in Western society requires an interrogation of its background in the social and cultural formations of individualism in classic modernity. These problems are inseparable if for no other reason than that the very notion of identity inheres in the rise of modern society, while under postmodernity identity as we have conventionally understood it seems threatened with extinction. It is not unexpected, furthermore, that identity should have become such a preoccupation in the intellectual atmosphere of postmodernism, since the problematization and deconstruction of identity is a precondition for arguing against modernist epistemological beliefs. The success or failure of this particular effort notwithstanding, changing conditions of identity formation can serve as fundamental criteria for distinguishing between the modern and the postmodern as historical formations.[1]

In what follows, I explore and contrast the nature of identity formation in modernity and postmodernity, identifying major variations that modern thinkers and observers of postmodernity have attributed to this process, indicating how these formulations are reflective of cultural and structural developments in society. In considering its changing sources and forms, I argue that identity in modern society has led an agitated existence, more divided and problematic than many postmodernists have supposed, however mythologized by modernists *and* postmodernists in unifying notions of Western individualism and the rational ego. The fate of identity as understood by modern thinkers has revolved around questions of the relationship between the individual and the group and community, specifically how the individual (and self) negotiates the social disruptions and uncertainties accompanying modernization and the rise of mass society. While these conditions persist unevenly into the present, a postmodern formulation of the problem of identity addresses the threat to self-unity and coherence posed by structures of consumption in a commodity-[2] and media-based society and amid growing social and cultural difference. While the problem of difference will be addressed in later chapters, this chapter adopts a perspective on transformations in theoretical constructions of identity and the actual conditions of identity formation. Using television as an example, my main concern will be to show how the social relational basis of identity formation, originating in modern notions of self-unity, has been undermined by technologically based commodity culture in ways suggestive of both liberatory and regressive consequences for selves, social actors, and communities.

Identity: A Concept of Modernity and Its Modern Formations

What we today call "identity" could have become a problem only following the emergence of large-scale society and the relative decline of traditional group life in the West. In traditional society, identity is largely pregiven through membership in the group and community, determined externally by systems of kinship and religion. In traditional cultures, identity is more or less fixed at birth and integrated into relatively stable structures of custom, belief, and ritual.

By contrast, with the cultural beginnings of modern society the locus of identity formation shifts to the inner life of the individual. As group ties weaken, individuals are distanced from collective beliefs and attachments and challenged to invent, change, or oppose society in accordance with their own visions and interests, independently of ritualized frameworks of belief. The rise of individualism, a phenomenon concentrated historically in the white Protestant bourgeoisie of early modern Europe (Weber 1958c), brought with it prescriptions of autonomy, freedom, and choice, and these values enforced a realization that the conditions of modern life required self-definition independently of, if not against, ancestral forms of thought and behavior. The term "individual" itself insinuated a new, self-conscious identity insofar as having or making an identity necessitated standing apart from others through the development of a unique set of personality traits.

Thus, the assault on traditional social structures gave rise to an individual called on to forge his (but seldom her) own identity independently of the ascribed characteristics inhering in one's placement in tradition and nature. Through the resources of self, this individual was seen as destined to receive, acquire, and fashion his own identity in an increasingly unknown, uncertain, and rapidly changing world. Negotiating the contingencies of time and place, this figure of self-creation was to achieve status within a more or less tenuous social order by means of his own willful and self-interested actions.

In view of the chaotic diversity and change accompanying modernity, however, the very notion of identity and its roots in a unified and coherent sense of self began to acquire the character of myth. As many nineteenth-century thinkers understood, real historical individuals were as divided as the social effects and ambitions of modernization itself, reflecting tensions and contradictions *inherent* in the project of modernity.[3] While often assumed to be a unified outlook inspired by Enlightenment ideals of progress, modernity as a cultural enterprise has been split historically into divergent and often opposing intellectual and moral tendencies (Baumeister 1986; Taylor 1989). This is demonstrated first of all by the production within modern society of *many* individualisms. As Anthony Cascardi (1992) argues, the subject of modernity stands at the intersection of a number of disjunctive discourses: "For example, the 'philosophical' subject understands itself in terms that are quite distinct from and indeed opposed to those evoked by the 'literary' subject, and both of these seek to differentiate themselves from the secular and political subject" (3). These subjects are to be further distinguished from the economic subject of the expanding industrial and consumer marketplace as manifested in the "possessive individual" of modern property relations (Macpherson 1962). The modern (European American) individual, thus, was always implicated in a number of *different* projects of self-realization and change.

Furthermore, to the extent that the modernization process was inseparable historically from the rise of nationalisms, colonialisms, and imperialisms, modernity inherently divided identities along nationalistic, racial, and ethnic lines. While defining itself as a universalistic project of human progress through development (Berman 1982), modernity drew deeply on the particularistic elements of past and present cultures to forge national identities capable of exercising new forms of global power while simultaneously generating new kinds of ethnic and racial conflicts (Anderson 1991). Approached as history, then, the modern period has not been at all as unified or universalistic in goals or outlook as some constructions of modernity have implied (R. Young 1990).

There is yet another kind of problem with the tendency to think of modern forms and conceptions of identity in unified terms. In the modern intellectual tradition it was not long before "the subject" acquired an ontologically, psychologically, and politically conflicted status. Since at least the time of Marx, the subject has been understood in terms of both agency and determination, as acting and acted on, reflecting the modern antinomies of spontaneity and order, freedom and alienation, activity and passivity, autonomy and domination. The individual's very capacity for a unified identity, then, was problematized by "theoretical" modernity through the articulation of forces antithetical to reason and self-knowledge. This has been the hallmark of theoretical traditions inspired by thinkers like Marx, Nietzsche, and Freud, all of whom saw the modern self as torn between the ideal of reason and the irrationality and discord surrounding elusive and unmet needs and desires.

These antinomies account for the variety of discrepant modern discourses about the subject, both optimistic and gloomy, and the repetitive efforts in modern thought and literature to reconstitute the subject in the face of threatened dissolution by forces beyond its control. The discovery of such forces, and the emerging theoretical understanding of the social, psychological, and cultural determinisms comprising them, gave rise throughout the nineteenth and twentieth centuries to various notions of "authenticity" serving to disclose the possibilities of human wholeness as salvation from modernity's unruliness (Heller, Sosna, and Wellbery 1986). For instance, the famous Marxist themes of alienation, exploitation, and ideology were counterposed by the goal of socialist reconstruction based on ideals of equality, freedom, community, and rationality. The unseemly forces of the Freudian unconscious were redeemed by a rationalist faith in the powers of psychoanalysis to enable self-realization and the exercise of reason and self-control. In the existentialist tradition, the anxiety, guilt, and sense of purposelessness engendered by the modern world were overcome by a freely chosen and decisive "leap of faith" shaped by an ethics of responsibility and commitment (Barrett 1958; Collins 1952). In these and other discourses, the contradiction between autonomy on the one hand and determinism, domination, or oppression on the other became the driving force behind the humanistic assertion of an authentic self.

Variations of this picture have been foundational to the major critical perspectives of modern social theory. For the classic social thinkers, the individual faced the threat of absorption by large-scale entities such as bureaucracy, the state, the factory, the market, and mass society. Marxist reification, Weberian formal rationality, Durkheimian state oppression, and Frankfurt School domination are major thematic examples of the destruction of identity and selfhood by the forces of modern capitalist social organization. In one way or another, the development of the classic social critiques was propelled by pessimistic diagnoses of and glimmering utopian hopes for the fate of the individual in the modernization process.

In the search for identity running through what might be called the "discourses of alienation" in modern theory and literature,[4] we can discern at least three strategies for the articulation of an authentic self. First, the individual was seen as constituted by a preexistent identity waiting to be found or discovered. In this view, identity is substantial, essential, and unchanging, as implied by Cartesian, Kantian, and other Enlightenment conceptions of a rational and "knowing" ego. Second, identity was to be found through a romantic or existential search for personal meaning on the part of an isolated individual pitted against or in retreat from society. In this tradition, the path to identity lay outside society and its oppressive constraints. Third, in the Hegelian tradition the self was construed as a product of social interaction, whereby identity was forged through manifold encounters with and appropriations of the external, "objectified" social world (Miller 1987). While certain kinds of social relations were seen as alienating, for instance, those of work and the marketplace, others were seen as potential sources of selfhood, for example, the relations of family, religion, and community. These three possibilities—singly or in various combinations—represent modern conceptions of self-retrieval amid overwhelming impersonal forces. The idea of the modern individual and its vicissitudes thus took shape within a divided intellectual tradition that sought grounds for reason and liberation as against the alienating conditions of modern life.

The problem of modern identity, however, is not simply reducible to the problem of alienation, understood as a loss of human powers. In terms of the social divisions and ruptures of a rapidly changing society undergoing atomization, the search for identity was less a redemption from alienation than an attempt to reconcile and overcome the multiple internal conflicts of a divided self. This divided self had sociological foundations, first of all, in institutional change. The historical rupture of God and state produced a new opposition between the identities of "believer" and "citizen," involving fundamental conflicts between the categories of sacred and secular belief. Across these divisions, and pushing them in a secular direction, modernity created a plurality of new "life spheres" by means of institutional processes of differentiation. Family, work, religion, education, the state, and other sanctioned patterns of social organization became sources of competing claims on the self. In addition to institutional differentiation, new forms of inequality within the structures of capitalist society linked transformations in identity to new modes of production and reproduction based on the exploitation of labor. Modern society thus forged new identities from within the class, gender, racial, and ethnic relationships emerging from a transformed division of labor. At both levels of social change—institutions and class relations—a multiplication of social roles and relationships within an expanding and secularizing market-based society became a volatile source of sociologically divided identities.

The overall shape of the changing bases of modern identity formation, however, is most comprehensible in relation to evolving stages in the social relations of capitalism. The evolution of modern identity can be seen most simply through a broad distinction between the early modern period of entrepreneurialism and the later period of economic concentration and corporatism. Corresponding to the period of realism in art, early capitalist modernity still offered strong support to notions of a unitary self, goal-directed and motivated by an inner sense of purpose. David Riesman's (1950) "inner directed" personality type describes a self attached to inner normative controls still capable of a certain unity and coherence during the early stages of capitalist society. With major structural shifts—from manufacturing to clerical, service, and other secondary forms of economic activity; the expansion of capitalism into the sphere of consumption; and the growth of large-scale bureaucracy—economic and social roles underwent extensive differentiation. Additionally, the transformation from rural to urban life and the emergence of a modern city landscape expanded the horizons of self-development. Economic growth and urban concentration thus led to a multiplication of social roles and relationships and a corresponding proliferation of identities within a growing multitude of social settings.[5] The resulting fragmentation of perception, experience, and self-knowledge corresponded to the decline of realism in art and the rise of aesthetic modernism, in which the theme of self-dissolution figures prominently, especially in twentieth-century literature and theater and in cubist painting.

These later changes ultimately resulted in a transformed conception of identity and its sources. With greater mobility, change, and role multiplicity, the formation of identity increasingly became theorizable in terms of the social interdependencies of the individual. A fully formed modernity thus contributed to the emergence of a social conception of self. While originally disclosed by Hegel and later elaborated by Marx, who saw the individual as defined by the "ensemble of social relations" (Feuer 1959: 244, "Theses on Feuerbach," VI), this conception developed more completely in the writings of thinkers like Georg Simmel (1950) and especially in the later work of George Herbert Mead (1934) and his contemporaries. Mead's view of the social relational character of identity formation can be derived from his theory of the social constitution of the individual within a community of action (see chapter 6). The realization that the social interdependencies accompanying growing institutional complexity required a strong orientation to the responses of others also provided the makings of Riesman's (1950) category of "other directedness," which he saw as historically supplanting the inner-directed orientation. Other directedness designated a form of social behavior that is mutually adjusting: individuals seek the approval of others through an anticipatory reading of others' behavioral and attitudinal responses. Riesman's type can be seen as an excessively instrumental and conformist instance of a more general social conception in which identity formation is once again located externally, this time in the socially defined processes shaping encounters with others.

According to the Meadian conception, however, the shift to a mediatory outside social world became only the shaping context for what continued to be *internal* processes of self-formation, which Mead saw as the governing mechanisms of behavior. In Mead's view, the individual acquired an identity by means of self-formation within a socially interactive framework of mutual recognition and adaptation, a process occurring within a structure of community norms. Importantly, however, Mead (1934) stressed that social influences are constituted as an "internalized conversation of gestures," which is the "essence of the self" (228). As we saw in chapter 1, more recent discourse-based versions of this relational conception of identity have taken power and representation into account, however disproportionately, in a way indicative of the growing powers of culture to structure social relations and the self. Under the conditions of developed modernity, however, the individual was seen in terms of interdependencies reflective of the exigencies and potentialities of social relations.

Finally, an understanding of modern identity formation would be incomplete without a consideration of important shifts of degree in the dominant types of roles and relationships accompanying social development in the West. Whereas in early capitalism the relations of production became a primary deter-

minant of identity, with the growth of consumer society, occupational identifications have slowly weakened relative to the ascendancy of consumption and
lifestyle.[6] The transition from kinship to occupation to consumption can be
taken as a schematic account of the trajectory of role development from the decline of traditional society to developed modernity and the beginnings of postmodernity. While accumulative as well as disjunctive, this trajectory represents
within the framework of modernity a series of shifts away from cultural roles
rooted in traditional belief systems toward economic and social roles based on
the developing system needs of modern capitalism.

It is evident from the foregoing that the intellectual and philosophical projects of modernity were greatly at odds with the actual conditions of modern social life (Horkheimer and Adorno 1972). Whereas a subjective rendering of the
experience of these conditions defined aesthetic and theoretical *modernisms,*[7]
which despite strivings for unity defined themselves through images of fragmentation insinuating a divided and conflicted self, classical social theory and philosophy derivative of Kant and Hegel have persisted in foundational beliefs in
unity, certainty, and an authentic and "knowable" experience of the world based
in objective reason and social recognition (Honneth 1992). This outlook has
largely dominated twentieth-century social theory and has continued to exercise
a profound normative influence over modern social and political thought.

The persistence of ideas of self-unity has been apparent especially in the social sciences, where conventional definitions of identity have emphasized unity,
consistency, coherence, and stability in the formation of self. The work of John
P. Hewitt (1989) exemplifies this paradigm:

> What does it mean to have "identity" in our contemporary, everyday usage of
> the term? It is to be like others and yet also to have qualities that make one
> different from them, so that one can have "Jewish identity," say, but also a
> more distinctive "personal identity" that is not defined in terms of group
> membership. It is to maintain a balance between similarity and difference in
> the face of individual development and changing social conditions, so that
> one can assimilate to the self demands for change or adjustment, but also ful-
> fill an inner desire for constancy. It is to be a whole and complete person, and
> not fragmented into roles and ruled by scripts. It is to be connected with
> others and yet true to oneself. It is to participate in a variegated and often
> fragmented social life and yet to maintain continuity and integrity. Persons
> with identity, we are apt to say, know who they are, what they are doing, and
> where they are going. (152)

This idealized conception of modern identity is held together by four key elements: continuity ("the feeling that one's experience of self makes temporal
sense"); integration ("a feeling of wholeness"); identification ("a feeling of

being like others"); and differentiation ("a sense of boundaries between self and others") (153).

While the normative criteria supporting this definition continue to invoke the mythology of the modern individual, Hewitt's formulation has the virtue of underscoring the centrality of self-other relations in identity-forming processes. Group memberships, social roles, social actions, connectedness to others—these provide the contents and boundaries of social and personal identity that impart an enduring sense of selfhood. Paradoxically, the concept of the modern individual, which began with the decline of traditional community and the construction of an inner world defined by character and personal will, ended in a world of social interdependencies in which identity emerged through the individual's relationship to objects *outside of* and *other than* the self.

As this summation of modernity suggests, in the past the problem of identity, while not called by that name, revolved around the overcoming of estrangement and the search for an authentic self. While never in reality as integrated or consistent as often alleged by modernity's critics, identity in modern society has been governed nonetheless *and for that reason* by a series of unifying myths of authenticity. Modern myths of identity lost and found have in this sense presupposed a "depth model" (Jameson 1984a) of alienation underlying a normative project to shape the world in the image of "man."

Modernity, Community, and the Individual

The problem of alienation in classical social theory has often been associated with theories of the dissolution of community. Arguments that modernization has destroyed community have implicitly attributed the loss of possibilities for either selfhood or group-based identity to a detachment and isolation of the individual from community life. This idea is implied in the work of theorists as divergent as Emile Durkheim (1964) and Mead (1934), both of whom saw membership in community as involving social relationships definitive and supportive of the individual. In modern conceptions of the self, then, the search for identity and authenticity has been linked to the task of re-creating and strengthening community and the forging of new relationships between the community and the individual.

Always controversial, the concept of community remains contested to this day[8] yet remains an essential basis for any critical assessment of modernity and the individual. Importantly, the normative tensions inherent in the modern conception of identity (for example, self-fulfillment versus commitment to others) stem ultimately from the *problematic relationship* that modernity created between community and the individual.

The disappearance of "organic" community, which provided stable boundaries and a sense of belonging in traditional society, is implicitly thematized as a model of lost wholeness in numerous critiques of modern capitalist society. While serving as normative markers for what modernity has destroyed, however, many of these critiques have overdrawn the crisis of community in modern society. As Hewitt (1989) has observed, the emergence of modernity *expanded* the boundaries of social life to include both society *and* community. In his argument, classical social theory has exaggerated the decline of community by failing to recognize a transformation from communities that were more "concrete and immediate" (110) into those whose boundaries are more distant, abstract, and diverse. In modern society, individuals are members of numerous, less cohesive and less enduring "nonorganic" communities, existing within a set of impersonal forces associated with large-scale organization and change. At the same time, the forces of modernization have actually *widened* the dimensions of community, expanding its scope (Gusfield 1975). These arguments imply that under modernity community does not so much vanish as persist in altered forms. Indeed, some studies indicate that modern conditions have in various ways actually supported and even strengthened communal life (Gusfield 1975).

Thus, the experience of modernity might be more fruitfully understood as a *contrast* and *contradiction* between what Ferdinand Tönnies (1957) called *Gemeinschaft* (community) and *Gesellschaft* (society). Rather than a disappearance of community, modernity might be better thought of as the uneasy, conflictual coexistence of community *and* society (Hewitt 1989: 114). Viewing the matter this way, we see that the modern individual is thus also split between a desire for communal life and an attraction to the liberating possibilities of the larger society. These contradictory impulses might be thought of as the sources, respectively, of an exclusive "social" identity that differentiates individuals as members of groups and categories and a more autonomous "personal" identity based on individual uniqueness and accomplishment (Hewitt 1989: 191–213).

Furthermore, while idealizations of organic community have provided a normative ground for modern discourses of alienation, these discourses have largely forgotten the contradictory tensions connecting two different images of traditional community. On the one hand, community captures the longings for shared experience and identification with others, a sense of purpose and place, and a source of meaning and order. On the other hand, community can become a figure of authority and obligation, and, indeed, community has been known to manifest itself as an instrument of coercion and oppression, suppressing individual differences, needs, and aspirations. Major dilemmas of the modern self can thus also be located within the social ambiguities inherent in communal life.

Community thus becomes the desired yet conflicted and elusive foundation of the quest for identity, creating a tension in modern notions of freedom and selfhood that is never completely resolved and perhaps irresolvable. As implied by Hewitt's conception, modern identity depends on a valued sense of permanence and wholeness derived from participation in communal life as well as the double process of feeling both identified with and differentiated from others. Identity formation thus takes place through and against community. At the same time, the goals of individuation necessitate involvement in the larger, more abstract and complex order of society extending beyond the boundaries of a single community. To construct a self free of the claims and obligations of community life, the individual is faced with renouncing identifications with the group for achievement and recognition within a broader, more impersonal public or audience (Hewitt 1989). The modern ideals of self-knowledge and development, then, depend on a degree of disengagement from community and a diffusion of individual aspirations across a terrain of social relations and activities involving many kinds and degrees of community participation.

The expansive possibilities of community contained in modernity represent the source of a potentially fulfilled self, but a self always under stress of conflicted definitions and meanings. Weakened forms of organic community survive in such institutions as the family and religion and are reproduced in such locally based structures as neighborhoods, schools, workplaces, and voluntary associations. Such forms offer a degree of stability and security in the face of rapid social change but can also incur major obligations on the part of the individual. As opposed to these more or less permanent but increasingly strained forms of community life, however, modernity engenders an array of less enduring but more individualizing modes of participation. Mass society produces such ephemeral forms of community as social and cultural movements, mass protests, national and local rituals, media events, fads and fashions, and lifestyle trends. These types of collective behavior form a continuum with less transitory, volatile, and more institutionalized forms of community (Hewitt 1989: 146) while extending the horizons of community formation beyond physical place. Such possibilities suggest that community can be highly mobile and replicated in a variety of forms and contexts. Thus, while modernity destroys older forms of community, it creates new ones, more invisible and amorphous yet more differentiated and extensive in reach. This further implies that modernity endows identity with a large degree of elasticity, reflecting both the novel conditions under which identifications can occur and the broadened scope of community formation possible in a mass society.

In both its institutional and collective forms, community now has enlarged possibilities, the source of which is in the "disembedding" process theorized by Anthony Giddens (1990, 1991), whereby social relations are extended beyond local, territorial structures by means of abstract meaning systems.[9] The extension of community through space corresponds to the increased mobility of information, images, and people made possible in particular by the disembedding structures of mass literacy, communications, and transportation. The disembedding of social relations and the concomitant autonomization of culture are the larger forces lending complexity and unpredictability to modern identity.

Indeed, Giddens's formulations offer major insights into the nature of modern identity formation, a summary of which might look like this. First, the basis of self-formation shifts from the immediate and concrete controls of physical community to the mediations of abstract and distant symbol systems. Second, a separation occurs between group membership and processes of identification, so that membership per se no longer serves as the determining factor in identity formation. The individual is now in a position to choose kinds and degrees of group identification independent of ascribed characteristics of birth and communities of origin. Moreover, following on the separation of social relations from physical location, disembedding facilitates a form of abstract-thought-enabling identifications with categories as well as groups. It is therefore possible for self-construction to proceed through identifications with "abstract others" who share common characteristics, needs, or interests, for example, those of a similar age or class background. This feature of modern life is the foundation of "reference group" theory, which allows for identifications with social units of which one is not a direct member but that "provides standards of conduct and models for the self" (Hewitt 1989: 139; see also Shibutani 1955; Turner 1956).

The proliferation of social groupings and categories and the competing demands these place on selfhood constitute the sociological roots of the burden of choice (Melucci 1996) attached to the modern individual. A vocabulary of choice runs throughout the literary and philosophical discourses of modernity, informing the modern concept of identity through such notions as *will, becoming, fulfillment, actualization,* and other terms evoking a creative self. As we have just seen, choice is inscribed in the profound enlargement of identity beyond the immediate circumstances of birth and habitation to the symbolic potentialities of mass society.

However, while an integral component of the modern conception of identity, notions of choice remain largely ideological. As suggested earlier, questions of the actual degree or range of choice embodied in modern social processes have comprised a major subtext of classical social theory from its inception. While implied in the weakening of ascribed roles and the plurality of alignments and orientations made possible by modern society, the idea of choice is richly contradicted by various determinisms. Engendering notions of choice, modernity has at the same time bequeathed new knowledges about the forceful or conditioning effects of nature, tradition, history, social institutions, and biography.

As argued in chapter 1, the effects of socialization and social control are aspects of social construction placing limits on self-determined identity. While always partially a product of conscious choice, modern identity is deeply determined by a thick and complex weave of personal, biological, social, cultural, political, and economic factors.

In addition to creating a set of potentially individualizing and freeing conditions, then, modernity has also propagated an ideology of personal freedom seemingly at odds both with its own substantialist notions of identity and its widely accepted (constructionist) theories of social learning and social control. Yet this is less of a logical contradiction than that propagated by the postmodernists, who by simultaneously celebrating the fluidities of identity (freedom) and attributing these same fluidities to the constitution of identity in the decentering effects of power, desire, and signification (determinism), locate freedom and constraint in the *same source*. In the modern conception, identity is forged in the encounter between a conscious and reflexive self striving for its own realization and the limits of biography, society, and history. By providing a picture of the *dialectical interplay* between self-determination and social determinism, this conception thus remains a major scaffolding of a social relational theory of identity formation. The philosophical problem of freedom and determinism therefore becomes a practical problem of willing and choosing selves acting historically and socially in a world of constraints.

Assuredly, modernity works to create a space of associational life and symbolic identifications in which there can be a development of identities that transcend social background and the constraints of physical community. However, while identifications with, say, family, ethnic group, or religion on the one hand, or mass movements or media celebrities on the other, might be consciously chosen, factors such as biology, biography, and culture are sufficiently "originary" to establish, along with community structures, the boundaries and terms within which these identifications take place.

Since, contrary to arguments for a break between modern and postmodern society, it makes sense only to speak of a continuity and merging of their structural and psychological features, modern definitions of the problem of identity formation obviously continue to have relevance in the present. Three observations are in order regarding possible linkages between the two. First, as we have seen, seeming contradictions have always abounded between the modern mythology of the individual and both social theoretical accounts of the actual experience of modernity and various theoretical, literary, and artistic discourses of modernism. Similarly but less satisfactorily, postmodern theory has displayed two contradictory faces of identity but without the redeeming presence of a concept of a self that partially transcends its own determinations. Second, while claiming to reject the culture of modernity, the discourses of postmodernism have recuperated modernism's fragmented view of the world while abandoning any hope of redemption as reflected in modernism's abstract gestures toward unity.[10] Postmodern theorists have instead celebrated the fragmentation of subjectivity as a breakdown of authorizing cultural hierarchies in favor of cultural difference, relinquishing the despair of alienation for the playfulness of an eclectic culture. Third, theorists of the postmodern *condition,* in contrast, have resituated modernism's fragmentation of experience and meaning in the new contexts of consumerism, mass media, and informational technologies, shifting the problem of identity formation from social relations to the effects of commodification and technology. In theories of postmodern society, the commodification process is seen as undermining the social relations of modernity in general, and traditional and modern agencies of socialization in particular. While previously constituted within the realm of immediate social relations such as the family and work, in this view identity-forming processes have been displaced from these relations, reconfigured and mediated by commercially and technologically based forms of cultural consumption.

Identity in Postmodernity: The Imperatives of Consumption

While embattled, alienated, and proliferating, modern identity was nevertheless destined to find its expression in distinct social roles and relationships within the productive structures of modern life. These structures have provided for an identity premised on relatively fixed boundaries of the self based on distinctions between interior and exterior, self and other. These boundaries, however, defined lines of both separation and connection between the individual and the outer world. The estrangement thematized by the discourses of alienation presupposed an inner life separate from or opposed to the society outside as well as ideals of unity and connectedness to others through which this inner life might achieve some structure and fulfillment.

In contrast, theories of postmodernity project an image of a fluid self characterized by fragmentation, discontinuity, and a dissolution of boundaries between inner and outer worlds. This tendency toward fragmentation and dissolution is linked to the vast and rapidly changing landscape of capitalist consumerism and the evolving means of signification constituting mass culture and informational society. In these theories, technologically mediated forms of culture tend (1) to occlude or obliterate social relations, and by implication the self (Baudrillard 1981, 1983a, 1983c), or (2) to decenter social identities toward an unstable, fragile, and fluid self dispersed by the representational processes of media and other technologies (Harvey 1989; Jameson 1983, 1984a; Lash 1990; Poster 1990).

This conjures a contrast between a modern form of identity anchored in the internal states of individuals but produced in multiple structures of social interaction and a postmodern form constituted directly in the effects of externally mediated forms of signification. These various forms of signification include consumer goods, telecommunications (for example, broadcast and cable television), and informational technologies (for example, computers and databases).[11] In this view, the source of identity has historically shifted from the internalization and integration of social roles to the appropriation of disposable commodities, images, and techniques, selected and discarded at will from the extensive repertoire of consumer culture. In this argument, to the *extent* that communication and information technologies supplant older forms of association, roles and identities lose their interactional quality, becoming an extension of the instrumental and performative functions of various cultural media.[12]

This instrumentalization of roles and identities is suggestive of a demise of the modern individual, especially as constructed by notions of reason, emotion, and other elements of an inner life. Moreover, to the degree that roles become objects of performance and commodity exchange, they would seem to threaten basic ethical precepts of Western society, which presuppose a ground of social attachments and commitments. In some writings about postmodernism, and in line with Fredric Jameson's (1984a) argument about a decline in "depth models" of subjectivity, these ethics are seen as inconsistent with a culture of "surface" and "multiplicity" playfully asserted and celebrated for their own sake (Dunn 1991; Jameson 1984a; Newman 1985; Russell 1985). This particular postmodern sensibility is reflective of a commodified and technologized culture that severs subjectivity from social process, reconstituting it in a realm of images or "signifiers." A related argument sees the collapse of stable and continuous processes of identification producing a detached and mobile "nomadic" subject endlessly negotiating different identities (Melucci 1996; Deleuze and Guattari 1983).

Within this cluster of postmodern notions, however, it is possible to delineate two different theoretical positions. First, in its "stronger" version the subject of the postmodernists is no longer an individual but a fluid set of effects produced by processes of signification or discourse. As discussed in chapter 1, the sketchy articulation of this position in poststructuralism has often taken the form of an attack on Enlightenment conceptions of a substantial self or ego and their substitution by discursively determined subject-positions. Repudiating notions of the individual, poststructuralists have proclaimed the "death of the subject," appealing to the various deconstructions of the subject in Freud, Nietzsche, and Heidegger, and the fields of semiotics and structuralism, the latter of which are the original sources specifically of Jean Baudrillard's apocalyptic claims about the disappearance of the subject in commodity society.[13] This conception collapses essentialist and unified notions of the individual into unstable structures of language, discourse, and power, rendering the subject a shifting set of "textual effects." Such a view verges on denying subjectivity and identity altogether, claiming their complete disintegration in processes of signification.

A "weaker," more compelling version of the postmodernist subject, however, speaks less of dissolution than of changes in the subject's formation. In this argument, postmodern society destabilizes the subject through the commodification of culture.[14] This implies the disintegration of integrated, productivist roles as the subject becomes fragmented by privatized regimes of consumption and leisure. Specifically, as a consequence of commodification, processes of identity formation undergo transformation in at least four basic ways. First, the individual is turned into a *consumer*, and increasingly a consumer of signs and images. While social identities persist (for example, employee, parent, student), these identities are now subsumed by the role of consumption, which increasingly shapes and conditions the individual's social orientations and relationships. Second, the *sources* of identity formation change as tangible, role-based relationships are subordinated to the disembodied visual images of mass culture. Third, identity formation is *exteriorized* in the sense that its locus shifts from the inner self to the outer world of objects and images comprising commodified culture. Identity formation in postmodernity (as in premodernity) thus deeply roots itself in culture but in the form of the commodity rather than the group (Lash and Friedman 1992). Fourth, and as a consequence, the self loses its sense of autonomy from the outside world. Assaulted by market-based systems of signification, identity now becomes chronically unstable, inconsistent, and incoherent. The fragmenting effects of the commodity form *problematize* the integrative and continuous features of self-identity as the self is absorbed by the disjunctive features of mass culture.

In the weaker version of postmodern identity, then, the self is transformed by a culture of consumerism and identity and self destabilized by technological processes of signification, reconstituted and reshaped by the commodity form.[15] Images, fashions, and lifestyles manufactured by the media industries become sources of self-image and vehicles by which the self perceives others. The "other-directed" orientation of developed modernity becomes fully absorbed in the mediations of consumerism, the media, and advertising. To the extent that we define ourselves through acts of consumption, our relationship to others and to ourselves is mediated by commodities and especially the form they take as images. In this view, mass culture tends to substitute ready-made images for identifications with "real" social objects. Social identifications are displaced by collections of image attributes consumed through television, movies, mass periodicals, advertising, and other cultural commodities.[16]

In this argument, the displacement of social relations by commodities has two consequences. First, consumer culture becomes a primary means for the construction of self. Style and fashion offer themselves as a source of incessantly changing and highly personalized identities. People "fashion" themselves through clothing, food, music, automobiles, television shows, and other commodities, in what Axel Honneth (1992) refers to as a "*process of fictionalization* of reality . . . through which the atomized individual becomes an imitator of styles of existence prefabricated by media" (165; emphasis in original). Second, the collective identities of class, gender, sexuality, race, and ethnicity along with conventionalized institutional social roles are weakened or replaced by more individualized and fluid "lifestyle" identities constructed in relation to consumer goods (Featherstone 1991; Shields 1992) and mass media images such as film stars, advertising persona, television personalities, and fictional media characters (Kellner 1992). To the extent this occurs, the moorings of the self in socially delineated statuses, roles, and relationships are weakened and processes of self-definition come to depend increasingly on an appropriation of the attributes of commodities. An integrated social conception of self is thereby replaced by a loose aggregate of personality traits assembled through the consumption of goods and images.[17]

In an older discourse of social criticism, the shift of identity formation from social roles to the packaged world of mass culture was seen as a breakdown of the socialization process and associational life.[18] In this earlier rendition of perceived threat to social values, the influence of family, church, neighborhood, and school weakens in the face of mass media, particularly television. In this view, centralized media systems undermine the authority of traditional socializing agencies responsible for the formation of stable identities and group memberships. Here, a market in cultural goods works to erode the social contexts and loyalties in which meaning and identity traditionally took shape, leaving the individual adrift in a world of commercialized distractions. Thus, identities are no longer influenced by the validations and controls of social groupings but are prefabricated and mass-marketed to consumers who appropriate them according to their personal needs and desires.

Subsequent changes in the production and consumption of culture, however, have significantly changed this earlier critique of mass culture. Whereas previously mass culture was condemned for its standardizing features—the dominant tendency in the early postwar years of economic expansion—recent decades have seen increased cultural fragmentation and dispersal, inviting a postmodern rereading of old criticisms (Collins 1989: 7). The increasing fragmentations of mass culture have provoked a more ambivalent and often celebratory attitude, in which a new sense of heterogeneity in cultural consumption is approached somewhat optimistically. The postmodernist construction of mass culture, then, attempts to preempt the formerly one-sided, negative view propounded by elitist critics. As a result, when measured against modern ideologies of identity, the actual impact of consumer culture now seems more ambiguous.

The more optimistic postmodernist view, on the one hand, sees in a continually changing marketplace of goods and images a realm of personal freedom, an alternative to established cultural and social norms. Honneth (1992) sees an underlying feature of the postmodern as the replacement of "self-realization," which presupposed "some life goal," by the Nietzschean idea of "experimental self-creation." In Honneth's words, "here, human subjects are presented whose possibilities for freedom are best realized when, independent of all normative expectations and bonds, they are able to creatively produce new self-images all the time" (167). Such self-creation is offered through the freedom to select from a wide range of goods and experiences, such as clothing, hairstyles, music, or television shows, without constraints of tradition or convention. Consumerism in this sense provides a potentially liberating experience, facilitating an expressive self by providing an arena of conscious experimentation and choice in the construction and elaboration of identity (Lash and Friedman 1992: 7).

The posing of such possibilities by consumerism and the media, along with the commercial co-optation of new cultural attitudes and values spawned by the sixties counterculture, has led many observers to proclaim ours an era variously of "self-fulfillment," "hedonism," or "narcissism" (Bell 1977; Bellah et al. 1985; Lasch 1979; Schur 1976; Turner 1976; Yankelovich 1981). While such concepts are of only limited value in characterizing present-day culture as postmodern, they clearly reflect the shift from the productivist values of modernity to the consumptionist ethos of postmodernity. At the same time, however, although such tendencies are obviously compatible with notions of self-creation, they also reflect the extremely individualistic and frequently self-seeking and pathological forms that this has often assumed in the United States (Lasch 1979, 1984).

Nevertheless, a postmodernist reading sees in the very nature of consumer culture expanded possibilities for the development of new kinds of identification. On one level, this can be seen in the various ways that consumer culture has *pluralized* style, differentiating and articulating new social and cultural identities around gender, race, ethnicity, age, and sexuality (for example, the independent woman; the youthful and fit senior citizen). On another level, and within these new vocabularies, this culture introduces multiple possibilities for the articulation of *personal* style, whether in the form of individually constructed lifestyle identities (for example, new looks in women's and men's clothing fashions) or as part of lifestyle identifications with collective groups and categories (for example, upwardly mobile, professional African Americans). On both levels, consumer culture provides a range of models to choose from in the construction of novel identities, be they commercially marketed styles or individualized constructions. This has been accomplished through increasingly segmented markets and sales strategies that target consumers with specialized tastes. The post-Fordist replacement of mass production and consumption with product differentiation, target marketing, and rapid goods turnover (see chapter 4) has thus overcome many of the leveling effects of standardization widely criticized in earlier mass society theory.

Contrary to the critics of mass culture and consumerism, the conditions of contemporary consumer culture have thus made it possible to contemplate the commodity as a vehicle for a more fully developed self. Daniel Miller (1987), for example, has argued that material culture provides the means of "sublation" in the Hegelian sense, whereby the externalizations or "objectification" of the world in objects is reappropriated by the subject in a creative "overcoming" of alienation (28). This view suggests that commodities, rather than functioning as instruments of domination or manipulation that distort and fragment the self, can potentially be appropriated as means of self-formation and realization.

On the other hand, the original (modernist) critics of mass culture have attacked consumerist ideologies of choice for masking the basic powerlessness of individuals in a corporate-dominated society. Choice in consumer goods and media images, this argument runs, represents a spurious compensation for a real decline in power and influence in politics and the workplace. Consumer individualism, additionally, serves as a pale imitation of "authentic" individualism based on the values of achievement and individual self-worth. Consumer choice, in this view, has replaced real social and political recognition, trivializing freedom through its reduction to the category of taste. Consumerism, to the extent that it privatizes choice by enforcing loyalty to the values of leisure and lifestyle, has a depoliticizing effect, turning workers—who might otherwise be solidaristic and militant—into consumers, and citizens—who might otherwise engage in collective action—into spectators (Alt 1975, 1976; Brenkman 1979; Debord 1977). Moreover, tendencies toward conformity remain inherent in a cultural system in which social success depends on criteria of style and fashion sanctioned by the media and other corporate institutions. While consumer culture often seems packed with novelty, in fact rapid stylistic turnover simply masks the underlying structures of predictability that are the foundations of commercialism. Personal choice is short-circuited by market-based norms of popularity and conformity, as illustrated especially in the strategies of mass advertising.

From this perspective the incursions of mass culture also pose troubling questions about the impact of ready-made cultural products on the formation of a social self. Cultural commodification makes the formation of personal and social identities increasingly dependent on the prerogatives of the corporate economy. In this view, new cultural articulations of gender, race, and so on, while recognizing difference and contributing to collective forms of identification, are nevertheless *marketed* identities. In a society shaped by the marketing of goods and images, the criteria of self-definition become instrumental, impersonal, and distant, and self-construction comes to depend increasingly on the agendas and strategies of large-scale corporate enterprises.

In summary, the externalization of identity-forming processes in mass culture can be seen as both liberating and problematizing identity and the self. On the one hand, the proliferation of commodities and the play of images promise seemingly limitless possibilities for creative self-expansion and experience. Despite their predetermined market character, the self in this view retains a capacity for making of commodified images what it will, reading and utilizing the meanings and pleasures inherent in these images in ways that cannot be anticipated or fixed in advance. On the other hand, the tendency toward the absorption of self-identity into a world of images can be seen as threatening the dissolution of the boundary between self and outer world, problematizing both (Lasch 1984: 153). If and to the extent that a distinction between inner self and outer world is no longer sustainable (Lasch 1984: 32), the self is reduced to a function of the operation of sign systems, and identity becomes as scattered and fleeting as market-based manufactured culture. In this scenario, the multiplicity of discourses, sensations, and messages flooding the culture overwhelms and fragments the subject, foreshadowing the demise of meaning and selfhood and a loss of freedom.

Television as a Commodity Form: Consumption and the Displacement of Social Relations

Among the numerous scholarly traditions in media research (behavioral effects, content analysis, institutional analysis, uses and gratifications, ideology critique), none has been more provocative than the cultural studies approach, which, unlike older theoretical strategies, has attempted to conceptualize the media in terms of "text" and "audience" (Fiske 1987, 1992; Hall et al. 1980; Hall 1980b; Morley 1980, 1986; Radway 1984). In this approach, media and their spectators are understood as located within discursive and ideological structures of power. In a departure from ideology critics, however, who tended to focus on patterns of ideological reproduction in the media, cultural studies theorists usually see these structures as inherently unstable. In this view, given the ambiguities of texts and the multiple social positionings of culture consumers, meaning remains always at least potentially contested. On the one hand, "polysemic" texts (Fiske 1987) open themselves to a range of ideological meanings; on the other hand, active audiences use various interpretive strategies, as conditioned by their specific social and cultural locations and interests, to construct their own "readings" of the media. In this model, the media are located within a larger domain of struggle over meaning, where ideology is continually being shaped and reshaped through the interplay of texts and audiences.

By limiting itself to a conceptualization of the media as relations of discourse and power, however, the cultural studies approach has attended mainly to the (usually subordinate) *structures* of identity, without addressing the actual *processes* by which identity might form or change. While understanding media as sites of meaning contestation in terms of subject positions, cultural studies scholars have often neglected the more difficult problem of the subjective processes by which meaning is actually *formed* through media experiences and, importantly, the extent to and ways in which this depends on capacities of the self. This limitation, furthermore, follows from the fact that, while shifting attention to audiences, cultural studies has continued to understand audiences or readers as derivative of the text (Lembo and Tucker 1990: 99), broadly understood as systems of cultural signification—both inside and outside media experiences—rather than in terms of the readers as relatively autonomous selves.

In reality, the ironic[19] power of television to undermine conventional social categories and identity structures focuses attention more broadly on certain deficiencies of both ideology critique and cultural studies. The basic claim of ideology critique has been that the media simply function as another socializing agency, reinforcing hegemonic attitudes and beliefs through the imposition of corporate ideologies. Cultural studies emerged largely as a response to the shortcomings of this model by demonstrating that mass media are not at all reducible to ideological apparatuses, as demonstrated in how members of audiences frequently filter or "decode" media messages through their own socially specific, nonhegemonic belief systems (Hall 1980a). But at the same time, cultural studies has tended to reduce media and their audiences to discursive relations or positions.[20]

When we consider television as a commodity form and examine the actual viewing practices of television spectators, the limitations of exclusively ideological and text-based approaches to media consumption become apparent. Along with actual viewing practices (Lembo forthcoming), television as a commodity form is one of the more poorly understood aspects of postmodern identity formation. Such a perspective would recast television viewing as a consumption relationship in which viewers *consume visual representations*. In this respect, television serves as a model of the effects of consumerism understood as a commodification of cultural meaning and experience. Here, the visual properties of television assume a significance that is equal to if not greater than its powers of ideological reproduction. This recasting sees television predominantly in terms of its reliance on images and the constitution of the viewing experience in the flow and fragmentation of these images (Williams 1975). Furthermore, *as* a consumer of visual images the television viewer is positioned partially *outside of* fixed social and ideological relations. This makes it possible to explore television from a perspective other than that of power and ideology and in a way that shows how the consumption of images produces its own level of effects.

By regarding television as a commodity form producing effects on the self in excess of those of ideological or discursive relations (Dunn 1986a), it is possible to begin exploring the effects of commodification on identity formation as well as questions about the liberatory as opposed to nullifying effects of mass culture on self-development. To begin, of all the mass media, television most reinforces the tendency of consumerism to democratize taste and social relations, both by its leveling effects and its eclecticism. This feature of television stems from its marketing requirements as a commodity and its basic characteristics as a broadcast medium. In numerous ways, television erodes hierarchical relations and models of identity premised on stable subject positions. Just as postmodern theorists have redefined the subject as an intersecting site of multiple social and cultural determinations, television can be conceived as a site of not only multiple *messages* but of intersecting images, genres, styles, experiences, and effects (Collins 1992). While dependent on stereotyping and ritualization to focus and structure content, fixing it in formulas, television is simultaneously called on to eclectically mix a vast amount of subject matter to satisfy a vaguely known but broad range of consumer demand. This eclecticism operates at the level of single shows, the flow and fragmentation of single channels, and the simultaneous operation of multiple channels. The resulting heterogeneity of television culture as a whole profoundly alters the parameters of self-experience and identity formation. In a phenomenological sense, television experience is thus a major departure from the daily life experience and social relational contexts in which identity has typically formed.

At the same time that terms like *heterogeneity* and *eclecticism* generally describe the conditions that comprise television as a *medium,* the requirements of formulaization produce a powerful homogenizing effect at the point of production. This has its source in the rule of the common denominator and the semiotics of television production strategies. As Baudrillard (1981) has argued, the signifying processes of the mass media reduce everything to their own logic. These processes obscure "use value" (the "signified" of semiotics), leaving the production of meaning to television's own codes and signifiers (Dunn 1986a). By reducing cultural representation to the possibilities and limitations of its own commercially and technologically shaped discourses, television effaces the inherited cultural categories of modernity, fusing subject matter, value, and taste into a "popular" mix of mundane and common meanings. Thus, social and cultural distinctions are collapsed and refigured to fit television's entertainment formulas and production values.

As one form of homogenization, mass audience formulas result in a merging, compressing, and restructuring of familiar patterns of social structure. For instance, in *No Sense of Place,* Joshua Meyrowitz (1985) argues that television overlaps social spheres and merges social differences, erasing customary behavioral distinctions. Two aspects of this seem especially consequential for questions of identity destabilization. First, in his words, "By bringing many different types of people to the same 'place,' electronic media have fostered a blurring of many formerly distinct social roles" (6). This includes such distinctions as private and public, masculine and feminine, and adult and child. While in this argument behavioral distinctions of many kinds are weakened by television, one of the most important consequences is the effacement of authority levels, especially that of age structure. As a form of universal access to information, television, as Meyrowitz (1981) points out elsewhere, collapses the "graded access" to information on which childhood socialization depends, implying a "disappearance of childhood" (Postman 1982) and a broad merging of child and adult roles in forms of entertainment that are inclusive of all age groups.[21] Second, the weakening of social distinctions undermines the boundaries and significance of social roles *in general.* A sense of permanence is lost as roles come to be "seen as temporary phases chosen by individuals rather than as natural developments" (Meyrowitz 1985. 156). The collapse of real-world social structure in the world of television thus throws the boundaries of social knowledge and the self into question.

Another form of homogenization is evident in the ritualistic stereotyping of characters, plots, situations, problems, and scenes in fictional programming and the familiar packaging of other kinds of programs in which aspects of life's raw materials are selectively processed for mass consumption through television discourse. At this level, television constructs itself in ways designed to satisfy and not offend, blending diverse beliefs, attitudes, values, styles, and opinions in a smooth and palatable consensus. As a consequence, television produces material that is easily digestible by everyone but that speaks distinctly to no one in particular. This formulaic neutrality effectively abolishes differences that exist in the real social world by reducing otherwise distinctive identity positions to a carefully managed and manipulated set of preprogrammed responses. Identity on television is thus manufactured for easy consumption by being packaged in diluted and ambiguous forms.

Regarded merely as mass broadcasting vehicles and systems of formulas for marketing manufactured entertainment, television and other media raise important questions about changes in the material sources of identity formation, such as the rise of celebrity in the form of packaged identity models. But given the relational nature of identity formation, it seems even more important to explore the technologically based effects of visual flow and fragmentation on the viewing experience, and how this in turn dramatically changes the *conditions* of identity formation. As a result of its very form, television broadcasting works against the unity and cohesion assumed by modern modes of representation and conventional sociological conceptions of identity. As a commercially driven commodity form, television exemplifies the transformation to consumption relations and the inherently fragmenting effects of a corporate-based consumer culture. Furthermore, television is a major form of mass privatization. Television presupposes an isolated viewer/consumer; viewing presupposes a certain withdrawal from the contexts of social interaction. Television spectatorship, then, can be thought of as a socially disengaged experience of a simulated, ongoing, and highly fragmented world of visual images. While television viewers often watch with others, the *act* of viewing necessitates disengagement from social interaction for an immersion in a fabricated world of visual stimuli. Furthermore, even though viewers might hold to an inner sense of self against which they measure or judge what they see on television, the decision to watch often comes from a desire for pleasurable distractions that enable the viewer to escape from self and other.

The "escapist" character of television viewing is inseparable from the simulational and constructed nature of the televisual world itself. While in various ways making claims to "reality," television in fact constitutes only ready-made representations, substituting for real social relations their artificial construction as images. To the extent that identification processes might still be at work in television viewing, they shift from social contexts of interaction to artificially created visual experiences.[22] Whereas in social interaction identity is shaped and sustained by the ongoing and mutually reinforcing responses of self and others, in television viewing the self enters into a fundamentally different process of reacting to and appropriating prefabricated messages. As such, identity is both opened to innovative possibilities and limited by the preformed meanings on which television as a mass medium depends. Television can unsettle identity, offering a fantasy world of action and desire that opens to the play of mind and the imagination. Needless to say, television also promotes a powerful form of social "realism,"[23] however artificial, by formulaically condensing and privatizing familiar aspects of social experience and by rhetorically prescribing ways of thinking and acting in the social world. But as commodity form, television binds the self back into structures of consumption inherent in its programming, formulas, and visual codes. While creating a realm of image play (Lembo forthcoming), television simultaneously conditions and adapts the self to participation in consumption relations by substituting for socially based identity formation a fragmentary and disorganized collection of *image-based* identities.[24]

Social interaction connects the self to others' actions and responses by means of an internally shared set of common and negotiated meanings. These continually emerging ties, as Hewitt (1989) argues, contribute to an individual's sense of continuity, providing a framework for self-identification and differentiation. The consumption relationship, in contrast, weakens and ruptures these ties. As a functional object, television elicits responses without itself responding (Baudrillard 1981; Debord 1977). Instead, television works to absorb the symbolic and social processes of lived interaction into industrially finished products, harnessing these processes for predetermined and instrumental purposes. It is in this sense that television as a consumption relationship externalizes processes of identity formation, shifting the locus of self-construction from the internal relations of interaction to the consumption of externally produced images.

The nonsocial relational character of the television viewing experience symbolizes the transformation of the problem of identity formation from the alienation of self-other relations to the isolation and fragmentation of the self in consumption relations. Although the implications of this situation for questions of identity are profound, its real effects are unclear. Two possibilities suggest themselves. On the one hand, television viewing can be seen as an activity relatively free of direct social and cultural constraints and thus offering experiential openings to new forms of identity that viewers construct in self-determining ways. Identifications are in one sense viewer directed and controlled, implying a kind of free-floating identity-making process that is buoyed by an endless supply of images and sensations. In this respect, television viewing as an act of consumption provides a potentially inventive and imaginative means of self-construction free of conventional social influences.

On the other hand, if the capacity for self-definition is by its nature social relational, dependent on the concrete encounters of group life, we might expect the experience of television viewing as privatized entertainment to impede or undermine identity-forming processes. Involved in privatized entertainment, the self forgoes social engagement for the visual and dramatic pleasures of the screen. While viewers might actively construct their own private meanings while they watch, thereby enhancing their inner lives, television as simulation displaces viewers from socially formative processes of interaction.[25]

While critical theorists of television's ideological effects have been preoccupied with its hegemonic influences on viewers, the fragmenting effects of television as a visual medium dramatically change the kinds of questions that need to be raised about the mass media. As the foregoing considerations indicate, an ideological effect might be of less consequence than other effects of television viewing. Not only is the experience of television largely inconsistent with the formation of stable and unified identities, a condition *presupposed* by the ideological effects model, but television's lack of cohesiveness might be incompatible with the development of a coherent sense of self. As a consumption relationship, television tends to undermine the unifying and differentiating capacities that have come to be associated with self-development. The fragmentation of experience, the temporary and disposable character of self-identifications, and the externalization of the self in signs and images thus deeply problematize modern conceptions of the means and possibilities of self-definition.

The Fate of Identity: Community, Consumption, and Mass Culture

Addressing the tenuousness of identity in modern society, many modern thinkers fashioned a normative conception of the individual allied to the newly emerging social potentialities of an expanding and institutionalized market society. Eventually, modern social theory came to focus on the decline of community, a legacy of the passing of traditional society, and to consider the rise of the individual and the formation of self. As we have seen, while the critiques of modernity overestimated the decline of community and its consequences, the forms and nature of community have nevertheless changed dramatically in this historical era. By addressing a detached, isolated, and anonymous individual, the rise of mass communications especially has threatened communal ties even while creating new symbolic possibilities of individual and community formation. In sum, whether or not modernity protects or generates forms of community life capable of overcoming the forces of alienation and isolation has become the enduring issue for many twentieth-century social theorists.

The question of community, however, emerges with even greater urgency in a time when culture is being increasingly transformed into an arena of technologically mediated consumption. Whether we are talking about remnants of "organic" community or modern forms of community life in the realms of work, neighborhood, learning, or other areas, in modern society community has been concrete and "substantial," a more or less immediate presence in the social lives of its participants. Modern forms of community, furthermore, have been structured around a sense of collective purpose and shared meaning. Community in this sense has provided a means of social interaction through face-to-face relations in natural or physical settings. In contrast, consumerism, mass media, and information systems are a major departure from substantial community, creating "artificial" or "virtual" communities based on novel modes of consumption and technology. Television viewing, computer networks, and video entertainment are forms of collective behavior constituted and mediated by technologies whose uses and contents destabilize our sense of place and time. These modes of participation represent a break from natural interactional settings, precipitating practices and forms of consciousness inconsistent with the kinds of expectations associated with conventional social relationships. The more abstract and ephemeral kinds of community created by modernity and mass society—movements, fads, lifestyles, and so on—have now been transformed into technologically mediated forms of consumption, or replaced altogether by virtual forms of communication, interaction, and experience (Poster 1995). Moreover, these new modes tend to abolish hierarchical authority relations, as we have seen with television, by technological extensions of and access to the means of consumption in entertainment and information. Electronic environments have increasingly come to mediate even what remains of print culture, in the form of books on tape, CD-ROM, and other technologies that convert conventional print information into electronic form. As a result of such changes, modern forms of community organized around social relations are threatened with replacement by more fluid and elusive postmodern forms based on the consumption of signifying relations or the construction of virtual experience.

A number of theorists have attempted to formulate the changed nature and dimensions of community formation in contemporary mass culture with such concepts as "interpretive communities" (Lindlof 1988), "thin culture" (Lichterman 1992), and "lifestyle enclaves" (Bellah et al. 1985), all of which designate to varying degrees the replacement of older forms of community by aggregate collectivities seeking substitutes for weakened communal ties. The *extent* to which older forms no longer have a place in people's lives or are substituted for by consumption relations remains highly debatable. Yet as these authors argue, the media do engender their own distinct forms of community that overlay and compete with other community structures. According to Thomas Lindlof (1988), for example,

> the prime referents [of interpretive communities] are not formal organizations, kinship structures, or any other natural collectivity. Rather, they come into being with the typically ritualistic or rule-governed enactment of communicative events whose sense for the interlocuters is located in the sharing of media technologies, content or software, codes, and occasions. Thus an interpretive community operates in a *virtual* form. . . . the concrete referents of an interpretive community are easily elided because they actually consist of on-going, situated communications. In effect, each interpretive community functions as a sort of overlay of information structure on the structures of kinship and social organization. (92–93; emphasis in original)

Lindlof outlines a conception of media-based communities that are based on the emergence of commonly shared norms of media use, in which groupings form around the processes and contents of communications themselves.

Another formulation of media-based communities is proposed by Paul Lichterman (1992), who, in a study of self-help book readers, employs the term *thin culture* "to denote the readers' shared understanding that the words and concepts put forth in these books can be read and adopted loosely, tentatively, sometimes interchangeably, without enduring conviction" (426). Lichterman emphasizes that thin culture "does not support a deep commitment from readers" (427), implying that self-help readers make up a loosely constituted aggregate in search of a "substitute" for "more traditional or more collective forms of cultural authority . . . [which are believed to have become] fragmented or inadequate" (442). This study clearly implies that such communities of interest consist of only weak attachments or loyalties. While Lichterman critiques and broadens Lindlof's conception, both address the tendency of mass culture to engender rather tentative and attenuated forms of commonality and association alongside more structured groupings. In their views, community reappears within mass culture but only in limited, situated, and diluted forms.

In yet another formulation of the effects of mass culture, Robert Bellah and colleagues (1985) implicate the important processes of commodification and privatization in the search for community. In their view, however, community has been largely replaced by what they call a "lifestyle enclave," which is closely linked to leisure and consumption and composed merely of "those who are socially, economically, and culturally similar" (72). They contrast the lifestyle enclave to community in fairly strong terms:

> Whereas a community attempts to be an inclusive whole, celebrating the interdependence of public and private life and of the different callings of all, lifestyle is fundamentally segmental and celebrates the narcissism of similarity. It usually explicitly involves a contrast with others who "do not share one's lifestyle." . . . Such enclaves are segmental in two senses. They involve only a segment of each individual, for they concern only private life. . . . And they are segmental socially in that they include only those with a common lifestyle. (72)

Although posing the lifestyle enclave as an overriding tendency in American life, and an ominous sign of the decline of the public sphere and genuine community, the authors concede that they "should not exaggerate this tendency" (74), arguing that most groups in the United States today probably embody elements of both a lifestyle enclave and community.

These and related efforts to assess the condition of community in contemporary Western society remain conceptually and empirically problematic, given the diversity and complexity of various substitute forms and their relationship to the values of traditional community life. For example, whereas most media programming tends to reproduce the role of passive spectator, call-in talk shows break this pattern, instituting more direct forms of participation, however mediated by technology, suggesting the formation of new communities in an electronically reconstituted public sphere.[26] This situation differs, however, from that of computer networking that, while seeming to epitomize the collapse of social relations, has through such practices as e-mail and computer bulletin boards demonstrated (at least for some) new possibilities for contact and interaction among individuals otherwise distanced and depersonalized by the structures of mass society (Poster 1995; Turkle 1995). Nonetheless, notions of mediated, situated, and virtual community within relatively anonymous collectivities capture the general state of affairs in postmodernity. Mass culture tends to generate the elements of both virtual and surrogate communities, both of which afford their participants new experiences of membership and belonging, however vague their temporal and spatial boundaries. At the same time, however, numerous questions remain as to whether such formations deserve to be called communities and in what sense. To the extent that such formations are incapable of functioning as authentic and enduring communities, the fate of identity would seem to hinge largely on the extent to which commodified and technologized forms of culture weaken more traditional social groupings and contexts of interaction.

Despite identifying new forms of community, real or potential, these and other writings on the continued search for associational life generally tend to understate the consumerist nature of these communities and their origins in mass culture. Consumer goods, mass media, and high technology converge in a similar positioning of the subject within the structures of consumption. The production of subjectivity in the processes of self-other interaction is narrowed and reduced by these media to the act of consumption inherent in the commodity form. It follows that despite observable continuities with earlier forms of community, the collectivities formed by these media offer only limited opportunities for genuine social participation. As illustrated most powerfully by television, consumption tends to displace social interaction. Though acknowledging the consumptionist nature of "lifestyle," even Bellah and colleagues fail to recognize that lifestyle enclaves are *constituted* in the very act of consumption rather than in social relations or activities. The contemporary search for community is thus severely restricted by the larger framework of consumption to which human activity is increasingly oriented.[27]

In conclusion, in postmodernity the search for identity has been relocated in the act of consumption and the fragmentary and fleeting experiences of mass culture and telecommunications. Through a proliferation of cultural and symbolic possibilities, mass culture provides new means and sources for the formation of social and personal identity. However, the temporary and situated nature of consumption relations denies to the self the grounding, definition, and validation afforded by social forms of community and the enduring ties enjoyed by members of traditional groupings. While some excitement and creativity might accompany the novelties of mass culture and the concomitant emergence of fluid, mobile, and unpredictable identities, the boundaries and capacities of the self depend to a large extent on forms of association precluded by the structures of mass consumption, at least in its present forms.[28]

The fate of identity would thus seem to hinge on distinctions between activities of consuming on the one hand and relating, interacting, sharing on the other, opposing tendencies that intermingle, combine, antagonize, reconcile, and merge in ever changing combinations. Thinking through the problem of identity in a postmodern society therefore would require analysis of the ongoing interrelations and tensions between the powers and pleasures of consumption and the search for social connectedness. In a commodified society, consumption and social relationality persistently contend as sources of selfhood and personal meaning, each alternately reinforcing and undermining the other.

At the same time, the transition from modernity to postmodernity involves an important shift in the mode of identity formation from social relations to the commodity form. To the extent that technologically mediated forms of experience position individuals as consumers of commodified culture, traditional and modern social structures gradually lose their effectiveness as reliable and stable sources of identification and meaning. Further, the inherently fragmenting effects of the commodity tend to *problematize* identity by situating consumers in spaces and sites of consumption that work against the construction and maintenance of unified and consistent definitions of self. While modernity places great strains on self-conception by expanding and differentiating the field of social relations, the technological and semiotic environment of consumerism invades, absorbs, fractures, and reconstitutes this field in ways that throw self-conception into question. The differences between modernity and postmodernity thus need to be considered critically as having consequences for the very possibility of self-definition and the articulation of one's place in the world.

3
On the Transition from Modernity to Postmodernity
Transformations in Culture

The defining moment of postmodernity is the emergence of fundamental changes in the scope and character of *culture,* a development widely thematized in postmodern thought and the underlying foundation of the field of cultural studies. Directly linked to the commodity form, these changes not only transform but more importantly *problematize* processes of identity formation. This can be seen in the ways that the commodity works to reduce culture to highly dispersed, market-based systems of semiotic exchange and their disunifying effects on the self.[1] The massive spread of signification through technologies such as television, film, video, and computers has given manufactured images and information a pervasive presence in the culture, threatening the stability of meaning and problematizing our very sense of reality.[2] The makings of a unified and enduring sense of identity begin to recede as concrete and immediate kinds of cultural experiences, as found in the sociality of family, religious worship, ethnic celebration, the workplace, schools, neighborhood, and other forms of communal and associational life, dissolve in a highly mediated, superficial, and elusive environment of reproductive technology. Significantly, this technology displaces the written word for an electronically based visual and oral culture, which in working to fuse its representational processes with the patterned activities of daily life re-creates in new forms many of the conditions of premodern and especially "primitive" society. Oddly, to the very degree that they efface social and physical space as a ground of cultural production and consumption, the new semiotic and informational systems begin to appear as a postmodern reincarnation of preliterate culture, as evidenced in mass television viewing and virtually communal forms of interaction and information dissemination (for example, the Internet). This is suggestive of an evolutionary reversal to structural features of an earlier, more collectivized mode of identity formation and cultural existence, captured in Marshall McLuhan's sentient term the "global village." Paradoxically, while high-tech mass culture personalizes and privatizes modes of identity formation, it simultaneously collectivizes the forms, sources, and technical means of this process. The result is a global mélange of electronic communities—of information, entertainment, trade, and politics—that have completely shattered both private and public space as these have been historically understood.

To understand postmodernity as cultural transformation and excess, it is necessary to dig more deeply into the modern-to-postmodern transition, tracing the underlying connections between these cultural types. A fully developed definition of *postmodernity* requires a comparison of its major cultural characteristics with those of *modernity*. A comparison might begin with some broad questions about the consequences of modernity for social relations and experience. This will provide a framework for contrasting modernity and postmodernity and establish a basis for formulating the concept of postmodernity as a set of cultural conditions problematizing identity formation.

Modernity and Postmodernity

Some writers have located modernity in identifiable systems of values, philosophical and moral outlooks, and intellectual and artistic projects and traditions (Calinescu 1987; Cascardi 1992; Habermas 1987b), whereas others have seen in modernity a set of conditions theorizable in various historical, social, and psychological discourses (Berman 1982; Frisby 1986; Giddens 1990, 1991; Harvey 1989; Lash and Friedman 1992). Whatever reconstruction is preferred, what seems to have emerged from the burgeoning literature on this topic is a consensual view of modernity as always divided against itself, existing in perpetual tension among contending social and discursive frameworks. Clearly, at least since the nineteenth century, modernity has unleashed a torrent of energies and forces, taking many forms and directions, both illuminating and dark, progressive and destructive, insinuating both freedom and order, liberation and oppression.

The ruptures and oppositions within modernity itself, and the contradictions between it and the promises of Enlightenment philosophy, formed the crucible from which postmodern thought would eventually emerge, creating a phenomenon that Terry Eagleton (1996) has (with a critical attitude) called "the idea of postmodernism as the *negative* truth of modernity" (31). Importantly, postmodernism as a theoretical movement has drawn extensively on what Jürgen Habermas (1987b) has referred to as the "counter-Enlightenment" tradition *within* modernity, represented by philosophers like Nietzsche and Heidegger, who cast a shadow on the ideals of scientific reason and progress long before the emergence of postmodern skepticism. The catastrophic events of the twentieth century, which have in some sense been a fulfillment of the prophecies of counter-Enlightenment thinkers, have further inspired the critique of modern notions of progress, especially among more conservatively and nihilistically inclined postmodernists.

However, although the sources of postmodernism in the intellectually "repressed other" of modern thought are relatively well known, the connection of postmodernity to the internal divisions of modernity is much less recognized. Without distinguishing between *postmodernism* and *postmodernity* as I do in this study, several writers have understood the postmodern as a state of mind that reflectively grasps modernity in its multiple and contradictory dimensions. Anthony Giddens (1990) has suggested that what is called "postmodernity" is "modernity coming to understand itself" (48). Similarly, Zygmunt Bauman (1992), who unlike Giddens finds the concept useful, interprets postmodernity as "fully developed modernity taking a full measure of the anticipated consequences of its own historical work," as "modernity conscious of its true nature" (187). Postmodernity is thought of by these thinkers as modernity redefining itself, resituating and repositioning itself against an accumulation of experience and knowledge that renders modernity no longer sustainable in its past, mythologized forms. Jean-François Lyotard has seen the postmodern even more closely connected to the modern, not a separate stage or period following the modern but, rather, a "cyclical moment" (Jameson, "Forward" in Lyotard 1984: xvi) between old and new modernisms (Lyotard 1984: appendix). In these conceptions, postmodernity represents a reflective understanding of the underlying divisiveness and ambiguity of modernity and its alternately corrosive and regenerative effects. With the possible exception of Bauman, postmodernity for these writers is a *phase* of modernity rather than a separate period, epoch, or era.

In contrast, other writers, such as Jean Baudrillard, David Harvey, Fredric Jameson, and Scott Lash, have established tentative grounds for periodizing the modern and the postmodern in relation to transformations in capitalist society, with implications of an important distinction between postmodernism as a theoretical or epistemological position and postmodernity as a cultural condition linked to structural and technological change. While this body of writing demonstrates in a rather convincing way certain disjunctures between modernity and postmodernity, for now I want to argue for a view of postmodernity that recognizes its continuities with modernity, returning to these writers later on.

A telling characterization of the divided nature of modernity is offered in Charles Baudelaire's comment, "Modernity is the transient, the fleeting, the contingent; it is the one half of art, the other being the eternal and the im-mutable."[3] As Harvey (1989) argues, modernism as an aesthetic movement has veered between these opposing sides of the spirit of modernity, capturing a tran-sitory modern existence (a modernism of the streets) while searching for eternal essences, or universals, that transcend and contain the ephemerality of the mod-ern experience (a modernism of the study, studio, stage, and concert hall).[4]

What should not be overlooked, however, are the *historical* tensions con-tained in Baudelaire's reflections. Modernity as a state of mind or attitude gener-ated its intellectual power from the drive to direct, control, and rationalize the effects of unbounded growth and development. While the Enlightenment proj-ect itself set modernity in motion, it also attempted to discipline its conse-quences through the imposition of bourgeois reason and rationality, an effort to impose order on chaos. This project was undertaken through a belief in progress and the presumption of human will and motivation on the part of self-made subjects. More broadly, modernity attempted to define itself philosophically, morally, and politically through the invention of what Lyotard (1984) has called the "master narratives," the construction of grand historical perspectives by means of which the crises of modernization could be surmounted by the enact-ment of universal claims, often by heroic collective movements. In this respect, the ideal of progress took the form of mythical beliefs in material achievement and became attached to the rise of new individual and collective identities des-tined to fulfill this ideal (for example, "citizen" and "worker"). Thus, modernity is a long story of ruptures, recuperations, and heroic inventions, where the dis-solution of society and tradition, and the rootlessness of industrial and urban ex-istence, were to be overcome by an intellectual faith in progress through reason and science and realized universally in a unified and reconciled human subject.

As a statement of modernity, Baudelaire's reference to the transitory nature of modern life evokes innumerable images of the experience of urban life and the age of industry, involving terms that capture the ephemerality of modern existence, such as *growth, novelty, flux, movement, fragmentation,* and *imperma-nence.* Such terms imply a *dynamic* modernization creating a state of perpetual motion, disintegration, and change (Berman 1982; Marx and Engels 1978). As evident in the writings of Marx and Engels, this view of the experience of modernity can be accounted for by processes of economic development. Inher-ently dynamic, the capitalist system subjects the individual to a powerful set of forces both promising and threatening, exhilarating and unsettling, in which meaning and identity are to be continually remade under conditions of constant material and social change.

In one construction, the notion of the postmodern has its origins in a new awareness and rethinking of these conditions, their consequences, and implications. Extending and embellishing Bauman, Giddens, and Lyotard, this notion of the postmodern can be thought of as a culmination of the modern. Thus, postmodernism entails an *ambivalent* recognition of the effects of modern life—an agnostic, searching, and sometimes cynical *reaction* against those effects as expressed in a privileging of the previously unacknowledged intellectual countercurrents haunting "official" modernity.

In a contrasting construction, Baudrillard and others have argued that postmodernity as a social and cultural condition represents a qualitative departure from modernity insofar as the *sources* and *nature* of the crisis of meaning and identity have been fundamentally transformed. From a Baudrillardian perspective, postmodernity is characterized by an essentially different set of threats and promises, corresponding to new technologies and economies that have transformed the structures and conditions of culture along a path hardly imagined in the nineteenth and early twentieth centuries.

The limitations of arguments for a break between the modern and the postmodern notwithstanding, dramatic changes have occurred in postwar cultural conditions as a consequence of economic and technological innovation. In this sense, the Baudrillardian conception of postmodernity, if adopted with major qualifications, poses a relevant and challenging set of arguments about the problems of identity in our time. Before considering Baudrillard and other theorists of a break, however, I systematically explore both continuities and discontinuities between modernity and postmodernity at the level of culture, concentrating on the incommensurabilities between the two and the implications for changes in identity formation.

Modernity and the Postmodern Crisis of Meaning: Fragmentation, Heterogeneity, Space, and Time

In describing the experience of modernity, Marshall Berman (1982) invokes the shock of the urban landscape, with its multitude of new experiences and cacophony of impressions. He presents a quote from the hero of Jean-Jacques Rousseau's 1761 novel *The New Eloise*, which summons up the experience of being overwhelmed by sensory events:

> I'm beginning to feel the drunkenness that this agitated, tumultuous life plunges you into. With such a multitude of objects passing before my eyes, I'm getting dizzy. Of all the things that strike me, there is none that holds my heart, yet all of them together disturb by feelings, so that I forget what I am and who I belong to. (in Berman 1982: 18)

The descriptions by Rousseau's character were echoed later using another vocabulary by the German sociologist Georg Simmel in his 1903 publication "The

Metropolis and Mental Life" where he says, "The psychological basis of the metropolitan type of individuality consists in the intensification of nervous stimulation which results from the swift and uninterrupted change of outer and inner stimuli" (Simmel 1950: 409–10). In Simmel's view, the modern individual can find nothing that "holds the heart" because of an ineluctable separation between the logic and growth of the forms of the external world (objective spirit) and the capacity of the individual to assimilate their contents at a personally meaningful level (subjective culture). For Simmel, this "tragedy" of culture was predicated on a split between subject and object, which created an inner subjectivity protecting the individual from the onslaughts of the outer world, producing at its extreme an "exaggerated subjectivism" that compensated the alienating effects of this world (Frisby 1988: 62, 80).[5] To a great degree, then, the experience of modernity has consisted of the unmediated experiences of incessant movement, stimulation, and change that often overwhelm the subject. As these and many other observers of modernity have testified, what is today referred to as "sensory overload" is inherent in the abundance of experience in modern life, the acceleration of time, and the episodic nature of urban life.

But urban life is only one realm we might search for the underlying nature of the experience of modernity. The urban environment itself can be grasped as the effects of a more fundamental process of economic development, the character and direction of which must be comprehended in the *institutional* changes brought about by the evolution of a capitalist economy and social system. Modes of perception and cognition have been fundamentally altered by structural transformations in the realms of production, consumption, and communication accompanying the growth of a market society. This has entailed basic shifts in our experiences of space and time resulting from the effects of modernization and producing corresponding changes in our relationship to culture. The lineages from modernity to postmodernity thus need to be reconstructed at both levels—in the ephemerality and heterogeneity of modern urban existence, and in the more abstract institutional and technological changes affecting the spatiotemporal positioning of the subject.

What most defines these lineages and thus establishes continuity between modernity and postmodernity is the advance of the commodity form. The commodification process constitutes the driving force of modernity but also explains the dominant cultural trends accompanying the formation of a postmodern society. Indeed, the experience of incessant stimulation and movement captured in the quotations from Rousseau, Baudelaire, and Simmel could be easily rewritten from the standpoint of historical growth in social commodification and the world of objects. It is thus in the impact of the commodity where we need to look first for the connections and contrasts between the modern and postmodern conditions.

In this respect, the common theme connecting modernity and postmodernity is that of the fragmentation inherent in the logic of the commodity form. An expanding consumer society develops through a multiplication of products and a growing plurality of markets, within which occurs incessant product differentiation. Furthermore, many of these markets intersect, converge, and evolve in complicated ways, infinitely dividing the commodity into ever more varied kinds of products and meanings. As a consequence, the commodity form decomposes and then reconstitutes the social world into an ever increasing number and variety of consumable objects and images. The ensuing visual and semiotic fragmentation is experienced by consumers in numerous ways. The spatial deployment of consumer goods in the marketplace contributes to the intensification of sensory experience while their temporal deployment produces a sense of discontinuity and disunity in daily existence as products, styles, and fashions change rapidly from one day to the next.

Notions of fragmentation are also at least implicit in theories of modernity that focus on generalized processes of differentiation and change in society as a whole. As the main founder of this theoretical conception, Emile Durkheim (1964) broadened (but simultaneously abandoned) the Marxist theme of the economic division of labor to theorize what he regarded as a more basic functional and structural differentiation of society resulting from the "dynamic density" associated with population growth. In Durkheim's view, the transition from traditional to industrial society presupposed an internal differentiation of social roles, functions, and norms. Durkheim saw the social conflicts and anomie characteristic of industrialism as manifestations of the strains and breakdown inherent in a rapidly changing society of specialized roles and identities. To the extent that the experience of fragmentation has been embedded in the processes of societal differentiation, the theme of the fragmented self can be understood partially through the Durkheimian version of modernization. While Durkheim understood the problem of fragmentation as an effect of institutional growth, not commodification, he nevertheless identified an important set of corresponding structural processes behind the growing heterogeneity of social and cultural relations shaping the modern period.

Finally, social and cultural fragmentation can be seen as inherent in the growth of mass literacy, communications, and transportation. The media associated with these developments intensify the accelerating effects of modernization on change and further fragment our experience of time and space. The mobility of information, images, and individuals contributes to the rupturing effects of the commodity form, adding to the experiences of discontinuity and contingency associated with the social life of the city.

Given these salient conditions of modernity, one reading of the postmodern condition might consist simply of extrapolating modern manifestations of fragmentation to a transformed social and cultural landscape of electronic technology and consumerism. The contemporary "mediascape" (rather than cityscape) could thus be regarded as merely an intensification of the fragmenting consequences of modernity already instituted by the market economy and industrial capitalism during the nineteenth century. Experiences of the contingent and ephemeral would therefore be common to both modernity and postmodernity, and the postmodern attempt to periodize on the basis of these features of contemporary life might thus seem futile.

What enables a distinction between the modern and postmodern experiences in this context, however, is the extensive commodification that has more recently occurred *in the realm of culture*. What is most distinctive of the postmodern condition is the fragmentation inherent in mass culture and the shift to new technologies of entertainment and information based specifically on electronic as opposed to mechanical media of reproduction and transmission. The *locus* of fragmentation has thus dramatically shifted to the market-based semiotic operations driving the widespread commercialization of culture and information made possible by new modes of electronic technology.

Thus, on one level, postmodernity is an intensified continuation of the proliferation of sensory stimuli accompanying modernity, and postmodernism could be correspondingly seen as merely a changed *consciousness* of the multitude of divergent objects and experiences of modern life and its articulation in new discourses and epistemologies. On another level, however, postmodernity can be understood as a novel set of conditions resulting from a massive economic and technological reconfiguration of culture around privatized consumption and electronic media. A further distinction can be made between the two in terms of the subjective *effects* of fragmentation. Whereas the crisis of subjectivity precipitated by modernity might be characterized as a crisis of (religious) *faith* following the erosion of traditional forms of belief and association, the postmodern condition entails a crisis of (secular) *meaning* based in sensory overload and the discontinuities and disjunctures engendered by new communication and information technologies.

The meaning crisis of postmodernity is an inextricable part of the immense expansion of systems of representation made possible by these technologies and a corresponding rise in the powerful hegemony of images threatening to crowd the spaces in which meaning arises in the social interactions among human subjects. The sheer materiality of the signifier thus overwhelms meaning as the sensory environment is inundated by sensations and messages of all kinds. An unprecedented multiplication and relativization of meaning result not only from the proliferation of images but more generally from an expansion of information and discourse. As culture becomes increasingly textual in character (see below), it loses its normative unity and structure. Meaning multiplies, extends, overflows, competes, and contradicts in ways that destabilize thought and action as well as truth claims regarding "reality." As an assemblage of texts, culture becomes increasingly tenuous and contingent, casting doubt on the very possibility of normative or epistemological consensus.

The contemporary destabilization of meaning is a problem of *structure* as well as material *quantity*. High technology problematizes meaning not only through an excess of signification but by a transformation of the subject's relationship to space and time. The fragmentation of time, knowledge, experience, and sense of place built into the dynamics of contemporary media and information systems is suggestive of what Mark Poster (1990) has called "a generalized destabilization of the subject" (15). Immersed in electronic media, the subject is stripped of a stable, privileged position or reference point, broken into a series of "subject positions":

> In the mode of information the subject is no longer located in a point in absolute time/space, enjoying a physical, fixed vantage point from which rationally to calculate its options. Instead it is multiplied by databases, dispersed by computer messaging and conferencing, decontextualized and reidentified by TV ads, dissolved and materialized continuously in the electronic transmission of symbols. (15)[6]

Whereas in the absence of a highly developed informational mode of electronic media modernity still offered a relatively stable cultural framework and the possibility of a privileged epistemological position, the condition of postmodernity is characterized by cultural dispersal and epistemological uncertainty generated by a multiplicity of technologically constructed positions and locations.

The fragmentation of time and space through electronic media might be readable as yet a further phase in the logic of modernity itself, as manifest in the structure of mass communications and capitalist exchange relations. The evolution of symbolic systems that these developments made possible gave form and content to what had already become "empty" categories of time and space that Anthony Giddens (1990) has argued were necessary for social development. As Giddens suggests, the dynamism imparted to modern society originally was an effect of the separation of the category of time from that of space, and in turn the removal of each of these from physical place. Whereas time and space were fused in premodern society, a precondition of modernity was their autonomization, especially as constituted in the awareness of time, a development made possible by the "emptying of time" by the standardized calendar and clock. Once emptied of its particularistic cultural beliefs, time became a universal category and thus a rational form for the development and organization of social life. Using the category of time as a "coordinating" device, modernity was then able to sever space from place through the formation of social relations constituted of "absent" others (17–19). Modernity in this sense could be defined as the extension through communication and exchange of social organization that transcends locale. Giddens theorizes what he refers to as this "distanciation" of time and space and their emptying of particularistic, local content as the precondition for the "disembedding" of social institutions, whereby social relations are "lifted out" of their local context by means of the invention of "abstract systems" such as money and expertise (1990: 21–29; 1991: 17–21).[7]

However, as reflected in its classical social theories (Marx, Weber, Durkheim), modernity has always deprivileged space in favor of *time*. Put differently, modernity's emphasis on progress through development is the source of modern thought's embeddedness in historical forms of consciousness. As Harvey (1989) argues, progress requires the "annihilation of space through time," and modern writings have accordingly emphasized "temporality, the process of *becoming, rather than being* in space and place" (205; emphasis in original). The separation and valorization of time in modern thought granted priority to the future, giving modernity a sense of itself as a historical project. Historical consciousness of the future thus reflected and gave form to the social, economic, and political developments emerging from modernization.[8]

And yet, while postmodernity develops within this same logic of detachment of time and space from place, it is constituted by an entirely different set of spatiotemporal conditions from that entailed by modernity. First of all, while time and space in modernity became vehicles for the expansion and rationalization of social relations, advancing technology has rapidly *compressed* time and space, as is evident especially in the realms of economic production and exchange and mass communications. This tendency has been intensified by flexible accumulation strategies, which emphasize an acceleration of economic production, exchange, and consumption (Harvey 1989),[9] as well as by the spread of electronic media. As a consequence of these transitions, the subject experiences ever greater distortions of the temporal and spatial senses. Second, while in certain respects preserving and containing time by regimenting it in accordance with market requirements, mass culture simultaneously fragments temporality by collapsing it into the visual immediacy of images. Jameson's (1983) metaphorical invocation of schizophrenia to characterize the destruction of historical time in consumer capitalism is based on what he describes as the "experience of isolated, disconnected, discontinuous material signifiers which fail to link up into a coherent sequence" (119). In visual media as in consumer culture generally, Jameson suggests, time is broken down into a series of perpetual presents.

Third, the other side of the fragmentation of time is postmodernity's dissolution of physical space through the transformation of experience into a series of spatially disconnected images. As Jameson (1983) affirms, pastiche is a manifestation of the collapse of conventional spatial structure through the random, dissociated juxtapositions of mass culture. Thus, the postmodern condition, far from being a further manifestation of the disembeddedness of social relations through the decontextualization of time and space, portends their technological *destruction*.

Finally, assuming that in actuality the categories of space and time survive in some form, postmodernity, as Harvey argues, reverses modern priorities by deprivileging time for an expansion of *space*. The collapse of a sense of historical time is paralleled by the extension of space, as manifested economically in the new globalization/localization configurations of capital and culturally in the aestheticization of everyday life through the commodification of culture in consumption. This spatialization of culture has been recognized in what Edward Soja (1989) has referred to as the "reassertion of space" in contemporary social theory, a shift away from the historical and temporal emphases of classical modern theory.[10]

The differentiations, fragmentations, and discontinuities inherent in the formation of modern society established a generalized logic of heterogeneity that has extended to the latest forms of commodification and technology comprising contemporary culture. However, whereas in modernity the experience of heterogeneity was largely confined to the urban landscape, the postmodern experience is defined by a "pure" and detached cultural heterogeneity. Thus, the position of the subject is continually problematized through the cultural fragmentation inherent in commercial systems of imagery and information. This fragmentation reaches far beyond the physical spaces of the city into the recesses of private life, undermining the figure of an integrated modern individual in favor of a multiply positioned and disunified postmodern subject, now situated as a consumer of multiple forms of media and other commodities. What defines this subject is less a consciousness of a lost past or anticipated future than its negotiations in an immediate, ambiguous, and perpetual present.

Visual Signification and the Aestheticization of Society: The Interpenetration of Capital and Culture

As is apparent in the observations of writers like Baudelaire, the makings of a culture founded on the visual senses began to emerge in nineteenth-century Europe, especially France, as part of a modernizing of the city. The Haussmannization of Paris, which created broad boulevards and other expansive public spaces expressive of the rise of the bourgeoisie, symbolized a growing visual awareness engendered by fashion, leisure, recreation, consumerism, the art market, and other elements of a newly ascendant commercial middle-class society (Clark 1984).

The visual pleasures of a bourgeois Paris, however, were soon to be transformed by the powers of the camera into full-blown capitalist modernity in what Guy Debord (1977) called "the spectacle." For Debord, the spectacle was made up of visual images that "fuse in a common stream" to constitute a "pseudo-world apart" from lived social relations. Debord saw the spectacle as a form of reification, and the technological construction of images as an "instrument of unification." Debord seemed to understand the visual mode of perception as a descendant of the commodity form, saying that the "degradation of *being* into *having*" was followed by "a generalized sliding of *having* into *appearing*" (paragraphs 2, 3, and 17; emphasis in original).

Debord's spectacle was an outgrowth of the privileging of appearance inherent in a commodified and modernizing urban landscape. But more importantly, it identified an inaugural moment of postmodernity, where the production of imagery through technology reached a critical mass, exhibiting autonomy from the reality it purported to represent. The early modernist prehistory of this process was the invention of photographic images, which contributed to the demise of realist art and the rise of a nonrealist and experimental modernist aesthetic preoccupied with processes of representation. With the rise of the motion picture, however, reality was no longer "represented" by the image but effectively replaced by it, as "the filmmaker literally . . . [produced] . . . a new reality rather than merely representing it" (Aronowitz 1979: 110). Filmic images thus constituted an anticipatory turning point in the transition from modernity to postmodernity insofar as they manufactured their own visual reality. Finally, television and video marked the full arrival of postmodern forms of visual experience. Unlike film, these media began to blur the distinction between reality and its visual representation by replacing the latter with continuous flows of imagery. These media not only changed the ways in which meaning was produced but threatened the very boundary between reality and its representations.

The spectacle comes fully into existence, then, with the extension of visual culture from the (modern) camera to the (postmodern) techniques of electronic reproduction and transmission. Based on its mechanical reproduction, its physical location in time and space, and its constitution of a (however limited) collective experience (moviegoers watching a film together in public), film remains a modern form of representation. As postmodern forms of electronic reproduction, however, both television and video produce images that circulate widely, rapidly, and densely to mass audiences, transcending the conventional barriers of time and space. These media effectively privatize cultural consumption within a separately constituted landscape of visual signification.

Scott Lash's (1990) distinction between different "regimes of signification" captures the nature and consequences of modern as opposed to postmodern modes of reproduction. In his argument, whereas modernity is based on "discursive" modes of signification, privileging linguistic and rational forms of expression, postmodernity is constituted by "figural" modes. Beginning with film and progressing to television and video, these latter modes give priority to the "nonrational," positioning the spectator within a precognitive realm of sensation, effect, and desire, aspects of what Freud referred to as the "primary processes" (175).

The origins of postmodernity in the triumph of visual signification can be demonstrated by tracing the transition from the modern to the postmodern semiotically. The sign is brought into existence by capitalism and modernism, which are built around generalized processes of representation. As Jameson (1991) has noted, this development is part of the problem of reification, "the very logic of capital itself" (96), which specializes, rationalizes, and separates, bringing "traditional reference" into being, as manifested in realism in art. As Jameson argues, however, reference itself eventually becomes reified, distancing the sign from its referent, or reality, as reflected in the emergence of modern art. This is "the moment of modernism" where culture and language are autonomized in a separate realm of the aesthetic, "thereby winning a certain negative or critical power, but also a certain otherworldly futility" (96). Yet the discursivity of the sign is lost when, in a third stage of reification, the sign itself is severed, disjoining the signifier from its signified, or meaning. This is the stage of postmodernity, where "reference and reality disappear altogether" and meaning is problematized if not lost entirely in the "pure and random play of signifiers." This is a predominantly figural realm (Lash 1990) characterized by a weakening or disappearance of cognitive, literary, and rational modes of thought.

The figural realm marks the stage in the development of capitalism in which economic exchange thoroughly penetrates culture, producing what Baudrillard (1981) called the "commodity/sign form," a structure of semiotic exchange that commodifies culture while simultaneously culturalizing the commodity (see chapter 4). This is the stage at which the aesthetic, only momentarily autonomized by modernity, is reintegrated into the realms of production and consumption in the technological reproduction of images, leading to a widespread aestheticization of society, culture, and politics. Oddly, at the moment of the aesthetic's reintegration into social life, the world of images gains complete autonomy, operating independently of any referents. Thus, the paradox and blasphemy of postmodernity: while the aesthetic loses its privileged position through reabsorption into everyday objects and social relations, the *vehicle* of aesthetic value—the image—is elevated by the commodity and, specifically, technologies of reproduction, to a plane of purely functional, instrumental logic, reautonomizing the aesthetic dimension *commercially* within the framework of consumer capitalism.

The aestheticization of society through images has been widely character-ized as a watershed of postmodern culture (Featherstone 1991; Huyssen 1986; Jameson 1984a, 1991). Little effort has been devoted, however, to systematically explaining this transformation and the various forms it has assumed. The most developed theoretical and historical account can be found in the work of Lash (1990), who theorizes the postmodern condition through the concept of "de-differentiation." Following Weber and Habermas,[11] Lash regards modernity as founded on a process of differentiation in which culture is autonomized in terms of a threefold separation of science, morality, and art. The potentials of these forms were to be developed according to the logic of each sphere, through the evolution of rules and standards for the cultivation, respectively, of reason, ethics, and beauty. This autonomization of spheres implied (1) the hierarchical constitution and institutionalization of culture and knowledge, and (2) the organization and elaboration of modern culture according to the principle of a specialization of functions. Habermas (1983, 1984) has cast this process as a structural and cultural differentiation among the theoretical, moral-practical, and aesthetic fields.

The collapse of cultural boundaries marking the beginning of postmoder-nity signifies a reversal of this historical process (Lash 1990).[12] First, realms of culture that were formerly separate and internally regulated according to their own norms of development are now susceptible to claims and influences from outside their normative domains. This reversal is marked in particular by a ten-dency for the aesthetic dimension to impose itself increasingly on theoretical knowledge (for example, science is redefined as "rhetoric" or "language game") and the realms of ethics and politics (for example, a reading of human action as dominated by "desire" and "power"; politics as "spectacle"). Institutionally, this reversal is manifested in the breakdown of disciplinary boundaries and the rise of mixed genres in academic scholarship. Significantly, this cross-disciplinary movement is marked by a tendency for literary production and consumption to become a model for academic knowledge generally.

Second, the cultural realm as a whole loses its autonomy from the rest of society. In one form of this phenomenon, the boundaries between "high" and "popular" culture are partially broken down. This occurs both with a mixing of forms and genres in the sphere of production (pop art, jazz compositions for string quartets) and with the mass marketing of high culture in the sphere of consumption (televised symphony concerts or art lectures). This involves a collapse of evaluative norms enforcing the separation of "serious" artistic production, defined by specialized elites, from popular expression and corporate-based products serving as "entertainment" for a mass market. Under these conditions, the modernist conception of culture as a specialized, class-based realm of aesthetic and intellectual value enters a state of decline as culture assumes the status traditionally conferred on it by anthropology: it becomes coterminous with the realm of everyday life and social practices.[13] Paralleling the disintegration of the boundaries between high and popular culture is the gradual dissolution of representation as a distinctly *separate realm* of signification. As Lash (1990) indicates, when representational processes come to permeate society, they lose their representational character, assuming the function of symbolism in preliterate societies. This is a return to the undifferentiated state of "primitive" cultures traditionally studied by anthropologists, where meaning and significance are infused directly into the objects and experiences of collective life and the various forms of the natural world. In this sense, symbols signify "immanently" whereas representations signify "transcendentally" (7). However, whereas for preliterate groups cultural and aesthetic meaning was attached to the objects of the external world, which in this sense served these groups as "symbols," today these same values have been transmuted into the semiotic attributes of media images and other commodities, losing their symbolic character. Nonetheless, once representational forms become ubiquitous, they merge with the social forms of everyday existence, returning culture to the more immanent state of preliterate society.[14] The increasing pervasiveness of representational forms, furthermore, contributes to the spatializing tendencies of postmodern culture. As Harvey (1989) points out, "any system of representation . . . is a spatialization of sorts which automatically freezes the flow of experience" (206).

A third dimension of the de-differentiation of culture involves the "cultural economy" (Lash 1990), which is the institutional locus of the interpenetration of cultural products and commercial interests. The commodity/sign form for all practical purposes obliterates distinctions between the commercial functions of the economy and the production and appropriation of cultural experiences and meanings. This is illustrated, for instance, by types of advertising that appropriate popular musical forms and nostalgic images of the historical and biographical family. Another manifestation of cultural commercialization is the recontextualization of high culture within the framework of consumption—whether in media, concert, museum, or other format—and high culture's increasing dependence on corporate sponsorship and marketing strategies. Taking yet another example, clothing fashions for youth have become vehicles of corporate promotion in the form of "message" T-shirts, designer clothing logos, and other means for visibly and personally identifying the consumer with the corporation by way of aesthetic strategies. Also, major spectator events—sports, recreation, rock concerts, parades, and other forms of mass popular culture—are increasingly held under the auspices of corporations and shaped by their basic interest in promoting consumption. These examples of the merging of culture and the economy through consumption suggest that "one is hard put to say where the commercial institution stops and where the cultural product starts" (Lash 1990: 12). Viewed at an institutional level, then, de-differentiation is a manifestation of the massive appropriation of aesthetic impulses and cultural traditions by corporate capital.[15]

Reader as Author, Consumer as Producer: Consumption as Deauthorization

Another aspect of change in the cultural economy of advanced capitalism is the collapse of the dichotomy between authors and readers, producers and consumers. The postmodern erasure of hierarchy reflects a decline of cultural authority in the wider society, as evidenced in shifting relations and transformations in both the production and consumption of cultural products. Indeed, postmodernity can in some sense be measured by a seeming disappearance in the distinction between cultural production and consumption.

A sign of this change can be discerned in the celebrated notion of the "death of the author" (Foucault 1977) prominent in the poststructuralist argument that everything is "representation" and that there is no such thing as an essential self existing prior to its social and cultural construction (Wakefield 1990). In this conception, the positing of "an author" of a "work" is untenable since "the subject" is only constituted in discourse, or more generally the "text," and subjectivity in general is inseparable from the processes of signification constituting the culture. This poststructuralist dissolution of the author/subject in representation registers a *real historical shift* toward a technological mode of cultural production and reproduction that problematizes single authorship and unified constructions of meaning. This shift has been thematized in the fashionable replacement of the concept of work by text. A text transcends a single work, such as a book, exceeding the vision and labor of a single author because a text is constituted in and through a plurality of works and disciplines (Mowitt 1992). Text thus becomes a postmodern articulation of the collapse of material spatial and temporal boundaries of cultural production and consumption and a disintegration of distinctions among works, genres, disciplines, fields, and periods. Text becomes a positively valenced description of postmodern culture, an active and multiple production, characterized by "unboundedness," and demonstrated or realized in "play, activity, production, practice" (Barthes 1977: 167).

The collapse of author or subject into text, or "cultural representation," can also be read as a manifestation of the principle of "performativity" pervading postmodern theory and culture. In an age when appearance or surface replaces substance or depth, performance becomes the major criterion of evaluative judgment. It is thus now possible to argue that to the extent that authors might still be said to exist, they are known only through their performances. The merging of author or artist with production, and the concomitant destabilization of identity relations this tendency implies, is a dominant trend in postmodern cultural productions, as illustrated by the photography of Cindy Sherman, the performance art of Laurie Anderson, and the popularity of biographical novels.

The weakening concept of authorship is apparent also in new theoretical conceptions of reception, whereby readers, listeners, and viewers are seen as actively constructing objects of consumption through their own readings and other practices. Under the rubric of reader response criticism, the move to conceptualize consumption in this fashion has been a distinctive feature of the field of cultural studies.[16] Congruent with notions of the text, consumers of literary objects are seen by practitioners in this field as active participants in the production of meaning through acts of reading. Users of the media likewise are defined as actively shaping, modifying, and using what they consume. This theoretical repositioning of the recipient of cultural objects constitutes the other side of the deprivileging of the author, a deauthorization of the work and its replacement by the "play" of the text as activated by the "reader." Textual meaning is now understood as a product of the mutual interaction of the producers and consumers of the object. More precisely, *consumers* become *producers*, producing the object as text through their own socially and subjectively inscribed active readings.[17]

It is important to note that this innovative understanding of active readers did not originate in the fields of literary criticism or cultural studies. Rather, this idea reflects very real transformations in artistic and media practices in the reshaping of the relationship between recipient and object during the twentieth century.[18] Marcel Duchamp's earliest works announced that what made an object a work of art was an attitude and willingness to construct it as such (Gablik 1984). Decades ago this subjectivistic definition shifted the meaning-making process in artistic production to the reception context. Following initial gestures on the part of Dada and surrealism to reintegrate art and life, and Robert Rauschenberg's experiments with everyday found objects, this was advanced further by pop art, which at the level of aesthetic practice became a major vehicle for a reintegration of the cultural and the social by means of a visual, material heightening of the experience of everyday objects and perceptions (Rauschenberg 1987; Tompkins 1976, 1980). The pop artists effectively replaced the authorial conception of art, in which the artist "represented" something, with the notion that the artist performed "a set of operations . . . in a field of signifying practices" (Burgin 1986: 39). By renouncing authorship, the pop artists decentered the meaning of the object, shifting it onto reception and thereby effectively equating recipient and author. Michael Fried (1968) theorized the aftermath of this shift as turning art into "an object in a *situation*—one that, virtually by definition, includes the beholder" (125; emphasis added), effectively arguing that art had been replaced by theater. Finally, Susan Sontag (1966) corroborated the shift toward the recipient as participant in her discussion of how "happenings," popular with artists in the sixties, focused attention on the audience, creating something *for* them *through* their own participation. As these examples suggest, the cultural studies turn toward reception and the death of the author in poststructuralism were preceded by much earlier and deeper changes in postwar sensibility, as presaged in U.S. art movements of the fifties and sixties.

More recently, the merging of production and consumption has been evident in various kinds of mass media practices that attempt to include the spectator in production processes. What Lash refers to as the inclusion of the audience as part of the cultural product is exemplified by this trend and even suggestive of possibilities for the formation of new media-based communities as discussed in chapter 2. In addition to the more obvious example of the radio and television talk show format are such trends as local newscasters encouraging listeners and viewers to call in with information or reports on new or developing stories and encouraging opinion letters and e-mail messages as forms of feedback. In these and other examples of reduced institutional barriers, the media have adopted an inclusionary strategy for audience response, blurring (at least in appearance) the distinction between producer and consumer by constituting the media product partially through the audience's own activity. Similarly, although more privatizing than community building, home video production, interactive television, and personal computer technologies suggest a replacement of the passive spectator of mass culture with new forms of participatory self-practices in which consumer is producer (Aronowitz 1994; Poster 1995). These developments tend to bypass the corporate agenda and structure of the culture industries, introducing the possibility of using institutionalized media as vehicles of personal and political expression.[19]

These trends serve to illustrate the homology between developments in academic knowledge and transformations in the artistic practices and structures of media reception in the larger society. Specifically, these examples are suggestive of causal links between changes taking place in both mass and elite culture and the way culture consumers are constructed by academic theoreticians. Regarding processes of de-differentiation, it might be argued that the dual shift in academia toward textual and reception studies (inherently in tension if not contradictory) registers transformations in the larger culture. Powerful new cultural forms have been constituted by complex media systems and their languages, privileging signification over social relations in the constitution of human subjects. As a corollary, culture as a whole has been undergoing a seemingly democratic shift from authorial conceptions to an emphasis on recipients (or "readers") as producers of meaning. Significantly, these trends in consumption threaten to collapse older categories of production and consumption (a further form of de-differentiation) in a way that reveals a major turn *away* from production to consumption itself. The transition to consumer culture is thus reflected in a shift in modes of cultural production privileging reader and spectator. Cultural decentering and deauthorization thus occur within and *because of* a firmly entrenched consumption framework, reflecting the inherent democratizing and populist tendencies of mass culture itself.

Simulation and the Postmodern "Crisis of the Real"

A crisis in cultural meaning and authorship/authority is one major consequence of the world of visual representation engendered by the commodity form, and this crisis has important implications for the hierarchical structures of modernity and its universalistic aspirations. The technological intensification of signification processes through consumerism, entertainment, and information systems, however, has raised the specter of a drastically transformed order of experience, whereby the problematizing effects of visual culture are surpassed for a state of affairs in which the foundations of meaning formation have been completely abolished. This marks a transition from Debord's problem of the spectacle, the abstracting and reifying powers of capital that convert everything into an image, to Baudrillard's theory of the simulacra, in which signification acquires a life and operational logic all its own, causing a mutation of the visual and informational world of signs and images into a transcendent order of simulation (Best 1994; Wakefield 1990).

Appropriating a concept from Marshall McLuhan (Kellner 1989), Baudrillard, celebrated theorist of the "crisis of the real," has characterized the reversal of cultural differentiation at the level of the mode of representation as a process of "implosion." The sign of semiotic theory was clearly delineated under modernity into signifier (image, word), signified (meaning, concept), and referent (reality), corresponding to the three autonomous spheres of culture (aesthetic, theoretical, moral-practical). With the collapse of these spheres, the structure of the sign itself collapsed, reducing the mode of signification to the signifier, abolishing both signified and referent and leaving a world of freely circulating and self-referential signs and images. Thus, not only has meaning been thrown into question, but representation and reality have been thoroughly problematized (Lash 1990). Visual imagery, which bears a close resemblance to the reality it represents, begins to replace that reality. Thus, signifier and referent begin to merge. Indeed, images can be so literal and immediate as to make them more real than "the real" itself, what Baudrillard (1983a, 1983c) refers to as "hyper-reality." But just as the hyperreal substitutes for the real, the social environment becomes so pervaded by the means of representation that reality in the sense of daily existence simultaneously comes to be composed of images (Lash 1990). Thus, signifier and referent invade each other's realms, threatening the distinction between the real and its representation.

Baudrillard extrapolates the subordination of reality to signs to an extreme degree, constructing the media, the culture and information industries, computer-ization, and other components of consumerism and high technology as elements of a vast system of simulation, which he calls the "simulacrum" (Baudrillard 1983a). This semiotic universe is purely "operational" in character (Baudrillard 1988a), devoid of any relationship to the real world for which it has been substi-tuted. For Baudrillard (1988a), the real reappears in this universe in mysterious, illusionary, and phantom forms, for example in Disneyland, which he exemplifies as "a perfect model of all the entangled orders of simulation" (171). Baudrillard recognizes the essentially technological nature of simulation, claiming this as a major rupture from modern capitalist society. In this respect he moves beyond even his own earlier writings on the system of objects and signification consti-tuting the semiotic exchange relations of consumer capitalism to invoke a new universe of regulation and functionality based on electronic technology. The earlier consumption world of "the scene and mirror no longer exist; instead, there is a screen and a network" (Baudrillard 1983c: 126). Where Lash still sees the postmodern landscape as "figural," emphasizing the psychological dimen-sions of an image-based culture, Baudrillard sees the psychological dimension as having vanished into the "ecstasy of communication," "a single dimension of information" (131).

The contemporary cultural scene is replete with examples of the techno-logical transformation of cultural experience into a simulated, artificial reality, and the displacement of direct, unmediated experience by simulated versions. There are a number of dimensions to simulation, however, that Baudrillard ig-nores in a dogmatic insistence on the disappearance of the real. First is the ex-tent to which reality becomes so thoroughly mediated as to threaten its displace-ment by technologically based images. This is illustrated by the deployment of video technology at sporting events, concerts, and other venues where spectators present at the event are provided video replays and various entertainments and commercials on a huge screen *while* they are watching the event itself. At ballparks, for instance, fans are often given larger-than-life instant replays of what the naked eye just witnessed on the playing field, as if video reproduction and amplification made the event more real, more material, and more legitimate. This replicates an earlier transition in media culture when television viewers were heard to comment that an event did not seem "real" until they had seen it on television. Taking another example, huge video screens often dominate the stages of rock concerts, such that "the monitors are grabbing almost as much attention as the actual performances."[20] Here, rock fans experience the pleasures of enormous video images of musical celebrities *while* the latter are performing in their physical presence. While in such examples the media do not literally replace reality, they are endowed by spectators with a power to verify and sanction it and a visual pleasure that makes reality subservient to its representation.

A second dimension of technological simulation bears on questions concerning the distinction between reality and illusion, truth and falsehood. For example, computerized electronic imaging of photography is a Baudrillardian development threatening to undermine the veracity of the still picture completely. Computerized alterations of visual images in the media, especially in photojournalism, are increasingly accepted in practice (Ritchin 1990) and even have emerged as a new form of entertainment. This is illustrated by a provocative and ridiculous visual reconstruction of Hillary Rodham Clinton as a dominatrix posing in the Oval Office, which appeared on the cover of *Spy* magazine in February 1993.

Visual media in general have the capacity to invent, construct, or modify reality in accordance with the goals of mass consumption. A pragmatics of effect occupies the very core of these media, and so by nature they operate to produce a desired result on their recipients. For example, television depends on "staging" to achieve its desired effects. In the case of news and documentary, the visual powers of television technology allow it liberties with the truth that are justified by the criteria of effective reporting or storytelling. A dramatic illustration of this principle is NBC's *Dateline* story of November 17, 1992, on an allegedly unsafe model of a GM pickup truck. NBC rigged a side-impact explosion of the gas tank on this vehicle to demonstrate the hazards of the controversial truck. While the fakery was discovered by GM sleuths and followed by a reprimand of and apology from NBC, the critical response to this purported fraud was basically misguided, missing the important point. Television is not in the business of accuracy but of effective storytelling and visual portrayal. NBC did not in any way falsify the facts of the case but, rather, manipulated the elements of a *demonstration* of the purported facts to guarantee the visual success of its own constructed version of the story. As everyone already knew, not all of the trucks with alleged defects blew up in collisions. NBC had to guarantee *theirs* did in order to make the story come alive on television. In this regard, NBC was hardly culpable but simply conducting business as usual—constructing a consumable commodity for its viewers, in this case a workable and therefore believable news story. In fact, evidence indicated that there *was* a serious danger with these vehicles. NBC producers simply wanted to dramatize that truth to their audience. The critical lesson of the NBC episode is that media constructions of the news are based less on veracity than on the economic and technical imperatives of mass consumption. The technologies of photography, film, and video are used in the context of mass entertainment and consumption to produce preferred outcomes in the audience. What this further implies is that, regarding notions of truth and falsehood, the simulational powers of technology need to be read within the context of their social uses and economic motivations, a point overlooked by Baudrillard and other technological determinists.

A third dimension of simulation is the most complex and perhaps unsettling of all. How does the emergence of a simulated order of visual technology affect the distinction between the "real" and the "imaginary," our very sense or understanding of reality? Perhaps the purest manifestation yet of the simulacrum is the arrival of what is variously called virtual or artificial reality. Employing manual and visual hookups enabling a person to be transported to other places and times, new computer technology literally creates another reality through a materialization of the person's movements on a computer screen. In this case, a total sensory environment is simulated electronically. Virtual reality is a literal, material realization of technological space-time compression. Other developments illustrate the powers of visual or informational technology to create their own orders of reality but also demonstrate a possibility about which Baudrillard is silent, namely, the effort to turn high technology into new forms of art. Consider the familiar example of MTV. As imaginary visualizations of music, this genre employs the most sophisticated techniques of visual production to construct a completely other world of play, eroticism, magic, the bizarre, and the phantasmagoric. Constructed from elements of social reality, MTV represents a high-tech version of romantic fantasy at its extreme, resulting in a complete obliteration of space and time. At the same time, MTV exploits many of the possibilities of video as an art form by transforming music into highly creative visual productions, adapting them to the structures of commercial television. Similarly, computerization has led to the evolution of vast informational networks and electronic communication systems that threaten to collapse everything into digitalized information appearing on a screen. At the same time, however, a whole new cultlike culture made up of computer hackers, musicians, artists, science fiction freaks, futurists, and others has formed around computer technology. Dubbed "cyberpunk" and hailed as a "counterculture of the computer age,"[21] this miscellany of rebellious visionaries and experimentalists is attempting to explore the virtues and artistic possibilities of artificially created environments. Turning high tech to their own purposes, the cyberpunks celebrate the fusion of humans and machines in a surrealistic world of computer technology.[22]

With regard to defining postmodernity, the collapse of the referent claimed in Baudrillard's writings is perhaps the most consequential of all transformations. To the extent that processes of commodification and technological advance have led to a simulated world in which signification and information systems become more real than their purported referents, reality itself is thrown into doubt. On Baudrillard's account, foundational modern categories of meaning and value give way to a weightless world of interchangeable and floating signifiers where both meaning and reality as we have understood them recede, if not disappear.

Culture Besieged: Spectacle, Simulation, and Identity

Among contemporary thinkers, Baudrillard remains the most provocative, clever, and insightful theorist of consumerism, media, and high technology and their dissolution of the social and epistemological structures of modernity. His argument that our current system of social and cultural reproduction has turned into a simulational order is powerful and subtle, lending more credence to the concept of postmodernity and yet carrying it further than other theorists. As many critics have alleged, however, Baudrillard's account of the informational society is excessively one-sided, reductionist, and deterministic.[23] What could be plausibly theorized as only *tendencies* in society, Baudrillard takes to be a *fait accompli*, posing rigid distinctions where one can only find mergings and blurrings. In addition to exaggerating the break of the postmodern from the modern, many of Baudrillard's formulations "take future possibilities as existing reality" (Kellner 1994: 13), reading an imagined state of affairs back onto a much less ominous and more mundane situation still full of a plurality of contending forces. At his worst, Baudrillard is apocalyptic, even "reckless" (Rojek and Turner 1993: xi), making wild and insupportable claims about the disappearance of all meaning, power, and reality.

In addition to extremism and inaccuracy, Baudrillard is susceptible to charges of conservatism for his postulation of a closed universe of discourse and functionality where subjective agency is no longer possible. While positioning himself as a post-Marxist radical occupying a space completely outside of political economy, Baudrillard posits a simulational order that effectively brings to an end the dialectic between subject and object informing the Western Hegelian tradition and modern philosophy generally (Kellner 1994). To take

Baudrillard seriously is to accept the defeat of the subject as agency and the elimination of any possibility of social and political opposition or subversion. Even without the theory of simulation, Baudrillard's earlier formulations about objecthood and semiurgy if read literally foreclose the possibility of stable identity or a social self still capable of conscious thought or action. But the substitution of a simulational order for social relations portends the dissolution of *any* possible identity since the boundary separating self and other, "inside" and "outside," is eliminated by the total absorption of identity into the signifying processes of technology.

It would be more reasonable to approach Baudrillard as having characterized as simulational in nature an increasing number and variety of media practices and technological forms constituting mass culture, politics, and the workplace, rather than as having established the replacement of reality by simulation. While the lived personal and collective experiences and meanings of a whole population have been imposed on and often dominated by these practices and forms, this is far from arguing a complete absorption of subjectivity and social action into the operational powers of high technology. The problematization of identity is more accurately a consequence of an extensive *intermingling* of the commodity/sign form and lived social reality, and to the extent that we can speak of two separate orders of experience, their possible *confusion*. The problem of identity in a postmodern society, then, is in the mediating effects of signification, and the recurring tendency of individuals to draw on or submit to the structures of the mass media and informational technologies and their various claims to legitimation. Baudrillard's discourse, then, *focuses attention* on those sites and spaces of technologically mediated experience and meaning that compete with social experiences of self and other and that threaten to subvert the social interactional processes on which they depend.

While falling short of destroying reality, the other cultural transformations that this chapter has addressed are suggestive of a pervasive set of forces undermining unified conceptions of identity. To the extent that such unity presupposes acts of individual consciousness, the problematization of identity resulting from the transformations in culture outlined above can be formulated in terms of a weakening or loss of continuity, integration, identification, and differentiation posited by Hewitt (1989) as constituting the major elements of identity. Unified identity, which in relation to the primary feature of continuity could be conceptualized as a problem of memory, is threatened by the strains placed on it by the fragmentation and excess of signification accompanying the commodity form.

This brings us to some general conclusions regarding the impact of cultural change on identity formation. First, privatized modes of consumption confuse and weaken identity through rapid change in goods and styles. The transitory and temporary sense of the world of objects experienced in a rapid-turnover consumer culture disrupts feelings of self-continuity and wholeness. Second, the multiplication of sites and spaces where identity and selfhood might form produces numerous discontinuities in the self's experience of itself and others. Third, the fragmentation of experience inherent in various forms of media and related technologies problematizes unified conceptions of self and other. Not only is temporality disrupted by new kinds of visual spatialization and disjunction, but identification processes shift to the consumption of fabricated images. Such discontinuities undermine feelings of wholeness and boundedness. Fourth, and closely related, consumerism and the media produce a present-oriented culture in which a sense of the passage of time and more generally history itself is often obliterated by the immediacy of objects and images and their claims to reality. Finally, a general withdrawal of the self from public or associational life into private spaces of consumption deprives the self of opportunities for identifications with and differentiations from others in the context of socially or spatially based community. This withdrawal, however, needs to be understood as the destruction of an older "public sphere" and its replacement by a new *kind* of public sphere(s) constituted by communications technologies and consumer culture.[24] This is attributable to the new spatializations created by consumerism and communications, whereby "public" space is increasingly occupied by sites of consumption (shopping malls, freeways), and what is left of the historical public sphere penetrates the private domestic realm by way of the direct intrusions of mass media (television talk shows). More to the point, the reorganization of society and culture around spatial relations effectively *abolishes* the conventional distinction between public and private. In this respect, the privileging of space in postmodernity problematizes the boundaries between self and other by questioning the norms separating the public and the private (as might be illustrated by the increasingly common practice of referring to public and media figures by their first names, and putting the private lives of politicians and other public figures under the magnifying glass of the media). The overriding tendency toward privatization is in this sense a more complicated matter of destroying the very concept of the private by eliminating the boundary between private and public in an unbounded, expanded space of signification and hedonistic consumption.

While culture has not yet been completely aborted by a simulational order of technology, the power of signification has destabilized identity and identity formation by blurring the boundaries of self and displacing or abolishing the older spaces in which self-other relations formed. Unlike Baudrillard, who presents a decontextualized analysis of hyperreality (the dense world of signs and simulation that becomes more real than reality itself), Debord offers a productive way of thinking about the conditions of this occurrence by connecting the spectacle to the dynamics of capitalist development (Best 1994). He correctly understands the spectacle to be a product of capitalist exchange relations, in which social life and culture have been deeply penetrated by profit-driven efforts to transform these into instruments of economic accumulation and control. The spectacle, then, is a reified product of human activity, not a totally autonomous operational system with its own logic: "The spectacle is not a collection of images, but a social relation among people, mediated by images" (Debord 1977: paragraph 4). The orders of signification, therefore, while often *appearing* to have reduced all meaning and experience to their own operations, have not entirely abolished the distinction between subject and object and their constitution in social relations. While standing apart from these relations, the spectacle refers back to them because it is ultimately constituted of them. In Debord's conception, the subject stands both inside and outside the spectacle, partially absorbed but retaining a sense of separateness and opposition.

Thinking about the destabilization of identity thus depends on a consideration of the consequences of cultural transformation and the particular direction and forms this has taken as a result of the economic and technological dynamics of an expanding capitalist society. While identity has been problematized, in the sense of a questioning of the boundaries of self, other, and outside world, the dominance of signification processes in the production and consumption of culture raises issues about not only the loss of self but the possibilities of regeneration within a consumption orientation that in many ways, paradoxically, shifts the balance of power to the consuming individual. The same forces that problematize identity, therefore, simultaneously create the conditions of possibility for a wider and deeper democratization of culture and society.

4 Explaining the Destabilization of Identity
Postmodernization, Commodification, and the Leveling of Cultural Hierarchy

Historical changes in identity formation can be linked most directly to the rapid commodification of culture inherent in the growth and impact of the electronic media as objects of consumption. The cultural changes defining postmodernity more broadly, however, are embedded in an extensive set of developments in the larger economic and political arenas of society. Capitalist reorganization, the concentration of corporate mass media, a new globalization of capital and communications and information technologies, and the emergence of new kinds of politics and social movements underlie the demarcation and formation of a new and multilayered cultural terrain. What most distinguishes this cultural terrain is the widespread erosion of notions of cultural authority and a dismantling of the cultural hierarchies usually associated with modern society. These changes are evidenced in the weakening of older cultural distinctions between "elite" and "popular" culture and a growing ethos of cultural populism. All of these developments I regard as part of what has been referred to as postmodernization (Crook et al. 1992; Featherstone 1988).

In turning to postmodernization, we look at the actual processes of change behind transformations in the realm of culture. To a large extent, these are *material* processes of change that are specifically economic, organizational, and technological in nature. Of course, the concept of postmodernization raises the same problem associated with the distinction between postmodernity and modernity: On what grounds can we justify a separate "post" phase of development? What are the continuities and discontinuities between these successive developmental stages? An outgrowth of modernization, postmodernization, I argue, is characterized by a series of disruptions in the unilinear patterns of development commonly associated with societies undergoing modernization. In particular, this involves numerous restructurings and consolidations in the most advanced sectors of capitalism as well as a major expansion and reconfiguring of capital on a global scale. Indeed, in certain respects postmodernization marks the entry of the capitalist system into a new phase of globalization. The structural and cultural shifts accompanying this phase can be seen as placing severe strains on nationalism and other forms of collective identity—ethnic, religious, racial, gender—definitive of the modern era.

Postmodernization thus presupposes the rise of a new set of domestic and increasingly global economic, social, and cultural relationships. Domestic changes in the United States, where the features of postmodernization are perhaps most intensified, have been occurring in conjunction with a larger set of economic and technological forces reshaping the "second" and "third" worlds and, most important, their *relationships* to the "first" world. Indeed, these larger transformations are of such scope and depth as to make such nomenclatures, including divisions of the world into "core" and "periphery" countries (Amin 1974; Wallerstein 1974), rather outmoded.[1] Furthermore, a glance at the global scene today shows a swift but uneven movement toward both greater *interdependency* and increased *disjunction* (Appadurai 1994) among countries, a state of affairs throwing general evolutionary models of developmental change into disarray. Finally, the rapid dissolution of older institutional forms within and among societies has begun to problematize the very concept of society as an identifiable structure or order of relationships with known and established boundaries (Bauman 1992).

Thus, the destabilization of identity in Western societies has its deepest sources in the transformation and increasing instability of cultural patterns associated with massive economic and technological restructuring on a world scale. At the center of this restructuring are new economic priorities and arrangements and informational and entertainment circuits and technologies operating in the service of a vastly expanded consumer capitalism. This changed capitalist regime has been undermining the status system of modernity and unsettling its institutional structures, dislocating older regimes of cultural production and consumption in favor of more pragmatic and fluid arrangements for the global marketing of culture.[2]

Modernization and Postmodernization

The familiar term "modernization" has typically been used to describe the economic, social, cultural, and political development of the West as well as the exportation of Western patterns to non-Western countries. Specifically, the term denotes the rise of science and technology as the major forces of production; the growth of industry, markets, and bureaucracies; the emergence of nation-states; and the spread of literacy through mass communications. Sociologically, "modernization" has commonly referred to the processes of urbanization along with the transformation of social structures following the formation of new class systems.

The central theme of theories of modernization has been "development," what Marshall Berman (1982) refers to as "creative destruction," the imperative toward growth realized in the demolition of everything deemed an obstacle to economic and social "progress." This calls attention to the disintegrative impact of capitalist development on traditional ways of life, which capitalism as an inherently dynamic and expansive system has relentlessly penetrated. Modernization in this sense must be understood as a predominantly economic process based on the simultaneously destructive and creative powers of capital, whose driving force is the development of markets through the production and exchange of commodities (Harvey 1989; Marx and Engels 1978).

While continuous with the changes set in motion by modernization, the conditions of postmodernity require an analysis of the corresponding category of postmodernization. This developmental process emerges within the structures of modernization and is in certain respects a matter of their extension and reconfiguration.[3] However, whereas modernization exemplifies the power of capital and technology to eliminate older ways of life in the seemingly inexorable historical transition from "traditional" to "modern" society, postmodernization introduces innovative twists and reversals into the processes of capitalist expansion, including new forms of social control and resistance.

In my usage, "postmodernization" refers to (1) changes in the nature and patterns of production and consumption; (2) the reconstitution of society and culture around the mass media; (3) a restructuring of capital and culture through a new wave of globalization; and (4) the rise of identity-based social movements. Taken together, these four dimensions of change signify conditions of social and cultural destabilization, which, while an outgrowth of modernization, spell the dissolution of the basic patterns of modernity. While we are witnessing massive domestic and global restructuring, the decline of modernity in this respect is reflected in a shift in vocabulary from *destruction* and *creation* to *destructuration* and *decentering*. This substitute vocabulary designates a series of disruptions in the familiar patterns of linear development, as expressed in Enlightenment notions of history and progress, and the appearance of new multidirectional and amorphous processes of change.

In the case of the United States, although the dominant historical patterns of modernization showed signs of waning during the postwar era of suburbanization, consumerism, and bureaucratic growth, the contours of postmodernization have become readily observable only since the seventies. The economic crises of this decade involved demonstrable shifts in economic policies, structures, and practices and innovative forms of organization and technology, indicating a new direction in capitalist enterprise (Barnet and Cavanagh 1994; Block 1990; Bluestone and Harrison 1982; Reich 1992). It was during this period that the effects of social, economic, and technological change began to manifest themselves in a new type of culture and society. With the collapse of postwar affluence and the gradual demise of sixties culture and politics in the seventies, the trajectory of Western modernity began to disintegrate, leaving in its wake a series of economic, social, and political problems and possibilities that could no longer be simply called "modern."

Importantly, postmodernization is an outgrowth of the same dynamic principles of commodity production and exchange that have driven the modernization process. However, while in this respect not a decisive break with modernization, postmodernization signifies the decline of modern regimes of economic, social, and political control and a disintegration of modern cultural patterns. Thus, what most defines the process of postmodernization is its destructuring effects on culture and social relations and its corresponding erosion of modern models of hierarchy.

In what follows, the process of destructuration and its destabilizing effects on identity and identity formation will be explored specifically in relation to changes in the character and patterns of commodity production and consumption, the impact of mass media, the new globalization of economic life, and the rise of new social movements.

Consumption and Flexible Accumulation: Economic Change, the Commodity, and Status Destabilization

Social roles, identities, attitudes, values, and the structures of daily life have undergone fundamental change as a consequence of a relative decline in the importance of production and the rise of consumption as a way of life. Conventional historical accounts tend to regard the turn to consumption in the modern age as a response to novel individual and group needs generated by the breakdown of traditional society. In this sense, the rise of consumption is both inherent in the ascendancy of personal desire and choice within a culture of individualism and abundance and a solution to the need for establishing social distinctions within an ever growing system of material goods. The far-reaching reorientation of economic life toward consumption, however, must also be understood as a reflection of capitalism's need to expand its markets incessantly. This has been especially true in the most advanced sectors of the West, where consumption has become a deeply entrenched pattern.

A significant cultural tendency in the early part of the century, consumption in the postwar era has come to define and dominate patterns of economic development, becoming the central means of accumulation and control in advanced capitalist societies. This was made possible, however, by means of a widespread *privatization* of consumption and the concomitant emergence of a consumer culture that has focused economic, social, and cultural life ideologically on the private purchase and use of commodities. As discussed in chapter 3, the tight demands of a consumption-based economy combined with the invasion of daily life by the means of signification have blurred the boundary separating the economic and cultural spheres of society, reconfiguring social and cultural experience in novel ways. A complete account of postmodernity,[4] therefore, would focus on strategic shifts in the operation of the economy during the seventies and consequent changes in the nature and patterns of consumption during that period.

In *The Condition of Postmodernity,* David Harvey (1989) argues that with the end of economic prosperity in the early seventies, capitalism began to face the "rigidities" of the Fordist system of production, which was organized around standardized mass production, and began to experiment with more flexible strategies in the production, marketing, and sale of goods and services. Changes in production and labor processes, labor markets, and consumption patterns, and the emergence of new markets and new kinds of services, characterized the response of capitalists grappling with falling production levels and profits as well as a generally stagnating economy during that decade. Most important was the intensification of "commercial, technological, and organizational innovation" (147). These changes ushered in what Harvey calls a regime of "flexible accumulation," the goals of which were adaptability to rapidly changing market conditions and increased ability to compete through cost reductions.

The central strategy of flexible accumulation is "an increasing capacity to manufacture a variety of goods cheaply in small batches" (155). This has been accompanied, importantly, by an accelerated rate of product innovation and specialization targeted at particular segments of the market. The net effect of these changes has been (1) a dramatic reduction in turnover time, a condition always essential to the realization of profit, but of crucial importance during a period of economic downturn, and (2) a new segmentation of the market, in which specialized customer needs and demands lead to a greater differentiation of products and services, replacing mass economies of scale with strategies of target marketing (see also Reich 1992).

The greatest consequence of the transition from Fordist mass production to flexible accumulation strategies is the implication of a new type of "speedup." While there have been some changes on the production side, reflecting the

Marxist notion of the factory speedup, the biggest changes have occurred on the side of exchange, involving numerous strategies intended to increase consumption rates. The rise of major industries in consumer research, marketing, financing, packaging, and promotion speaks to the voluminous growth occurring in the consumption circuit of the capitalist system. More importantly, whole industries have established themselves around the symbolic and aesthetic functions regulating the consumption process, for example, advertising, fashion, design, and the various media that serve as their vehicles. With the consolidation of these industries, the exchange process has been embedded in a culture of consumption that shapes and conditions consumer behavior by resituating the commodity in a complex system of social and personal meanings. The dynamics of this culture are attributable to a remarkable decrease in production turnover time. As Harvey suggests, flexible accumulation requires strategic industries like fashion and advertising to target select parts of the population to facilitate consumer motivation and choice in ways consistent with an accelerated production and marketing of goods. In effect, rapid turnover is dependent on highly differentiated and fast-changing consumer demand. In response to the need for ever greater competitive maneuverability, the economy has effectively elevated consumer culture to a position of dominance in the creation of new purchasing patterns and investment and marketing strategies. The rudimentary consumer culture that appeared decades earlier through the efforts of a nascent advertising industry and a rising urban middle class (Ewen 1976; Ewen and Ewen 1982; Fox and Lears 1983) and that later burgeoned in the suburbs and shopping districts of the United States during the prosperous economic expansion of the fifties and sixties has been turned into an elaborate system of carefully managed control over consumer demand.

As an index of postmodernity, the accelerating and segmenting effects of flexible accumulation have moreover transformed the *character* of consumer culture. First of all, economic speedup leads to an accelerated circulation of goods. Novelty, a product of modernization, has now become the driving force of the marketing system and the key psychological mechanism governing consumer demand. Consumption speedup requires that styles appear, disappear, and then reappear with great rapidity, generating a powerful sense of instantaneity and ephemerality in the marketplace.[5] Second, market segmentation leads to growing fragmentation and heterogeneity of styles and fashions and a resulting emphasis on diversity and difference within the marketplace of cultural goods. On the one hand, stylistic differences become increasingly distinct to reflect targeted segments of the population. On the other hand, although factors such as class, age, race, and gender still broadly influence the overall shape of the market, stylistic differences begin to operate more and more independently of conventional social structural categories. The production of style is linked instead to a continually shifting array of market "niches" carved out in response to specific trends in popularity. This can be illustrated by fads and fashions in, say, entertainment and fitness, or sensationalized publicity surrounding the (mis)fortunes of media celebrities. Third, as a consequence, the consumer is confronted by an extraordinary array of constantly changing appeals and choices in consumer goods and services. The overall effect of these changed marketing dynamics is growing complexity in the meanings attached to consumption practices and a concomitant destabilization of the status order.

By implication, consumers are now positioned in the commodity system in more multifarious and unpredictable ways than previously, their choices complicated by the changing needs of capital, volatile trends in the determinants of mass popularity, and the mere vagaries of a rapidly evolving marketplace. The construction of personal and social meanings around the purchase of commodities, on the part of both consumers and marketers, thus becomes increasingly fluid and idiosyncratic. In this sense, the rapid circulation of commodities and the segmentation of markets undermine the influence that social structure has traditionally exercised over the flow of consumer goods and their meanings. In effect, the marketing of goods and services has been "decoupled" from institutionalized status norms. This structural shift makes the shaping of social relations and social differences by the system of commodities ever more complex and unpredictable.

Before elaborating the consequences of this change, it is important to recall the critique of commodity society launched by members of the Frankfurt School, French thinkers such as Baudrillard, and others who have seen mostly the negative impact of consumption (Adorno 1957; Alt 1975, 1976; Baudrillard 1981; Berger 1972; Debord 1977; Dunn 1986a, 1986b; Horkheimer and Adorno 1972; Kellner 1983; Leiss 1976; Marcuse 1964). Among other things, these critics have claimed that the commodity form corrodes identity and social relations through a system of commercialized manipulation exhibiting irrationality and the creation of "false needs" (Marcuse 1964). Further, according to this critique the system of commodities characterizing capitalist society is designed to immunize capitalism against opposition or collapse, thus comprising a "total administration" of society (Horkheimer and Adorno 1972). In this school of thought, commodities are seen as deceptive strategies of power.

While the exaggerations and mistakes of this critique have been widely commented on, these earlier views of mass culture nevertheless offer a continuing basis for reflection on the nature of the commodity form. Reminiscent of the early Frankfurt School, Baudrillard (1981, 1988a) has emphasized the nonreciprocal character of commodities, suggesting this as a source of their power and mystery. Whereas interactions among human beings are predicated on social and symbolic exchange, our relationship to commodities is one of appropriation. Commodities present themselves to us as finished products, objects ready to be purchased, used, and "wasted."[6] Furthermore, despite varied forms of resistance on the part of active subjects, commodities demand compliance, attempting to turn subjects into agents of the coded meaning of the commodity itself. To the extent that the commodity as sign form (Baudrillard 1981) inscribes itself in our practices as consumers, it unilaterally assigns us a place in the social and cultural system. Importantly, although consumption occurs within a framework of social relations (buyer and seller), and often in an interpersonal context (family, friends), it is in its nature an act on the part of isolated, privatized subjects. Responding to and constituting an ethos of personal choice and individualism, privatized consumption contravenes many of the influences and identifications of group and community. Since the goal of consumption in capitalist culture is the private acquisition, possession, and use of consumable objects, the vast preponderance of consumption practices occurs in private settings. The commodity, then, seems to be a major threat to socially shared forms of interaction and experience, especially beyond the contexts of interpersonal life and the family.

The basic structure of the consumption relationship could be thought of through what Jean-Paul Sartre called "seriality" (in Brenkman 1979). A series defines the relationship between the individual and the collective as one in which, paradoxically, people are connected only by the commonness of their isolated activities, as illustrated by moviegoers standing in line to purchase tickets, followed by their subsequent collective/isolated consumption of filmic images inside a darkened theater. The commodity system, it could be argued, conspires—in the name of social and personal fulfillment—to weaken and displace the collectivity (Brenkman 1979).

Furthermore, consumption can be understood socially and psychodynamically as appealing to the consumer's search for pleasure, security, and power. By defining consumer goods as objects of desire, the system effectively instills commodities with the power to gratify our deepest wishes. Yet as many critiques have pointed out, it is in the nature of the commodity system to simultaneously frustrate consumer desire (Berger 1972; Leiss 1976). While an aspect of this dynamic has been labeled by economists as "marginal dissatisfaction," under a regime of flexible accumulation as defined by Harvey the frustration of consumer desire might be more appropriately described as a state of "perpetual dissatisfaction." Extreme product differentiation and rapid turnover tend to create a generalized state of crisis in need satisfaction. This results both from an amplification of desire through consumer culture and from a continual extension of the horizons of the marketplace. While the social and political implications of this state of affairs are debatable, it is at least plausible that need dissatisfaction strengthens dependency on the commodity system. Consumption thus begins to appear as a self-reinforcing process, whereby consumers repeatedly turn to it as a means of satisfying their needs and desires in response to previous disappointments with commodities, as well as from expanded motivation to buy. To the extent that this actually occurs, consumption tends to displace social relations as a source of personal meaning and satisfaction, becoming a substitute for the pleasures of sociability and thereby threatening social ties to the group or community.

More broadly, privatized consumption not only reflects our relationship to material goods but becomes an underlying principle of social organization in general. Thus, we consume not only clothing and automobiles but also entertainment, politics, education, health care, fitness, sex and sexuality, and even personal relationships. The commodity system relentlessly turns these and other areas of contemporary society into profitable markets for capital, large and small, threatening not only the replacement of social relations with private goods consumption but the commodification of *all* areas of social and cultural life, a process that has been referred to as "hypercommodification" (Crook et al. 1992).

Despite the considerable force of these critiques and abundant historical evidence of major shifts from associational to privatized modes of consumption, a perhaps more plausible argument is that the commodity form does not so much destroy social relations as mediate, attenuate, and displace them, changing their character and weakening their influence. As argued in the conclusion of chapter 2, consumption behavior and the continuing search for social connections coexist in uneasy tension, undermining and reinforcing each other.

The weight of their insights notwithstanding, the Frankfurt and Baudrillardian critiques are limited by their modern assumptions about the negative effects of commodification on the character and unity of the individual, not to mention the totalizing and undifferentiated nature of these theorists' views. For my purposes, these critiques serve as background to the theory of post-Fordist economic practices put forth by Harvey, which provides an approach to the effects of commodification that raises newer and more immediate social and political issues within the context of postmodernity. In this respect, a major implication of Harvey's analysis is that the commodity form exerts complex and paradoxical effects on the *status* system it has been both praised and condemned for propagating. Curiously, the very power of the commodity as sign form has endowed it with the capacity to disrupt the same system of status signification it has allegedly bolstered. As the use value of commodities is transferred to their functionality as signs (Baudrillard 1981), they acquire the ability to autonomously inscribe so-cial meaning on the whole system of market exchange, defining various con-sumption practices independently of institutionalized expectations and social customs. With an increase in market segmentation and rapid turnover of cul-tural goods, the system of social distinctions is thrown into a state of disarray, eroding older status distinctions and signs of social difference. Ironically, the dis-ruption of social and cultural meaning attached to consumption practices in-heres in the dynamics of consumption itself as a marker of social standing. The logic of the commodity in this respect is inherently self-contradictory insofar as it both constructs *and* abolishes social distinctions.

Modern models of inequality have generally based themselves on the social and cultural structures of Europe and the United States during the nineteenth and early twentieth centuries, a period when status distinctions reflected the growing affluence and hegemony of the upper and middle classes of modern capitalism and the increasingly institutionalized tastes and resources of these classes as reflected in the separation of high and popular culture (Levine 1988). These models have accurately seen the commodity as an important indicator of social status, especially class position, during a time when the commodity func-tioned to demarcate a system of differences in a slowly evolving social structure characterized by a system of class inequality encoded in cultural objects of ex-change and display. Throughout modernity, in other words, the system of social differences marked by the commodity has been relatively stable, hierarchical, and universal, in the sense of being widely recognized and shared by socially visible and "legitimated" groups.

A variant of this conception can be found in the work of Pierre Bourdieu, especially his influential study *Distinction: A Social Critique of the Judgement of Taste* (1984). According to Bourdieu, each social class and social class fraction in society develop their own classificatory schemes of taste in cultural goods, which he calls a "habitus." The habitus consists of certain predispositions, preferences, and practices marking a class's position culturally and symbolically in relation to all other classes in the same society (for example, with regard to taste in art or food). The value in Bourdieu's general analytical scheme resides in its formula-tion of the fundamental relationships between class position and the symbolic processes attached to the consumption of cultural goods. To the extent that class differences in consumption persist in the United States, the notion of classifica-tory schemes and struggles illuminates the cultural dynamics of class relations, providing a means of dealing with the ever shifting boundaries of the contempo-rary class system.

While considerable attention has been paid to Bourdieu's notion of the rise of a new cultural petite bourgeoisie that attempts to impose its "postmodern" tastes on the rest of society (Featherstone 1991; Lash and Urry 1987), the general thrust of Bourdieu's study is to reestablish the significance of class "taste cultures" (Gans 1974). When situated in the framework of consumer culture in the United States, however, numerous problems arise with this approach, reflecting important differences between the social structures and culture of France (and Europe generally) and the United States, and the extent of the postmodernization processes already well under way in the latter country. Specifically, Bourdieu's analysis ignores the decline of class cultures in the United States and the disintegration of taste cultures generally in a plurality of fluid, shifting, and segmented markets. Bourdieu's emphasis on distinction exaggerates the role of consumer culture in marking class differences while ignoring the other side of commodity logic—the *erasure* of these differences.

The collapse of status distinctions in the postwar United States has been analyzed and documented in some detail in the work of Paul DiMaggio (1987, 1991). In a statement broadly reflective of the destabilization of modern status hierarchy, DiMaggio (1991) argues that

> changes in social structure and the rise of an open market for cultural goods have weakened institutionalized cultural authority, set off spirals of cultural inflation, and created more differentiated, less hierarchical, less universal, and less symbolically potent systems of cultural classification than those in place during the first part of this century. (134)

The major social structural changes DiMaggio mentions are the emergence of a national elite whose authority is based in large organizations and the rise of a large, upwardly mobile college-educated middle class for whom taste and style in cultural goods are "important emblems of identity" (143). He sees the "open market for cultural goods" arising from the decline of private patronage and what he calls a "managerial revolution in the arts" (143). While DiMaggio acknowledges that the source of destabilization in modern cultural hierarchy ("declassification") is the market economy, he pursues other explanatory paths on the grounds that the market alone cannot account for the demise of class-based high culture in the past thirty years or so. While not in any way *reducible* to the marketplace, however, the processes of destabilization that DiMaggio explains in institutional and structural terms cannot be grasped in their immediate cultural and social impact except by reference to the ways in which the commodity form erodes modern schemes of classification.

Similarly, in a major empirical study focusing on the distribution of cultural institutions in the United States, Judith Blau (1992) has found that any class-supported distinctions between high culture and popular culture had largely collapsed due to increasing urbanization, rising educational levels, and lowered class inequality during the twentieth century. Generally, Blau finds diminishing social differences in the production and consumption of culture. Further, she argues,

> this investigation of cultural institutions and products in U.S. cities concludes that in a variety of ways they exhibit little structure and order. That is, there are few fundamental differences in the ways that high and commercial cultural products and institutions relate to their urban environments. . . . This study suggests that large-scale social forces promote a decline in the differences in the conditions that account for the distribution of both high and popular arts, and also a decline in the differences in the opportunities that individuals have to enjoy them. (2)

In an acknowledgment of the destructuring effects of commercialization and market growth, she asserts that "findings of this study suggest that both institutionalized popular and elite culture are governed by about the same social and economic conditions" (166). And implicitly referring to the inflationary effects of education and commercialization on the disruption of cultural distinction, she states, "the very ubiquity of all forms of cultural institution provides a partial explanation for the loosening of fixed conventions, the mobile meanings of art, cross-over styles, and broken codes that are described in contemporary analyses of art" (177). Blau appreciates an important contradiction in the development of modern culture when she observes that "the very social conditions that shape institutionalized culture also erode distinctive cultural meanings as these meanings have become universal and are widely shared in modern society" (1). Overall, the findings reported in Blau's study diverge from our conventional expectations of patterned social and economic differences in the availability and consumption of various kinds of culture and the differences between the distribution of high and popular culture. Yet while these findings, too, indicate a blurring or erasure of differences in cultural consumption, like DiMaggio's approach this study fails to recognize the source of this de-differentiation in the logic of the commodity form.

The leveling effects of commodification have operated historically on a number of different but interrelated levels. First, from its inception, the modern commodity contained within itself an inherently democratizing logic. As part of a system of equivalences of market exchange, the commodity introduced the notion of a universal abstract principle governing all "free" transactions among members of society. As an ideological form, the commodity has often promoted the notion of a "just" exchange between legally free agents. Despite its role as marker of distinction, there has therefore always been a powerful tendency within the commodity to *diminish* social class differences, insofar as the act of consumption reduces (*and* elevates) everyone to the common level of *consumer*. Second, the commodity form evolved within the structures of standardization and uniformity characterizing a mass-production and mass-market economy. Within the Fordist strategy of accumulation, this meant that mass markets have worked *against* the perpetuation of material class distinctions, as economies of scale have stubbornly expanded the size and composition of the consuming population, creating at least the *appearance* of a common culture of consumer goods. Third, the historical transition from production to consumption has resulted in a major ideological shift from occupational to consumer roles, followed by the conversion of the latter into vehicles of "lifestyle" affiliation rather than class standing, turning privatized consumption into the primary source of identity and shared culture. As a result of all these changes, class consciousness has been weakened and greatly diminished in its consequences as the occupants of unequal class positions have been reduced to the common denominator of consumers, creating in effect a "democracy" of consumption (Baudrillard 1981).

The democratizing tendencies inherent in consumption have been rapidly accelerated in the postwar period by the massive extension of consumer credit. Indeed, the impact of the credit industry on the class system in the United States is one of the least recognized and understood aspects of advanced capitalism. Through increased consumption rates and an expansion of taste levels made possible by a widespread rise in purchasing power, the relationship between objective class position (as measured, for example, by income and occupation) and lifestyle position (as gauged, for example, by entertainment preferences and home furnishings) has been substantially weakened. Through credit, members of lower income brackets can now effectively purchase the lifestyle of the middle class (however partial and strained), just as the middle class can avail itself of elements of an upper-class lifestyle.

Yet even when the credit system fails to reduce gaps in purchasing power effectively, the commodity system itself provides a semblance of growing equality by providing a democratization of style. This involves the familiar process of "marketing down" to lower levels of the class system styles (for example, in clothing and automobiles) originally coded for the higher strata. Thus, members of the lower-middle class are able to purchase cheaper versions of goods reflective of upper-class taste and lifestyle. This strategy evolved under Fordist principles but has been increasingly perfected under conditions of target marketing for the sake of capturing larger market shares among lower-income consumers. The net effect of marketing down is to spread the signs of affluence more widely throughout the society (only the discerning eye can tell the difference between the real thing and its cheap imitation), thereby simulating the conditions of growing social equality.

Consumer culture, therefore, operates according to a simultaneously discriminating and democratizing logic. This logic has undoubtedly proceeded furthest in the United States, where the material and cultural conditions for consumerism as a way of life have been most developed and where the traditional class distinctions of European society have been largely bypassed for a more commercially based and fluid system of social differences shaped by an array of nonclass factors.[7]

As this account suggests, modernity displays tendencies toward a destabilization of social and specifically class relations to the extent that the commodity form equalizes the terms of these relations. However, what is crucially significant about the transition from Fordist mass production to the strategy of flexible accumulation is that cultural leveling has been *intensified* by replacing standardization with its opposite. In short, flexible accumulation rests on a strategy of *difference*. Whereas mass production and consumption democratize by making things and people seem more identical, flexible accumulation democratizes by elaborating their differences. Yet while engendering a "democracy of difference," the strategy of target marketing differentiates social and cultural distinction so extensively as to create a new and, by modern standards, indiscriminate cultural heterogeneity. Paradoxically, this occurs through a *furthering* of the very dynamics of distinction formulated by Bourdieu, whose scheme fails to recognize the contradictory consequences of distinction when pushed to its logical extreme by post-Fordist market segmentation and turnover. Also contrary to Bourdieu, the differences elaborated under this new system are not those of class as traditionally conceived but of *lifestyle* as differentiated by income, gender, family status, ethnicity, race, age, and sexuality. This system has introduced a new level of signification and coding of social and cultural difference, valorizing difference for its own sake. Thus, the signifying powers of the commodity disrupt older social hierarchies, leaving in their wake a multitude of new codes. As a consequence, consumption is yet further distanced from the reproduction and reinforcement of existing social structures, class or otherwise. The erosion of distinction is aggravated by the novelty accompanying a high-turnover, competitive marketplace, where cultural goods circulate with increasing speed.[8]

The social and cultural destabilization of consumer goods resulting from an overworked post-Fordist commodity/sign form might be characterized as a problem of "inflation" in the cultural economy.[9] In contrast to Baudrillard's claim that *simulacra* form a cultural break with the modern, in this argument it is the *accumulation of cultural excess* that distinguishes postmodernity from the relatively ordered social hierarchies of modern society. The social structural changes outlined in DiMaggio's account of cultural destabilization assume that the creation of high demand for cultural goods is "a predictable result of [the] intimate relationship" between social structure and culture (DiMaggio 1987: 452; see also Gans 1986). Here, DiMaggio rejects Daniel Bell's (1977) argument that the erosion of cultural boundaries is due to a "disjuncture" between social structure and culture. However, as the preceding account suggests, the post-Fordist economy *dissociates* the marketing of goods and services from the constraints of social structure and organization, "freeing" both the commodity and consumer for speedy and socially unhindered changes in the advertising, packaging, and distribution of new products. Furthermore, DiMaggio overlooks (1) the extent to which demand itself is driven by these marketing strategies, (2) the democratization of style inherent in the changed cultural economy, and (3) the effects of consumer credit in pulling lower-income groups into the higher taste levels. Although the incessant innovation required of flexible accumulation presupposes a high-demand society and thus a degree of cultural inflation prior to economic strategizing, small-batch and rapid-turnover marketing cannot but create material and stylistic excess. Under such conditions, products undergo regular devaluation in social and cultural status, just as money becomes devalued when there is too much currency circulating in the economic system.[10]

A devaluation of status and meaning in the commodity system in turn leads to a greater investment of effort in the creation of *new* meanings that can give renewed life to the commodity and invigorate its powers to confer status and identity. Inflation becomes a hindrance to the status system insofar as it requires consumers continually to seek new status symbols capable of both differentiating them from the rest of society and offering means of identification with others. This drive to reclaim the markers of status is a special problem for members of higher groups, whose identity is crucially dependent on "invidious distinctions" (Veblen 1934) separating them from groups lower down the ladder. The fact that status devaluation through consumer democratization is largely a pseudo-form of upward mobility hardly changes the symbolic and psychic significance of the downward transfer of status markers from their original class habitus. Status reclamation thus leads to a continuous replacement of older codes by newer ones, producing a state of perpetual semiotic change in the constitution of cultural products.

The dissolution of status boundaries resulting from the constant turnover of products and marketing images produces what Mike Featherstone (1991) has called a "paperchase effect" (18), whereby higher social groups are forced to invest continually in new cultural objects simply to maintain the preferred distance from others. This in turn explains the tremendous expansion in the knowledge- and information-producing sectors of the economy. The disruption of status distinctions leads to a demand for cultural specialists who can map the ever shifting terrain of symbolic goods while developing new vehicles of status for the more privileged and educated. These specialists act as "cultural interme-diaries" (Bourdieu 1984) who produce and disseminate information, largely through the media, and who also themselves create new styles and products to enrich the increasing flow of cultural goods (Featherstone 1991).

The rise of cultural intermediaries reraises the question of the extent to which the demise of modern culture is related to changes in social structure. The alleged emergence of postmodern styles has been attributed by some writers to the rise of a new middle class linked specifically to these cultural functions (Pfeil 1985; Featherstone 1991; Lash and Urry 1987). In this argument, post-modern cultural goods are to be located in stylistic tendencies reflective of the experiences and positions of what has been variously called the "professional-managerial" or "new middle" class. The breakdown of cultural boundaries and hierarchies, specifically between high and mass culture, and the postmodern traits of ironic detachment, eclecticism, irreverence, and fragmentation that characterize the affluent worlds of media, fashion, travel, architecture, and cui-sine are seen as manifestations of the social and cultural practices of this class. These authors thus read postmodern sensibility and taste as the invention of a trendy and highly educated generation of producers and consumers belonging to a newly arrived middle class making their living and leisure from high-tech consumer capitalism.

While this argument raises important questions about the class bases of postmodernism, both as a cultural phenomenon and philosophical movement, a direct linking of postmodern culture to class structure oversimplifies the dynam-ics of postmodernity. First, it follows too closely the Bourdieuian conception of class culture and reproduces the deficiencies of that scheme when applied to the United States. Second, and more important, to reduce the postmodern as a cul-tural category to the phenomenon of class is to oversimplify the larger cultural and social dynamics of a developmental phase of the capitalist economy. While the logic of this development might produce new classes and affect members of different classes and other social groupings differently, it exists independently of its class manifestations, producing other effects. Moreover, as we have seen, the dominant tendency of post-Fordist forms of commodification is to subvert cul-tural and social expressions of class through a ceaseless fragmentation and re-shaping of consumption codes along nonclass lines.[11] Third, to connect post-modern culture to a particular class or class fraction is to reinvoke the modern notion of "taste" with all of its implications of institutionalized class boundaries, whereas postmodernization replaces class-based taste with the phenomenon of "style" (Crook, Pakulski, and Waters 1992).

The strategy of target marketing occupies a curious and self-contradictory place in this disintegration of class status. On the one hand, market segmentation strongly diminishes the translation of class into consumption patterns as class categories and codes are broken down into a multitude of other social and cultural categories related to entertainment and leisure styles. On the other hand, under conditions of status destabilization the targeting approach becomes indispensable, as seen in the rise of demographics as a response to the increased need for a continual remapping of the status boundaries of the marketplace. Thus, market segmentation is a simultaneously self-perpetuating and self-defeating strategy, constantly reasserting difference just to keep ahead of itself. The competitive crunch giving rise to flexible accumulation requires a continual demographic redrawing of the consumer, an endless resignifying of social differences directed toward the generation of profitable new markets.

An understanding of the dynamics of this process clarifies the reasons why the concept of lifestyle, or merely style, has assumed such importance in contemporary discussions of consumerism. The notion of lifestyle has been linked to consumer culture on the grounds that it designates how people spend their money, and this concept has long served as a sociological description of variable consumption patterns among different social groups, especially classes. The notion of style, however, acquires special significance under conditions of status instability. With spiraling inflation in commodities, status boundaries can only be renegotiated and reestablished through the assertion of stylistic difference. Lacking fixed and reliable indicators of class, the consumer resorts to lifestyle construction as a means of signifying a position within the current trends and fashions defining popularity and status in the consumption system. Increasingly, this task is borne by the marketing system itself, which packages lifestyle *for* the consumer, as exemplified by magazines targeted for specific leisure groups— runners, cyclists, gardeners, fitness buffs, collectors, campers, and so on. Lifestyle thus is the main product of the new information and knowledge industries, providing the basic framework within which the struggle to redefine and reclaim status is waged.

In summary, the regime of flexible accumulation is the source of a transformed consumer culture within which the experience of postmodernity becomes fully apparent. The excess, turnover, and ceaseless differentiation of commodities characteristic of this mode of accumulation produce an eclectic and rapidly shifting mixture of cultural goods and significations competing for consumer attention. Most of these products can offer only temporary pleasures and identifications since they are soon replaced by new commodities in the ceaseless redrawing of status lines necessitated by an accelerated search for profits. The flooding of the marketplace by swiftly recycled fashions creates an atmosphere of novelty and diversity and a sense of excitement over shopping for, purchasing, and using commodities to satisfy personal desires and status needs. At the same time, eclectic and rapidly changing styles create a sense of endless difference in the flow of consumer goods, and thus consumer *in*difference. The resulting erosion of class hierarchy intensifies the search for status distinctions through the appropriation of goods from an expanding marketplace of lifestyle identities and the valorization of appearance within a generalized semiotics of difference in which style takes precedence over taste. Consumers thus face a heterogeneous, capricious, and often ambiguous landscape of symbolic goods. While class factors such as income and education still play an important conditioning role in particular cases, flexible accumulation strategies effectively decouple consumption from social structure (Pakulski and Waters 1996), segregating the production of "status symbols" from the class structure. This entails a major shift in perception from class to lifestyle criteria and more generally from patterns of differentiation within the *social* sphere to the production of differences in the realm of *culture*. Thus, in a manner of speaking, "Bourdieu's 'distinction' gives way to Derrida's 'différence'" (Crook et al. 1992: 133).

As consumer culture forecloses the articulation of class identity, the awareness of class difference recedes behind the expression of other kinds of identity driven by a volatile consumer marketplace. The weakening and loss of class identities, however, is accompanied by three further developments. First, we can safely assume that a certain fragmentation of self is inherent in growing cultural heterogeneity and especially the incessant changeability of status symbols. Second, the "core" identities of class, gender, race, ethnicity, age, and sexuality are culturally deconstructed as part of the dissolution of modernist hierarchies of cultural authority stemming from consumerism and the inflation of cultural goods in a high-demand, excessively differentiated society. Yet while the market breaks down older identities, it also introduces new fluidities in identity, facilitating its redefinition along more inclusionary and democratizing lines. Third, a tendency is set in motion for identification processes to shift generally away from core identities to consumer roles. However, while individuals increasingly see themselves and act as consumers, far from replacing core identities consumerism *reshapes* or *inflects* them in new ways, providing new contexts for their construction and reconstruction.

Electronic Media and the Commodification of Images

Technology always has been integral to the needs and fortunes of the capitalist economy and so is inseparable from the processes of commodification driving modernization. Today, the social and cultural effects of technology and the system of commodities are deeply intertwined. Not only has technology assumed a constant presence in daily life, but the commodity form and technological form are increasingly indistinguishable, so that our connection to technology is bound up with our relationship to commodities in general.

This is most evident in the technologies of cultural reproduction and especially electronic reproduction in the form of mass media. These media are extensions of the commodity system, and their operations replicate the logic and effects of cultural commodification. The act of consumption is given in both the structure of the mass media and their function as corporate enterprises. As technological forms, the media serve as delivery systems for programs and advertisements that are consumed by members of a mass audience. As corporations, the media produce, market, and sell their goods (ultimately, selling audience attention to advertisers) according to the same dictates of profitability governing the sale of other commodities. It is mainly through their technological forms, however, that the media create new kinds of consumers—readers, listeners, and spectators of packaged goods.

Commodification in the sphere of mass media is based on a twofold process. First, the media produce cultural objects in technologically manageable and economically marketable units, establishing a distribution system for the consumption of these objects by mass audiences. The objects of communication—concretely, words and images; less tangibly, ideas, messages, information, and so on—are converted into consumables for media recipients. Second, as commodities, media objects work to construct passive audiences. Structurally, mass media are one-way communication systems. As such, they foreclose direct social participation, absorbing and reproducing social and cultural exchange within the confines of their own functional logic. Television spectators, for example, visually consume social exchange taking place among the characters in formulaized situation comedies. Mass communications thus in their very nature replicate the consumption relations characterizing the market.

Visual media embody the very experience of the commodity as an object known through its semiotic properties. In a sense, commodification reaches its apogee in those media that rely on filmic and video technology. Representation in these technologies is shaped by a manufacturing process in which symbolic production generally follows the form of industrial production. Accordingly, cultural expression as we know it through the media assumes the shape of fixed and finished products. These products possess a certain claim to reality by virtue of their materiality as consumable objects, that is, as "things" in our field of experience.

The commodity form in mass communication is exemplified by television, whose technological and economic characteristics make it the most commodified of all electronic media. The technical and commercial requirements of mass visual broadcasting impose relatively fixed structures on both visual and programming production. The small screen, for example, demands a large degree of visual regimentation (close-ups, interior scenes). Marketing requirements demand the imposition of format and formula on television programs (Gitlin 1979), leading to predictable routines and structures from one show to the next, including recognizable stereotypes. Flow, the central feature of the medium (Williams 1975), necessitates strict scheduling and segmentation of programs and advertisements, commodifying time itself in compact, interchangeable units (Gitlin 1979). In all these ways, television reproduces the basic structures and rhythms of industrial production.

The greatest impact of visual technology, however, has been in the creation of a material world of images, and this constitutes the shift to a postmodern experience of mass culture. The means of mechanical and electronic reproduction have transformed images into ubiquitous and freely circulating objects, decontextualized in time and space from any originals they might represent. Images originate and operate within the logic of the commodity form, synthesized and deployed solely for purposes of stimulating economic activity through the consumption of advertising and commercial entertainment. Disseminated electronically, mass images have a unique capacity to multiply and migrate indefinitely.

The inner structural relationship of commodity and image has been theorized perhaps most fully by Baudrillard (1981). His notion of the commodity/sign form presupposes an expansive consumer culture in which images have acquired a life of their own as part of the commodification process. His argument that the commodity has an inherent capacity to function as a sign (for example, of "status") is suggestive of a "culturalization of the commodity" in which the commodity becomes part of a semiotic language governing consumption and social relations. In the obverse of this process, mechanical and electronic reproduction constitutes the sign as a commodity, leading to a "commodification of culture" in which cultural constructions are reduced to the status of commodities. Signifiers are thereby strategically linked to meanings and products in accordance with the marketing and political needs of the media industries. The drive to increase consumption through media advertising has the predictable effect of semiotic saturation in which "signs" shrink to the status of "free-floating signifiers," a flood tide of visual images detached from meaning and referent.[12] The proliferation of images thereby parallels and intensifies the inflationary tendencies of consumer culture more generally. An oversupply and rapid turnover of images have the effect of reducing their meaning quotient, inflating the semiotic currency.

As an aspect of the commodification of culture, the proliferation of images, connected primarily to electronic media, dramatically changes the character of culture, leading to fundamental shifts in perception and consciousness. The first and most obvious trend is toward cultural eclecticism. Television aesthetics epitomize the experience of juxtaposition inherent in a rapidly changing consumer culture and the extensive differentiation of taste and style necessitated by flexible accumulation. Television creates pastiche, mixing subject matter and genres, moods and messages, resonating (while seldom addressing directly) many of the unresolved tensions, inconsistencies, and contradictions of the larger society, patching together a national culture fashioned from a plurality of often discrepant information, styles, and traditions.

Second, the market requires television to play a populist role within the larger culture. In addressing the needs and desires of large audiences, television democratizes by appealing to popular tastes, leveling many of the social hierarchies and distinctions enforced by modern culture. Paralleling the effects of the consumer goods system, television thus destabilizes institutionalized norms of social and cultural expression. This is manifest in television's lowest-common-denominator codes (programs must address a heterogeneous audience and not offend anyone), its varied menu of entertainment, and its wide access to mass audiences.

Third, the visual culture of television works in conjunction with the culture of consumer goods to elevate objects to a dominant place in everyday life. The power to "objectify" inhering in the commodity has been greatly expanded by the power of electronic images. The image's capacity to absorb and code lived experience within preestablished technological and material forms is a major source of its power. While the responses of media recipients to this reified world are complex and problematic—theory and empirical research suggest that media content is internalized but also variously ignored, subverted, transformed, or opposed[13]—the image nonetheless possesses a certain objective power through its sheer facticity and presence. To this extent, images endorse a positivistic attitude, privileging surface, appearance, and sensation over understanding, experience, and other essentialist epistemological categories. Thus, the privileging of appearance in mass culture is reflected in the postmodernist epistemological rejection of essentialist forms of knowledge. To the degree that images circulate as part of a whole system of visual forms—in television, film, video, photography, computers, and other media—they constitute their own reality, acquiring their own life despite what individual subjects might make of them. This is suggestive of a parallel between mass culture as image-constituted discourse and the linguistic turn in contemporary philosophy (Mowitt 1992), particularly the instabilities of language and meaning celebrated in theories of deconstruction (Culler 1982). Through images, communications media have created languages and discourses having an autonomous yet pervasive presence in society. As components of technological systems, images circulate with a certain regularity and according to their own laws, much like coded language and rituals in the structuralist theories of Ferdinand de Saussure and Claude Lévi-Strauss (Lane 1970). At the same time, images tend to proliferate in unexpected ways. While images reify, they also exhibit a certain instability and contingency, as do language and discourse in the arguments of poststructuralists. While single images can fix meaning, the saturation of society by a great multitude of images can disrupt and dissolve meaning.

Fourth, images are inherently democratizing, sharing with other commodities the capacity to reduce meaning and value to a common denominator. Images perform this function visually, rather than economically, collapsing distinction and difference into a common reproductive form and semiotic code. Whatever is convertible into an image is susceptible to losing its uniqueness, its qualitative difference from other things with which it might be compared or contrasted. The image thus serves instrumentally to provide a common visual discourse for the absorption and reshaping of cultural meaning. All television fare, for example, is the same insofar as it is constituted in a televisual image and accorded a visual and symbolic status within television's own system of commercially determined signification.

Fifth, visual media like all commodities exhibit powerful tendencies to reconstitute culture as a psychological idiom. Weak on narrativity, conceptual development, and logical argumentation, the image world is fundamentally figural (Lash 1990) and nonlinear. Given the economic and entertainment agendas of commercialized media, images work to deprivilege the cognitive level of awareness for appeals to desire and emotion. Based in visual experience, mass culture provides consumers entry into the realm of the unconscious (Wood 1982), where drives and instincts prevail over reasoning ego. Devoid of truth value, visual imagery thus constitutes a world of pleasure based on the stimulation of affect and the senses. Visual culture thus constructs the spectator as a pleasure seeker responsive to preconceived effects.

Finally, media culture is instrinsically parasitical and therefore intertextual. Mechanical and electronic reproduction effectively abolishes modernist notions of creative originality for an emphasis on technological and economic efficacy. Therefore, as reproductive technologies, the media constitute and perpetuate themselves by feeding off preexisting traditions (storytelling, drama, melodrama, games, fantasy) as well as each other (spinoffs, remakes, sequels, quotations). Those traditions and devices that have met the criteria of popularity in the past—that is, have worked with mass audiences—are used over again in seemingly endless recombinations, aptly captured in Todd Gitlin's (1983) notion of "recombinant culture." The technological reproduction of culture thus results in a paradoxical tension: media systems are compelled to create trends and fashions to attract and hold audiences but can accomplish this task only through "traditional" appeals. These circumstances generate a state of generalized cultural eclecticism and exhaustion. The media, like the goods-producing economy, trade in popularity and therefore must sustain a climate of novelty. But they can only accomplish this effectively through a system of recyclable products whose meanings and effects are predictable, thereby creating the feeling of a second-hand culture.

As extensions and intensifications of consumer culture, the technologies of mass communication, like the goods-producing economy, create a cultural landscape both eclectic and fragmented, weakening class and destabilizing other collective identities. Extending the erosion of taste and status boundaries to the realm of entertainment, mass media hasten the disintegration of modernist hierarchies by promoting a recycled and heterogeneous culture in which identities are multiplied and reconstructed almost infinitely, although always within a familiar set of conventions. To a large extent, the demise of the modern theme of progress can be seen in the recyclable character of media culture and its persistent tendency to reconstruct the present, in all its immediacy, through fragments of the past. Recyclability can further be seen as playing a part in the shift from goal-oriented identity formation to a smorgasbord approach in which identities are constructed through an assortment of mass cultural images. More generally, the contemporary conception of identity as shifting and fluid, and absorbed in discourse, is largely attributable to the pervasive and autonomous power of images to define and shape cultural experience.

Globalization and the New Cultural Geographies

In highlighting the destabilizing features of post-Fordist consumerism, the previous sections have focused on structural and cultural changes related to the U.S. domestic economy. These changes, however, need to be placed in the context of the new globalization (Barnet and Cavanagh 1994; Featherstone 1995; Friedman 1994; Reich 1992; Schiller 1981), a complex of world economic and technological changes that have unleashed a set of forces subversive of the older cultural boundaries of nationalism and ethnicity. Previously local, ethnicity has become a "global force," moving in increasing surges across and within borders (Appadurai 1994). But this is only one of the more significant changes implied by the concept of globalization.

While technology has played a key role in its development, all of the changes loosely designated by the term *globalization* have fundamentally economic origins. To begin, the shift in emphasis from production to consumption in the U.S. economy is part of a broader economic transformation worldwide involving an overseas corporate relocation of productive activity during the past thirty years. In search of cheap labor, U.S. multinationals have moved an increasing proportion of their manufacturing operations to Third World countries, accelerating the trend toward a domestic economy geared to consumption and the production and distribution of information and services (Harvey 1989; Bluestone and Harrison 1982; Reich 1992). These tendencies have hastened the transition in the United States from technologies of production to technologies of reproduction in the form of information and communication systems (Schiller 1981).[14]

The export of manufacturing operations, however, is only the more visible aspect of a major restructuring and intertwining of economic relationships between the U.S. domestic economy and an emerging global economy. The dominant trend in this regard has been a globalization of capital involving major shifts in the flow of investment, finance, labor, and goods and services. These shifts have created entirely new configurations and experiences in international and intergroup relations on a world scale, transforming the landscape of multinational capitalism.[15]

The globalization of economic life can be readily seen, first of all, in an internationalization of investment. The transnational character of corporate ownership is by now a familiar feature of multinational capital.[16] Also, a global financial system has arisen, making the financial markets of different countries highly interdependent (for example, the stock exchanges of major capitalist countries are now mutually reactive). Labor markets similarly have undergone a massive internationalization and degradation. While cross-national labor flows have been common throughout the twentieth century, in recent decades immigration into the more economically advanced countries has dramatically accelerated, as capital effectively imports cheap labor through the loosening of restrictions on immigration and lax enforcement of immigration laws. This has been the case especially in the United States and Europe, where subaltern migrant groups, crossing borders in response to labor demands in foreign countries, increasingly find themselves in situations reminiscent of the colonialist and imperialist relationships of their countries of origin. This is evident in the alarming revival of traditional kinds of labor practices alongside conventional modern practices. As Harvey has observed, the contemporary U.S. economy has witnessed a surprising rise of "domestic, familial, and paternalistic labour systems" (Harvey 1989: 187), as exemplified by a resurgence of sweatshops in such places as New York and Los Angeles. Finally, the production and flow of goods are no longer predominantly national but, rather, international in scope and character. Single commodities now have multiple national origins (for example, American automobiles made of parts from Mexico, Canada, Japan, and Europe), and goods within a single market are manufactured in a plurality of locations (for example, textiles and clothing made in the Far East and Latin America). Furthermore, the import business in the United States is now a booming industry, as ethnically stylized goods from other countries accompany the migration of entrepreneurs who produce and sell them or are shipped through corporate outlets for imported commodities. Overall, the expansion of global markets and the newfound mobility of multinationals have threatened to eliminate altogether the importance of nationality in the manufacture of products and the flow of consumer goods and services (Reich 1992).

The new geographic mobility of finance, labor, and consumables has already resulted in a discernible blurring of national identities, especially in the more mobile population centers of the West. In these regions, travel, job mobility, and high-tech communication are rapidly effacing national borders, creating an increasingly cosmopolitan ethos of cultural diversity,[17] along with growing enclaves of "borderland" ethnic and cultural identities. Metropolitan populations have been undergoing a dramatic diversification as groups of varying ethnic backgrounds migrate to new labor markets and social settings in advanced countries. Significantly, as part of this process, increasing numbers of people, mostly workers but also professional/managerial and scientific/technical personnel, have been crossing cultural borders from non-Western into Western societies. The consequence is a growing multiplicity and fragmentation of identity (Featherstone 1995), especially for migrants undergoing an intensely borderland experience of cultural crossings and encounters but also for native Westerners confronted by new kinds and amalgamations of immigrant cultures and communities.

Consumer culture has been substantially affected by these changes, reflecting the new ethnic population mixes of Western societies as well as the increasingly multinational origins and multiethnic character of consumer goods, information, and images flowing around the world. The availability of a widening range of ethnically diverse and eclectic styles means that in many metropolitan centers of the West (cities like London, Paris, New York, Los Angeles, and Miami come to mind) one can consume food, clothing, music, and entertainment from numerous cultures in the course of a single evening. Thus, in addition to becoming eclectic in other ways, consumer culture has become more ethnically and nationally heterogeneous. Correspondingly, the personal and collective experiences of urbanized Western populations have begun to register a sense of new ethnic "otherness" as natives and migrants begin to intermingle, allowing for a new exchange of cultural goods and meanings within an increasingly hybrid culture.[18]

To a considerable extent, this constitutes a dramatic reversal of the cultural processes of modernization, which involves an export of Western culture (with its "universalistic" and "universalizing" values) into non-Western nations. The tendency of modernization has typically been a homogenization of culture on a world scale, as Western cultural practices spread around the globe, flowing from core to periphery countries.[19] Alongside a continuing process of Westernization, however, there has recently emerged a powerfully opposite importation of non-Western styles into the urban centers of the West, from periphery to core countries. This reverse movement is suggestive of a breakdown of universalistic perspectives and the rise of "particularisms" within the experience of Western populations, as various ethnic traditions and communities, or fragments thereof, reappear and are recontextualized within Western centers of power. The sense of "otherness" engendered by encounters between Westerners and non-Westerners *within the context of the West* thus places strain on inherited structures of thought and feeling and many of the legitimating ideologies of Western culture, short-circuiting the hegemonic influences and universalizing ambitions of the Western powers.

It is important to remember, of course, that modernization itself has always generated a world of contrasts within those countries whose traditional patterns of life have been disrupted by the cultural invasions of the more economically advanced countries. U.S. popular culture, for example, has for years been massively entering Europe by way of television, film, and the recording industry, juxtaposing contemporary industrial forms of U.S. culture with older forms of European culture. Thus, ancient, medieval, Renaissance, modern, and postmodern forms may coexist in the same city (for example, television and ancient ruins in Rome, Andy Warhol and the Cubists at the Pompidou in Paris) or locale (for example, Disneyland in the French countryside). When non-Western countries experience modernization, cultural exports from Western societies penetrate the daily lives of their inhabitants, creating a pastiche of cultural motifs and beliefs (for example, Coca-Cola and Levis in Buddhist societies). Thus, while the dynamics of modernization generate universalizing *tendencies,* traditional cultures often display resistance and adaptation to Western styles, creating an eclectic mix of modern outlooks and technologies with sacred, local, and particularistic patterns of living.[20]

The new globalization is a phenomenon embracing these opposing tendencies toward homogeneity and heterogeneity (Appadurai 1994; Friedman 1994). While commodification continues to impose uniformity on countries throughout the world, pluralistic and eclectic cultural formations appear in more and more places as a result of the movement of symbolic goods in and out of Western enclaves. This dual movement registers the possibility of a truly global marketplace unhindered by national boundaries. Controversially, this prospect lies at the center of the economic policy push by Western capitalist nations for the elimination of all trade barriers, enshrined in recent treaties such as the

North American Free Trade Agreement (NAFTA) and the General Agreement on Tariffs and Trade (GATT). Such treaties threaten to fully impose the "free market" on massive sectors of the world's population, irrespective of the indigenous rights and needs of sovereign countries or the environmental risks of overdevelopment. Regardless of aggressive trade policies, however, the intensified global movement of people and goods is transforming the overall configuration of cultural development throughout the world.

Paradoxically, the formation of a multinational world economy has been occurring during a time of resurgence in small-scale enterprise at the local level. To some extent, this has been evident in the manufacturing sphere, but in retail and service sectors the U.S. economy in the past twenty years or so has been witnessing what appears to be an entrepreneurial renaissance.[21] To the extent that this trend is real and not merely ideological, the revival of small business has a number of sources: the massive shift from manufacturing to a retail and service economy, the flight of multinational capital to overseas locations, and the growing practice of corporate subcontracting. Yet it is probably the case that the revival of small business has been more celebratory than real, perhaps reflecting a conservative reaction against the threat posed by large-scale corporate capital, as expressed through a wish to reaffirm the traditional values of early entrepreneurial capitalism.

Nonetheless, as if to balance or compensate a new scale of globalization, the interest in smallness is in great evidence. This is apparent, for example, in the small shop or boutique movement commonly found in suburban shopping malls and the trendy upscale retail complexes prominent in the fashionable and tourist-oriented sections of big cities.[22] Even when the small shop is corporately owned, through lease or franchise, its reemergence is suggestive of an attitude shift in consumer relations, specifically of a new affirmation of personableness, intimacy, and other values associated with precorporate settings. In this sense, there has occurred a real resurgence in small-business culture. Also, a return to earlier entrepreneurial approaches that is often couched in a premodern emphasis on kinship and place is apparent in the rise of domestic and familial patterns of business and labor. Corporations themselves have "downsized" and localized manufacturing and other operations as a result of flexible accumulation strategies requiring smaller and more adaptable production units, although these practices are certainly not carried out in a spirit of entrepreneurialism. But at an entrepreneurial level, these changes can be seen as part of a more general countertrend toward localism within the social and cultural dislocations of a globalizing economy and a reassertion of place against the disembedding and disembodying effects of global communications technology and globalized consumerism.

Whether carried out by the independent entrepreneur or the corporation, the trend toward small size is part of a post-Fordist decentralization of the economy representing a reversal of the modernization process. Both in the revival of small entrepreneurship and in the narrowly short-term outlooks and sometimes ruthlessly cost-cutting practices of large corporations, the turn to smaller, more localized operations signals a departure from, if not in some cases a reaction against, highly centralized, large-scale mass production. In this sense, despite continued and even growing patterns of centralization and concentration of ownership, we are witnessing the reintroduction of past forms of capitalist organization in production and labor processes.

The contrasting trends of globalization and localization place a great strain on older concepts of a national economy, and a national identity. Whereas the Fordist strategy of accumulation was organized around centralized nationalist principles, flexible accumulation requires a high rate of resource mobilization and a highly fluid conception of how to organize labor and production processes as well as marketing operations. This strategy recognizes no physical or social limitations to the movement and deployment of capital, and no firm loyalties or commitments at any level of social organization—local, regional, national, or international. The emergence of global technologies and communications networks, furthermore, creates a new cultural space (Jameson 1984a) in which to negotiate a less predictable economic terrain. This space transcends national boundaries in ways that strain the collective sense of national identity and belonging.

In this context, the mass media acquire special significance, especially in their role as new cultural intermediaries. As globalization and localization combine to erode the foundations of a national economy, the mass media attempt to constitute, or reconstitute, a national culture. Local and regional cultures have always weakened under the impact of these media, and thus a struggle ensues between newly strengthened local and regional loyalties and the renationalizing tendencies of the mass media.[23] As we have seen, however, the national culture that emerges through the media is made up of a patchwork of discourses, a fragmentary and eclectic array of collective representations signifying the needs of a commercial system of broadcasting more than the contours of an authentic national culture. Through the media, a national culture is constituted insofar as it is able to facilitate the advertising, marketing, and packaging of commodities and consumerism as a way of life. Further, despite a new emphasis on cultural diversity, the consumer is still predominantly constructed as "an American." But here, too, the strains on national identity are apparent since consumer culture is unable to avoid the new polyglot realities of migration and cosmopolitanism.

Although the new globalization is economically driven, it needs to be defined largely in terms of its technological basis. Whereas classic modernization took place primarily by means of an expansion in the "mode of production," the new globalization is characterized by expansion in the "mode of information" (Poster 1990). This includes a vast network of electronic communication systems, including older technologies such as radio, film, and television, but more important, the newer telecommunications that are capable of rapid information movement on a global scale. Although the mode of information plays an important role in the production process, it is absolutely crucial to the globalization of finance, marketing, and other operations in which rapid access to information becomes a necessary condition of corporate power and control on a world scale. Global information systems facilitate a degree of economic coordination and integration unheard of with earlier communications technologies, leading to an unprecedented compression of time and space along with fundamental shifts in cultural, social, and political perceptions. Further, while older communications systems once contributed to the consolidation of the nation-state and national economies, telecommunications and information systems contribute to a fragmentation and dispersal of economic resources and cultural styles, across and within national borders.

As a result, global homogeneity is on balance giving way to heterogeneity, as elements of national, local, and folk culture are torn from their indigenous settings and scattered throughout the global marketplace according to the needs of commerce and tourism. In the process, Western culture gradually begins to lose its legitimating functions (Tomlinson 1991) as mixtures of national and ethnic culture, detached from territorial and historical context, migrate across large regions of the world. To the extent that a new global culture might be emerging from such trends,[24] it is at present a predominantly commercialized culture, devoid of origins or place.

The contemporary globalization process raises the specter of a complete disintegration of cultures as we have known them, a loss of all authentic, indigenous cultures. Nevertheless, insofar as a new cultural openness might be emerging from contacts among ethnic communities and between them and the larger commercial culture, the prospect continues of a more genuine global culture that is eclectic but also socially and physically rooted in place. In this respect, a theory of the effects of globalization would have to examine the nature of the interplay between commercialized communication systems and real groups and communities.[25] While its commercialized forms seem to portend the complete destruction of indigenous cultural values and traditions, and their oppositional themes, globalization also creates the conditions for reconstituting and extending these cultures in new and unforeseen ways. Such possibilities suggest themselves especially in the ethnically and racially mixed cosmopolitan cultures and border spaces of the Western metropolises, where varieties of traditional, popular, and oppositional cultural practices appear in new commercial and technological contexts.[26]

The New Social Movements

The period marked by the rise of economic and technological forces eroding the modern cultural order has witnessed major social and political upheavals no less significant than the emergence of post-Fordist consumerism. Postmodernization thus must also be defined with reference to the rise of the "new" social movements opposing the prevailing value systems and dominant structures of social and political authority in the West during the sixties and seventies (Boggs 1986; Darnovsky, Epstein, and Flacks 1995; Epstein 1991a; Evans and Boyte 1986; Freeman 1983; Touraine 1985; Tucker 1991). For the most part, these have been nonclass movements. Grassroots and often spontaneous in character, these movements have challenged patterns of social hierarchy and domination, particularly along the lines of gender, race, ethnicity, and sexual orientation, as well as in the form of local structures of power in neighborhood and community settings. Peace, environmental, and ecology movements have launched challenges to the structures of economic and political power on a national and international scale while focusing attention on the more devastating global consequences of modern science and technology. Many of these movements have had an urban basis and constituency, involving neighborhood organizing, housing rights, welfare rights, and other issues of particular significance to racial minorities and poor whites. While the new movements have been basically oppositional in character, this period has also seen the emergence of a variety of groups, inspired by the strategies and tactics of oppositional movements, that are more affirmative but still critical of the establishment, illustrated by consumer-oriented groups in areas such as product safety and health care. At first glance, one sees in these movements a potpourri of special interests and particularistic issues. Yet the sixties and seventies gave birth to a new consciousness of opposition to the "system" as a whole and to a commitment to broadly based social and cultural change.

The major movements of the sixties and seventies signaled a new era of doubt over basic cultural values, giving rise to a set of collective demands for a more egalitarian society. Thus, a new antihierarchical orientation had already begun to develop within the social and political activism of sixties culture. This contributed to a general decline in class politics and their replacement by a set of political demands more social, cultural, and personal in nature. Beginning within a new political discourse of rights and justice, these movements gradually evolved into a politics of local control, empowerment, and self-determination.

Significantly, the dominant theme running through these movements was democratization, along with strong overtones of populism. Despite the range of issues and demands raised, the movements that emerged during this period shared a common impulse to overcome what were regarded as oppressive relations of authority and domination and to share more equally in the material, social, and political resources of society. Issues of autonomy and self-determination were central to the politics of the groups comprising these movements, and all sought greater degrees of participation in the processes of self-governance. Unlike the older labor movements, which were hierarchical, bureaucratic, large-scale, and focused on a fairly uniform and narrow set of economic issues, the new movements represented a multiplicity of nonclass democratic values and aspirations. The politics of these movements were framed by social struggles outside the workplace, and they were concerned primarily not with economic redistribution but with a reallocation of power and control, along with a transformation in society's values. While this amounted to a weakening of class politics, it signified the beginning of a more widespread and diffuse politicization, the emergence of a new "micropolitics" that highlighted a large number of discrete but interrelated problems affecting the everyday lives of diverse segments of the population.

Many of these movements could be categorized as political movements insofar as they were antibureaucratic, antistatist, and generally anti-institutional (for example, the student antiwar movement). But the most influential of these movements were predominantly cultural in nature, in that they sought to challenge the basic ideas and values through which the dominant social powers operated. Ultimately, they accomplished this task by raising broad questions concerning collective identity and personal selfhood.[27] A strong dimension of these movements, furthermore, was the assertion of personal values as against the impersonal powers of large bureaucratic organizations. Although it was in the nature of the new social movements to combine political with cultural or personal issues, the overriding tendency was thus toward a "culturalization" of the process of political protest. Relatively weak on political strategy and organization, these movements found their strength ultimately in their ability to address questions of culture and to affirm the importance of self-expression and governance. During the seventies, this assumed the form of a more specifically cultural critique, including questions concerning the ways in which women and minorities were socially constructed by the dominant culture and its institutions. This led to a new concern for the "politics of representation," including issues of personal- and group-identity formation through cultural struggles against hegemonic institutions, including the state, education, the family, and the mass media. The turn toward these broader and more differentiated types of issues gave rise to identity politics (chapter 1) and cultural politics (chapter 5), both of which challenged underlying authority and power relationships as they were manifested in cultural institutions and practices.

Gradually, cultural and identity politics became the modus operandi of historically marginalized groups. The importance of the ecology and environmental movements notwithstanding, the subordination of women, people of color, gays and lesbians, youth, and others denied positive identities formed the political focus of the opposition movements of the seventies. Emerging from the politics of subordination was a critique of the dominant European framework of beliefs and values legitimating patterns of social inequality and oppression. The critique of this framework launched the now almost formulaic attack on the white, patriarchal, middle-class structures of discourse and power in Western society and their exclusionary effects. The attack on Eurocentrism has proven to have implications even beyond the politics of subordination and exclusion. The critiques of rationality, science, progress, and other Enlightenment ideals emerging from these oppositional movements have contributed demonstrably to the current crisis in modern thought, most notably the growing disillusionment in academia with the epistemological and disciplinary structures of Western knowledge.

Compared to earlier periods of protest, the new social movements were unusually diverse and amorphous in character. In composition, they included people from an extraordinary range of backgrounds and circumstances, and in their styles and goals they tended to be relatively informal and structureless. While sharing a common sense of purpose in their opposition to the existing society and culture, they nevertheless spread themselves over a wide set of causes. The eclectic character of these movements gave expression to a new plurality of voices that emerged following the initial protests for civil rights among blacks, and the subsequent protests against gender inequality among women. This new plurality constituted a multifaceted challenge to the establishment and its exclusionary policies and practices and to a large extent contributed to a breakdown of Cold War consensus around basic values and institutions that became manifest after the fifties.

Although the tone of these movements was visibly antibureaucratic, as argued in chapter 1 the new social movements can be interpreted also as a reaction against consumerism and mass culture. Taken together, the new social movements thus represented a major alternative to the dominant trends toward a concentration of corporate and state power and the related imposition of the prerogatives of commercial culture. In these movements, the theme of community stood as a protest against the uprooting effects of modernization and the social isolation and atomization characteristic of a modernized society.

Significantly, as part of a process of a dramatically different nature from that of consumerism or the mass media, the rise of the new social movements registered a similar dissolution of hierarchically ordered attitudes and modes of thought. Whereas the culture of consumption has tended to level hierarchy by means of a weakening of a sense of place, status, or identity, the new movements have challenged hierarchy by attempting to pluralize and decenter the social and political process. In the first instance, commodification has eroded the class foundations of hierarchy, while in the second instance social and cultural movements have directly attacked the very notion of hierarchy in the name of the political values of autonomy, equality, and self-determination. In this sense, the new social movements have in a very different way contributed to the same tendency toward the destabilization of social and cultural relations already under way as a result of the commodification process and subsequently intensified under post-Fordism.

Postmodernization and the Transformation of Culture

The changes discussed in this chapter point to a broad set of material forces contributing to a transformation in the nature and functions of culture and to a corresponding disintegration of the patterns of modern culture in particular. The multiple causes of these changes can be summarized as follows. First, economically, these changes are among the effects of the shift to flexible accumulation as a strategy for differentiating and accelerating the exchange of goods and services in the context of consumer capitalism. Through intensified consumption, cultural symbolism has become an arena of volatile contestation over social status and social meaning. Second, technologically, these changes can be attributed to the effects of the relative shift in economic priorities from production to reproduction, in particular, the transition to a mode of information based on electronic media and telecommunications systems. With growth in the means of mechanical and electronic reproduction, modernist categories of taste, judgment, and value have been increasingly overshadowed by a rapidly circulating mass culture of goods and images. By transforming culture into an ever expanding world of consumable images, reproductive technology has contributed to a collapse of old cultural barriers. Through the media, culture has been turned into a system of effects, sensations, and pleasures derived from the power of the image. Third, as a result of new trends in economic, social, and cultural globalization, the cultural configurations of modern society have begun to disappear, as manifest most directly in a weakening of national boundaries as a basis of economic and cultural relations. Fourth, as a consequence of the new social movements, culture has become a contested terrain, an arena of struggle over conflicted meanings and disputed identities. Taken together, these changes represent a challenge to the values of modernity and the supremacy of Western culture, calling into question its underlying structures of individual and collective identity.

While the structures of economic, social, and political hierarchy have remained largely intact and have in some cases grown more confining, the processes of postmodernization have brought about a generalized leveling of cultural hierarchy by extending and elaborating the inherent tendency of consumerism to democratize the cultural realm. This is evident in the weakening of normative patterns supporting the transmission of status and specifically class distinctions. At the same time, the generalized blurring of status is both cause and consequence of a broader questioning of identity, including gender, race, ethnicity, age, and other bases of affiliations. Overall, the erasure of older distinctions by post-Fordist consumerism and a new proliferation of cultural styles have problematized identity formation on both personal and collective levels by disrupting conventional categories of identification.

The emergence of cultural eclecticism and the consequent introduction of instability into the status system pose both dangers and opportunities. On the one hand, the misleading appearance of social leveling distracts from the real worsening of inequalities that has been occurring throughout the class system, both domestically and on a world scale, as a result of massive economic restructuring. Behind this false appearance of equalization lurk disturbing questions about the reduction of culture to an array of instrumental functions (means of control) dictated by the commercial and political economy. Finally, post-Fordist consumerism provokes questions about the fate of culture, in particular artistic and intellectual values, in a marketplace where anything goes. The inflationary effects that are the other side of cultural leveling thus pose difficult issues for the future of cultural values and meanings.

On the other hand, the new regime of consumerism has arisen at the expense of elitist models of cultural production and control. The disruption of class codes in the realm of consumption and the displacement of class politics by gender, racial, and other kinds of politics have thrown open the question of the social bases of cultural representation and have both allowed and necessitated diversification and innovation in cultural expression, within and outside commercial contexts. The implosion of cultural hierarchies through the rise of mass culture and the new social movements has been cause and consequence of the exposure of the classist, sexist, and racist foundations of modernity, as found particularly in the exclusionary structure of the distinction between high and popular culture.[28] Relatedly, this development has led to a revitalization and expansion of consumer culture in potentially disruptive ways. The commercial system of media and advertising has been forced by the market into increased dependency on the appropriation of popular cultural forms, which are frequently those of subordinate or oppositional groups (Clarke 1991). More generally, by creating a realm of meaning and behavior beyond the control of established and organized institutions, the rise of consumer culture has directly threatened the authority structures of modern society, leading to a weakening of authority per se. While the breakdown of authority may be an unwelcome and widely controversial development, especially in areas like the family, community, and politics, in the realm of culture it opens new spaces for artistic creativity, social and political struggle, and new modes and sources of identification. Finally, as a vehicle of new collective identifications and a means of mediating and articulating cultural difference, a nonclass-based consumer eclecticism can contribute to the formation of culturally amalgamated communities, facilitating the development of innovative, pluralistic, and mixed cultural practices.

Theoretically, the importance now attached to the reproduction and reception of culture and the struggle over cultural forms and meanings needs to be understood as a consequence of the destructuring, disruptive, and potentially liberatory effects of postmodernization. The destabilization of identity and values stemming from economic and technological change has generated multiple and contradictory responses to the decline of modern authority, both conservative and progressive, creating a novel and ambiguous ideological landscape. The decline of the older exclusionary hierarchies of modernity and the seeming exhaustion of modern culture have created possibilities for a genuinely global and universalistic culture built on recognition and inclusion of difference. As chapter 5 will show, however, the exhaustion of modernity has *also* led to various revivalist movements and other often ambiguous returns to premodern beliefs and practices.

5
Identity, Politics, and the Dual Logic of Postmodernity
Fragmentation and Pluralization

Running through the disparate discourses of both postmodernism and postmodernity are recurring themes of the differentiation, dispersal, and decentering of cultural meaning and experience. The postmodern condition begins with the cultural density and heterogeneity resulting from structural transformations in the capitalist system of production and marketing, the impact of media technologies and aesthetics, and a massive expansion of private consumption. Writers like Harvey (1989) and Jameson (1983) have focused on the consequences of time-space compression accompanying cultural commodification and the processes of cultural fragmentation embedded in economic and technological development. These theorists along with Baudrillard (1981), Lash (1990), and others have called attention to the problems of sensory overload and meaning dispersion resulting from a massive proliferation of objects and images in the sphere of consumption, a situation referred to by Featherstone (1995) as an "overproduction of culture." The fragmentation of culture resulting from its absorption by the commodity form leads to a leveling of institutionalized taste hierarchies in a highly differentiated and rapidly changing marketplace of cultural goods and images. Given these conditions, postmodernity is an often disjunctive and sometimes jarring experience of multiplicity and fluidity, disturbingly incongruous and disorienting yet full of exhilarating possibilities.

However, theorists characterizing postmodernity in terms of heterogeneity and difference usually obscure a crucial distinction. On the one hand, and this has been the focus of my analysis so far, heterogeneity can be thought of specifically as a manifestation of processes of *fragmentation*. This suggests that social and cultural experience is shattered, disconnected, and incoherent, as social relations and cultural meaning disintegrate. Fragmentation thus carries connotations of lack, confusion, or loss accompanying a discontinuity of experience. On the other hand, heterogeneity can refer to an entirely different kind of phenomenon. As alluded to in previous chapters, postwar U.S. society has propagated numerous social, cultural, and political groupings and movements in search of new kinds of identification, self-fulfillment, and community, involving an enlarged domain of collective practices and group organizing. To speak only of fragmentation, therefore, is to overlook the equally important historical resurgence of group *pluralism*. A familiar idea in social and political theory, pluralism usually designates the constitution of society and politics through the recognition of a plurality of diverse social and cultural groups, often thought of as competing interest groups. More broadly, pluralism implies multiple group differences and heritages, whether they be ethnic, racial, economic, national, religious, gender, sexual, regional, or ideological in nature. To return to the introduction and chapter 1, the stirrings of postmodernity thus stem not only from cultural fragmentation but the rise of a new identity and cultural politics. We can now better interpret identity and cultural politics not only as a politics of recognition (Taylor 1992) but as a response to the disruptive and disintegrative features of postmodernity. The disorientation and sense of emptiness accompanying cultural turmoil give rise to a search for compensation and redemption through identifications with and membership in various groups and communities. Thus, postmodernity generates both a sense of ephemerality and loss associated with cultural fragmentation *and* movements of cultural renewal as manifested in an expanded field of cultural and political practices.

A rising sense of heterogeneity, therefore, is a manifestation of two separate, contradictory, but closely intertwined logics. Commodification can be taken as the cause of an unsettled social and cultural existence characterized by a fleeting and superficial landscape of consumer goods and images and an anxiety-filled evacuation of meaning. In contrast, a pluralizing logic based in established democratic traditions of voluntary association and group participation, by allowing new collective formations, works *against* the condition of privatized consumption to overcome its fragmentation and rootlessness. A loss of connection and coherence thus drives the creation of new communities promising renewed social bonds, personal and social fulfillment, and coherent, however multiple, identities.

While perhaps uncontroversial, this distinction has significant theoretical and political consequences. First and foremost, it focuses attention on a basic opposition between what could be called commercial and political postmodernities and postmodernisms.[1] Whereas commercial postmodernity can be defined by its origins in the commodity form and its manipulative and depthless aesthetics, political postmodernity is manifest in identity and cultural politics and the search for new forms of authenticity and place. Second, this distinction captures both the *de*stabilizing and *re*stabilizing features of contemporary cultural phenomena. While the postmodernity of consumerism and the media poses a problem of fragmented identities, the postmodernity of groups and movements, left and right, can be seen in diverse efforts to redefine and reconstitute identity through political and discursive struggles over group and societal meanings and values. Third, at the base of the opposition between these two postmodernities is a domain contest over the meaning and constitution of difference. Commercial mass culture appropriates, commodifies, and markets difference in the form of style. As Douglas Kellner (1995) has succinctly put it, "Difference sells." In contrast, the task of cultural politics is to invoke difference in the name of group identities and cultures. At the same time, however, the far-flung contemporary search for identity is apparent in efforts to create new forms of culture and group life both from within *and* outside the worlds of consumption and technology, by means of consumerist strategies in the marketplace *and* through participation in cultural and political movements and communities. The search for identity thus spans the intersection of the contradictory currents and impulses of commercial and political culture.

The frequent conflation of these distinct logics can be seen as a failure to adequately sort through the scattered democratizing tendencies of postmodern culture. The distinguishing features of today's cultural landscape—the fragmenting and leveling effects of the commodity form, and the formation and reformation of new and old social groupings—are outgrowths, respectively, of (1) the ineluctable process of cultural democratization necessitated by capitalist development, and (2) the political contract at the foundation of the liberal state. Whereas in the modern elitist conception of mass culture, democratization referred to a degrading process of standardization through mass production and consumption, from the standpoint of postmodernization as discussed in chapter 4 mass culture designates a valorization of *particularity*, specifically a recognition of the cultural needs and aspirations of particular groups and categories of individuals and their construction as marketable goods. To some extent, this is a process inherent in the logic of the market. As Kellner (1995) observes, "Capitalism must constantly multiply markets, styles, fads, and artifacts to keep absorbing consumers into its practices and lifestyles" (40). But this tendency is also a consequence of capitalism's growing dependence on consumerism, media technology, new labor markets, and new regulative mechanisms of artificial opposition and "repressive tolerance" (Marcuse 1965). Thus, despite itself, capitalism necessarily sweeps away older hierarchies and universalisms in favor of more particularistic appeals, however commercialized. In the words of Terry Eagleton (1996),

> As the capitalist system evolves . . . —as it colonizes new peoples, imports new ethnic groups into its labor markets, spurs on the division of labour, finds itself constrained to extend its freedoms to new constituencies—it begins inevitably to undermine its own universalist rationality. For it is hard not to recognize that there are now a whole range of competing cultures, idioms and ways of doing things, which the hybridizing, transgressive, promiscuous nature of capitalism has itself helped to bring into being. (39)

Ironically, whereas in the realm of consumption, capitalism creates the appearance of a classless society, in the realm of politics the liberal state has been forced by identity movements and a politics of recognition to acknowledge the persistence of social inequality and group subordination. Capitalist society thus defends against its social contradictions through a combination of cultural classlessness in the marketplace and carefully circumscribed political concessions to particular communities of interest in "civil society." However, while thereby actually perpetuating underlying inequalities, the capitalist system is by these very same means both commercially and politically compelled to endorse and *intensify* persistent impulses toward equality by regrouping itself around points of particularity and difference. This results in a palliative that might be called "democratic particularism," a substitute for social equality in which *culture* is democratized through a semiotics of difference.[2]

Within the realm of culture itself, however, the forces of commodification and the practices of cultural politics work at cross-purposes, attempting to undermine each other's agendas. The commercialism of consumer culture works to obliterate real cultural difference by integrating it into the prevailing social logic of capitalist accumulation. Consumerism constructs difference in the interest of the market, dispensing packaged, corporate versions of human diversity, including what Kenneth Gergen (1991) has called "ersatz community." In contrast, the thrust of cultural politics is the articulation and assertion of difference as individual and group identity, based on real (spatially and socially rooted) community. As opposing tendencies, however, consumer culture and cultural politics interact in complex ways: the former attempts to absorb and exploit the latter, while the latter attempts to deconstruct and displace the former. In the last analysis, however, attempts to retrieve authentic meanings and experiences, and to reclaim or reconstruct authentic identities, are waged largely on a terrain defined by the imperatives of commercial culture itself. Cultural and identity movements have been forced by and large to operate in an environment dominated by the prevailing modes of capitalist consumption and technology and the priorities of a corporate economy.

The dialectical encounters between the commercial and political tendencies of postmodernity are reflected, finally, in an ideologically contingent and ambiguous politics. Today, the marketplace, liberal democracy, populism, neo-conservatism, and traditional modes of belief mix in uneasy and unpredictable ways, visibly blurring the lines between economic and social liberalism and conservatism. While the destruction of traditional and modern forms of culture by commodification leads to innumerable attempts at reconstruction, the competing logics and goals of commercial and political postmodernism make this process increasingly complex and undecidable. The deployment of various notions of tradition and heritage among both supporters and critics of the present economic and political systems has turned these into contested concepts, complicating the familiar ideological landscape of left and right.

Looking for Difference in Postmodernity: Fragmentation or Pluralization?

The valorization of difference in postmodernist academic discourse, while presumably a move against the universalizing and totalizing modes of modern thought (the "grand narratives"), needs also to be read as a refraction of the cultural heterogeneity of contemporary society. While almost ritualistically invoking the theme of difference in discussions of culture, identity, and politics, post-modernists seldom if ever articulate the idea of difference in structural and institutional contexts. While privileged in movements to demarginalize subordinated identities and cultures, difference has not been seen in relation to social and cultural forces in the larger society. In this respect, postmodernists have generally failed to connect their claims to a diagnostic perspective on social and cultural transformations. A reflexive postmodernism, I argue, would have to position itself more explicitly as a response to the societal and cultural transformation toward particularity and difference captured in the concept of post-modernization discussed in chapter 4.[3]

The structural and cultural fragmentation of experience and meaning undermining identity and self-coherency is a neglected source of the awakening to difference pervading contemporary postmodern theory. While thematized in identity and cultural politics, difference is also a feature of the proliferation of meanings and styles characterizing rapid-turnover consumer capitalism. The commodity form that reduces both labor and culture to an exchange relation paradoxically multiplies and disperses cultural difference, increasingly a common denominator of everyday personal and collective experience. An intensified awareness of difference is thus tied to the extensive fragmentations and spatializations of commodity labor and culture. This kind of difference is produced by the marketplace of workers, goods, and images and inseparable from an expanding global capitalism.

As discussed in chapter 2, to the extent that consumer culture markets a variety of styles and imagined identities it offers ceaseless opportunities for self-elaboration, experimentation, and personal fulfillment. Ultimately, however, within a corporate economy difference is presented for the sake of difference, as mere novelty. Furthermore, the experience of difference is to a large degree a phenomenon of fragmentation itself, a by-product of the disjunctive effects of technology and the marketplace. While commercial postmodernism celebrates this kind of difference as a form of freedom—a relativizing thus allegedly subversive explosion of style, belief, and value—it is in reality more of an "indifferent difference." It is an individually inscribed difference of personal choice and style circumscribed by the limits of the consumer marketplace.

The particularity and difference inherent in mass culture are thus to be kept distinct from those of cultural politics. As an attempt to *overcome* fragmentation, the politicization of culture and identity follows impulses to reclaim and reconstruct communal and group-based definitions of experience and self, and such impulses are expressive of the need for connections and meanings obviously deeper than those of commodity culture. In this sense, cultural politics represents an attempt to assert *authentic* difference, an effort to recognize particularity in a plurality of groups and movements whose members are seeking viable new affiliations and identities. These efforts are manifestations of a political postmodernism that strives to articulate new forms and modes of identity formation by reconstructing the collapsed social and cultural spaces of consumer society.

Contemporary cultural politics was born in the pluralist impulses, collective struggles for autonomy, and critiques of representation that in convergence with the post-Fordist marketplace have contributed in the past half of the century to the erosion of modern cultural institutions. As a pluralizing phenomenon, however, cultural politics is rooted in forces as old as modernity itself. Movements of class, ethnic, and religious groupings infused early modernity with a sense of plurality reflecting a multitude of different social interests seeking resources, power, and position in the creation of a new social order. Of course, the dominant tendency of modernity has been to subjugate social and cultural difference under class-controlled economic rationality. The spread of capitalism, rooted in the exploitation of labor, necessitated the triumph of a worldview that justified and rationalized a social order congruent with bourgeois class interests. Difference was suppressed by capitalist ideology, a falsely universalizing form of thought subsuming the particularistic claims of subordinate groups under the "general interest" of the bourgeoisie.

Notions of plurality remained implicit, however, in the liberal traditions and politics of revolt accompanying the evolution of modern capitalism and the liberal state. Such traditions were strongest in the United States, which witnessed slave rebellions and various movements of women, workers, and people of color against the prevailing system of inequality.[4] Given its democratic traditions and complex social composition, the United States—despite capitalism's autocratic features—has been historically exceptional in its capacity to generate and accommodate a multitude of social and cultural movements and experimentations. Glacially, the formal norms of democracy and the historical struggles of various groups led to the assertion and construction of numerous and complex social and cultural identities. This has had dramatic political consequences for marginalized groups. Beginning with the rise of a militant working class, economic and social developments within modern capitalist society—including upward mobility and rising expectations, the formation of new collectivities, large-scale organization, and monopoly capital—set the stage for a decline of the "bourgeois subject" and the emergence of other subjects. The contradictions between the propertied white male figure signifying personal success and social progress and the interests of the subordinate social groups who built the United States through their physical labors generated class-based struggles from the early nineteenth to the mid-twentieth centuries. In our own time, the divisions of race, ethnicity, gender, age, and sexual orientation have risen to the surface of political life, providing grounds for new pluralist and oppositional challenges to hegemonic social and political structures. In both periods, while the reduction of social inequality has often been only minimal, protest movements have led to the formation of new identities and communities.

While a reaction against trends of cultural conformity in the fifties (chapter 1), the upsurge of pluralistic impulses beginning in the sixties was also largely attributable to the consequences of modernization in the economy and, especially, higher levels of education. During the seventies, however, these impulses were strengthened by processes of postmodernization. The formation of new global relationships and a heightened sense of global interdependency, rapidly changing structures of production and consumption, major changes in the structure and social composition of labor markets, the collective impact of the new social movements—all contributed to, and reflected, the destabilization of modern forms of culture and identity and the concomitant rise of new groupings and movements. Earlier models of order, in which containment of social contradictions was sought through various "normalizing" practices, became increasingly ineffective during this period, including not only what Foucault (1979) called "disciplinary" practices but also mechanisms of the economic marketplace, state-sponsored cultural and political strategies, and other means of social control.

From this perspective, the postmodern condition represents a legitimation crisis (Habermas 1975) precipitated by a breakdown of modern universalistic values. The resurgence of pluralism characterizing cultural politics registers a major shift from universalistic to particularistic modes of thought and expression. To the extent that culture has become an arena of struggle over contested meanings and identities, pluralism now implies the affirmation of cultural difference.[5]

It is now possible to understand identity politics as an emergent form of the legitimation crisis of modernity and to recapitulate its origins in two interrelated developments of the sixties. First, the rebellion of youth, student activists, and counterculturalists during this decade was an indication that the individualistic and apolitical expressions of fifties youthful alienation and discontent had finally taken a collective form. This "value revolt" led to a new emphasis on spontaneous personal and collective expression as well as a pluralizing of popular styles and sentiments antithetical to the suburban white middle class while reflective of other social experiences, namely, those of blacks and working-class whites (Ferrandino 1972). Second, the growing awareness of racial and gender difference and oppression accompanying the civil rights and women's movements contributed to new forms of black and feminist consciousness and protest. Black opposition to white institutions eventually led to racial and ethnic pluralization, involving separatist impulses to recuperate or fashion alternative cultures and institutions reflective of the experiences of people of color. Similarly, the women's movement contributed to a pluralization of social and political attitudes governing relations between men and women and the formation of new conceptions of gender and its social organization. Clearly, the revolt against middle-class values and the racial, ethnic, and gender oppositions that followed generated a new ideology of pluralism, providing the framework for the social and cultural movements arising from the sixties rebellions.

A certain bifurcation *within* postmodernist writings between an emphasis on cultural eclecticism, on the one hand, and a focus on cultural and identity politics, on the other, has prevented more informed distinctions and relations to be drawn between the separate processes of fragmentation and pluralization I have outlined. Indiscriminate use of these terms has often resulted in the conflation of fragmentary mass culture and cultural and identity politics, or simply a disappearance of one or the other term in debates about the postmodern. The weakening of modern forms of cultural authority has thus typically been seen as a wholesale disintegration of cultural and social forms in general. However, whereas mass culture has an atomizing effect on groups and their cultural heritages, the fading of modern identities has been accompanied by collective attempts to forge *new* group identities based on popular aspirations and cultural traditions and innovations beyond and in opposition to the intrusions of the consumer marketplace.

Failure to recognize and theorize these opposing tendencies is also related to the fundamental antihierarchical and particularizing impulses of *both* processes. The leveling effects of the commodity form and the inclusionary demands of diverse social and cultural movements make common democratizing claims against the universalizing foundations of modern society. Both partake of a relativizing assault on the elitist institutions of the modern order, whether in the realms of art, education, science, politics, or religion. Both developments contribute to a destabilization of older social positions and to an erosion of established epistemological, moral, and aesthetic categories. For instance, in conjunction with mass culture but in a radically different way, a pluralizing politics subverts modern notions of authorship and authority by questioning their social and cultural bases. Commodification and pluralization, therefore, while manifestations of mutually opposing dynamics and impulses, converge in their undermining of modern forms of culture and identity.

How these processes work to overcome modernity's suppression of difference might now be summarized. On the one hand, the dynamics of mass media and consumer society undermine firm identities by fragmenting and dispersing the subject in consumption and spectatorship. Here, mass culture strives to enlist social and cultural difference in the interests of the market, transforming "otherness" into new forms of novelty and pleasure for mass consumption (hooks 1992). More generally, mass culture obliterates authentic difference by creating a "democracy of consumption" in which difference and particularity act as merely other common denominators among consumers. On the other hand, while mass culture *appropriates* and *manufactures* difference, feeding it to consumers as packaged personal identity, in cultural politics attempts are waged to *articulate* and *politicize* difference in the form of collective identities. Here, silenced groups seeking autonomy and self-determination form diverse cultural movements. This involves challenging prevailing media representations of dominants and subordinates by invoking alternative collective histories and experiences along with newly constructed identities.

This is only a schematic model of the dynamics of postmodernity. In reality, despite the appeal of cultural politics, the commodity form is so pervasive and powerful as to dramatically shrink the space in which oppositional politics can effectively be practiced. The fate of movements struggling for autonomy and identity in a consumer culture is ultimately dependent on their capacity to overcome the fragmentariness and distance built into a continually expanding system of market-oriented production. Harvey (1989) has commented on the dilemmas of oppositional groups, which he argues "are relatively empowered to organize in place but disempowered when it comes to organizing over space. In clinging, often of necessity, to a place-bound identity, however, such oppositional movements become a part of the very fragmentation which a mobile capitalism and flexible accumulation can feed upon" (303). It should be pointed out that while this statement might accurately characterize the predicament of movements, it ignores the many possibilities and actualities of oppositional *practices* based on the creation and intersection of new kinds of spaces. Also, Harvey overlooks the many alternatives to identity dependent on place, as exemplified by the virtual communities discussed in chapter 2 or the resurgence of cultural identities of widely scattered populations encompassing whole regions of the world, for example, Jews, Muslims, and others. Still, by contextualizing movements in the spatializations of capitalism, he draws attention to the problem of maintaining their coherence and autonomy in the face of market forces. This problem might be considered from the standpoint of the distinction that Raymond Williams (1977, 1980) makes between "alternative" and "oppositional" cultural tendencies. This distinction is problematized to an extreme by the continually shifting marketplace of capitalism and its persistent absorption of oppositional culture into the dominant commercial framework. The central tendency of commodification is to convert political opposition into alternative lifestyle, rendering threats to the dominant system of consumption relatively harmless by turning potential subversion into new consumer products.[6]

The fate of movements is somewhat more positive, although still mixed, when considered in the context of mass media. Despite the difficulties imposed on movements by their representation in the media, by packaging them for national consumption the media often endow popular or oppositional movements with life and credibility, drawing attention to and amplifying their ideologies and actions. In the very process of constructing them for mass audiences, the media often *contribute* to the formation of new movements and identities, in part by publicizing and circulating popular ideals and utopian visions (Jameson 1979). In their newsmaking function, furthermore, the media often draw *attention* and generate *responses* to the plight of oppressed groups.[7] But while lending them a degree of legitimation, the media are at the same time compelled to contain and domesticate these movements (Gitlin 1979, 1980). Oppositional groups are therefore required to position themselves within an ongoing system of commercial media interests, constituting and "selling" themselves within the frames and mediations of mass culture.[8] This culture renews and extends its own hegemony by feeding off popular traditions and innovations, co-opting struggles for authentic meanings and identities that might otherwise flourish beyond the boundaries of the corporate system. Movements are thus largely unable to form and develop independently of their constructions in the mass media. Futhermore, criticism of commercial culture can as a rule be effectively launched only through the media themselves.[9] While commercial media and cultural politics operate in a state of mutual tension, then, the advantage tends to lie with the defining powers of corporate institutions, which repeatedly attempt to construct movements in accordance with their own economic and political needs.[10]

The Antitheses of Fragmentation: The Search for Moorings

The opposition between cultural commodification and cultural or group plural-ism provides a general framework for considering a countermovement to frag-mentation that includes, but is more deeply and broadly configured than cul-tural politics alone. This countermovement has been variously characterized as involving "hypersimulated" or "nostalgic" reality (Crook et al. 1992), "the search for personal and collective identity" (Harvey 1989), "ersatz being" (Gergen 1991), "a generation of seekers" (Roof 1993), and "resacralization" (Wexler 1996). These characterizations refer to a variety of reactions and responses to the crisis of meaning engendered by the rationalizing and isolating effects of con-sumer culture. Against the intensities, uncertainties, and emptiness of a hyper-differentiated and hyperrationalized society (Crook et al. 1992), and specifically the sensory overload of a saturated cultural environment,[11] this countermove-ment entails a widespread and sometimes fervent search for immutable truth. Just as this search fills the other half of Baudelaire's formulation of modernity (Harvey 1989), it is also the complementary other of postmodern fragmenta-tion. Whereas aesthetic modernism launched this quest in the sphere of art, today we witness a widespread personal and collective search for meaning and purpose in the contexts of everyday life. As a response to the erosion of culture as "a lived unity of experience," such efforts enable "individuals and groups (to) believe that they have access to a deep reality around which a unity of experi-ence, a real culture, can be rebuilt" (Crook et al. 1992: 72–74).

The pursuit of experiential unity and depth has been undertaken not only to recover a sense of purpose and meaning but correlatively to re-create stable and more enduring structures of self and identity. As older social norms and forms dissolve under the impact of commodification and the atomization of mass soci-ety, individuals and groups seek to construct new identities or to reconstruct old ones, with and without the trappings of consumer culture. Such efforts, however, seem primarily motivated by a wish to renounce the world of commodities for alternative experiences and frameworks of meaning. The rise of cultural and identity politics, therefore, needs to be seen in the context of a wider and more diverse quest for self in the midst of cultural attenuation and loss.

This countermovement, moreover, exceeds the disintegrating effects of postmodernized culture, reflecting a disillusionment with modernity itself. To a large extent, it represents a revolt against the larger historical trend of rationali-zation shaping modern society, including both its "disenchantment of the world" through the machinery of bureaucracy (Weber 1958a), and the horrors of modern technology, as exemplified by weapons of mass destruction and the devastation of the environment. While the search for moorings might in the most immediate sense be a response to the instabilities of postmodern culture, it is driven also by a more basic rejection of the more deleterious and ominous features of modernity. Indeed, postmodern culture in this respect recuperates many of the elements of premodern culture, as evidenced in the rise of revivalist values and the new popularity and legitimacy of "tradition."

The manifestations of the search for a sense of certitude and unity are varied and far-ranging. A major cultural phenomenon reflecting this trend in the United States is New Ageism, a potpourri of movements and sensibilities constituting a nebulous worldview based on notions of self-awareness and spirituality, evident in pop psychologies, Eastern religions, mysticisms, astrology, new eclecticisms in music and the visual arts, and cultivations of the body and other sensuous experiences. The often cultlike character of these phenomena of discovery and renewal connotes a generalized religious awakening without the institutionalized trappings of organized religion. The juxtaposition of past and future orientations in these movements is suggestive further of a repudiation of the momentary present and an attempt to reconstruct the past mythically, in a way often prefigurative of a visionary future.

The general outlines of a countermovement opposed to high-tech consumption, however, are more apparent in the revalorization of tradition. One of the more disturbing aspects of this turn has been the resurgence of various forms of authoritarian politics in both the United States and Europe. The rise of neoconservative and reactionary politics in the United States has often been regarded as a fearful and defensive postsixties reaction to the transgressions and turmoil of that decade. But the conservative resurgence needs to be understood more broadly as an attempt to reinstate traditional values and beliefs in the midst of ongoing cultural crisis, of which the sixties was only a major symptom and that has since appeared in the "culture wars."[12]

Regardless of how the rise of conservative politics might be interpreted, they have clearly surfaced alongside a revivalist culture that is seeking to reinvent tradition out of the fragments of commercialism and social decay. A move to revive basic institutions such as the family, religion, the state, and the community has been widespread in the United States and other Western countries. The resonance of "family values," the dramatic growth of fundamentalist and evangelical religions,[13] the moral crusade against abortion rights, the war on drugs, the rise of right-wing populism and nationalism, and the mythologizing of the state are among the more fervent and extreme examples of a broad trend toward the reassertion of traditional values in many societies of the West. Despite the inevitable problems of interpreting such broad and complex trends, evidence suggests that an antisecularist revival of traditional values and institutions is a widespread phenomenon in the United States today, cutting across numerous demographic categories.[14]

Another and more troubling development is the revival of intense national and ethnic loyalties throughout much of Europe and the former Soviet Union since the end of the Cold War. The fierce reaffirmation of ethnicity in these regions is inter alia an extreme and volatile expression of the resurgence of cultural particularisms in the wake of the collapse of communism's forced modernization and its destructive impact on traditional identities and cultures. Another though less warlike and nationalistic version of ethnic revitalization has been occurring in the United States. While the controversial ascendancy of white European ethnicity can be interpreted as a case of backlash against the gains of people of color and the perceived threats of immigrants, the revival of ethnicity in this country is in part a reaction to a different type of modernization, the market-oriented "mainstreaming" of diverse cultural groups into the white middle class. Here again, however, countermovements are a complex response both to modernization, in this case the suppression of ethnic identity coupled with compulsory identifications with commercialized WASP culture, *and* to postmodernization, specifically the destabilization of identity, the new openings and forms of resistance developed within cultural politics, and the new migration.[15]

A further sign of revivalism is the search for historical roots, which is symptomatic of the destructive effects of both modernization and aspects of postmodernization on social and personal life. The celebrated seventies television miniseries *Roots* was significant for its own historical reasons, but its title elicited a mass emotional response that became emblematic of a longing for a personal past, particularly in the family. The specific forms of this phenomenon are multifold but include an interest in family trees and histories, an intensified appreciation of the values and objects of home and family (heirlooms, antiques, photographs), and an emphasis on the home as a "place" offering refuge from the commercial environment. Efforts to root the self in history have also emerged in more organized public forms. Heritage and historical societies, commemorative events of various kinds, and other institutionalized efforts to reestablish connections to the past have flourished in the past twenty years or so. Yearnings for the past have also taken the form of escape into fantasies of premodern times. Consider the Society for Creative Anachronism, an international organization that promotes the chivalrous ideals of the Middle Ages. With a reported two thousand members in northern California and twenty-five thousand worldwide, this organization provides "not just a sense of community but a code of conduct, a purpose—a veritable cosmology."[16] More commercialized versions of such phenomena are annual events such as the Renaissance Faire in California, which packages the pleasures and romantic fantasies of medieval life for weekend family consumption, and various kinds of theme parks that manufacture escape to other times and places. The increased incidence of such efforts to retrieve the past is reflective of a desire to recover a lost sense of history (Jameson 1984a) resulting from the spread of consumerism, mass media, and high technology.

All of these phenomena are examples of the nostalgia mode pervading postmodern culture. An aspect of every movement celebratory of the past, nostalgia has become a commodity in its own right, whether as an attribute of consumer goods or as a motif in advertising images, television formulas, or political campaigns. Also, since the early seventies nostalgia has become a prominent feature of Hollywood film (Jameson 1983), evoking sentimental longings and imaginings through backward glances to previous decades (the thirties, the fifties, the sixties). Nostalgia has not only become an important element of commercial cinema but has provided the inspiration for a whole new genre of film, the period piece.

Finally, a characterization of this countermovement would be incomplete without mention of the search for community. Whereas community has long been regarded as the antidote to the atomized and anonymous individualism of modern urban life, while itself undergoing major attenuation by consumerism and mass media (chapter 2), the politics of community were reinvigorated along new lines by the wave of activism and counterculturalism emerging from the sixties. Community building has since been a recurring part of efforts to reestablish the bonds of group life. This is illustrated by "communitarianism" (*Telos* 1988; Etzioni 1994), an ideological response to a perceived threat of social disintegration, cultural and moral decay, and a growing sense of powerlessness across the political spectrum. Whether as a revival of traditional forms of community, such as in a revitalization of the extended family, traditional forms of religion, or cult membership, or as merely an attempt to revive a sense of community in formal or voluntary associations such as neighborhood groups or professional organizations, the desire for a sense of belonging and direct participation and control has become widespread in the contemporary United States.

While clearly in part a manifestation of the search for stable structures of meaning and association, identity politics stands in a complicated and equivocal relationship to the broader trends toward revivalism and tradition. There is often an implicit appeal to tradition in the assertion of ethnic and racial identity. But in contrast, feminist and gay and lesbian politics are demonstratively built on a renunciation of traditional ideologies governing gender and sexuality. At the same time, identifications with group and community and the affirmation of a collectively shared culture are common to all identity politics, which in this sense can be compared to the more widespread search for moorings. As a manifestation of racial, ethnic, gender, and sexual pluralism, identity politics reveals the powerful subjective and political dimensions of the particularistic identifications with group and community prevalent in society in general. In a curious twist, however, by disrupting established attitudes and social relations, identity politics has itself bred feelings of rootlessness and displacement, feeding on itself in contradictory and unanticipated ways. This is apparent in the strong identifications with inherited traditions that have often been provoked by the politicization of gender, race, ethnicity, and sexuality, as illustrated by the phenomenon of white backlash, specifically the assertion of white ethnicity and aggressive reassertions of traditional stereotypes of masculinity as provoked by feminism (Faludi 1991; Jeffords 1989). In this respect, group loyalties have been intensified in response not only to the impact of commercial culture but to threats posed to *older* identities by identity politics itself.[17]

Endeavors to reintegrate a sense of purpose and meaning in daily existence represent yet another side of the trend toward de-differentiation discussed in chapter 3. In the aestheticization of society, the aesthetic dimension is brought into the realms of production and consumption, appropriated by consumer capitalism through the merging of culture and the commodity. Revivalism can be seen as an aspect of this aestheticization insofar as it reflects a new expressivist tendency within a turn toward traditional cultural practices and artifacts. Revivalism, however, also retrieves the *moral* elements of tradition, including "family values," religiosity, spirituality, patriotism, loyalty, obligation, personal responsibility, and other "virtues" associated with the moral discourses of the past. Moral values, formerly embedded largely within religious institutions and personal life, have spilled over these boundaries into the institutions of public life, as exemplifed by the push to abolish the separation of church and state through school prayer and the antiabortionist crusade to impose personal religious beliefs on others in violation of the laws governing reproductive rights. These are particularly zealous manifestations of what Philip Wexler (1996) has called "re-sacralization" and other observers have noted as a return of personal and group spirituality. Such developments obviously represent a further collapse of the boundary between public and private life, in this instance through a politicization of personal life issues. The pressures to desegregate morality and ethics evident in these developments place unusual strain on the long-standing modern dichotomy between the sacred and the secular. Remoralizing trends are also indicative of the extent to which the pursuit of personal meaning has become an ideological vehicle of identity politics. Right-wing religious groups have appropriated morality as one means of establishing their particular identities, just as the defense of secular rights such as choice and freedom *from* religion has recently served as a partial definition of the identities of those on the left side of the political spectrum. Whether or not in the service of identity politics, the revitalization of moral and ethical debate, and the encroachment of the sacred on the secular, are further instances of the culturalization of society. Here, personal beliefs and values come to define a new terrain of ideological and political struggle in which cultural questions increasingly overlay political life.

The contemporary social and cultural landscape is replete with attempts to reconstruct an authentic culture beyond the reach of consumerism and its various incarnations. Contemporary movements and sentiments opposed to rationality and commodification invite comparison to Raymond Williams's (1977, 1980) important distinctions among dominant, residual, and emergent culture, and his closely related concept "structure of feeling." According to Williams, while every culture has certain prevailing and determinate features (dominant values, beliefs, and cultural practices), such hegemonic patterns are not exhaustive of human activity (Gramsci 1973), which also includes residual elements from the past and emergent tendencies reflective of new values, practices, and relationships that are continually being formed in the present. Clearly, the rise of cultural politics signifies an activation of both residual and emergent elements as against the dominant culture, depending on whether we have in mind a retrieval of tradition or the construction of new meanings and identities. As I have suggested, however, what is significant about the current period is the almost promiscuous intermingling of these different elements. Contrary to what seemed to be Williams's conceptual intent, cultural politics and its broader context of purposeful searching are to a large extent exemplified by the resituating, reinterpretation, or reconstruction of residual culture *within* emergent forms, a recuperation of tradition within a context of the regeneration of meaning and identity. In these circumstances, the residual is given new valences, thus complicating if not obscuring the very distinction between residual and emergent. The larger search for meaning extending beyond but cutting across cultural politics, however, would seem to be a manifold expression of a new structure (or structures) of feeling. These structures are aimed at revitalizing a sense of "place" (Harvey 1989) and "presence" (Wexler 1996) within a framework of renewal, whether or not of a reactionary nature. The emphasis that Williams (1977) placed on the "affective elements of consciousness and relationships . . . in a living and interrelating continuity" (132) seems to fit the burgeoning awareness and consciousness of the need to re-create culture in the face of disintegration. Williams's stress on the close relationship between structures of feeling and emergent formations, furthermore, is reflective of the multifarious movements and tendencies characterizing postmodern society in the United States.

As I have suggested, however, this search repeatedly succumbs to the forces of commodification, an aspect of what Williams (1980) called "incorporation." Under existing conditions, the possibilities for the retrieval of identities and meanings that are not already contained within the structures of the commodity, already formed by the mediations and simulations of media-based culture, remain problematic. New selves and modes of life are difficult to pursue except on the terrain of consumption itself, where they are packaged as lifestyle and marketed like any other commodities. In addition, judging the "authenticity" or "autonomy" of a trend or movement is no easy task in a culture of blurred boundaries, where hardly anything is immune to imitative recycling. The search for authenticity is thus extremely problematic in a society in which everything is vulnerable to immediate commodification.[18]

Efforts to resuscitate tradition are particularly difficult and obscure in a culture that is increasingly sealed off from the past. Not only is a sense of historical continuity problematic in a rapidly changing and technologically mediated society but whatever knowledge we have of history now comes predominantly from the mass media and other outlets of commercialized entertainment. Indeed, tradition is easily packaged for commercial consumption. As Harvey (1989) argues,

> The irony is that tradition is now often preserved by being commodified and marketed as such. The search for roots ends up at worst being produced and marketed as an image, as a simulacrum or pastiche (imitation communities constructed to evoke images of some folksy past, the fabric of traditional working-class communities being taken over by an urban gentry). The photograph, the document, the view, and the reproduction become history precisely because they are so overwhelmingly present. (303)

As Harvey points out, none of these means of representing history is immune to *mis*representation, given sophisticated technical means of image construction. And yet historical accuracy and authenticity are hardly issues in an age of theme parks, period movies, collectors' reproductions, and other simulacra. These are forms of entertainment and symbolic expression in which accurate representation of historical events is clearly less important than the pleasures of entering an imagined and idealized past, with its simulated possibilities for heroism, romance, and adventure.

In this respect, the paradoxical transformative effects of technology on culture are truly remarkable. Although we continue to think of it as modern in the sense of representing the "latest," most "up-to-date" developments, technology in fact undermines the "realist" epistemology and experience of traditional and modern cultures by creating a realm of *reproduction* that abolishes direct unmediated experience. The capacity to endlessly recirculate fragments of the past through an experience of the present is the persistent source of an inescapable cultural pastiche and eclecticism in which our very access to history is mediated by a technology that simultaneously destroys history. Reproduction is not merely tied to the past but collapses past *and* future into the present, obliterating our sense of the *passage* of time and therefore of real historical connection and development. Overall, technology both produces and perpetuates the dilemma of choosing between an empty present and an artificially recuperated past. It not only reduces experience to the momentary presence of the image, it *constitutes* our very access to the past, mediating our every attempt to recover a "true" sense of history.

The pursuit of authentic experience thus stands in a complicated relationship to the process of commodification. On the one hand, the susceptibility to commodification has become so omnipresent that certain kinds of consumption have become ritualized in the sense of becoming "act[s] of dedication" (Crook et al. 1992: 74) to, say, the environment,[19] cultural traditions, experiences of the self, and other forms of authenticity, in which the act of consumption is believed to serve the preservation of cherished values. Such ritualized behaviors are means of recuperating a larger sense of purpose *within* the commodity form, an effort to preserve or protect authentic values and forms of experience despite their absorption by the marketplace. On the other hand, the quest for community, tradition, and self continues to operate partially beyond the sphere of consumption. Not all human practices have been (or can be) subsumed under the commodity form. And yet consumer culture tends to condition experience in general, shaping background and context for even the most private search for meaning.[20] To some degree, the mere pervasiveness of consumerism and the media can turn such quests into acts of resistance. At the same time, such quests can be robbed of any qualities of authenticity merely through the *threat* of appropriation by the commodity form.[21]

Kenneth Gergen (1991) has explored the fall from authenticity through the concept of "ersatz being," which he defines as "the capacity for entering immediately into identities or relationships of widely varying forms" (183). He sees the possibility of potentially endless substitutability of identity in relation to what he calls "the technology of saturation" (182), which makes cultural traditions, especially those of relationships, available on a mass scale. The sheer availability of diverse models of the self and of social and personal relationships through mass culture "sets the stage" for the appropriation of all sorts of identities, among which the individual may choose over a lifetime. This possibility has even led to the development of "industries of *identity production*" (184; emphasis in original), in which the individual develops and markets her/his identity by commercial means (educational programs, career counseling firms, and so on). Mainly, ersatz being implies the ever present potential in a media-based culture of acquiring or changing identity as circumstances dictate or allow. Gergen's notion speaks to the power of commodified culture to offer innumerable choices in the consumption of commercially packaged identities as well as to the individual's dependence on commercialized culture for a sense of options in the search for self.[22]

The crisis of authenticity in commodity culture is continuous with the crisis of reality precipitated by the image, a problem that feeds on itself in curious and contradictory ways. As Baudrillard (1988a) has pointed out, the loss of "the real" drives an incessant effort to recuperate reality and the past that only worsens the situation by reinstating these on the representational terms of the media:

> When the real is no longer what it used to be, nostalgia assumes its full meaning. There is a proliferation of myths of origin and signs of reality; of second-hand truth, objectivity and authenticity. There is an escalation of the true, of the lived experience; a resurrection of the figurative where the object and substance have disappeared. And there is a panic-stricken production of the real and the referential. (171)

The media, having dehistoricized our collective experience and problematized our sense of reality, pursue every conceivable kind of information, mythology, history, human interest, and voyeuristic pleasure so as to "inform" and reconstruct a sense of historical and social reality.

An example of the quest for reality in television is the docudrama, a typical postmodern genre blurring fact and fiction through televisual dramatization. The rapid proliferation of such shows in the United States, especially the hard-core action type featuring actual footage of law enforcement officers in pursuit of offenders, while perhaps a reflection of their relatively low production costs is also suggestive of a craving for the most sensational kinds of reality, of "lived experience." The popularity of these serialized shows might also be indicative of a reaction against studio-produced forms of theatrical entertainment and a felt need to reinstate "real-life" action in the experience of mass culture. Nevertheless, real life in these shows is turned into voyeuristic entertainment where, as Baudrillard argues, substance is replaced by figuration. The dramatization of real-life episodes is also illustrated by the recent Hollywood penchant for making both television and large-screen movies about the misfortunes and heroic deeds of actual people in a variety of contexts including wilderness adventure, sophisticated crime, political careers, or family tragedy. Such trends are reflective of more than just the usual demand for human interest stories but suggest as well a longing to witness the making of personal biography and history. The irony of these trends is that the deprivation of authentic experience can only be overcome through commercial and technological simulations. This predicament has its metaphor in the figure of the televangelist. The revival of religion, while a real development, is transformed into show biz, turned into a staged event in which the minister is transmogrified into a television actor.

Thus the search for tradition and authenticity is recurrently commodified. The return of a sense of time and place is experienced at a remove, through a highly mediated set of images consumed in an artificially constructed and commercially programmed cultural environment. Technologically based images of the past collapse history into a timeless present, and our relationship to cultural objects remains imprisoned in the pastiched forms of mass culture. Thus, the paradox that novelty and change are everywhere while the culture remains "perfectly static" (Calinescu 1987).

Cultural Populism, Tradition, and the Political Ambiguities of Postmodernity

A delineation of the two major tendencies of contemporary culture, the commercial and the political, is implicit in the diverse discourses about the postmodern. I have concentrated in my analysis on writers who have theorized the new forms of consumption and cultural goods, media and advertising aesthetics, the highly stylized and eclectic character of mass culture, and the simulational character of technological representation (Baudrillard 1983a; Featherstone 1991; Harvey 1989; Jameson 1984a; Lash 1990). Just as often, however, the term "postmodern" has designated tendencies of a political nature: the revival of tradition (Harvey 1989); new forms of reactionary and progressive politics (Arac 1986; Bauman 1992; Foster 1983; Habermas 1983; Jameson 1984b); and a decentering and differentiation of identity within the dynamics of difference and otherness (Anzaldúa 1990; Butler 1990a, 1990b; Fuss 1989; Malson et al. 1986; de Lauretis 1986; Lash and Friedman 1992; Nicholson 1990; October 1992). While these varied constructions serve as a useful reminder of the multiple features of the postmodern condition (and perhaps an excessive and indiscriminate use of the term "postmodern"), they refract various aspects of the dynamics of postmodernity as a new constellation of economic, cultural, and political relations structured around this distinction.

Theorizing the dual tendencies of commercialization and politicization enables a social understanding of the contradictions and troublesome political and ideological ambiguities posed by the democratization of culture implied by both tendencies. In the remainder of this chapter, I attempt to identify these problems, leaving for chapter 6 and the conclusion a fuller discussion of theoretical responses to postmodernity.

The democratization of culture and specifically the erosion of the hierarchical attitudes and institutions of modernity have been a recurring theme in my analysis of postmodernization and postmodernity. I have used the term "democratization" with reference to the leveling effects of consumer capitalism and the commodity form, which tend to destroy codes of cultural consumption sequentially. I have also applied the term to the pluralizing process characterizing identity and cultural politics, which promote the reconstruction and assertion of new identities. While opposing tendencies, these developments share a common *inclusionary* impulse, expressing a general trend toward the elimination of hierarchical barriers to cultural expression and participation, as expressed most directly in the collapse of the distinction between high and mass culture. In this sense, the concept of democratization, bearing a long and uneven history, now primarily designates a process taking place in the realm of culture.[23]

The nature and consequences of cultural democratization are at the core of the conflicting ideological responses to postmodernity and postmodernism. While this form of democratization seems to have been embraced by many writers (Baudrillard 1983a, 1983b, 1983c, 1988a; Chambers 1986; Derrida 1976, 1978; Lyotard 1984; Venturi et al. 1977), it has been attacked by others as a "false negation" of culture (Habermas 1983), an exhaustion of the avant-garde (Bürger 1984; Crane 1987; Huyssen 1986; Levin 1988; Newman 1985; Russell 1985; Tompkins 1988), and a corrupt relativization of truth and value (Anderson 1984; Callinicos 1990, Norris 1990). It is no surprise that the antagonists to the debate have by and large identified themselves with either postmodernism or modernism, while theorists of postmodernity (Bauman 1992; Harvey 1989; Huyssen 1986; Jameson 1984a; Lash 1990; Lash and Urry 1987; Smart 1993) have remained more neutral or equivocal. Regardless, the fading of familiar epistemological and ideological positions inherent in cultural democratization has generated a disputatious intellectual atmosphere.

Links between postmodernity and cultural democracy have been invoked by a growing acceptance of the term *populism*. The currency of this word in postmodern writings reflects a recognition of the new legitimacy of the desires of "ordinary people," illustrated originally in charges of an alleged betrayal of common tastes and traditions by modern architecture (Jencks 1984, 1986; Venturi et al. 1977; Wolfe 1981). Some of the social and political issues raised by postmodernism have been most clearly and forcefully stated in this field, and attacks on the elitist and technocratic pretensions of the Bauhaus style are no exception. The populist tendencies of postmodern culture in general, however, seem to be a more complicated matter. While a number of writers have loosely described postmodernity as populist (Chambers 1986; Frith and Horne 1987; Huyssen 1986), Fredric Jameson (1984a) has deployed a specific designation, "aesthetic populism." Jameson here refers to the collapse of the modern dichotomy between high and popular culture, seeing the postmodern as an exchange between "serious art" and "commercial entertainment" that privileges the latter.

Although it has been appearing with greater frequency in contemporary cultural discourse, however, "populism" is more commonly a political term. As Jim McGuigan (1992) has pointed out, furthermore, "populism" has often been used imprecisely and with vaguely derogatory connotations of mass mobilization or demagoguery. According to McGuigan, the negative meanings of the term have been carried over to cultural discourse, where it has come to imply "popular approval and commercial success" (2). While oversimplifying, McGuigan is basically correct that a strong populist perspective has surfaced in cultural studies. Cultural populism is thus what McGuigan refers to as the currently dominant tendency in cultural studies in both Britain and the United States to conceptualize culture primarily in terms of consumption (see chapter 3). Here, he says, the strategy of hermeneutics is employed to "uncritically endorse" and privilege the tastes and pleasures of "ordinary people" over those of elite groups. McGuigan takes exception to this shift, arguing that it wrongly severs consumption from production and, more generally, political economy, in favor of a position consistent with that of economic liberalism, namely, "consumer sovereignty" (5–6). By implication, it could be argued that the overall direction of cultural studies as a theoretical and empirical field thereby refracts the expansion of consumerism in society at large. Increasingly, scholars in this field have uncritically adopted the socially prevailing consumptionist ethos and its correlative relativization of taste and value as an epistemological stance in ethnographic readings.

I endorse McGuigan's assessment of cultural studies and his proposal to reestablish links between consumption and production. However, once we begin to sort through the political implications and complications of postmodernity, it becomes apparent that populism is not just an issue for cultural studies but also poses stubborn problems as a political and ideological category. Populism generally has been a conflicted ideal, attaching itself to movements across the political spectrum depending on particular historical and political circumstances. Having a continuing appeal throughout U.S. history, populism evokes the economic interests of the "common person"—historically, small farmers and businessmen—as against powerful elites and "establishments" as well as identifications with certain cultural styles lower down the class hierarchy (Kazin 1986).[24] As a set of feelings or impulses, however, populism has seldom supported political distinctions between left and right, preferring instead to divide the world into the powerful and powerless. Indeed, "populist discontent has a way of shifting sides" (Kazin 1986: 102), as illustrated by the way the supporters of former governor of Alabama George Wallace, a renowned southern racist, threw their political support to Robert Kennedy, a friend of Martin Luther King Jr. and strong advocate of civil rights, after Wallace's political career ended following an assassination attempt. While appealing to the democratic sentiments of the "average American," populism is in some sense apolitical and nonideological, bereft of particular loyalties and suspicious of politics in general. It is nonetheless and perhaps paradoxically a powerful and volatile force in U.S. politics. Since the seventies it has enjoyed a remarkable resurgence, resonating the cultural mood of traditional, small-town America implicit in conservative varieties of identity politics and manifest in Reagan-era politics.

Efforts to attach a *cultural* meaning to this term, however, engender numerous problems. Besides possibly invoking the sentiments of the white petit bourgeois groups to which populism was originally attached, to cast postmodernism as *populist* is to reproduce the political vagueness of the term in a more complicated context. Thus, for example, cultural populism as postmodernism can mean giving people whatever they want, however base, trivial, or commercialized; or it can mean claiming equal worth for indigenous forms of folk and popular culture as against the modern bourgeois art forms of Western Europe. Furthermore, the use of *populism* to describe postmodern culture replicates the problems involved in interpreting the political loyalties to which this mood might become attached. Support for family values and antiabortion legislation and attacks on elite art institutions for failing to recognize street artists and local indigenous cultures could be construed as populist but constitute rather disparate political acts. Indeed, the former are more likely to be labeled "conservative" or "reactionary" and the latter "progressive." To describe postmodern culture as populist is thus to obscure important ideological questions by simply extrapolating to cultural analysis the inherent political ambiguities and instabilities of the term. Nonetheless, the term often seems an apt description of cultural reality. Indeed, the surge of populism in the realm of culture is largely responsible for the growing ideological confusion across the political landscape.

Culturally, populism in the current period seems to reveal two faces. The collapse of an avant-garde reflective of the oppositional and critical spirit of modernity and its replacement by a market-oriented consumerism are obvious manifestations of the reduction of cultural issues to matters of popular taste and style. Concomitantly, the populist mood opens the door to an expression of grassroots sentiments and a shift in our conception of democracy from formal political participation in the state (for example, voting) to new forms of empowerment through participation in local communities and the redistribution of cultural resources down the social hierarchy. In and of itself, then, populism offers no clear and distinct political direction but only a loose assortment of "anti-"

impulses that can attach themselves, sometimes indiscriminately, to a range of cultural and political practices, equally feeding consumer capitalism and cultural politics.

Yet a further complication is the way that the ideological ambiguity of populism reproduces itself *within* both the commercial system and cultural politics. In the context of mass culture, populism has often become a commercial ideology in the name of which anything commodified, however retrograde, attains legitimacy, verging on a popular ideology of normlessness or "anything goes." In this respect, the marketing of difference is a thoroughly populist strategy. At the same time, however, populism has the potential, though seldom realized, for serving as an ideological vehicle for the expression of popular aspirations and demands against elitist interests. As a signifier of popular needs, populism has been an important force in the rise of consumer protests, such as movements in the United States against violence on children's television and the sale of dangerous toys, indicating a source of opposition to a concentration of power in the culture industries. Moreover, populist sentiments inhere in the longings and ideals recurrently encoded in popular culture (for example, "the good life," and community, personal, and social success). Thus, despite its earlier identifications with white nativist groups and its contemporary association with the masses and commercial success, there is nothing *inherent* in the concept of populism that prevents it from acquiring oppositional overtones. As these examples suggest, notwithstanding its partial absorption into the commercial system, populism seems to have retained an anticorporate meaning as a manifestation of unfulfilled and widely shared popular aspirations.

The ambiguous meaning of populism is no less apparent in the domain of cultural politics. We have seen that the popular aspirations of specific movements, especially ethnic movements, can take the form of powerful reaffirmations of ascriptively based groups. Group loyalties can easily acquire reactionary overtones, setting the stage for a particularistic revival of old rivalries, thereby reducing self-determination to a tribalistic play of power. Moreover, in the counterpart to the marketing of difference, the celebration of difference for its own sake is a populist gesture that can postpone difficult questions about the relations of power and inequality operating *behind* cultural difference as well as the direction a cultural politics of difference ought to take in addressing such problems. Yet in contrast to these possibilities, populism has acquired a certain symbolic significance for all popular struggles for self-determination. Despite its legacy in the often reactionary revolts of small rural farmers and other white nativist groups, the populist impulse in principle is expressive of the pitting of popular aspirations against the powers that be. This impulse is evident in a range of political practices from identity politics to cooperative movements. Furthermore, through its implications of popularity and commonness, the concept retains a potential for broad collective appeals to those at the bottom of society, a social "lowest common denominator" (McGuigan 1992: 1) that can unite a spectrum of oppressed interests.

Thus, both commercial and political postmodernisms carry populist strains susceptible to both reactionary and progressive tendencies. Mass culture is both a marketplace for anything that will sell as well as a vehicle of popular, utopian longings. Similarly, cultural and identity politics carry the potential for competitive and absolutistic group power claims and the shrinking of tradition and difference to ritualistic celebrations, but they also create a framework for subversive challenges to an exclusionary social order. Populism therefore transcends and obscures conventional ideological divides, disrupting the familiar political categories of left and right in unpredictable and diffuse ways. Whether or not populism, in culture or politics, is capable of sustaining a universalistic vision or is by nature fated to represent only particularistic interests, devolving the ideals of recognition and popularity onto particular groups, remains unclear.

Yet the obscurities of populism should not preclude some kinds of political distinctions and judgments regarding postmodern culture. Probably the most apt and promising distinction has been made by Hal Foster (1983), who contrasts a "postmodernism of reaction" and a "postmodernism of resistance" (xii). For Foster, the former "repudiates" modernism to celebrate the status quo, rejecting any adversary culture for a defense of existing interests and relations with pragmatic disregard for a questioning of cultural values. The latter attempts to "deconstruct" modernism and resist or attack the status quo, setting itself up as a countermovement to both while retaining the critical oppositional spirit forged within modernism. The contrast between these postmodernisms seems in Foster's view to hinge largely on the appropriation of tradition. Reactionary postmodernism is "a return to the verities of tradition," whereas resistant postmodernism seeks "a critical deconstruction of tradition," "a critique of origins, not a return to them" (xii). Foster clearly implies an affinity between resistant and what I have called political postmodernism, which he firmly dissociates from "an instrumental pastiche of pop- or pseudo-historical forms" (xii).

We find definite differences in Foster's account between a backward-looking, anticritical postmodernism that seeks a revival of tradition that can be imposed on cultural disintegration and flux, and a forward-looking postmodernism that deconstructs both modern and traditional forms of culture for new adversarial forms. While Foster's definitions come close to retaining familiar ideological contrasts, however, we have to question whether the distinction he draws is empirically or practically feasible. He gives few criteria for distinguishing the two postmodernisms other than actual examples, and these are lacking in his construction of resistant postmodernism.

But the more interesting question is how we are to regard tradition. Foster recoups the conventional meaning of tradition, which in the vocabulary of modernity is positioned in opposition to progress. In the context of postmodernity, however, the concept of tradition loses its fixity and earlier meanings in the wake of the disintegration of the notion of progress itself. While the revival of tradition always at least bears the implication of reactionary politics and, indeed, frequently takes this form, as a protest against instrumental rationality and the horrors of "progress," tradition more recently has acquired more liberatory overtones. The meaning of tradition has changed significantly also within the framework of resistance to commercialism and the weakening of communal institutions such as the family. In contemporary cultural politics, we find evidence not only of rigid and autocratic reassertions of traditional values but also a revalorization of the personal and social sustenance that cultural tradition can offer. Against a backdrop of growing meaninglessness and narcissism, tradition now carries a certain appeal as a vehicle for the revitalization of social and personal relations, implying possibilities for an emotional and symbolic reinvigoration of the relationship between self and other. Furthermore, it is important to consider specific types of historical tradition, especially those based in class, gender, racial, and ethnic cultures of protest. From this vantage point, a reading of tradition as ineluctably conservative or reactionary seems problematic. On the contrary, as Stuart Hall (1981) has remarked, historically tradition has been "one of the principal sites of resistance" (227) to capitalism's intermittent efforts to transform popular ways of life and class cultures to fit its changing needs. Accordingly, we can perhaps no longer afford to regard tradition *only* regressively but need to consider its critical potentiality as a basis of opposition to commercial culture. In this sense, tradition raises the prospect of as yet unarticulated possibilities for a progressive politics. Thus, tradition could at least begin to serve as a defense of communal values, even if this must occur as part of the current ideological contest taking place over such institutions as the family and religion. In this respect, the political problem of postmodern culture no longer seems to be a matter of choosing between tradition and its various enemies but, rather, the construction of a new set of understandings about the meanings and *uses* of tradition.[25]

The fate of oppositional cultural politics is somewhat less obscure, at least for the foreseeable future, than the political meanings of the populist turn in culture. As suggested in the earlier discussion of pluralization, despite the continuation of cultural protest and experimentation, the commodifying forces of post-Fordist capitalism are strong enough to forestall and dampen even the most vigorous challenges to the hegemony of consumerism and advanced technology. While the breakup of modern culture has created new spaces and contexts for the formation of oppositional movements, these movements seem to quickly run their course, rapidly absorbed by the commercialized structures of the mass media and the organizational forms of mainstream society. Among the many reasons for their demise, as I have been arguing, the impact of mass culture and the fragmentation of daily life are fairly significant. As we have seen, the quest for authentic experience and meaning is itself fragmented, typically carried out in solitary circumstances within the structures of privatized consumption against which this quest is counterposed. Despite their newly found ideological powers, the group and community remain fragile entities. The search for meaningful identity thus frequently takes the form of personalized and privatized withdrawal into highly specific, particularistic, and even esoteric loyalties and roles. Thus, while cultural politics offers numerous examples of collective challenges to the hegemony of consumer capitalism, the reconstruction of identity just as often takes an individualistic or familistic form, thereby becoming an apolitical accommodation to existing conditions.

This type of response is in turn inseparable from the demise of a shared sense of history. While ultimately a theoretically shallow notion, the death of the subject in poststructuralist thought does capture something of the real collapse of a feeling of living *in history*, of people as members of groups and communities actively engaged as agents in the making of their own history. Because it connects us to a past, the revival of tradition is in part symptomatic of this loss. The commodification of history itself, however, belies the real problem—consumers are no longer historical actors. The packaging of pseudohistory in commercial culture presupposes the absence of a real historical present in which people *could* act outside their roles as consumers. The return of tradition and a sense of past therefore seems possible only through the commodity form. Widespread resort to commercial images of a lost past is merely indicative of the destruction of *real* historical time by technology and an endlessly recycled culture. Ironically, the accumulation of stored information through visual images, the printed page, and CD-ROM has made a "knowledge" of history available on an unprecedented scale, even if in a commodified form. The longing of which this information overload is a partial reflection, however, hardly compares to the actual distance that now exists between us and real history.

Moreover, just as mass culture reflects an aestheticization of society, so does history undergo aestheticization as it is retrieved and recycled through images and stylistic transformation. In effect, history becomes pastiched, a history of successive *images* of the past and a history of all the aesthetic *styles* of the past. This is nowhere more apparent than in architecture, where we find perhaps the purest form of postmodern theory and style, where past styles have been intermixed with the modernist style to create a pastiche of architectural history. This architectural version of the text takes the form of a "double-coding" of traditional and modern styles, a strategy of reconciling the conflicting requirements of professional elitism and an educated minority taste with the populist sentiments of the public (Jencks 1984, 1986). As is the case with pseudohistory in general, postmodern architecture, while perhaps satisfying a hunger for popularity, humanism, and the vernacular, registers a sense of the exhaustion of subjectivity and historical progress. Substituting for economically risky originality, pastiche as imitation of past and present styles in this sense represents an accommodation to the needs of the marketplace (Foster 1984).

At the same time, there might exist a more promising set of possibilities. Despite the overriding tendency toward cultural pastiche, commercial or otherwise, it is nevertheless true that the critical attention given the effacement of the categories of high and mass culture within the commodity form has often been at the neglect of popular art forms that have been only incompletely usurped or destroyed by eclectic commercialism. Moreover, even if they could be read as unequivocally conservative in nature, which seems unlikely, the revival of older forms of popular or folk culture has occurred in the midst of significant *innovations* in popular art, including street theater, political filmmaking, video art, mural art, performance art, mobile sculpture, and "cross-overs."[26] While some of these forms are more commercial and pastiched than others, these examples suggest continued creativity in the realm of popular and oppositional art. Additionally, Foster (1983) has pointed to cases of artistic resistance to the commercially eclectic stylistic tendencies of postmodernism even in architecture, citing Kenneth Frampton's (1983) "critical regionalism," a counterinfluence to pastiche that distances itself equally from modern myths of progress and romantic appeals to the preindustrial past (20). For Frampton, a truly postmodern architecture would avoid both nostalgia and decoration for a deconstruction of and mediation between the universalizing forms of a world culture and the vernacular of a local culture that mutually recognize each other. As these and other examples attest, the marketplace still falls short of exhausting the range of contemporary cultural innovations.

Nevertheless, there is no escaping the drift of postmodern culture toward accommodation with existing arrangements of power and the connections between cultural difference and capitalist market relations. However, the sense in which postmodern culture is attributable to "the cultural logic of late capitalism" (Jameson 1984a) and the consequences of this need to be carefully considered. Two opposing arguments present themselves. The first argument maintains that the postmodern celebration of heterogeneity and the reliance on pastiche in

contemporary culture are highly congruent with and therefore reinforce com-
modity/market relations. While this is true by definition for commercial postmodernity, political postmodernity, too, it could be argued, risks succumbing to
the logic of commodification as a consequence of its own privileging of particularity and difference and its experimental violation of cultural boundaries. Postmodernism as *stylistic* practice—whether in architecture, art, literature, media,
music, or politics—if not homologous with market relations at least refracts and
mimics them in its eclectic and indifferent mixing of disparate elements, reproducing *as cultural discourse* the fragmented condition of the marketplace. While
often considered a political response to the incorporation of sixties activism and
counterculture, and the rise of neoconservatism, the mood of resignation on the
left can also be read as both cause and effect of this failure to extricate cultural
discourses and expressions from the workings of the market. By implication,
aspects of political postmodernism fall victim to the prevailing social logic, as reflected in the decline of an adversarial avant-garde and the marginalization or incorporation of incipient political cultures. In this argument, pastiche and eclecticism have become "dominants," the main constituents of a new hegemonic
cultural order in both consumerism and politics.

By contrast, the second argument maintains that the very characteristics of
pastiche and schizophrenia through which Jameson (1983, 1987) characterizes
postmodern culture threaten imminent disruption of the dominant order. Here,
Frankfurt School and Baudrillardian notions of a totally administered and manipulated society are discredited by arguments about the antihegemonic effects
of the very fragmentation of meaning and experience inherent in commodification. Jameson's account draws attention to a significant paradox: in closing the
universe of discourse, the commodity/sign form of Baudrillard simultaneously
fragments it. As argued in chapter 2, the conditions of fragmentation cast serious doubt on widely accepted notions of the "ideological effect" in the media
and other cultural forms. Thus, commodification produces a lack of cultural coherence. In this view, precisely because everything *is* now "cultural" (Jameson
1984a), postmodernism poses a more total threat to the established order than
did the subversive attacks of modernism (Lash 1990: 14). To the extent that
postmodernity creates an open field of signification, an emphasis on a "play of
differences," a sense of contingency and provisionality, and a demand for recognition and accessibility, it engenders an undifferentiated sense of freedom and
possibility subversive of dominant codes and power relations. Finally, Baudrillard
(1983b) himself takes this process one provocative step further, pointing to an
"implosion of meaning" and an "end of the social" in which through the abolition of all ideology and social relations the masses become utterly silent, thereby
withdrawing support for the existing order of things (Chen 1987).

Neither of these arguments, I suggest, offers a very satisfactory position on the politics of postmodernity and postmodernism, and to embrace either would be to repeat the mistake of choosing between a wholesale denunciation of postmodernism as decadent and politically regressive and a simple celebration of its progressive or utopian potentials (Jameson 1984b). While in certain respects plausible portrayals of the conditions and possibilities of contemporary culture, both views lack dialectical structure and grounding in the realities of capitalist society. On the one hand, the commodification of culture can never be totalizing insofar as culture is by nature a meaning- and identity-making process that always exceeds the dominant beliefs and practices of society. On the other hand, the almost metaphysical faith that the polyvalent conditions of cultural heterogeneity and breakdown will in and of themselves lead to collapse and collective renewal seems overly facile and historically unwarranted.

Since the second argument seems to enjoy strong appeal among some advocates of postmodernism, it is deserving of critical attention. I would argue, however, that the scenario of disintegration is less convincing as an assessment of cultural conditions than as a prognosis of *social and economic life*. The now almost total collapse of the social contract in the United States has resulted in economic insecurity, despair, and spreading violence (especially among racial minorities but also among poor women and white male workers) perhaps far more threatening to the system than cultural normlessness. Indeed, a more powerful argument is that the system actually benefits from cultural fragmentation among the underlying population. While the sense of possibility engendered by cultural anomie might be expected to stir radical and utopian visions of change, the consequences of social and political anomie would seem more real and strategically promising.

The intimation of openings in a fragmented culture suggests yet another important connection between the condition of postmodernity and the appearance of new theories not always fully cognizant of their material conditions of existence. Literary versions of postmodernism have often allied themselves with conservative-leaning theorists of deconstruction, who valorize the internal inconsistencies and overall heterogeneity of language and discourse. However, as Charles Russell (1985) has argued, literary postmodernism has been largely formalist and idealist, focusing on the "mechanics" of semiotic systems rather than their "functions" in social and material life, thereby erasing the presence of ideology and politics. This brand of deconstruction is encapsulated in an apolitical world of textual relations, taking the form of an analytical game removed from the productive apparatuses of society and the consuming and political practices of its members.[27] In contrast, the notion of deconstruction found in the writings of Jacques Derrida (chapter 6), who develops the poststructuralist premise of discursive instability into a theoretical/political strategy of critique based on the concept of difference, has been appropriated by some contemporary critics as a strategy of *cultural* deconstruction. Without necessarily harboring illusions about the fragility of the existing order, these writers adopt a deconstructive stance toward culture and politics, challenging dominant meanings as oppressive, arbitrary, and fictional and therefore inherently unstable and susceptible to transformation. Drawing also on the ideas of Michel Foucault, the best of this work understands deconstruction as a disruptive and subversive attack on hierarchical relations of power, extending the idea of deconstruction to institutionalized social and political relations.[28]

The task of translating even politically conscious deconstructive practices into collective struggles, however, remains supremely difficult. Realistically, politics and history lose much of their effectivity and imaginative grasp under highly differentiated and amorphous cultural conditions. Whether the liberatory impulses and openings implicated in the heterogeneous condition of postmodernity can be formed into viable oppositional practices and movements will depend on the ability of individuals, groups, and communities to translate discontent and utopian longings into organized action. Contrary to Baudrillard, this presupposes a field of social relations and an ideological terrain on which various alternative and oppositional practices are able to emerge and exert pressures for change. Indeed, an "end of the social," aside from being an ontological impossibility, would portend an intolerable passivity and stagnation or, worse, a dangerous political vacuum. While the widespread culturalization of society creates the conditions for renewed struggles over meaning, the success of such struggles depends on a sense of connectedness, collective purpose, direction, and political organization that only vital social relationships can provide. Properly waged, the contest for culture requires a socially articulated "difference within unity," a recognition and inclusion of cultural difference within a social community of political actors.

The postmodern celebration of cultural dissolution and decentered subjectivity partakes of Nietzschean-inspired images of "experimental self-creation" based on an "aesthetic concept of individual freedom" (Honneth 1992: 166–67). This rendering of the postmodern world imagines a self that is being continually reinvented through the dispersals and intensities of a fragmented and overloaded culture whose center cannot possibly hold. As Terry Eagleton (1996) argues, however, this seems a rather dubious "freedom," implying a postmodern subject that is "at liberty to drift." It remains unclear how politics survives or undergoes renewal under such conditions, since in a political context "freedom" in the positive sense implies an ability to act in concert with others in a determinate set of conditions. The paradox of freedom is that it requires closure, an idea toward which postmodernists express reluctance if not hostility (Eagleton 1996: 42). The penchant for deconstruction, even in its political versions, while a promising response to totalizing modes of thought, risks the paralysis of disunity. As Steven Best (1989) has put it, "while poststructuralists rightly deconstruct essentialist and repressive wholes, they fail to see how repressive and crippling . . . [it can be to valorize] . . . difference, plurality, fragmentation, and agonistics. . . . The flip side of the tyranny of the whole is the dictatorship of the fragments" (361).

Such images of freedom, furthermore, fail to grasp the necessity of social relationality and intersubjectivity to projects of self-realization. In this respect, Honneth (1992) has argued for the continued relevance of the Hegelian concept of recognition in addressing the consequences of a postmodern dissolution of the social. What postmodernists regard as the freedom of aesthetic pluralization thus might be defined as a "serious crisis in the structure of recognition in highly developed societies" (Honneth 1992: 169). Political and other forms of identity formation, thus, depend on "intersubjective recognition" (Melucci 1996: 29).

For progressive change to occur, it is necessary for there to be a connection between cultural practices and collective movements and struggles in the form of organized political practices. The social is indispensable to the formation of the conditions under which culture can be freed of the commodity form and enlisted in movements capable of overcoming the inertia stemming from a restless and shapeless life of privatized consumption. Only then might it be possible to move beyond a performative postmodern politics, limited to "the reallocation of attention" (Bauman 1992: 200), to a form of politics involving a socially based reallocation of meaning, identity, purpose, and economic resources, a politics directed toward the inseparable goals of social and cultural renewal and material redistribution.

6
Redeeming the Subject
Poststructuralism, Meadian Social Pragmatism, and the Turn to Intersubjectivity

Postmodern theory broadly defined sees the world as heterogeneous, composed of a vast plurality of interpretations in which knowledge and truth are contingent and therefore ultimately undecidable. In this world, identity is inherently decentered and fluid because constituted in unstable relations of difference. Read optimistically, this "worldview" evokes a sense of creative freedom, of seemingly infinite possibilities for the invention of new knowledges and identities. On a more negative reading, the postmodern stance involves an imposing relativization, a fragmented Nietzschean universe where, since everything is interpretation, knowledge easily defers to the rule of power. Whether regarded positively or negatively, postmodern theory marks a fundamental epistemological shift, a radically new set of strategies and practices for apprehending a world that can only be grasped in its multifariousness (Dews 1987; Clifford and Marcus 1986; Habermas 1987b, 1992; Harding 1991; Lyotard 1984; Nicholson 1990; Rosenau 1992; Seidman and Wagner 1992; Wellmer 1985).

A major purpose of my discussion has been to suggest that as an epistemological shift, postmodern theory could be read as a *refraction* of underlying socioeconomic changes and cultural transformations constructed in theories of *postmodernity*. But establishing a context and framework within which postmodernism could be more fully cognizant of the conditions of its own existence, and articulating the underlying structural and institutional changes that impart social content to the postmodern debate, will not entirely suffice as a critique. Postmodernism as an epistemological position is *on its own terms* an inadequate response to the postmodern *condition*. I argue that a decentered world is ultimately problematic and thus not in itself a satisfactory model of intellectual and political renewal, or of new theories of the subject.

The theme of decentering in postmodernism had its origins in the sixties French "antihumanist" attack on inherited Cartesian and Kantian conceptions of the subject (Descombes 1980; Ferry and Renaut 1990; Poster 1975). A major paradigmatic shift from which theoretical postmodernism has drawn its strength, this attack has provoked new epistemological arguments over the status of the subject. Armed with philosophical ideas from Nietzsche and Heidegger, and some of the determinisms of psychoanalysis, structuralism, and semiotics, French thinkers and their followers launched a major assault on models of a unified and rational subjectivity tied to Enlightenment thought, drawing on themes from what Jürgen Habermas has called "the counter-Enlightenment tradition" and specifically its implications of an unconscious life. While the immediate targets of the French attack were the alleged metaphysical fictions and essentialisms of Marxist humanism, existentialism, phenomenology, and neo-Hegelian philosophy, the main enemies of these and subsequent critiques have been the foundational belief in first principles and notions of a unified epistemological standpoint. Often overlooked, however, is the fact that assaults on the centered ego of Enlightenment philosophy, culminating in proclamations of the death of the subject, were only a final provocation in a prolonged philosophical and ideological crisis of the individual precipitated generations earlier by Kant himself and manifested in the cataclysmic material and social changes of the nineteenth and twentieth centuries (Eagleton 1983; Megill 1985).

Thus, despite obvious continuities between modernity and postmodernity (chapters 2 and 3), some postmodern theory has cast itself as prosecutor, witness, and judge in an ongoing trial of the modern myth of ego-centered identity. The alleged epistemological crime of imposing a unified subjectivity on a chaotic and alienated existence was committed, according to postmodernists, to conceal an inherently multiplicitous and opaque subject, dispersed in the social and discursive contingencies of its particular, varying, and historically conditioned circumstances. In the fictions of wholeness and totality driving the project of modernity, "reality," "knowledge," "truth," and "progress" have been among the major offenders. This interrogation, however, has borne a certain irony. As suggested in chapter 3, postmodern thought can be read as the experience of modernity catching up with itself theoretically. In their troubling over the subject, modern and postmodern thinkers *alike* have nurtured skepticism toward foundational and universalizing beliefs (Best and Kellner 1991: 257). Furthermore, to the extent that contemporary critiques of the subject are informed by highly partisan readings of earlier thinkers who were critical of some

Enlightenment ideas while still committed to others—one thinks of Marx, Freud, or Lévi-Strauss—the distinction between modern and postmodern thought appears elusive if not arbitrary. Attacks on notions of a sovereign and rational subject can thus be seen as derivative of modern thought itself. When it comes to the philosophical problem of the subject, it is less the construing than the prognosis and response that have changed, from a modern optimism to a postmodern agnosticism and pessimism toward Enlightenment conceptions of reason and knowledge and the possibilities of progress through universalizing forms of thought.

Moreover, the postmodern opposition to foundationalism and, specifically, preoccupations with notions of a decentered subject have obscured the many ambiguities contained in the term "subject." The divided subject of modernity (Cascardi 1992) betrays persistent splits and dilemmas at the base of modern philosophy, reflecting unresolved tensions in how modern thinkers and social actors understood themselves and others as subjects. This is readily apparent in the shifting meanings of "subject" and "subjectivity" across different theoretical discourses and disciplines throughout modern thought. Within Enlightenment discourses, the term "subject" has been inseparable from the capacities of reason, truth, and knowledge attributable to a consciously thinking ego. Within the discourses of modern social theory, however, the subject has acquired a double and contradictory meaning. On the one hand, theorists have given the subject certain voluntaristic overtones, linking the subject to notions of agency within an action or interaction framework through which individuals and groups are seen as operating as agents of social reproduction and change. On the other hand, the subject has taken on an opposite meaning, that of determination by more or less unconscious forces. This latter notion of being "subjected to" has been a central assumption of the social sciences since their beginnings, enjoying a long career in sociology under the label of social determinism, a notion ultimately traceable in its most compelling forms to Marx and Durkheim. In our own era, the structuralist method and the field of semiology generally have invented a new linguistic determinism. Originating with Althusserian-influenced versions of British cultural studies, which relied heavily on the notion of discursively determined "subject-positions,"[1] this notion of the subject subsequently surfaced in French-poststructuralist-influenced textualist studies derived mainly from Foucault's writings on discourse and power. Finally, within conventional philosophical, psychological, and artistic discourses informing modern bourgeois individualism, "subjectivity" has typically referred to the cognitive and evaluative irreducibility of the internal mental states of individuals, to solitary consciousness. Traceable both to Romanticism and liberal bourgeois ideology, the subject in this sense has been understood in terms of individual creativity and spontaneity and therefore as the wellspring of cultural innovation. Subjectivity here denotes an incommensurability of perception, thought, taste, and judgment that is accommodated pluralistically within a market-based society espousing consumer choice and political ideals of personal freedom.

As this inventory suggests, subjectivity has been theoretically constructed in more or less two broadly opposing directions. On the one hand, the term has borne the Enlightenment heritage of the volitional individual who is the source of innovation, progress, and change. In this view, the category of subject designates autonomy and free will, implying a capacity for conscious identifications, reflection, choice, and control. This sense of the subject also includes notions of expressiveness rooted in Romanticist-inspired artistic notions of originality, genius, and authorship. On the other hand, the subject has implied just the opposite condition of determinacy and constraint. This determined subject is a basic category of Western science, especially strong in its positivistic versions, which postulates the constitution of the actor by a range of antecedent forces and limiting conditions beyond intentionality or rational choice. Whereas the Marxist and psychoanalytic traditions have employed both conceptions of the subject, equivocally positing both freedom and constraint, the structuralist tradition has predicated itself on a subject governed exclusively by unconscious forces or "laws" operating behind the back of the subject.

By situating subjects in the structural relations and conditions of language and discourse, both structuralism and poststructuralism privilege some version of the determined subject. An emanation of the linguistic turn in twentieth-century philosophy, these approaches have displaced the Cartesian ego and its humanist presuppositions (or pretensions) with the alleged determinisms of discursive systems. Importantly, by positing an externally determined subject, structuralism and poststructuralism have reinvented positivism in a novel guise by locating the subject in the facticity of discourse. It is ironic that this approach has secured a place for itself in the humanities, which have traditionally been considered "interpretive" and thus hostile to the positivistic and antihumanistic leanings of the social sciences. Nevertheless, despite important differences between structuralism and poststructuralism (Best and Kellner 1991), to be discussed below, both take the subject as semiotically or linguistically constructed, as a product of forces external to human consciousness.

However, by eliminating consciousness, these approaches abandon the modern *tension* between the subject as agency or actor and the subject as determined effect—a tension distinctive to the thought of Marx and Freud as well as the pragmatist tradition of Mead and subsequent social theories emphasizing the active dimensions of agency. To return to chapter 1, while it can be argued that the paradigm shift from a consciousness-based subjectivity of identity to discursively structured relations of difference represents an advance beyond earlier phenomenological and hermeneutic conceptions, textualist approaches pay little if any attention to the constitution of identity and difference in the social relations of intending, reflexive, and interacting selves. As a result, these approaches efface the dialectical tensions structuring social and cultural processes that are captured in such conceptual constructions as agency and structure (Giddens 1984), freedom and alienation (Marx 1978), reason and repression (Freud 1961), and "I" and "Me" (Mead 1934).

In this final chapter, I sketch the fundamental contradictions, dilemmas, and absences of theories in which subjectivity is absorbed in the determinations of discursive structures and practices. I see such theories as reductive and as unjustifiably reifying the fragmented and dispersed condition of postmodern culture and identity. My critique of poststructuralism and the broader positions of postmodernism, while striving for balance, will take these approaches to task as limited accounts of human subjectivity and practices and as insufficient rejoinders to the postmodern condition. The main vehicle of my critique will be an encounter between poststructuralism and the ideas of George Herbert Mead. I illustrate some of the more original and provocative claims and insights of poststructuralism through a critical reading of Judith Butler, whose version of this perspective simultaneously reiterates and departs in revealing ways from the central tenets of Meadian thought. I use Butler both to demonstrate the strengths and weaknesses of poststructuralism and to indicate the relative advantages of a Meadian approach to issues of discourse, self, identity, and difference. Finally, I re-present basic Meadian concepts and arguments, along with a summary of the closely related work of V. N. Voloshinov on the social nature of language, indicating how these redress major gaps in the poststructuralist account of discourse. I argue that Meadian ideas can be effectively deployed in retheorizing the poststructuralist theme of cultural instability, specifically with regard to questions of identity and difference. While poststructuralism and postmodernism ultimately succumb to the older dualism of subject and object, Mead's social pragmatism overcomes this dualism by transforming the Hegelian subject-object dialectic into a social psychology of self. From the standpoint of my treatment of postmodernity, I advocate a shift in emphasis from a textual or discursive focus to an engagement with the social relations of culture, using Mead to consider how we might reconceptualize the subject in the context of the structural and cultural conditions of postmodern society. While some poststructuralists have been attentive to the social and institutional contexts of the subject, I attempt to establish a yet stronger theoretical case for the social roots of discourse by arguing for the inseparability of discursive and social practices and the indispensability of a concept of a social self.[2]

Structuralism and Poststructuralism: The Attack on the Subject

A salient theme in postwar French theory, the dissolution of the subject in the workings of language, power, and desire has become a hegemonic idea in academic theory in the United States. The theoretical movements at the base of this idea, however, have precipitated sharp intellectual divisions, with devout followers and stubborn dissenters, a polarization characterized by uncritical loyalties, on the one hand, and unfriendly neglect and sometimes bitter attacks, on the other. In this respect, poststructural theory marks a major exclusionary break with earlier traditions, a radical paradigm shift giving rise to antagonistic theoretical and political camps. Yet those who would simply repudiate poststructuralist theory as mistaken or obstructionist miss the challenge and complexity of poststructuralist arguments while denying the failures of the older philosophy of consciousness. Importantly, poststructuralism has invented new possibilities for the project of reconstructing a "postmetaphysical" conception of the subject. Unfortunately, the textual bias of poststructuralism has often interfered with meaningful debate and further theoretical advances in cultural analysis. Indeed, poststructuralism sometimes exemplifies some of its own more controversial claims about the world it purports to comprehend. In practice, it frequently assumes the form of a language game, a performance, a self-validating epistemology and style that at its worst operates as a self-enclosed system of discourse and power.

An assessment of poststructuralism needs to begin with a brief consideration of the new terrain opened by structuralist methods and an identification of their main victims, the metaphysical and historical subjects. The rise of modern individualism entailed the notion that "man" was endowed with a "mind" or "consciousness" that was thought of as the individual's access to knowledge. The individual was further seen as epistemologically unitary and reflective, as occupying a centered position in a world capable of being known and experienced with a priori certainty. As Habermas (1987b, 1992) has pointed out, this conception depended on an unconditioned subject that constituted itself internally through a split between subject and object, inner and outer worlds, a dichotomy that since Kant has served as the epistemological foundation of Western thought.

The structuralist perspective attempted to cast doubt on this model of the subject, and the conception of a thinking ego has since been rejected by poststructuralists as a theoretical fiction consisting of metaphysical categories (substances, attributes, ideas, ideals, thoughts) that, as a priori elements of consciousness, serve as false foundations of truth. Implicitly, structuralists and poststructuralists argue the insupportability of such metaphysical notions from a positivist position.[3] According to these theorists, the problem with the Enlightenment subject is its presupposition of an autonomous mental life governed by reason, involving a sovereign consciousness prior to already existing structures of discourse. For poststructuralists, this impossible subject pretends to exist independently of desire and the limiting conditions of language and power.

Despite the obvious origins of this theme in Nietzsche and aspects of Marx, the most direct challenge to the rational subject came from Freudian theory, which constructed the rational ego as besieged and divided by the irrational forces of id and superego (Wellmer 1985). However, it was not until the linguistic turn in philosophy that rationality as understood by modern thinkers was seriously questioned. With the invention of semiotics, interest in theories of human behavior shifted radically to the nature and structure of language, namely, how thought and behavior were constituted linguistically. As language was increasingly accepted as a model for social and cultural analysis, the transcendental ego was replaced by the sign system. Lévi-Strauss's structuralism challenged the free and reasoning ego by positing preexisting deep and universal structures of the mind as the origins and foundations of unconscious ritualistic patterns in social and cultural development (Kurzweil 1980). The merging of structuralist thought with semiotics produced an even more potent critique of philosophies of consciousness. Whereas for the latter, meaning originated in consciousness—in the intending subject who communicated and acted *through* language—for the former, meaning was already present *in* language, specifically the structure of the sign. The language revolution thus revealed a coded social universe in which preexisting semiotic relations determined the structure and contents of human action. In structuralism, the subject lost its rational unity through a dissolution into "structures, oppositions, and differences" (Pheby 1988: 51) that conformed to the universal operative rules of language. In poststructuralism, the subject was further dissolved in the *instabilities* of language apparent in its actual practices and its substrata of desire and power.

The procedure known as deconstruction associated with Jacques Derrida (1976, 1978) represents the major move beyond structuralist assumptions about the stable and universal character of the structured relationships constituting the subject. In Derrida's critique of the "metaphysics of presence" an attempt is made to remove any remaining sense of certainty involved in the philosophy of consciousness by denying direct linkages between signifiers and signifieds, thereby rejecting the existence of a realm of stable or absolute meaning (signifieds). Signs, Derrida argued, operated by means of a continual deferral to other signs, creating the possibility of an infinite regress of meaning. Writing (as opposed to speaking) demonstrates that language is an imperfect container of meaning, that the user of language lacks control over the way language actually produces meaning. Derrida's major insight was that language worked by means of inclusionary and exclusionary processes (the hierarchies of which deconstruction exposed), leading to a perpetual "absence" within language in practice and therefore a habitual tendency for language to undermine itself through its own gaps. In Derrida, the system of "difference" that structured language in Saussure's theory was replaced by a process of "deferral" (the French word *différance* signifying both to "differ" and "defer"). The ongoing generative and degenerative aspects of language imply a subject that is forever being reconstituted within the play of signs and a self rendered incoherent by ruptures in linguistic meaning. Deconstruction, then, points to the discursively constructed character of discourse and self, and of culture in general.[4]

Another kind of decentering of the subject has appeared in the writings of Gilles Deleuze and Félix Guattari (1983, 1987), who effectively reessentialized the subject as a fragmented "desiring machine" (Best and Kellner 1991: 78). This more explicitly biological conception derived from Nietzsche postulated "desire" as a prediscursive, irreducible force in human behavior, a strong counterconception to Freudian notions of ego and representation, that tended to reduce the subject to willful and immutable forces in the psyche. Desire also played an important part in some of the earlier Nietzschean formulations of Lyotard, who denounced the language philosophers for ignoring the world of sense. For Lyotard, desire emerged in the gap left by language's exclusion of "what it seeks to possess" (Dews 1987: 118).

Of all the poststructuralist thinkers, Michel Foucault (1980) has perhaps most extensively explored the role of power in the production of the subject. In Foucault's staunchly antihumanist and antirationalist work, the subject disappears in discourse/power. Foucault's critique of Cartesianism consists in arguing against a "contractual" or representational theory of power by demonstrating that power inheres in the institutionalized discursive formations accompanying the emergence of various knowledge disciplines in Western society. For Foucault, who introduced power explicitly to counterpose it to semiological models (Dews 1987: 200), discourse and power are inseparable, since every discourse through its very functioning produces "power effects." Foucault (1980) sees "manifold relations of power" everywhere in society. Power, he argues, is not a phenomenon of individuals dominating others but is, rather, something that "circulates," such that individuals serve as "vehicles" of power, not as its agents but as "one of its prime effects" (Foucault 1980: 98).

The expulsion of the subject as a centered, metaphysical entity has been accomplished by privileging forces presumably beyond individual control, and this has typically taken the form of a dissolution of the self in discourse. But this maneuver has its counterpart in another type of critique that calls into question the historical subject. The radicalization of Enlightenment reason in the work of

Hegel and Marx transformed the rational ego into a collective subject whose actions shaped the course of history and whose totalizing reason turned "history" into "progress." This conception of the modern subject is perhaps most associated with the traditions of the French Revolution and revolutionary Marxism.

A dismissal of this historical subject is the centerpiece of Lyotard's (1984) questioning of the "master narratives" he claims serve as legitimating archetypes of modern science and nation-states. Part of Lyotard's polemic is directed against the "myth" of the unity of knowledge connected to the idea of a centered ego. But he also attacks these narratives' legitimating notions about the emancipation of humanity through heroic class actions. In this critique, launched in the context of post- or anti-Marxism in France, Lyotard questions the role that grand historical narratives have played in justifying various movements and authorities, whether reactionary or revolutionary. Lyotard observes a "delegitimation" process in which historical narratives are in decline as a result of scientific and technological development, and he argues for the destruction of humanist and speculative philosophy and its replacement by what might be called "microscience." In his words, "we are all stuck in the positivism of this or that discipline of learning" (Lyotard 1984: 41). Similarly, in his studies of disciplinary power, Foucault dispenses with collective ideals of the subject, both by subordinating subjectivity to the operation of power and by implicating the subject in particular discursive formations that rise and fall at determinate points in history. Foucault's archaeological and genealogical methods historicize the subject in ways antithetical to the universalizing and totalizing features of nineteenth-century philosophy and politics, resulting in a micropolitical model of change. No less than Lyotard, but by different methods, Foucault strives to undermine systematizations of knowledge whose purpose it is to rationalize and universalize history.[5]

Poststructuralism thus wages war on the transcendental subject on two fronts. On the one hand, it attempts to displace metaphysical conceptions of consciousness with notions of textuality, power, and desire. On the other hand, it rejects grand teleological schemes in favor of heteronomous accounts of historical development. In place of historical agency, poststructuralism posits a series of particular discursive formations and practices in which linear progress gives way to historical contingency and incommensurability.

While earlier thinkers had already cast a shadow over autonomous reason, those who have promoted structuralist and poststructuralist methods have claimed to turn reason into a myth and metaphysics into an illusion. The intellectual appeal of poststructuralism, however, has had less to do with its attacks on metaphysical reason than with a broader postmodern critique of what has been absent from the Enlightenment heritage. The discontinuities of language and knowledge argued by the poststructuralists have resonated with a new generation of academic scholars and activists of a postmodern bent who see only particularity and difference where modern thinkers have presupposed a priori conditions of universal knowledge. In addition, as identity politics opened onto a new terrain of epistemological doubt, especially in relation to the emphases on fluidity and multiplicity engendered particularly by the gay and lesbian movements and more generally coalition politics, the poststructuralist postulation of the disunity of identity suddenly became attractive. The relocation of the subject within the instabilities of discourse and power added insight and strength to the political struggles over identity and to new doctrines of contingency and relativity serving these struggles and the wider attack on established political, cultural, and scientific authority. Further, as suggested in earlier chapters, in a culture saturated by signification, a textualist epistemology easily gains a privileged place over consciousness-based philosophies of knowledge that imply the possibility of unified and self-knowing individuals.

Despite the obvious power of its critique of modern epistemology, however, poststructuralism has by and large left the problem of the subject unresolved. Habermas (1987b) has traced this failure to poststructuralism's continued dependence on presuppositions from the very philosophy of consciousness it attempted to overturn and in which it remains trapped by dilemmas of the subject-object dualism. Because poststructuralism developed through a largely negative relationship to the philosophy of consciousness, he argues, it has been unable to overcome the recurring difficulties of the latter. There are actually two problems here. First, poststructuralism has waged a relatively unsuccessful struggle against the binary oppositions of Hegelian thought and structuralist method. Second, theories that reject unified or universal standpoints invariably fall victim to the logical contradiction of attempting to make knowledge claims while simultaneously denying that we can "know" reality in a coherent or comprehensible fashion. Poststructuralism has evaded the problem of how it is possible to make statements about the world without assuming an epistemological and theoretical *position* on some object(s) believed to be knowable, and how such a position can be anything but "unified" if it is to be theoretically recognizable. In other words, poststructuralists dissolve the subject into discursive heterogeneity while still claiming to speak from the position of a knowing subject.

Ironically, in the very attempt to postulate a disunified world, devoid of moral and rational intention, and full of flux, dispersion, and difference, poststructuralist thought, far from destroying it, ultimately *reinvents* metaphysics for its own purposes. In the argument of Peter Dews (1987), this problem is traceable to Nietzsche, whose influence made it possible for the poststructuralists (with the exception of Jacques Lacan) to break with structuralist and prestructuralist assumptions of a unified knowledge. According to Dews, what many critics regard as the paradoxes of Nietzsche's thought actually reflect a genuine dilemma running through his work. On the one hand, there is a strong positivist element in Nietzsche that regards philosophical inquiry as having been permanently undermined by modern science, including the possibility of philosophy providing any assessment of the adequacy of knowledge. On the other hand, Nietzsche repeatedly returns to the idea of an ultimate reality through his notion of the biological or psychological drives, employing such concepts as "will to power" and "eternal return of the same." Thus, while denying the metaphysical principle of "appearance" versus "reality" by reducing knowledge to particular and divergent concepts and languages (perspectives), in the end Nietzsche reaffirms a ground of reality. In Dews's assessment,

> Nietzsche's critique of philosophy, therefore, of the "knowledge of knowledge" drives him towards a perspectivism which equates what is real with what is given in a form of knowledge, while his critique of all perspectives which see through their own "illusory" nature pushes him towards a reinstatement of the distinction between appearance and reality. . . . Hence Nietzsche is obliged to develop his own conception of ultimate reality in order to possess a means of judging the adequacy of perspectives. (178–79)

Both structuralist and poststructuralist approaches have tended to reproduce this Nietzschean dilemma.[6] In the hands of Lévi-Strauss, structuralism recreated the dilemma by replacing the "metaphysical subject" with "deep mental structures" that, in the guise of scientific discourse, merely established another metaphysical entity. Similarly, Derrida's critique of a "metaphysics of presence" depended no less importantly on the elevation of the *différance* of language to the status of a metaphysical ground for deconstruction. In Lyotard, we find a revival of metaphysical thinking through the distinction he draws between language and sense or desire. In his earlier work, Lyotard takes a strong stand for a prediscursive ground of desire against which language works and on which its limitations are revealed (Dews 1987: 112–13). The work of Deleuze and Guattari exemplifies what Lévi-Strauss grudgingly referred to as a "metaphysics of desire." In all these authors, then, we find various metaphysical moments in the attempt to reconstruct subjectivity, whether understood as mind, desire, or will.

The tension inherent in theoretical efforts to dispense with unified conceptions of knowledge and the subject is illustrated perhaps most dramatically by the work of Foucault. To a greater extent than other poststructuralists, Foucault inherited the positivist tendency in Nietzsche, partially grounding his work in concrete historical and social phenomena. But as Dews points out, Foucault's positivist commitment, like Nietzsche's, competed with the conviction that "forms of knowledge do not simply constitute, but can also obscure and obliterate reality" (Dews 1987: 181). In *Madness and Civilization* (1965), for instance, Foucault attempts to argue that the science of psychiatry eliminates unreason in the name of reason, thereby repressing a source of truth. But Foucault cannot remain a perspectivist and still criticize psychiatry for imposing its own perspective. To do so presupposes a reality that according to Nietzsche's doctrine of perspectivism cannot be known. The critical dimension of Foucault's thought, therefore, heightens the problem of positivism. While his premises require that meaning and knowledge be determined by discourse and power, his political critique requires a normative standpoint outside these determinations, a ground he in fact lacks (Dews 1987: 185; see also Best and Kellner 1991; Fraser 1989). According to Habermas, this problem is the reproduction in a new guise of the dichotomous subject-object relationship at the core of all philosophies of consciousness. The knowing, autonomous subject stands apart from and against the world of known objects in what Habermas (1987a) refers to as "the transcendental-empirical doubling of the relation to self" (297). In repudiating the centered subject, poststructuralists have simply reproduced this split or doubling in new metaphysical terms on the side of the object.[7] Thus, in their rejection of modern metaphysics, poststructuralist thinkers invent their own metaphysical positions. In the words of Albrecht Wellmer (1985), "the philosophy of total unmasking still lives from the very rationalistic metaphysics which it set out to destroy" (353).

The inability of poststructuralism to escape some form of metaphysics is one side of the impossibility of eliminating a role for consciousness in accounting for human practices, whether theoretical or otherwise. The other side is the reductionist consequences of textualist constructions of subjectivity and meaning. By replacing consciousness with language and discourse, poststructuralists negate the processes of self-reflection and self-formation in the *creation* and *shaping* of structural relationships, thereby positing a conception of structure bereft of human and social significance. Constructing a new metaphysics of the text, poststructuralism leaves the subject-object dualism untouched by simply privileging the object in the form of the "always already" constituted determinations of language and discourse. This poses a number of problems at the level of language alone. The theoretical enclosure of the subject in language precludes an accounting of the sources of both diversity and change in the structures and usages of language. The very presence of linguistic structure in cultural phenomena goes unaccounted for in the absence of an explanation of its subjective and symbolic origins. The identity of the subject is a necessary condition for the communication of meaning, which depends on and in turn facilitates linguistic closure. In Maurice Merleau-Ponty's argument, "without some conception of a subject which expresses and comprehends meaning through language, and therefore which provides a point of departure and return," language would imprison us in an "infinite regress" (Dews 1987: 32). Indeed, the nature and functions of language are incomprehensible without social subjects who use it for identifiable purposes (Eagleton 1983). The reduction of meaning to language and discourse thus results in a radically dehistoricized and desocialized subject. Poststructuralism thereby tends to occlude will, choice, freedom, and interests as grounds for individual and collective action.

Within the paradigm of discourse theory, attempts have been made to rescue the subject from these untenable implications. One such attempt is instructive. Paul Smith (1988), in an engrossing and important study titled *Discerning the Subject,* argues that resistance to the determining effects of discursive practices has its source in the "contradictions" and "disturbances" among all the "interpellations" of the individual. In his view, "choice" is a by-product of the way in which different "subject-positions" are negotiated within the individual. Maintaining that individuals are a product of ideologically determined subject positions, he states that, nonetheless, "where discourses actually take hold of or produce the so-called 'subject' they also *enable* agency and resistance" (40; emphasis in original). Importantly, however, Smith never explains the processes by which this occurs. Choice and action seem to remain embedded in the workings of language and ideology, and the process of negotiation itself along with the mechanisms of meaning and action are left a mystery. Smith's argument demonstrates the fate of subjectivity and agency within theoretical frameworks that refuse to leave the discursive realm and enter the world of concrete social relations and selves. Similarly, Foucault's reduction of the subject to the effects of the operation of power leads to a nonrelational and astructural conception that effectively ignores the underlying range of concrete social goals and interests motivating the exercise of power.

The postmodern theme of desire is employed in yet another critique of the Enlightenment subject but in its own way performs a similarly reductionist function in French theorizing. In the work of Deleuze and Guattari (1983, 1987), power is reduced to an energistic force, a pure and undifferentiated biological will that, unlike Lacan's "desire" (Turkle 1978), resists structuring by language. The category of desire as derived from the biological and psychological drives central to both Nietzsche's and Freud's views of the psyche is suggestive of a prediscursive ground of action existing prior to the repressions of representation and a "symbolic order." But while the account of Deleuze and Guattari contains possibilities for a way out of the enclosure of the subject in discourse and power found in other poststructuralist writings, it simultaneously poses its own problems by *voiding* the effects of representation and its politically liberatory potentials. Similarly, in positing a gap between the discursive and the nondiscursive, Lyotard opens a path for seeing desire as a source of drive and indeterminacy in a not yet fully constituted subject. In both cases, desire is posed as a subversive alternative to linguistic determination, pointing to the unformed and formative dimensions of subjectivity, but both arguments also commit the error of omission by bracketing both the power and emancipatory effects of discourse.

Within this varied corpus of ideas, poststructuralism constructs a subject that is heterogeneous and unstable in character. On a strong note, notions of the play of the text, the circulation of power, and the metaphysics of desire loosen meaning and identity in potentially emancipatory ways. The poststructuralist celebration of difference and otherness marks a departure from unitary notions of knowledge and an identity logic that encapsulates meaning and identity in fixed forms. The French subject, however, suffers serious lack. The subject that French poststructuralism destabilizes usually remains a socially disembodied, discursively constructed and disconnected subject, devoid of self-identity, historical context, or social relationality. Despite the social and political perspectives that have been incorporated into some poststructuralist work (chapter 5), theoretical poststructuralism tends to remain abstracted from any recognizable field of social relations.

In sum, French poststructuralism marks the displacement of a socially and symbolically endowed subject by an imposing set of linguistic idealisms and positivisms. The overriding reductionist tendencies in both structuralism and poststructuralism typically result in a subject stripped of particular social location and the social capacities of communication and action. As an articulation of the particularities, instabilities, and incommensurabilities of a world fragmented by the power effects of discourse and desire, poststructuralism tends to forget the underlying material and social forms and purposes embodied in discursive practices and power. Further, by locating the meaning of discursive practices exclusively in already constituted, objectified textual structures, poststructuralism closes itself off from the unformed and imaginative dimensions of subjectivity.

Commonalities and Contrasts between Two Philosophical Defectors

The writings of George Herbert Mead have recently enjoyed long overdue attention, most notably in the work of Jürgen Habermas (1987a, 1992) but more widely in a revived interest among scholars on both sides of the Atlantic in the place and promise of pragmatism in twentieth-century social thought (Aboulafia 1986, 1995; Diggens 1994; Joas 1985, 1993). This is a significant development, considering that pragmatism has been more closely associated with thinkers like William James, John Dewey, and Charles Sanders Peirce. While Mead was always the lesser philosophical figure (although he exerted considerable influence on Dewey),[8] the lack of attention paid to Mead also partly reflects the complex and unfinished character of his pragmatism and its lack of fit with established disciplines. But perhaps most telling, despite remarkable similarities between Mead and poststructuralists, which might partially account for the Mead revival, Mead's social theory of pragmatism is ultimately at odds with the basic presuppositions of the poststructuralist project. With few exceptions,[9] the ruling postulate of textual difference and instability in poststructuralism has lent support to those who characterize it as a postmodern epistemology, if not doctrine. Mead, however, occupies a more ambiguous position in the contrast between the postmodern and the modern. While a philosopher of plurality, recognizing the contingent, transitory, and unstable character of human behavior and experience (including scientific practice), he steadfastly held to the ideal of universal knowledge through the development of science as a social enterprise devoted to an investigation of the natural and social worlds. Furthermore, despite his theoretical reliance on the centrality of language and his strong awareness of the multiple and changeful character of human existence, Mead had an ultimately *social* understanding of the nature and functions of language, which he saw as serving the purposes of community formation.

If a revival of pragmatism is under way, this can only be understood as part of the same decline of older functionalist and Marxist paradigms and the arrival of postsixties, postmetaphysical outlooks that have made poststructuralism itself so popular. But interest in pragmatist theory might at the same time be suggestive of a growing discontent with certain features of poststructuralism and the search for alternative approaches to the problems of subjectivity, identity, culture, and politics. While a "neopragmatism" has already been claimed on a variety of postmodern fronts (Rorty 1979, 1989; Lyotard 1984), a more systematic reappropriation of earlier pragmatist philosophers is perhaps on the horizon.

If so, it is no accident that Mead should be a part of this renewed interest. On the one hand, it was Mead (1934: 165) who remarked many years ago that "language . . . makes possible the existence or the appearance of . . . situation(s) or object(s)," an obvious precursor to structuralist and poststructuralist perspectives and an originary statement in the twentieth-century linguistic turn. But this is only one of many suggestive parallels between Meadian thought and contemporary theoretical developments, especially poststructuralism. Additionally, both traditions place strong emphasis on the multiplicity and fluidity of signification and meaning and the processual, tentative, and contingent character of communication and action.

Intellectual reasons for the similarities between Mead's theories and post-structuralism are not hard to find. Both emerged in the context of radical critiques of Hegelian reason and the turn from philosophies of consciousness toward linguistically oriented epistemologies (Butler 1987; Descombes 1980; Ferry and Renaut 1990; Habermas 1992; Joas 1985; Miller 1973). More broadly, both theoretical developments originated in reactions against well-known nineteenth-century metaphysical pieties. Here, a comparison and contrast are apparent between the pragmatist denial of conceptual dualisms in favor of a processual model of problem solving and the poststructuralist rejection of binary oppositions for a more fluid and dispersed notion of language, conceptualized as unstable relations of difference. Taking his cues from Charles Darwin, Mead's general approach to the problems of knowledge, self, and behavior was governed by the principle of emergence, or the idea that life forms are in a continual state of evolution. This meant that for Mead knowledge was provisional because contingent on time, place, and purpose. Along a different route, poststructuralist thinkers similarly regard truth and knowledge as provisional and contingent. For them, the interpretation of meaning is a process entangled with the workings of language and discourse. In this view, the gaps and absences inherent in language leave open the possibility of ongoing contested meanings and therefore chronic discursive instability. Both approaches thus recognize the emergent properties of human practices, and for both meaning is always tentative in the sense that absolute and fixed points of reference are unavailable in an inherently dynamic, constantly changing, and therefore unstable symbolic environment.

Another common feature of poststructuralism and Meadian pragmatism is a shift from notions of innate consciousness to a strategy of locating the subject in a system of external relations, a relocation of subjectivity to the exterior world of collectively shared symbols. As we have seen, poststructuralists understand the subject as being constructed by discursive practices. Contrary to the Meadian view, this position has often led to claims that the subject is nothing but a fiction disguising the construction of social reality through discourse. Foucault's (1979, 1980) arguments about the embeddedness of power relations in discourse are a further elaboration on the idea that social relations and formations are a product of the institutionalization of discursive practices. Mead, in contrast, locates the subject firmly within a social process defined and shaped by symbolic interaction. In both cases, a belief in innate consciousness, whether prelinguistic or presocial, is replaced by a postulation of relational influences operating on the subject. Both theories thus see meaning as objectively given in the outer world, in Mead's case in the form of the "objectivity of perspectives" (Mead 1932), and for poststructuralism in the autonomous workings of socially and politically inscribed texts.

On the other hand, in a major divergence from poststructuralism, Mead (1934) expresses an important qualification that language is only *part* of "the mechanism whereby" situations or objects are created. What Mead has in mind here is the mechanism of social interaction: language specifically serves to embody the social meanings of the act as generated in this interaction. Discourse, then, takes a social form and is inseparable from the social context in which it is located and functions as discourse. While outlining the rudiments of a theory of language, Mead, contrary to poststructuralist thinkers, concentrated on transforming the dialectical relationship of subject and object into an intersubjective field of communicative social action. Furthermore, in Mead the subject is redefined as a self, understood as a product of socialization through role taking. By resituating the subject-object problem in a social psychology of the self, Mead is able to postulate an objective basis of meaning while retaining a notion of subjectivity as a source of *conscious* meaning and the possibility of its modification or transformation. Poststructuralism instead adopts an objectivistic conception of a discursively determined subject, eliminating conventional notions of subjectivity for the performative enactments of "subjects" and "bodies." Consciousness thus serves no useful purpose for poststructuralists, since meaning inheres exclusively in textual objects incapable of the structural unity and coherence that consciousness presupposes.

The Poststructuralism of Judith Butler: A Meadian Critique

These similarities and contrasts between Mead and poststructuralism can be illuminated through the work of Judith Butler, who presents an especially compelling appropriation of poststructuralism that reverberates dramatically with Meadian theory. Butler develops an engaging set of arguments for a signification theory of the subject and of identity, and her carefully constructed arguments that identity is constituted in relations of discourse and power illustrate many of the salient strengths of the poststructuralist position.

In her seminal work, *Gender Trouble* (1990b), Butler raises a series of provocative theoretical and political questions regarding the categories of sex and gender. In her discussion, Butler adds to the poststructuralist emphasis on discourse the notion of "performativity,"[10] a notion she effectively deploys in her arguments about what she considers a regulatory regime of heterosexuality. According to Butler, this institutionalized regime enforces fixed identities of sex and gender through a discursively produced *fiction* of interior and substantial identity that she argues is performatively constructed. Her position is explicated in the following passage, from a related essay that contains the major elements of her theory of identity formation:

According to the understanding of identification as fantasy, however, it is clear that coherence is desired, wished for, idealized, and that this idealization is an effect of a corporeal signification. In other words, acts, gestures, and desire produce the effect of an internal core or substance, but produce this on the surface of the body, through the display of signifying absences that suggest, but never reveal, the organizing principle of identity as a cause. Such acts, gestures, enactments, generally construed, are performative in the sense that the essence of identity that they otherwise purport to express becomes a fabrication manufactured and sustained through corporeal signs and other discursive means. That the gendered body is performative suggests that it has no ontological status apart from the various acts which constitute its reality, and if that reality is fabricated as an interior essence, that very interiority is a function of a decidedly public and social discourse, the public regulation of fantasy through the surface politics of the body. In other words, acts and gestures articulate and enacted desires create the illusion of an interior and organizing gender core, an illusion discursively maintained for the purposes of the regulation of sexuality within the obligatory frame of reproductive heterosexuality. (Butler 1990a: 336–37)

The remarkably Meadian tone of this passage can be underscored in a number of ways. First, Butler says that identity has a performative basis in "acts and gestures," reminiscent of Mead's behavioral conception of the development of the self. Second, these acts and gestures are constituted within a "public and social discourse," a socially generated and shared language that provides a common frame of meanings, akin to Mead's "community." Third, Butler's characterization of discourse as inherently normative contains suggestive overtones of Mead's concept of "the generalized other."

In addition to its Meadian parallels, however, this statement is important for other reasons. First, it is an expression of Butler's argument that language, as the means of discourse, becomes a vehicle for the articulation of normative prescriptions. In other words, discourse serves as a system of social control. Second, and more significantly, this passage polemically renounces any claims of identity as an "interior" and "organizing" principle. For Butler, the repetitive enactment of discursively produced identities only creates an illusion of an inner sense of identity. This is consistent with other poststructuralist writings that theorize subjectivity in terms of the unstable structures of discourse. However, by introducing the concept of performativity, Butler adds an important behavioral and social dimension, saying in effect that discursive practices are also social practices. Her concept of performativity here invites comparison to the work of Erving Goffman (1959, 1967), who stressed the dramatistic or theatrical character of social behavior, albeit while retaining a conception of an interior identity (the "backstage" as opposed to the "frontstage"). Deviating from the central tendency of poststructuralism, Butler thereby seems to leave some room for notions of agency. This is apparent in the concluding chapter of *Gender Trouble* (1990b), where she attempts to clarify and systematize her position. Against "the foundationalist reasoning of identity politics," she argues that an identity need not "first be in place" in order to engage in "political action," and therefore by implication any kind of action. In her words, "My argument is that there need not be a 'doer behind the deed,' but that the 'doer' is variably constructed in and through the deed" (142).

For Butler, then, action is linguistic in character, constituted in the discursively based performances through which actors *construct* identities by means of their own actions, as opposed to *expressing* identities that are interior and "pregiven." Butler's poststructuralism proceeds from the commonplace that discourse takes a behavioral form. The use of language or other sign systems is inseparable from the behavioral activity they produce and that they symbolically inscribe with meaning and significance. Identity is not "substantial" or "essential," according to her argument, but a product of the articulation of discourses *about* identity and sustained through the operation of these discourses and their behavioral effects.

Thus, along with other poststructuralists, Butler regards thought, meaning, and behavior as constituted in and by discourse. Yet she recognizes that discourse receives its embodiment and power in the concrete performances of human actors. Through her notion of performativity, then, she turns poststructuralist theory in a social direction, effectively joining the concept of discursive practice to more behaviorally congealed notions of subjectivity and identity.

Butler's reworking of poststructuralism positions it rather closely to a Meadian perspective by valorizing the notion of performativity and therefore more explicitly addressing how identity is constructed behaviorally. Butler thus offers a more socially dynamic version of poststructuralism than can be found among its French founders. Despite overtures to the social, however, Butler strives vigorously to disclaim the nondiscursive elements of behavior, elements that lie at the very foundation of Mead's philosophy of emergence and that define the larger project of pragmatism of which his work was a part. In short, Butler's project illustrates how, despite its contributions to our understanding of the inherently unstable nature of meaning, cultural relations, and the subject, poststructuralism reaches its limits at a practical understanding of social relations and the self. Although striving to impart a behavioral dimension to the operations of discourse and the constitution of subjectivity, Butler nonetheless remains entrapped in a theory of discourse bereft of any conceptualization of the manifold social and individual sources of meaning, identity, and agency.

This is evident, first, in her rejection of identity as an interior and organizing phenomenon of self. While Mead never spoke of identity as such, his theory of the self offers a set of more fruitful counterclaims to Butler's insistence that identity is constructed solely by discursive means. For Mead, role-taking behavior (Butler's performativity) is *internalized* through a symbolic process taking place reflexively in the self. Discerning the difference here between Butler and Mead hinges on how we understand the meaning of "internalization." Mead sees the person as forming attitudes and dispositions taken from others, which become a basis of how one sees oneself as a social entity as well as a means for developing an identity. Thus, one's relations with others become grounds for a conception of self. Mead does not seem to understand self-conception as essential, that is, innate, but neither does he deny that it occupies an important and substantial place in one's interior sense of self. But, in fact, for him self-conception was *not* fictive insofar as it was rooted in the capacity to make an object of oneself as a real person and was materially based in the perceived social responses of significant others, which became part of a person's perception of and relationship to self. Whereas Butler's argument re-creates the poststructuralist evasion of consciousness, Mead, sensing its indispensability, retains a weak version of consciousness, refashioning it in accordance with his idea that the self is structured as subject *and* object ("I" and "Me"). In his conception, consciousness is a site of reflexive, symbolic awareness and activity, that is, it represents a state of internal responsiveness (self as subject, or I). But consciousness is also dependent on social experience and is specifically constituted in social relations, being externally formed (self as object of both others and oneself, or the Me).

Dramatically unlike Mead, while offering it lip service, Butler seems to dispense entirely with the self, regarding it as merely an effect of discourse. For instance, "There is no self prior to the convergence . . . [of discursive injunctions]" (1990b: 145). Compare this to Mead's (1934) remark that "the language process is essential for the development of the self" (199). In the first statement, the self seemingly has no basis or existence *apart* from language, specifically its controlling functions, while in the second statement language is a *necessary but insufficient condition* of the self. Mead posits *other* conditions, most notably the capacity of self-consciousness and the ability to objectify one's experiences in order to transform them into objects of reflection and redefinition. Additionally, Butler's account is preoccupied with the *injunctive* character of signification, whereas Mead would understand discourse as exhibiting two faces, closed and compulsory (normative) *and* open and facilitative (innovative). On both counts, while disavowing this position, Butler seems to be assuming a more deterministic stance toward the effects of signification than Mead does. By allowing the self to be absorbed in the workings of discourse, she supposes change to be an ever present—but ultimately unexplained—possibility inherent in the instabilities of the hegemonic discursive system itself. Finally, in addition to her vagueness on the status of the self and its relation to discourse, what remains unclear in Butler are the grounds on which she justifies claiming an inner sense of identity as being an illusion and, what is another side of the same problem, why the impossibility of imagining identity as forming outside of discursive practices precludes postulating its internalization in the self.

Significantly, where Mead talks of the self, Butler speaks of the body. The body is the site at which the discursive becomes performative; the signifying practices of the normativizing culture operate through bodily behavior, or corporeal signs. For Butler, the body has no "ontological status" apart from the acts that constitute (or "gender") it. In his behaviorist mode, Mead, too, at least initially focused attention on the body. In this regard, it could be said that the term *performativity* in Butler's lexicon is a postmodern term for behavior, but with a significant difference. Performances are scripted, already prescribed (prescripted) in the discourses of the culture, and are then enacted or performed by recipients of the script. Behavior, in contrast, is a purely physical or mechanical event that requires interpretation. In her early work, Butler understands performativity as a culturally induced and restricted effect produced on the surface of the body, whereas Mead understands behavior in a social sense as a bodily manifestation of the socially shared symbolic acts of group members. However, by postulating a crucial distinction between the body and the self, arguing that bodies can only be objects while selves possess cognitive and moral capacity and are therefore capable of being both subjects *and* objects, Mead made his social behaviorism conscious and intelligent. Where Butler's performance seems dictated by the discursive powers of cultural authority, Mead's behavior originates in reflexively produced and defined acts embedded in a process of social interaction.

The difficulties engendered by the exclusion of a self in Butler's account are revealed in a particularly strong way in the quotations about the absence of a "doer behind the deed." While the last half of her statement—that the "doer" is "constructed in and through the deed"—might seem reasonable, the first half seems entirely implausible. The question poses itself: how can there be "deeds" without "doers"? It is difficult to imagine predicates such as "constructed" apart from acts that are carried out by actors. Put differently, language "uses" actors only in the most metaphoric sense of the term. While doers may be constructed through the deed, they are in an important sense the agents of their own, and others', construction. Butler *seems* to be claiming that identities are constructed out of the whole cloth of discourse, absent a subject occupying a physical or material space existing prior to (or at least simultaneously with) discursive construction. A Meadian formulation would seem more credible: human actors are subjects with purposes, intentions, needs, drives, and the like, all of which arise as motivational "causal" factors working *in* and *through* practices that are both discursive *and* social in nature.

In contrasting Mead and Butler, we see that the theoretical problem of the self, specifically the excess over discourse that is represented by the very concept of a self, can be joined in terms of arguments about a "nondiscursive" realm. In the following statement Butler (1990b) theoretically refuses any prediscursive basis of self-formation:

> This is not a return to an existential theory of the self as constituted through its acts, for the existential theory maintains a prediscursive structure for both the self and its acts. It is precisely the discursively variable construction of each in and through the other that has interested me here. (142)

Being "interested" in discursive variation, of course, is not to disprove a prediscursive ground of self or identity. But her negations of this prediscursive realm are, in fact, ultimately mystifying. Besides being theoretically and philosophically questionable, such negations seem irrelevant to her arguments about the discursive construction of identity. Finally, not only does her denial of any prediscursive elements in identity deplete her account of the subject, but it fails to withstand empirical scrutiny (for example, the consequences of biological and anatomical difference on gender identity).

Here, we find poststructuralism's peculiar aporia and its major divergence from Mead's pragmatism. The latter posits a prediscursive level of meaning located in the evolutionary development of life forms, the problem-solving conditions of social life, and the formative activity of the "I." Indeed, one of the accomplishments of Mead's pragmatism was to demonstrate that the constitution of meaning and experience in signifying systems—culture—necessarily presupposes prediscursive, ontological conditions of existence. Mead notwithstanding, it is in any case unnecessary to perform the impossible feat of "getting outside" language and discourse to demonstrate the existence of a prediscursive ground of social reality and culture.

The enduring question of "agency" also hinges largely on whether and how we theorize a self. Butler argues that the problem of agency has usually been understood in a binary fashion, whereby culture and discourse "*mire*" but "do not constitute" the subject (1990b: 143; emphasis in original). Here, she seems in substantial agreement with Mead in her argument that to be constituted in discourse is not to be determined by discourse, if "determination" is taken to mean the impossibility of agency. However, she disagrees that agency depends on "recourse to a prediscursive 'I.'" In her conception, identity is only "asserted through a process of signification, . . . is always already signified"; "in other words, the enabling conditions for an assertion of 'I' are provided by the structure of signification" (143). But Butler does not explain what these "enabling conditions" are or what precludes a preexistent or simultaneous "I." Far from being merely a word, in the Meadian view the "I" is an internal experience of reflexivity that *precedes* the sense of linguistic reflexivity imparted by signification (Wiley 1994). Mead gave ontological primacy to the subject-object relation designated by his terms "I" and "Me," seeing this division and relation as the source or ground of grammatical structure in language. The grammatical structure of nominative and accusative cases in language, then, could be understood as a reflection of the subject-object duality inherent in the self.

Furthermore, if we take the I in a Meadian fashion to mean simply the *activity* of the self, its *assertion* within a discursive structure, there seems to be no need to deny a prediscursive element to agency in order to maintain a discursive theory of identity formation. Indeed, it hardly seems possible to *have* such a theory without conditioning it on some concept of consciousness in which an I or its functional equivalent serves as agency of identity and behavior. While in basic agreement with Mead that language is not a mere medium or instrument of behavior but, rather, in some sense constitutive of it, Butler nonetheless wants to exclude from consideration any social or psychological processes of nondiscursive elements operating *behind* the linguistic process. Since "enabling condition" must imply a *something* that is enabled, Butler's denial of the prediscursive becomes an elliptical argument. Although the position that "everything is discourse" might serve as a rallying point against essentializing modes of inquiry and primitive forms of identity thinking, it also represents an unnecessary limitation on theory, an implausible absence that overly exercises the place of discourse in theories of behavior and identity.[11]

Rather than *reducing* the self to language or discourse, it would seem more fruitful to establish *connections* between them in a way that demonstrated their relative autonomy and mutual interpenetration. While Mead himself paid insufficient attention to language (Denzin 1988), his notion of the "internal conversation" is in this respect highly suggestive. The internal conversation of the self arises out of the reflexive relationship of the "I" to the "Me." As active, subjective dimension of the self, the I carries on a "conversation" with those already formed aspects of the self—those past, socially determined elements Mead designated as the Me, which is the "object" of the I's deliberations. In criticizing poststructuralism, Norbert Wiley argues that "the internal conversation is 'structured like' rather than being identical with language" (1994: 59). In fact, modeling the internal structure of the self linguistically provides a point of possible accommodation with poststructuralism. Mead's metaphor of conversation is suggestive of a homology (implied above) between the internal structures and processes of the self and the workings of language, and it further suggests the dependency of self-reflexivity on an appropriation and use of language. Thus, the self can be understood as structured in and through discourse without being thoroughly reduced to it.

Butler's position on the problem of the prediscursive as well as constructionist modes of argumentation receives greater attention in her later work, *Bodies That Matter* (1993). Here we find fleeting acknowledgment of the limitations of the discursive conception of sex and gender. Butler argues that to claim that the subject is produced "as a gendered matrix of relations is not to do away with the subject, but only to ask after the conditions of its emergence and operation" (7). To overcome the dilemmas and contradictions of existing constructionisms, which she argues falter on questions of the body and the subject, Butler proposes replacing the idea of construction with that of materialization, as "a return to the notion of matter, not as site or surface, but as *a process of materialization that stabilizes over time to produce the effect of boundary, fixity, and surface we call matter*" (9; emphasis in original). Reminiscent of Mead's notion of emergence, Butler's materiality captures the temporal essence of the manner in which discursive practices construct identity while at the same time destabilizing it through its own activity. In her words, "Construction not only takes place *in* time, but is itself a temporal process which operates through the reiteration of norms; sex is both produced and destabilized in the course of this reiteration" (1993: 10; emphasis in original).

However, it remains unclear what the introduction of the notion of materiality resolves. First of all, this overly vague concept adds little to our understanding of how construction actually occurs, and it postpones dealing with the problem of the prediscursive by simply casting it in another mold. Indeed, after conceding the existence of "the alleged [!] facts of birth, aging, illness, and death" and the material realities of physical sexuality (anatomy, hormones), Butler immediately reverses herself by saying that to concede the above "is always to concede some *versions* of 'sex,' some *formation* of 'materiality'" (1993: 10; emphasis added), suggesting that the very discourse through which the concession occurs is "itself formative of the very phenomenon that it concedes" (10). Once again, Butler refuses the possibility of ever escaping linguistic construction.

Second, by locating power and resistance in the "reiteration of norms," Butler simply poses another set of unanswered questions. She attributes both the authorizing power of discourse and the possibilities of its subversion to the condition of repetition itself, to the need to repeat and therefore perpetually constitute in this repetition a fixity of identity, a process that takes the form of normative regulation (Foucault's "regulatory ideal" [Butler 1993: 1]). Nowhere, however, does she explain how this instability actually manifests itself, except through arguments about the exclusionary and prohibitive demarcation of boundaries that normative reiterability necessitates. In arguing against Foucault that "repression" can operate as "a modality of productive power," Butler implies, but does not demonstrate, that the repressions of the body (and therefore identity) involved in the discursive drawing of boundaries around compulsory behavior are the source of resistance or opposition to what she alleges are intrinsically limiting structures of identity. Beyond implying a simple "return of the repressed," Butler provides no account of the dynamics of discursive instability, leaving us with a simple deferral to her earlier comment in *Gender Trouble* that "'agency' . . . is to be located within the possibility of a *variation* on that repetition" (1990b: 145; emphasis added).

Furthermore, at the very core of Butler's theory that discourse works by means of exclusions we find an inevitable contradiction with her basic position against the nondiscursive. In arguing that "materialization is never quite complete" and that "bodies never quite comply with the norms," she is effectively postulating the ontological limitations of signification, implying a realm of experience or material reality *beyond the reach of existing discourse.* The repressed presupposes a realm of nondiscursivity set apart, in her words, by "exclusionary means, . . . through a set of foreclosures, radical erasures, that are . . . refused the possibility of cultural articulation" (Butler 1993: 8). Gender construction has the consequence of demarcating a discursive inside and a nondiscursive outside: "The construction of the human is a differential operation that produces the more and the less 'human,' the inhuman, the humanly unthinkable. These excluded sites come to bound the 'human' as its constitutive outside, and *to haunt those boundaries as the persistent possibility of their disruption and rearticulation*" (8; emphasis added). While the nature and location of these "excluded sites" remain vague, their existence would seem to necessitate a prediscursive realm, for how else could they present the "persistent possibility" of disruption?

Butler creates a similar kind of confusion over the problem of "intentionality." She claims that performativity is not to be understood as a "singular 'act'" (1993: 12) but, rather, as a reiteration of norms that takes place through their continual "citing." Solipsistically (who or what does the citing?), she argues that "the citation of the (symbolic) law (of sex) is the very mechanism of its production and articulation" (15).[12] Thus, the process by which materialization occurs is "a kind of citationality, the acquisition of being through the citing of power, a citing that establishes an originary complicity with power in the formation of the 'I'" (15). But at the same time, in arguing that the power of citationality is "not the function of an originating will, but is always derivative," she presents a quotation by Derrida in which he states in seeming contradiction that "*the category of intention will not disappear; it will have its place, but from that place it* will no longer be able to govern the *entire* scene and system of utterance" (13; emphasis added).

The reluctance of poststructuralists, including Butler, to incorporate a concept of self is at least partly attributable to the critical stance toward the Western idea of the self assumed by many theorists who write from subordinate subject positions. Many poststructuralist authors, including Foucault and Butler, have drawn our attention to the power relations inscribed in modern constructions of the self, which often implicitly bear the traits of domination and hierarchy (whiteness, maleness, heterosexuality, class privilege). Yet the absence of a concept of self, as exemplified by Butler's denial of any moment of indeterminacy or creativity in what Mead refers to as the I, effectively precludes the possibility of accounting for potential sources or forms of normative destabilization, by negating any notions of agency. Moreover, despite poststructuralists' deconstructive critique of the socially hegemonic structure of the "modern" self, there is a case to be made that the pragmatist self is in fact thoroughly democratic (Wiley 1994). Voluntarist and egalitarian, Mead's conception of the self is relatively immune to accusations of dominant positionality. On the contrary, as a pragmatist Mead was seeking a theoretical model of the self supportive of democratic ideals of individual autonomy and participatory community life.

Debates surrounding postmodern thought have suffered another kind of confusion regarding the conceptual status of the self. Poststructuralism has frequently been characterized as a position that decenters the self by relocating or dispersing it within a larger set of structures and forces, most notably (as we have seen) discourse, power, and desire. Close readings of the poststructuralists, however, show that "they do not so much decenter the self as eliminate it" (Wiley 1994: 29). Indeed, an important distinction is to be made here between decentering and reduction: the former involves increasing explanatory elaboration and complexity whereas the latter merely "explains away." Emanating largely from poststructuralist theory, the postmodernist fashion in decentering tends to involve formulaic attempts to rid social and cultural theory of the self rather than to sort systematically through the various external and internal theoretical dispersals necessary for an understanding of the cultural and social constituents of the self.

Pragmatist conceptions seem even more promising when considered in this context, since they attempt to decenter the self by *combining* external and internal dispersals in a way that leaves the self intact (Wiley 1994). On the one hand, they break down its Cartesian isolation by partially constituting the self in social relations. The Meadian concept of a *social* self thus mutes postmodernist attacks on the modern conception of the autonomous and rational ego by linking the self to the normative (and cognitive) structures of community. On the other hand, pragmatism sees the self as dispersed internally among the I, the Me (Mead), and the You (Peirce) (Wiley 1994). Unlike the poststructuralist reduction of the self to language and discourse, the pragmatist conception differentiates the self into multiple internal relations of meaning.

Against the backdrop of dominant theoretical trends, the pragmatist decentering of the self remains a seldom noticed yet challenging intellectual perspective. Indeed, the cultural turn in academia could find enormous benefits in a rehabilitation and rereading of pragmatist theory, especially that of Mead and Peirce, the latter of whom provided important missing elements in Mead's self theory. As the recent work of Wiley (1994) demonstrates, when Mead's theory of the self is combined with Peirce's conception, the result is an integrated and powerful pragmatist understanding of the self as a system of semiotic relations. Whereas Mead's model of the I and the Me limited the temporal dimensions of the self to the present and past, Peirce provided a much needed future orientation through his concept of the You. In combination, the Meadian and Peirceian views of the self yield a triadic Me-I-You semiotic relationship and a corresponding threefold temporal delineation of past, present, and future self-orientations. As Wiley (1994) explains in his synthesis of these thinkers, Mead and Peirce together established the self as a temporal structure organized around the reflexive relationship of the I to the Me and the direct relationship of the I to the You (43). Whereas Mead's Me is in the past, Peirce's You is in the future. Peirce thus adds an important dimension of both "otherness" (You) and "contingency" (the future) that is lacking in Mead's view of the self. As Wiley shows, a Mead-Peirce synthesis lends more complexity to the problems of internalization and the internal conversation by more fully situating the self in a structure of social relations. For example, although the Me is the internalized You, the You is not always internalized but often remains a figure external to the self. Put differently, in an ontological sense Mead was more focused on the self while Peirce brought more focus to the self-other relationship. In this respect, Peirce stands in a somewhat similar relationship to Mead as does Herbert Blumer (1969), who likewise shifted focus toward the interactional processes implicating the self in relations with others.

This broadened conception of the self, which places added emphasis on social interaction, offers an even more appealing alternative to poststructuralism and its efforts to account for meaning instability by reference to discursive structures and processes. Between the reflexive relationship to its past and the more direct encounter with its potential future, the social self of Mead and Peirce offers a more credible and fruitful basis for theorizing identity, behavior, and social and cultural change.

And yet, to return importantly and finally to Butler, there are in her presentation few major claims that are in principle incompatible with Meadian philosophy or social psychology. Brilliant in its way, Butler's work illustrates significant points of compatibility between poststructuralism and Meadian thought while nevertheless demonstrating the odd and cumbersome omissions of textualist approaches. Although rigorous and sophisticated in its probing argumentation about the powers and oppressions of discourse, Butler's work exemplifies the pitfalls of attempting to account theoretically for the formation and destabilization of identity exclusively within a linguistic paradigm. Butler rightly recognizes the temporal and processual character of discursive practices and the importance of theorizing them in terms of the performances through which discursive meaning is behaviorally inscribed and reproduced in social practices. At the same time, however, her rigidly discourse-based account of production and change in identity lacks the crucial element of social subjectivity. Critically, this is related to her failure to recognize the *social* matrix of discursivity by means of which processes of self-reflexivity and social interaction themselves generate the conditions of both normative reproducibility *and* instability. Lacking these elements, Butler is unable to account for how identity actually forms and re-forms, how situationally and conditionally subjects both are constructed by others and construct themselves. The manifestation of instability in the discursive reiterations of the normative order requires the presence of a self in which conscious reflection leads to humanly wrought redefinitions of the situation and corresponding changes in intentionally and motivationally based lines of social interaction.

Meadian Philosophy: Sociality, Intersubjectivity, and the Self

The foregoing critique of Butler indicates some tentative lines along which Mead's theory of the social self could serve as a basis for theorizing identity and difference. Before assessing his contributions to such theorizing, however, I present a more general overview of Meadian philosophy. In what follows, I attempt to demonstrate the originality and ingenuity of Mead's solution to the subject-object dualism and its preferability to the poststructuralist abandonment of the problem. The strength of Mead's solution, despite its limitations,[13] resides in the implications of his "naturalistic" philosophy. Mead grounds the subject-object dialectic in an understanding of the practical constitution of the self in social relations, thus creating an interactive and intersubjective social psychology.

Customarily regarded as a uniquely American form of thought, pragmatism as a philosophical discourse inherited the difficulties posed by Hegelianism and was thus ineluctably shaped by the problem of the subject-object relationship of inner and outer worlds of experience. What distinguished pragmatism in its efforts to transcend Hegelianism, however, was the transformation of this problem into a theory of the practical import of knowledge in the context of problem solving. Mead himself was perhaps more deeply influenced by nineteenth-century German idealism and the issues it took up than the other pragmatist thinkers.[14]

Nonetheless, despite the strong influences[15] from that direction, a predominantly Hegelian reading of Mead would be ultimately mistaken. Rather, it was to Darwin[16] that Mead looked for a way out of the impasse of the subject-object dualism created by the Cartesian concept of mind and left unresolved by the Hegelian dialectic (Joas 1985; Miller 1973). In short, it was a transfigured Darwinian evolutionism that opened the door to Mead's new conceptualization of the problem. For Mead, Darwin's model of an organism adapting to its environment demonstrated the mistake of positing a rational mind or self prior to a structured world of biological and social activity. Darwin's conception of a struggling species enabled Mead to locate mind and experience as developing *in* nature (Lee 1945: 84) and to understand knowledge as necessarily founded in behavior, as situated in the "necessary conditions set by nature on the organism's reproduction of itself" (Joas 1985: 53). As a pragmatist, Mead had come to see the adaptive accomplishments of animals as a "primitive analogue" to human behavior and intelligence. He correspondingly saw the "procedure of the experimental sciences" as directed toward an "active reshaping of the environment" through the "self-reflective control" of the evolutionary process (Joas 1985: 53). This view equated the solving of problems with the making of adjustments, understanding both as the source of novelty or "emergence" in both biological and social life. Darwin's theory further offered an alternative to troublesome teleological and mechanistic accounts of evolution by demonstrating the "possibility of qualitatively new forms of organisms" (53), or the emergence of new life forms through adaptive transformation. Mead thus found in Darwin's work the major components of a biologically rooted naturalistic understanding of human society and a functional theory of mind and behavior.

It is only from this Darwinian foundation that Mead's thought in both its particulars and as a whole can be properly grasped. In Mead's view, Darwin represented the triumph of the experimental method of the natural sciences over both Christian and Cartesian worldviews and prevailing materialistic and idealistic philosophies, which failed to recognize the close relationship of mind to the natural "life processes" of evolution. The development of Mead's concept of action as behavior directed toward the performance of problem-solving tasks would have been impossible without Darwin's notion of the centrality of adaptation to changing life conditions in the struggle of natural species to survive. Darwin's work on the expressive behavior of animals was influential in the importance that Mead attached to the communicative gesture as the means by which humans interacted symbolically. Relatedly, in Mead's view the constitution of meaning was inseparable from the problem-solving situation in which communicative acts occurred and the broader set of life circumstances in which individuals changed the forms of their social existence through processes of adjustment.

Of considerable consequence, the theory of evolution, along with that of relativity, also provided Mead with a general model for locating mind and action in the relationships of past, present, and future as phases in the temporal formation and transformation of social relations and the self. This is nowhere more apparent than in *The Philosophy of the Present,* based on lecture notes in which Mead formulated his most general and foundational ideas shortly before his death. Although developed after his better-known social psychological theories in *Mind, Self, and Society,* this final part of his work provides the unifying philosophical conceptions of temporality and relativity from which his unique conception of the social arose and through which we get a sense of Mead's comprehensive understanding of the dynamic character of human life and culture.

According to Mead, "reality exists in a present" (Mead 1932: 1). What we call "the past" and "the future" are nonexistent in the sense that they have a reality only through a present from which they both emanate (Miller 1973: 173). For Mead, the present contains "everything," so to speak, insofar as human experience only takes place *in* a present. Mead's discussion of the relationships among past, present, and future was an attempt to follow through the implications of the scientific theory of relativity. Consistent with a foundational approach to relativity, and contrary to Nietzsche, whose perspectivism implied subjectivistic interpretation, Mead sees new perspectives[17] arising in the natural passage from an older to a newer set of conditions, a position that David Miller (1973: 184) refers to as "objective relativism." Thus, the past undergoes continual change as a function of the passage of time and the succession of novel events that constitute an ever emerging present through which the past is redefined according to objectively changed conditions. Our sense of the past, therefore, must forever remain tentative. By implication, Mead maintains, "we must have the same hypothetical attitude toward the past that we have toward the future" (Miller 1973: 175). By this account, evolution offers a theory of emergence, or novelty, a conception implying that previous states are unable to completely explain the rise of new ones because of the indeterminate consequences of change. Emergence, then, is an objectively creative process generating new problems and adaptations and corresponding forms of life and consciousness. Within this framework, Mead regards mind and action as developing within experience itself as formed by a continually emerging present. Just as nature in the Darwinian perspective is continually evolving in a way that shapes and conditions change in organisms, so does the social life of the individual undergo a process of evolutionary development. As Mead put it, "the social and psychological process is but an instance of what takes place in nature, if nature is an evolution" (Mead 1932: 173–74).[18]

Contained in these assertions is the outline of a comprehensive philosophical system based on the principle of what Mead called "sociality," which he referred to as "the principle and form of emergence" (Mead 1932: 85). It was perhaps Mead's boldest and most innovative move to construct a conception of the social from the ideas of temporality and relativity inhering in the evolution of nature, and correlatively to see the social as part of the natural world while conversely understanding nature as operating according to what he came to regard as inherently social principles. For both, although on different levels of intelligence and expression, life is governed by the principle of emergence, and it is within the phenomenon of emergence that the social resides: "The social nature of the present *arises out of its emergence.* I am referring to the process of *readjustment* that emergence involves" (Mead 1932: 47; emphasis added). Sociality, then, describes the phase of transition from an older order or state of affairs—what Mead calls a "system," in apparent reference to a "referential system" (Joas 1985: 182)—to a newer one as facilitated by acts of adjustment. Mead here is positing *the social as the defining characteristic of any situation in which change necessitates processes of adjustment among different entities* (biological organisms, persons, social groups) that as a result of evolutionary development *belong simultaneously to more than one system.* The social arises and has its very existence and raison d'être in adaptive evolutionary processes requiring acts of mutual adjustment among separate beings.

The historical and transitional character of the adjustment process means that the social is intrinsically *multiperspectival* since it is generated within the passage from one perspective to another: "The social character of the universe we find in the situation in which the novel event is in both the old order and the new which its advent heralds. *Sociality is the capacity of being several things at once*" (Mead 1932: 49; emphasis added). Being able to take two or more points of view simultaneously and to recognize the relationship among them is not only the origin of the problems addressed by the theory of relativity (Joas 1985: 188) but constitutes the very beginnings of the social. Thus, the social is inherently heterogeneous, dependent on the ability of the organism to adopt several viewpoints, attitudes, and understandings at a time, or to assume what today might be called "multiple positionality." While multiple positionality might only be ascertainable at a given point in time, a feature of "the present" that is our lived reality, it is clear that Mead understood its genesis to be temporal by nature and thus part of a situationally based historical process of change. Moreover, the multiple positionality of the organism is clearly *necessitated* by the task of adjusting perspectives and practices in the sequential shift from one system to another and is therefore *built into* the very condition of sociality. Put differently, without change and its accompanying demands to adjust, the condition of multiplicity and therefore the social could not arise.

Mead's theory of sociality serves as a solution to the problems associated with defining consciousness as something inwardly and immediately given in the experience of the ego. Consciousness in Mead's view comes into existence *outwardly* as a result of the passage of events in the sensuous world and the experience of newness inherent in the duration of time. Thinking occurs only when novelty disrupts habitual patterns, calling for adjustment to a new set of conditions (Miller 1973: 194). As Mead (1932) stated, "It is here that mental life arises—with this continual passing from one system to another" (85). Consciousness is genetically and functionally based in the objective necessities of the life process itself, emerging as a strategic mental response to changing conditions and situations, that is, to new perceptions and information.

Such a conception of mind and consciousness is by itself a significant accomplishment in the search for a post-Cartesian model of the subject. Mead takes the decisive step toward this goal, however, by linking the formation of consciousness to social interaction. Thought is activated not merely or even primarily through the reflexive capacities of the mind itself but, rather, in response to the presence and attitudes of *others*. There is nothing innate or essential about a consciousness that is socially produced. Mead's concept of sociality thus leads directly to a theory of intersubjectivity (Habermas 1987b, 1992; Joas 1985) based on a self-reflexive process of taking the attitudes and roles of others in organized social situations. For Mead, the consequence of sociality is that subjects are constituted *interactively* in a shared and mutually responsive process of adaptation. Evolutionary adjustment in thought and behavior necessarily takes place within a community of action.

What Mead effectively proposes is a social theory of "practical intersubjectivity" (Joas 1985: 13) founded in a naturalistic model of the mutual interdependencies created by evolutionary processes of adaptation. Given its implications for a theory of society, culture, and politics, and its diverse origins in a critique of the philosophy and science of his time,[19] his understanding of intersubjectivity is perhaps Mead's greatest achievement.[20] By defining sociality in naturalistic terms and regarding mind as "only the culmination of that sociality which is found throughout the universe" (Mead 1932: 86), Mead establishes intersubjectivity as the ontological ground of all thought and action. This makes it possible to posit consciousness in the form of a functional entity constituted by the social relations of problem solving. The solitary ego is thus abandoned once and for all for a subjectivity that has its genesis in relations with others and through organized communal actions. Not only are thought and meaning socially produced and mediated, their social production both generates and depends on the capacity for self-consciousness. As Mead demonstrates, social interaction is thus also the genesis and foundation of a reflexive self. Cognition and rationality, therefore, are based in the self's ability to take others *into account* while determining through internal mental deliberations one's *own actions.* This assumes, further, the socially shared possession of symbolic systems of communication. As Habermas (1992) states, "Symbolically mediated interaction allows one to *monitor and control one's own behavior* through self-referential cognition" (179; emphasis in original).

In contrast to contemporary constructionisms, Mead's approach demonstrates that social processes not only shape subjectivity and identity but in turn depend on perceptual and definitional processes inherent to the self, processes without which social construction would be blind and mechanistic. At the same time, his intersubjective model of the self purges subjectivity of idealistic tendencies while preserving its "meaningful" components. Thus, Mead is able to save the subject within a constructionist framework by demonstrating the social bases of subjectivity, on the one hand, and the bases of action in self-reflexivity, on the other.

What finally grounds Mead's view of the subject is his theory of the self, the important category that translates sociality into an action framework. Temporality inheres in the self, of course, since the self is *aware* of and thinks and acts in relation to past, present, and future (Miller 1973: 47). It is in this sense that the self is the concrete embodiment and manifestation of sociality, that is, the self, constituted in the social process, exists logically and psychologically in time. In the following passage, Mead locates the self ("the social reflective individual") in the temporal structure of sociality:

> The biologic individual lives in an undifferentiated now; the social reflective individual takes this up into a flow of experience within which stands a fixed past and a more or less uncertain future. . . . The immediacy of the now is never lost, and the biologic individual stands as the unquestioned reality in the minds of differently constructed pasts and projected futures. (quoted in Joas 1985: 189, from the appendix to *Mind, Self, and Society*)

The past is the source of the present attitudes of the self, but *as* selves individuals in the present are continually reconstructing the past in order to anticipate and plan for the future. Mead thus sees all action and the self referred to the future (Joas 1985: 192).

Of course, as the very word *self* indicates, what distinguishes the self is its *reflexiveness* (Lee 1945: 66). In a well-known statement, Mead (1934) asserts, "The self has the characteristic that it is an object to itself, and that characteristic distinguishes it from other objects and from the body" (200). A consciousness of oneself as an object in the world is the very basis of that reflexiveness that internally and actively connects the individual to others. As Miller (1973) argues, "to be an object to oneself is to be aware of the meaning one's gesture has to the other participant (or participants) in the social act" (46). It is, further, "to be aware of one's behavior as a part of the social process of adjustment" (47). Self-reflection, therefore, similarly has a temporal structure, and selfhood means "the continuously active, reconstructive processing of occurrences and the planning of actions" (Joas 1985: 192).

The self "arises in social experience" (Mead 1934: 204) in the sense that the self internalizes the exchange of stimulus and response that occurs in the "conversation of gestures" (Mead 1934: 205) constituting social interaction.[21] This capacity of being both subject *and* object, then, is what defines the self and is where its social nature is to be located. The individual acts as a self by symbolically stimulating and responding to itself *from the standpoint of others*. Here we find Mead's argument that the self develops and operates through a process of "taking the role of others" (1934: 216). This process involves an awareness both of the influence of others on one's own behavior and of how one's behavior shapes the responses of others. Role taking means that in gesturing to oneself through internal conversation, "one's implicit response is functionally identical with the response that that gesture evokes in the other" (Miller 1973: 48).

The constitution of the self in social experience has at least three important consequences. First, it means that the self is fundamentally a *social* self in the explicit sense that mind and behavior are an expression of the larger community of normative or consensual action to which the individual belongs. This is captured in Mead's notion of the "generalized other," the commonly shared social meanings of the group that guide the behavior of the individual. Mead makes it clear that the generalized other is the locus of social determination:

> It is in the form of the generalized other that the social process influences the behavior of the individuals involved in it and carrying it on, that is, that the community exercises *control* over the conduct of its individual members; for it is in this form that the social process or community enters as a *determining* factor into the individual's thinking. (Mead 1934: 219–20; emphasis added)

Further, it is the generalized other that serves as the source of abstract and rational thought. Indeed, Mead argues, "only by taking the attitude of the generalized other toward himself . . . can [the individual] think at all" (1934). Second, Mead sees the generalized other as imparting to the individual a "unity of self" (218), implying that the self *is* a unity and that self-identity has a unity that stems from an internalization of the socially organized attitudes of the group.

Third, by implication, the identity of the individual (self-image) has its source in the internal responses of the self to the gestures/responses of others (Joas 1985: 110). Identity is thus unequivocally socially determined. The individual knows him/herself only through the social responses of members of the group or community. In a statement in which he attempts to recognize a distinction between the particular and universal dimensions of social otherness, Mead (1934) observes, "The individual experiences himself as such, not directly, but only indirectly, from the particular standpoints of other individual members of the same social group or from the generalized standpoint of the social group as a whole to which he belongs" (202).

The framework of temporality informing Mead's conception of the self, finally, provides him a conceptual discourse about its internal structure and process that addresses the chronic problem of indeterminacy versus determinacy (chapter 1). The generalized other represents the determining social influences of the past, the self as constituted and shaped through previous referential systems. By understanding the generalized other as the presence and influence of the group in the self, Mead attributes to this influence the normative controls shaping behavior. These controls present themselves in a phase of self-functioning that Mead (1934) refers to as the Me, which he defines as "the organized set of attitudes of others which one himself assumes" (230). This is the socially determined self whose actions are in conformity with social norms. However, Mead recognizes "the sense of initiative, of freedom" (232) in the acting self and that the future-oriented outcomes of action are more or less uncertain. The phase of novelty in self-reflective action, then, he labels the I, which he defines as "the *response* of the organism to the attitudes of others" (230; emphasis added). The I is the active, creative phase of self-functioning, the "movement into the future" beyond what is given in the Me (232). While Mead's own account of the relationship between the I and the Me raises numerous problems,[22] the distinction is a rare attempt to conceptually recognize and systematize the poles of freedom and constraint within a social psychology of the self. It serves, further, as a compelling example of Mead's insistence on a processual and functional approach to the self that is reflective of the principle of emergence: "The self is essentially a social process going on with these two distinguishable phases. If it did not have these two phases, there could not be conscious responsibility and there would be nothing novel in experience" (Mead 1934: 233). Thus, the self is seen by Mead as an intersection of past and future, constraint and freedom, through which the social determinations accompanying membership in organized society encounter the unformed, creative impulses of the active organism.

Gesture, Symbolic Interaction, and Meaning:
Mead and Voloshinov on the Social Nature of Language

Mead's consideration of language seems insignificant compared to the extensive developments in linguistic theory in the twentieth century and the strong predilections toward language and discourse analysis in the textual approaches of recent work in cultural studies and related fields. While falling short of the achievements of the language philosophers, Mead's ideas are nonetheless remarkably similar to the claims of these thinkers, many of whom likewise came to recognize language as an objective vehicle of thought whose domain was the entire complex of social practices. The resemblances between Mead's writings and Ludwig Wittgenstein's later work, for example, moved David Miller (1973) to comment, "Parts of the *Blue Book,* the *Brown Book,* and the *Investigations* read as if Wittgenstein had been communicating with the deceased Mr. Mead but had received only Mead's conclusions and not the experiential basis of arriving at them" (76).

Something similar could be said of a comparison between Mead and the obscure Russian writer Valentin N. Voloshinov.[23] Despite the Marxist thematics and inflection of his *Marxism and the Philosophy of Language* (1973), Voloshinov develops a series of arguments about the social character of language that are so astonishingly parallel to Mead that one imagines the former author as having simply read and paraphrased the latter's work.[24] Both thinkers acquire special significance at a time when the preoccupation with language has been burdened by a failure to recognize its inherently social character and functions. Mead's social psychological approach in combination with Voloshinov's forceful arguments for the social nature of language, therefore, provides a provocative corrective to the prevailing textualist paradigm.

Because he understood language as integral to the social process, Mead's remarks on this subject are thoroughly interwoven with his social psychological analyses.[25] Mead posits language as a fundamental condition of social life and as serving an essential function in interaction, through which it is constituted along with mind and self. The underpinnings of Mead's understanding of language are his social behaviorism and the essentially social functions he sees language performing. As Habermas (1987a) has shown, Mead demonstrates the evolution and social functions of language as following three developmental stages. First, Mead reduces language to its nonsymbolic behavioral rudiments in nature—the gestures and responses of animals. Borrowing from the psychologist Wilhelm Wundt, Mead (1934) defines the gesture as "that part of the social act which serves as a stimulus to other forms involved in the same social act" (154). Gestures are beginnings of social acts that call forth responses in others, which in turn become gestures, in a back-and-forth exchange that comprises the conversation of gestures mentioned above. In this early phase of communication, the meaning of an act is constituted naturally and objectively in "species-specific environments" (Habermas 1987a: 7). Second, when gestural exchange attains the level of human interaction, stimulus-response mechanisms are transformed into symbolic meanings. This involves a subjective "internalizing of objective structures of meaning" (Habermas 1987a: 7–8) whereby reflective subjects come to understand the meanings of each other's gestures symbolically and intersubjectively. When an initial gesture arouses an intended response in an other, thereby evoking an identical *idea* or *meaning*, it becomes a "significant symbol" (Mead 1934: 157). For Mead, communication occurs when a response reflects a gesture, in the sense that it gives reciprocal behavioral expression to the *same meaning*. In Mead's understanding, the basic function of language is to stimulate action in the social process of adjustment, in the form of "responses that lead to the completion of the act" (Miller 1973: 73). In Mead's view, language thus serves a strictly behavioral function; behavior could not possibly occur without language, and it would be difficult to imagine the latter except in the context of a field of action. Third, but less clearly worked out by Mead, actors learn appropriate social behavior through the process of role taking, which involves the structuring of language by social roles. In this final stage, symbolically mediated interaction is further transformed into "normatively regulated action" in which the socially functional use of language by actors acquires a "normatively binding" character (Habermas 1987a: 8).[26] The evolution of language is thus seen by Mead as paralleling the development of the symbolic capacities of the self made not only possible but necessary by the evolution of social relations themselves.

In the work of Voloshinov, the situatedness of language in social relations is stated even more strongly, but from a standpoint that complements the behavioral emphases of Mead with a semiotic stance. Language for Voloshinov is not the condition of a social psychology of behavior but the theoretical point of departure for a more general (and "revisionist") view of social and cultural production. Influenced strongly by Saussure, Voloshinov gives primacy to the idea of language as a system of signs whose meanings are shaped by their ideological content. But Voloshinov is interested in showing the inseparability of language from the social process itself and thus immediately places language in the context of social or group interaction, equating the "sign function" to the "social function" (Voloshinov 1973: 29).[27] In effect, he is searching for a theory that is at once semiotic and sociological, positing language not as a system, as in Saussure, but a process operating within the contingencies of social existence. Like Mead, Voloshinov regards language as an inherent part of the social dynamics of group life, seeing language as involving the active participation of speakers and writers.

In remarkable analogy to Mead, Voloshinov equates "verbal interaction" to "social interaction," saying that the specificity of language "consists precisely in its being located between organized individuals, in its being a medium of their communication" (12). Furthermore, Voloshinov shares Mead's view of the external origins of both consciousness and language, sounding literally like Mead in his claim that "social psychology . . . is not located anywhere within . . . but entirely and completely *without*—in the word, the gesture, the act" (19; emphasis in original). However, where Mead makes gesture the main unit of language, Voloshinov refers to the "utterance" as that which "is constructed between two socially organized persons" (85). Indeed, in the introduction (dated 1929), Voloshinov characterizes "*the productive role and social nature of the utterance*" as "the fundamental idea of our entire work" (xv; emphasis in original).

For both thinkers, language embodies and reflects the emergent character of social life, specifically its changing situations and meanings. Voloshinov elaborates this conception more fully than Mead, arguing that if we were to consider language objectively, "we would discover no inert system of self-identical norms. Instead, we would find ourselves witnessing the ceaseless generation of language norms" (66). And in a further echo of Mead on the same page, Voloshinov states that "language presents the picture of a ceaseless flow of becoming."[28] Language thus evolves along with the social "life process," and its norms change in accordance with the norms of society. At the same time, while acknowledging its processual character, both thinkers recognize in language the locus of social structure and vice versa. For Mead, this follows the rather vague boundaries of the generalized other, which limits the exchange of gestures to a common normative framework given by the community, whereas for Voloshinov social structure is conceived more schematically and textually in the ideologies, interests, and situations structuring the "dialogue" among social individuals. However, Voloshinov nonetheless understands language and its social conditioning in a fundamentally Meadian fashion, referring to the "word" as

> the product of the reciprocal relationship between speaker and listener, addresser and addressee. . . . I give myself verbal shape from another's point of view, ultimately, from [that] of the community to which I belong. . . . *The immediate social situation and the broader social milieu wholly determine—and determine from within, so to speak—the structure of an utterance.* (86; emphasis in original)

Throughout his study, the semiotic influence is apparent in Voloshinov's mention of the *sign* in discussions of the social ideological content of language, but he would hardly disagree with Mead's contrasting use of the word *symbol* in accounting for the nature and consequences of social interaction.[29] Although neither thinker used the term, the concept of *symbolic interaction* captures the essence of the social workings of language and its foundational role in social reproduction and emergence.[30] From Mead's account of the conversation of gestures, it is apparent that he understands the symbol in behavioral terms but as constituted only in *social* relationships, as a vehicle for the meaning of *shared* gestures and attitudes:

> The internalization in our experience of the external conversations of gestures which we carry on with other individuals in the social process is the essence of thinking; and the gestures thus internalized are significant symbols because they have the *same meanings* for all individual members of the given society or social group. (Mead 1934: 159; emphasis added)

As "shared meanings," then, symbols function as means of communication in the social process of adjustment. Their purpose is to evoke and facilitate action by *constituting* objects of action in the conscious awareness of the individual. Language as external gesturing, or "body-related expressions" (Joas 1985: 115), thus becomes internalized in the form of symbolic meaning. Relatedly, for Voloshinov language exists externally in the social relations of its use: "The organizing center of any utterance, of any experience, is not within but outside—in the social milieu surrounding the individual being" (1973: 93). Voloshinov focuses on the socially active dimensions of language: "*The actual reality of language-speech is not the abstract system of linguistic forms . . . but the social event of verbal interaction implemented in an utterance or utterances*" (94; emphasis in original). Leaving no doubt as to the interactive character of language use, he concludes, "Thus, *verbal interaction* is the basic reality of language" (94; emphasis added). Finally, Voloshinov expresses the ongoing nature of language as symbolic interaction even more explicitly than Mead, stating, "Any utterance . . . is only a moment in the continuous process of verbal communication" (95). The emergent character of verbal communication is to be explained, moreover, not in terms of the formal semiotic workings of language but in relation to the changeful and productive character of social life itself. Communication is therefore, in turn, "only a moment in the continuous, all-inclusive, generative process of a given social collective" (95).

Meaning, or that which is conveyed by the gestural acts comprising language, is for Mead inseparable from the social act as a whole. Meaning does not inhere in language, and certainly not in the psychical states of individuals, but, rather, originates in a field of action. Meaning is the "central factor" in the adjustive relationship between gesture and response among organisms, but it is given primarily in the *response* that completes the social act (Mead 1934: 163). As Mead phrases the matter, "Response on the part of the second organism to the gesture of the first is the interpretation—and brings out the meaning—of that gesture" (167). These formulations make it clear that for Mead the origins of meaning are purely social and inseparable from the intents and purposes of social actors and the completion of their acts. Meaning arises, then, in "the relations among actors that are established by their actions" (Joas 1985: 100). In other places, Mead strives to define meaning also in terms of the problem-solving tasks toward which action is directed (Joas 1985: 101). But the implication of Mead's social psychology is that meaning is generated only *interactively*, immediately produced by the social situation, and thus only indirectly a function of language.

The concept of meaning is troublesome under any circumstances, and Mead's social psychological formulations of meaning sometimes lack clarity. As with much of his thought, Mead's treatment of language and meaning is highly general and abstract. Moreover, he tends to reduce language to gestural exchanges among organisms and the symbolic mediations of social interaction, neglecting the structural relations and substance of language itself.[31] Yet Mead sets forth a provocative conception of the pragmatic implications and nature of linguistic meaning by situating it directly in social interaction. By means of this strategy, and in congruence with his basic theoretical approach, he defines meaning objectively as having its own existence outside the mind: "Meaning is thus a development of something objectively there as a relation between certain phases of the social act" (Mead 1934: 163). As Habermas (1987a) claims, for Mead, "meaning is systemic" (7). Meaning, Mead goes on to argue, "need not be conscious at all, and is not in fact until significant symbols are evolved in the process of human social experience" (1934: 168). Meaning thus originates prelinguistically, existing prior to consciousness in "the objective structure of the active relation of an organism to a determinate component of its environment" (Joas 1985: 116).

While seeing himself as a critic of philosphical idealism, Mead was not completely immune to charges of idealism and formalism in his social psychology.[32] This is evident in the primacy he gives to the role of socially generated symbolic meanings in the shaping of consciousness and perception. To Mead (1934), the world of objects is literally created through the social meanings we attach to them: "Objects are constituted in terms of meanings within the social process of experience and behavior" (164). The objects inhabiting our experience of the world are not only made accessible to consciousness but are literally brought into existence by the social definitional process:

> Symbolization constitutes objects not constituted before, objects which would not exist except for the context of social relationships wherein symbolization occurs. Language does not simply symbolize a situation or object which is

already there in advance; it makes possible the existence or the appearance of that situation or object, for it is a part of the mechanism whereby that situation or object is created. (Mead 1934: 165)

Our very sense of reality, including the material world, therefore undergoes change as a result of the emergence of new meanings, understood as generated within the social process. In perhaps his most direct concession to the powers of language, Mead claims that the symbolizing process constitutes experience, shaping and conditioning our perceptions and definitions of the world of objects.

Meadian Sociality and the Social Production of Identity and Difference

The companion themes of identity and difference have occupied a central place in poststructuralist work, the burgeoning fields of cultural and sex and gender studies heavily influenced by poststructuralism, and the wider arena of postmodern thought. Given its curiosities in the instabilities of language and the constructed and constructing character of discourse, poststructuralism has posed a number of provocative questions about the nature of identity and difference in the context of social and cultural relations. As we have seen, poststructuralists have challenged not only popular and scholarly conceptions of identity but the very idea of identity itself, thematizing in its place various politicized notions of difference, particularity, and otherness, understanding these primarily in terms of the discursive or cultural relationships between dominants and subordinates.

The theory of self is the logical place to begin an analysis of identity formation as this occurs in relation to social and cultural differences. Yet an even stronger starting point, and one that certainly includes the self, is Mead's important concept of sociality. This concept provides a penetrating understanding of difference as an inherent feature of social relations and change. The remainder of this chapter completes the critique of poststructuralism by unveiling in Mead's sociality the basic rudiments of a theory of difference. This concluding discussion also suggests ways in which Mead's pragmatism can be reread as anticipating many of the issues raised by postmodernists while offering what might be regarded as "revisionist" modernist solutions.

By shifting the focus of philosophy to the realm of practical problem solving, Mead's pragmatism established movement and development as the sine qua non of human existence. In this view, meaning remains in a continual state of flux as a consequence of processes of adjustment to changing social conditions. While poststructuralists see plurality and instability as inherent in discursive practices, manifested as "particularity" and "difference," Meadian pragmatism has always apprehended particularity and difference as necessary features of a social world in motion.

As indicated in the discussion of his philosophy of the present, the overlapping of what Mead thinks of as "referential systems" created by the passage of time produces a naturally multiperspectival social order. For Mead, *change* is the underlying dynamic of the social world—that is, multiplicity is generated temporally. The ongoing succession of perspectives implied in the principle of emergence points to an inherently differentiated and discontinuous symbolic order constituted of multiple meaning systems. If, as a consequence, sociality is in the words of Mead "the capacity of being several things at once" (1932: 49), then the subject is necessarily multiply positioned. Mead would thus see relations of difference as the temporal intersections of history giving structure to the self. But Mead would understand these relations of difference as *constituting* identity rather than *fragmenting* it, as in the poststructuralist and more generally postmodernist versions.[33] In this respect, Mead would be in basic agreement with Diana Fuss, who has argued that poststructuralists have tended to locate difference *outside* rather than *inside* identity, dispersing it in heterogeneity (1989: 103). In contrast, Mead theorizes difference as implicit in the shaping of the subject within the temporality of social relations. Thus, the phenomenon of difference is *incorporated into* the formation of self-identity. In place of the disunities of the subject that poststructuralists attribute to discursive practices, Mead posits a unity achieved through a socially integrated but multiply determined self. Mead understands multiplicity, then, as the underlying structuring principle of identity. Here, the particularities of objects and situations are subjectively *internalized* as the elements from which self-identity is being continually formed *through* its encounter with difference.

Mead's concept of sociality, furthermore, presupposes that the differences shaping the adaptive responses of the self have relational characteristics. The differentiation of experience engendered by and engendering perspectival change can therefore be conceived of as "internal relations of difference" within the self, insofar as the self assumes many points of reference simultaneously. While having a very different understanding of the processes involved, Mead therefore tacitly recognizes the *relational* status of meaning and identity presupposed by semiotics, structuralism, and poststructuralism. The social for Mead, however, arises *within* and *because* of the play of difference generated by *change*. The attribution of meaning, then, is part and parcel of its determination by the relational differences comprising any given situation. In short, meaning is produced by difference, but this meaning is always *social*. Whereas in the structuralist perspective meaning production is a function of the formal relationships of language, and in poststructuralism the social, cultural, and political instabilities of discourse, Mead understands meaning and difference as inherent in processes of social adaptation. By defining it as sociality, Mead effectively demonstrates that the social—the basis for the development of the self—necessarily exists in difference, and vice versa. Social relationality, therefore, implies difference just as difference presupposes social relations.

Mead's conception provides the elements of a model of intersubjectivity that transposes the problem of the subject-object relationship into the problem of identity and difference. Peter Dews (1987) has argued that in our present theoretical situation the task of reconciliation now belongs to a working out of the "interplay of identity and non-identity" (231). Whereas poststructuralism fails to engage this new dialectic properly by positing either objective processes of textuality, power, and desire, on the one hand, or a subjectivized perspectivism, on the other, Mead implicitly attempts to demonstrate the necessary interdependence of identity and nonidentity in the constitution of the self. In doing so, he reformulates subjectivity as a problem of social relations, moving toward an intersubjectivity that would retain, in Dews's (1987: 232) words, "the relation to the other which is constitutive of subjectivity." Mead contributes profoundly to an understanding of the ways that the formation of subjectivity depends on social encounters. The socially shared process of symbolically mediated adjustment could be understood as providing precisely what poststructuralism lacks, what Dews (1987) describes as "a concept of individuation as an identity which is developed and sustained through the awareness of nonidentity" (233).

Mead's translation of his philosophy of emergence into a practically based social psychology of action positions him historically as the original constructionist. In his view, the evolution of life forms and the succession and multiplicity of perspectives, while immanent to nature, are more centrally a product of the activity of social selves individually and collectively pursuing their practical interests. Mead demonstrates that consciousness, far from pregiven, is formed in practical problem-solving activity, in the social relations of adjustment, and in the symbolic constructions of language as they reflect and shape these processes. For Mead, then, human consciousness, while manifest only in discursive acts, is actively constructed—and even more importantly *re*constructed—through social interaction. Discursive practices would be understood by Mead as social practices with a practical intent, and the construction of self and identity as a product of socially structured and continually evolving problem-solving relations among actors. The legacy of symbolic interactionism within the field of sociology, indeed, has been to affirm a counterargument against structuralist and macro-oriented theoretical models (for example, structural functionalism) by arguing that *structure* is simply a name for the patterned effects of social action, an argument forcefully made by Mead's student Herbert Blumer (1969). Within this tradition, furthermore, we find a strong precedent for contemporary constructionist thinking in what has been called "labeling theory," which understands the construction of identity as an effect of the discursive practices of social authorities attempting to regulate and control the behavior of subordinates and marginals (Becker 1963, 1964; Erikson 1966; Matza 1969; Rubington and Weinberg 1978; Sarbin and Kitsuse 1994). Thus, while converging with poststructuralism in the idea that identity and difference are constructed, Meadian theory offers a more comprehensive and potentially grounded framework by focusing attention on the *social processes* of construction.

As suggested earlier, Mead and the poststructuralists find common ground in their shared idea of the epistemological primacy of language and the related concerns of social meaning and interpretation. Yet poststructuralism persistently deprivileges the social and subjective elements of language and discourse. This is linked to a recurring problem of poststructuralism: while arguing that identity and difference are constituted in discourse, poststructuralists seldom if ever demonstrate, either theoretically or empirically, how real or potential instabilities (whether understood as resistances, subversions, deviancy, and so on) might arise within actually existing human practices. Most poststructuralists seem to divorce the structuring of identity and difference from the actual social practices and material sites of action and struggle around which identities and differences get defined. At the same time, poststructuralists have substantially advanced our understanding of the intimate connections between culture and power. The mutually constitutive effects of power relations and discursive formations provide an account of the hierarchical structuring of identity and difference in society and the particular cultural forms this takes. In this respect, Mead and the symbolic interactionist perspective generally need to be faulted for a neglect of questions of power. Here, it is important to acknowledge that the voluntaristic pragmatist emphasis on action, interaction, and community might seem from this angle more like an idealistic vision of democracy than a realistic and concrete assessment of social and cultural relations.

Mead nevertheless presents a fertile and provocative alternative to postmodernist and poststructuralist theories of identity and difference. Beginning with a naturalistic theory of language as gesture and response, Mead develops a conception of language as symbolic interaction and social control, stressing the communicative functions of language through the sharing of common symbols. Clearly, his remarks on language are still made from within an assumption of consciousness as a necessary ground of action. Also, by privileging the notion of *communication* he concentrates on language as a vehicle of universal understanding, taking seriously the etymological connection between "communication" and "community." Thus, in contrast to the poststructuralists, who emphasize the dispersive effects of language, Mead perceives language as a vehicle of shared symbolic meaning, a set of practices with formative and unifying effects. In a modernist vein, then, Mead regards language as a path toward universal knowledge, however tentatively won. While his conception of sociality as multiple positionality could be read as an anticipation of postmodern identity, Mead sees language as enabling a unity of self. For him, language accommodates and synthesizes disparate meanings, making it possible to negotiate the transition from one perspective to another. In place of discursive fragmentation, Mead therefore sees a linguistic potential for shared understandings, unity, and organization. By implication, it is through the use and workings of language as a symbolic system that difference can be contained and recognized *within* identity.

What distinguishes Mead's thought in this regard is its reconciliation of flux with a structuring of experience as social meaning, a resolution without loss of social difference within social identity. Mead presents a distinctive conception of the inherent instability of meaning that allows for social continuity and provisional unity. First of all, giving it a naturalistic foundation—locating it in the social relations of adjustment—Mead sees symbolic meanings as continually generated from within the objective conditions of change but as simultaneously shaped by the social actions and meanings that *facilitate* this change. The problematization of meaning is thus socially shared and overcome as the precondition and resultant of the act (1934) as carried out by social subjects. Second, while thus given an objective basis, meaning is nevertheless constructed symbolically by actors. Situationally shaped, adjustment is still an interpretive process resulting in the discarding of old meanings and the formation of new ones. The I of Mead's self is an interpretive figure, opening the door to a continuous process of interpretation and reinterpretation of the social meaning of objects and events. On both objective and subjective levels, then, meaning is drawn into a dialectical process of problematization and reconstruction as a means of moving action forward. Action, therefore, is marked by alternating phases of symbolic disjunction and integration.

Identity and difference thus dwell within sociality. Unlike the many postmodernists who see only fragmentation and disunity in social and cultural life, Mead saw a multifariousness rooted in the principle of emergence and contained within the unifying and universalizing potentialities of language and self. Refusing to take "sides," Mead viewed plurality and unity as alternating and ongoing *phases* of the social universe. Significantly, his very concept of the social presupposed difference, but it was this difference that provided the materials for the constitution of a social self and, by implication, of identity.

Conclusion: On the Rejoining of Subjects and Objects

The dilemmas of the poststructuralist position originate in a displacement of the earlier idealisms, which sanctified innate consciousness, to an objectified realm of textuality where the ego is dispersed in discourse. Instead of constructing a conception of the relations of subject and object that might reconcile them, poststructuralism simply reverses the Cartesian order of privileging, creating an objectivistic idealism/materialism in which the very concept of meaning is forcefully reduced to discursive relations of difference. This new "metaphysics of the text," as it has been called, leaves the perennial problems of consciousness unsolved. Without a theory of how consciousness is constituted socially and symbolically, it is impossible to account for identity formation or to reflect on the dynamics and consequences of difference.

The naturalistically and symbolically based pragmatist social psychology of Mead provides the tools for theorizing how identity develops within a social process while appreciating its discursive character. As Mead demonstrates, the idea of a self remains a necessary precondition for redeeming subjectivity in the face of objectivistic and culturally reified accounts that, while revealing the power of signification, ultimately imprison our understanding of human behavior within the boundaries of language and discourse.

Conclusion
Postmodernity and Its Theoretical Consequences

Theory refracts without necessarily speaking to or beyond the limits of its times. This seems especially true of the era of postmodernity. Popular varieties of postmodernism and poststructuralism exhibit strongly reifying attachments to the social and political contexts in which they arose and the broad cultural changes privileging discourse and notions of particularity and contingency in contemporary academic work. While appropriately preoccupied with questions of identity and difference, much contemporary theory not only neglects the structural and institutional aspects of these questions but lacks a critical perspective on social and cultural change.

In a sense, the inadequacies of theory today are a problem inseparable from the overly culturalized and fragmented condition of postmodernity itself. Ironically, what poststructuralism alleges theoretically of discourse could be claimed as well for the circumstances of *theorizing about* discourse. The dominant modes of theorizing today are often unduly conditioned by the workings of contemporary culture itself, uncritically reproducing the basic structures, conditions, and values of consumption society. The prevailing focus on culture, and the reproduction of the consumptionist stance in work on culture, is itself a structural problem, in a number of senses. Consumer culture has foreclosed certain theoretical possibilities, limiting the terrain on which theorists work, reframing the problems they work on, and relocating the "subjects" they study. To the extent that society and politics themselves have been absorbed in the cultural field, it is difficult for scholars to avoid doing cultural analysis. But the unprecedented concentration on issues of culture and discourse and the specific manner in which they have been addressed are partially attributable to the social class and disciplinary structures of contemporary academia as well as the "politically correct" interests of theorists and researchers whose training and political experience predispose them to certain kinds of problems and theoretical conceptualizations. This has been exacerbated by the relatively slow response of the social sciences and particularly social theory to the issues emerging around the concept of the postmodern situation, allowing the cultural turn in academe to be shaped largely by the perspectives and methods of the humanities. Thus, while a concentration on culture represents an appropriate response to a culturalization of society, this concept has become too exhaustive (and exhausted), too overworked and encumbered by special intellectual and political preoccupations, absorbing that which surrounds it in a fashion reminiscent of the larger society. Accordingly, we should question whether theory has lost a desired critical perspective in becoming too identified with the actually existing society and culture.

Writing as a social theorist, I have attempted to draw connections between social and cultural change and underlying transformations in economic and technological structures and conditions in order to synthesize major features of the work of such scholars as David Harvey, Fredric Jameson, Jean Baudrillard, Scott Lash, and others who appreciate the material and historical conditions of cultural production and transformation. I see this body of work and my own writing as in certain respects a continuation of the epistemological and methodological stance of the sociology of knowledge. Accordingly, I am here situating theory itself as part of the larger ties that bind cultural transformation and its material foundations.

But I have attempted in this work to reintroduce the sociology of knowledge as a method and ground of social and cultural critique. My rather sweeping look at salient features of postmodernity is an attempt at diagnostic intervention in the problem of identity. While not sociological in the conventional sense, my discussion has sought to establish a sociohistorical ground for addressing questions of identity and difference that translates the issues raised by *postmodernism* into a series of analytical problems of *postmodernity* as a set of cultural, social, and political conditions. Looking behind identity politics to the larger societal changes generating them, my analysis has focused on the problematization of identity in the transition from modern to postmodern society as this has occurred in the postwar United States. I have attempted to show that with transformations in the social and cultural conditions of identity formation resulting from technological and economic change there has emerged a generalized condition of identity *destabilization*. The closely interrelated but distinct and separate processes of cultural fragmentation and pluralization intrinsic to this destabilization constitute the basic postmodern problematic of identity and difference and represent the axes around which identity politics has arisen and foundered. While recognizing the limits of periodization, a theory of postmodernity, I have argued, must ground itself in the economic, technological, social, cultural, and political dynamics of these processes. As a theory of identity crises, a theory of postmodernity would account for how fragmentation and pluralization have contributed to a decline in modern conceptions of identity, on one level, and how these processes have transformed the means and goals of identity formation, on another level. The destabilizing effects of both changes, I have argued, illuminate the peculiar configurations of a culture in which the commercial and political aspects of postmodernity elaborately intersect. Across this intersection we find a signifying terrain in which identities have become fragmented by mass culture as well as reinvigorated and reunified by strategies of cultural renewal both revivalist and innovative.

It is into this particular fray that I believe theoretical and cultural critique must venture. Theoretical gaps and conflicts in our understanding of identity and difference reflect the tensions and dilemmas surrounding them in the real world, calling for more materially and institutionally grounded analyses. As a modest beginning, I have proposed reconceptualizing the postmodern themes of identity and difference in terms of social as well as discursive relations. Despite my emphasis on the social, by arguing that social and discursive practices mutually constitute each other, I have suggested deploying a social relational approach not to replace but, rather, to *complement* and thus strategically *resituate* the reigning textualist approaches to culture. The suggestive affinities between poststructuralism and Meadian social pragmatism at this historical moment would seem to be in large measure a reflection of the pertinence of each to the sense of contingency and possibility surrounding the proliferation of discourse characterizing postmodern culture. The stress that both place on language and discourse, the multiplicity of meaning, and the emergent features of cultural practices makes them natural allies for a theory that addresses the issues raised throughout this book. In addition to resonating the concerns expressed in my analysis, the introduction of Mead into the theoretical terrain now dominated by poststructuralism produces a necessary corrective. If we are not to lose a *social* perspective on the commodification of culture and our immersion in discourse, it seems imperative to recognize the *mutually* productive, reinforcing, and deconstructive effects of social and discursive relations and practices.

What does it mean in this context to have a "social perspective"? First of all, it suggests a need to pursue problems of identity and difference within a context of structural and institutional analyses of society. Studies concerned with identity and difference ought to tie experiential and cultural constructions of these concepts to analyses of concrete changes in the institutional means of identity formation. Identity and cultural politics should be regarded as conditioned by material and social change and, specifically, the needs generated by structural shifts to new modes of identity formation resulting from economic and technological development. The politicization and theorization of identity, then, should be more explicitly understood in terms of the problematization of older models of identity *in the context of historical change.*

Second, and more important, adopting a social perspective involves a recognition that culture is just as much a product of social relations as it is constitutive of these relations. The emphasis on language/discourse/signification frequently forgets the underlying social bases and purposes motivating and shaping discursive practices in given societies at particular times. Theory today has invested culture with a formative and controlling power that just as surely belongs to social relations and practices themselves. It is time once again to ask where culture comes from and to explore the relationship between its production and consumption. Importantly, *production* is to be understood here not merely in a limited material (Marxist) sense but also as referring to the social capacities and actions of actors who actively shape their own and others' lives. It is in this sense that a Meadian perspective on the social interaction processes *constitutive* of cultural production and consumption can become a basis for reconceptualizing questions of identity and difference along more fertile lines. Mead's approach construes these questions socially, regarding culture as a socially produced outcome. Culture in this sense is a matter of interactively based definitional and social processes involving selves, in which cultural and social processes are understood as interdependent.

Third, and closely related, introducing a social perspective requires refocusing the themes of identity and difference on a theory of the self. Conceptualizing social relations with reference to the self not only (dare it be said?) "humanizes" social processes but provides explanatory and interpretive links between society and individual, normative regulation and emergent creation, and limiting and facilitating conditions of action—connections that textualist models leave unclear. While my analysis of postmodernity has not always given sufficient attention to the self and, indeed, has often suggested its demise, my discussion of the formative dimensions of postmodern culture associated with the process of pluralization presupposes a multiply constituted self in search of identity and meaning. In order to think the innovative and generative possibilities of postmodern culture, then, the concept of a reflexive and active self is indispensable.

Throughout my analysis I have endeavored to pose questions about changing processes of identity formation in terms of the enduring problems of freedom and constraint in theories of human behavior. The historically specific possibilities that postmodernity presents for both personal choice and limitation—self-formation and -deformation—are a recurring theme in my assessment of the impact of commodification and technology on identity-forming processes. Additionally, my analysis has attempted to address the political possibilities and liabilities of the complex relationship between processes of fragmentation, which I argue on balance thwart the self and social relations, and pluralization, which represents a set of conditions for reconstruction and reunification of identity at the level of the group and the community. A comparison and contrast of poststructuralism and Meadian social psychology have demonstrated the importance of a social conceptualization of these problems. Whereas poststructuralism seems to locate the conditions of freedom in discursive exclusions, without saying how these conditions are actually materialized, in Mead's theory freedom and constraint are relational phases of the self, ontological conditions of action. For Mead, the problem of determinacy is always only definable through the presence of real social entities. Postmodernity calls for a formulation of this problem in terms of the effects of commodified culture on the formation and functioning of social selves, the particular ways that selves are constituted, or not, in the commodified structures of discourse and technology in which an experience of self develops. While social and cultural fragmentation, specifically the attenuation of community, carries ominous implications for Mead's conception of self, the pluralizing features of postmodernity would seem to strengthen especially those parts of his conception that emphasize the play of difference in the constitution of identity. The self-determining features of the pluralizing dimensions of identity formation, with their implications of diverse and self-styled behavior, resonate with Mead's I, while the search for community and place would reflect his insights into the rootedness of the self in normative structures, or the generalized other.

It is now possible to situate Meadian thought more explicitly within the condition of postmodernity. We have seen the multiplicity inherent in Mead's conception of the socially constituted self and the intimations of difference accompanying his philosophy of a temporalized and provisional world of ongoing adaptive activity. In his efforts to structure the self into Me and I, Mead was struggling with the relationship between identity and difference in the context of social adjustment. For him, identity was achieved through difference as mediated symbolically and socially in the role-taking process. But this identity was always tentative and problematic, shaped by the plurality of perspectives defining sociality. As such, Mead could be regarded as incipiently postmodern in his view of self and society.

But at the same time, to situate Mead in the context of postmodernity, and to juxtapose him to poststructuralist renditions of culture, is to position him as a philosopher and theoretician of praxis, a thinker who saw individuals and groups struggling through their own actions to redefine and change the conditions of their lives and to reshape the forms and contents of their identifications. The active dimensions of the self conceptualized as the I, Mead implied, were an important source of social emergence through self-activity. Although his theory of the self was focused on individuals, from the corpus of his work it is clear that Mead was thinking of "collectively constituted goals in coordinated activity" (Joas 1993: 249). A Meadian notion of praxis thus describes social relations as actively constituted and changed through what actors *do*. This stands in contradistinction to a social and cultural system structured by the commodity form, in which economic and technological modes of signification have increasingly absorbed those spaces where actors would otherwise directly engage each other through communicative interactions. The absorption of social and discursive practices by mass culture places a huge weight on Meadian notions of a reflexive, role-taking self. The condition of postmodernity thus lends a strong critical dimension to a Meadian conception of praxis, insofar as postmodernity implies a set of conditions under which the self tends to fragment and atrophy.

Woven throughout my discussion of postmodernity are observations of the ways in which theory is shaped by culture. On the negative side, theory performs a reifying function, and here I have characterized postmodernism and poststructuralism as in major respects replicating the problematic features of contemporary culture. Modes of thinking and representation emphasizing fragmentation, discontinuity, and incommensurability (O'Sullivan et al. 1994: 234) reflect the eclectic features of mass culture and the disunities of identity in a world pervaded by the experience of fragmentation and difference. On the positive side, the hegemony of signification *does* require us to think of power and resistance in cultural terms, in terms of the powers and subversions of discourse. The rise of postmodern and poststructuralist theory is thus expressive of a shift to a politics of discourse in which oppositional practices are now rightly conceived in relation to prevailing modes and means of signification in society at large.

But regarding poststructuralism, there is a point at which homologies appear between the theory or method and its object, with the result that the theory comes to falsely universalize a particular set of historically specific conditions, a circumstance in which poststructuralism contradictorily departs from postmodernism. To the extent that it is premised on the presupposition that "everything is discourse," poststructuralism in this sense is turned into a reification of mass culture. This has several consequences. First of all, it binds theory to a consumptionist conception of culture, in which an exclusive concern for the effects of discursive practices reproduces the consumerist orientation of mass culture and thereby the ideology of a system in need of deconstruction. Whenever it as-

sumes an "always already existing" system of discourse, poststructuralism forecloses concerns for the production of culture, understood not just materially but
symbolically as the definitional and interpretive processes by which social selves
construct meaning in their lives, whether on the side of power or opposition. As
I have argued, a concern for resistance within cultural studies has led theorists to
address the active production of meanings at the point of consumption, a move
that further distinguishes postmodernism from poststructuralism. Because of its
limited focus on the effects and instabilities of discursive relations, however, the
latter is fundamentally ill equipped to comprehend the actual processes of cultural formation on both sides of power. In the absence of a socially formative
conception of culture, poststructuralism runs the risk of appearing as a de facto
certification of the normalizing functions of discourse. Thus, without a conception of social praxis, a tacit acceptance of the prevailing system of discursive relations seems unavoidable.

Second, while many of those committed to a progressive cultural politics
have found the poststructuralist emphasis on difference and decenteredness appealing, the premise of discursive instability stands in a problematic relationship
to other features of the postmodern condition that inhibit political struggle.
When privileged as an end in itself, difference tends to become sheer heterogeneity, directly playing into the fragmentations of commodity culture. The
themes of instability and fissure in poststructuralist thinking thus come close to
replicating the logic of commodification. As Peter Dews (1987) has argued in
relation to a discussion of Theodor Adorno,

> Post-structuralism does indeed seek for difference, but it does so through an
> immersion in fragments and perspectives, not perceiving that this splintering is
> itself the effect of an overbearing totality, rather than a means of escape from it.
> In other words, post-structuralism can be understood as the point at which the
> "logic of disintegration" penetrates into the thought which attempts to com-
> prehend it, resulting in a dispersal into a plurality of inconsistent logics. (233)

A thoroughly fragmented and disunified subject reflects a theoretical dispersion
of difference beyond its capability for providing an articulation of complex and
competing values and interests within a field of social and political struggles. The
destabilizing play of difference privileged in poststructuralist thought implies
a fragmented subjectivity that turns out to be no subjectivity at all but merely a
reified expression of a fragmented and divided social and cultural existence in
which discourse seemingly operates independently of human will or purpose.

This version of the poststructuralist subject ironically presents a figure that
positivistically reflects society's major modes of domination. This is illustrated in
parts of Judith Butler's work that, like that of Michel Foucault, take up the ques-

tion of resistance in an unfortunately vague and elusive manner. For the most part, these thinkers' modes of argumentation preclude any articulation of the dynamics of resistance and the conditions under which they might develop. As Dews (1987) suggests, this is a consequence of a fundamental contradiction at the core of poststructuralist thought between its attempt to theorize power discursively while simultaneously combating normative frameworks that would critique and challenge power (169–70). Indeed, by postulating the play of difference at an abstract, almost metaphysical level, poststructuralism is complicit in the very power it theoretically enunciates since it is through the social conditions of fragmentation and dispersal that discursive and other forms of power are able to hold sway. This problem could be described also in terms of the relativistic implications of the Nietzschean influence on contemporary theory. The appeal of Nietzsche's perspectivism in poststructuralist thought both reflects and reinforces a fragmented view of the world as conditioned by the *real* consequences of the commodity form. Indeed, as suggested in chapter 6, the poststructuralist appropriation of Nietzsche's perspectivism ignores his apparent misgivings about the relativistic implications of his own doctrine, against which he later developed a conception of ultimate reality that could serve as a means of "judging the adequacy of perspectives," a task fulfilled by his doctrine of the "eternal return of the same" (Dews 1987: 179). The poststructuralist use of Nietzsche, then, has tended to play too easily into the workings of a society that has become organized around the instrumental logic of commodities with its consequent fragmentation of subjectivity and social relations, in which stable points of reference seem to have all but disappeared.

In his penetrating treatment of the relationship of poststructuralist theory to the early Frankfurt School, Dews (1987) argues that the formation of a second generation of critical theory has revolved around a rejection of Adorno's pessimistic view of the "totally administered society" in favor of a theory of intersubjectivity, as seen in Habermas's work and the influence of his notion of "lifeworld," which he posited as a limit on the instrumental reason that Adorno saw culminating in a "logic of disintegration." The poststructuralists, Dews rightly maintains, have been preoccupied with the same problems of domination engaged by the early Frankfurt theorists but share in common with the second generation a repudiation of Adorno's *Subjektphilosophie* in favor of a language-based paradigm. However, unlike Adorno, who questioned claims to absolute identity and was in fact seeking another form of subjectivity, poststructuralism "lacks any sense of the *interdependence* of identity and non-identity" (Dews 1987: 230; emphasis in original). This results from the reduction of subjectivity to the repressively unifying functions of language, in which emancipation can only take the form of an explosion into fragments, the repressed returning in the form of heterogeneity. The poststructuralists, in Dews's view, are consequently even more tied to a philosophy of consciousness than Adorno and therefore generally fall short of a standpoint that could both transcend subject-object relations and preserve, contrary to actual social development, a dialectical relationship between universal and particular.

It seems to be Dews's conclusion that the poststructuralist turn has been largely wrongheaded and wasteful, while the contemporary Frankfurt theorists, as represented by Habermas and Albrecht Wellmer, have succeeded in transcending the aporias of Adorno's philosophical position by pursuing a linguistic paradigm in which inherently dominating identity logic is decisively surpassed in an intersubjective model of communicative reason. While in considerable agreement with his critique, I nevertheless see Dews as failing to appreciate the strengths of poststructuralism as an acknowledgment of the ascendancy of discursive power relations in modernity and a characterization of the proliferating and fragmentary signifying practices of mass culture in the sociohistorical field of postmodernity (Poster 1995: 75). While in some sense Dews counterposes later Frankfurt theory against Adorno's earlier version as an advance toward linguistic intersubjectivity still within a framework of modernity, I have counterposed Mead against poststructuralism as a solution to the unreflective extension of uncritical and instrumentalist modes of thought in the works of writers like Foucault, Derrida, and Butler in the context of postmodernity. Without forgetting that Mead has been appropriated (albeit highly selectively) in Habermas's linguistic reconstruction of critical theory, Mead's concepts of sociality and self seem more applicable not only to the problems confronting the theoretical strategy of intersubjectivity but also to the development of a social theory consistent with the postmodern thematics of contingency and difference.

Albrecht Wellmer (1985) has made an argument for viewing the relationship between modernism and postmodernism dialectically in terms of "a genuine 'postmodernist' impulse towards a self-transcendence of reason" (360). By this he means a rethinking of Enlightenment universalist ideals that would reflect the pluralizations of postmodern thought. He calls for a "localization of reason" within a plurality of discourses ("language games"), a move that would involve "the mutual 'openness' of the discourses to each other: the 'sublation' of the one reason in the interplay of plural rationalities" (360). In this fashion, Wellmer implies, the subject is prevented from disintegrating into a multiplicity of nonrational determinations while a plurality of thought and discourse is preserved within a set of "basic orientations and meanings of a second order" (359). What Wellmer is proposing is a model of the "mediation" of different language games (360) as a means of overcoming the gap between universal and particular.

This model of reconciliation is suggestive of a postmodern conception of reason in which communicative strategies facilitate a mutuality of meaning, a locating of reason and understanding in the dialogic transactions among a plurality of discourses in which difference is being continually negotiated in an interactive process of democratic give-and-take. Like Habermas, Wellmer projects a linguistically based intersubjectivity in which the universal and particular are reconciled in the form of certain "agreements" (359) on principles, rules, and so on within a democratically formed consensus. In basic compatibility with this projection, a Meadian conception of intersubjectivity would define postmodern discursive plurality as having *social* parameters, contextualizing local reason in the purposes and goals of particular groups and collectivities. The mediation of linguistic viewpoints, of knowledges, for Mead would take the form of mutually acceptable rules of social adjustment. The dynamics of mediation would be located in problem solving. Meadian intersubjectivity would thus place more emphasis on the social relational nature and production of linguistic modalities and the functions of the self in responding to competing or discrepant discursive claims. Finally, Mead's concept of sociality provides the theoretical horizon of normativity required of critique. Where a linguistic model of intersubjectivity would posit ideal conditions of speech as the normative basis of communication (Habermas 1971, 1984), Mead would see problem-solving adjustments among individuals and groups as the foundation of a normative framework for judging different discursive claims.

Finally, the always unresolved problem of power eludes even the most provocative and thoughtful of theorists, old and new. The illusion of a general theory of power has not seriously interfered with the tasks undertaken by any of the writers I have dealt with here but nevertheless remains a seductive goal of social theory. Despite a new interest in power stimulated by Foucault's work, it would seem that very little progress has been made on this front since the time of Marx and Weber or, in the less distant past, C. Wright Mills (1956, 1967). The poststructuralist understanding of discourse as a form of power, of power as a manifestation or effect of discursive practices, certainly has to be reckoned with and is one of the enduring legacies of Foucault. Yet the widely criticized limitations of Foucault's conception of power and Butler's overly abstract and vague treatment of this phenomenon leave us wanting. While offering a resolution of the dilemmas of the old philosophy of the subject, theories of intersubjectivity such as those of Mead, Habermas, and Wellmer ultimately miss the realities of power, a topic about which these thinkers have few words. As a constituent of identity formation and relations of difference, power can be neglected only at a high cost to social and cultural analysis. Perhaps the condition of postmodernity has so disseminated the workings and effects of power as to make its analysis the ultimate theoretical challenge.

Notes

1. Regrounding Theory: The Social Relations of Identity and Difference

1. The growing importance of the new identities, especially race and gender, is attributable to numerous factors and can perhaps be traced originally to transformations in the industrial labor force during and after the Second World War, when blacks and women were for the first time accepted in skilled manual jobs historically held by white males. Following the war, women were relocated in the home and returned to traditionally "female" jobs, but a condition of unease and anxiety in gender relations that emerged during the war persisted in the new world of the suburban nuclear family, laying part of the groundwork for the second wave of feminism. Similarly, new tensions between blacks and whites, rising to the surface during and following the war, when pressures for integration began to build, set the stage for the civil rights movement. In both cases, the forties was a transformative period, leading to new cultural and political identities and rising expectations among both women and blacks. Additionally, the rise in a politics of race and gender can be partially attributed to the relative losses suffered by minorities and women in the postwar labor-management bargain, which mostly benefited white male workers. In a sense, the rise of identity movements during this period was a manifestation of how class came to be increasingly lived and experienced through race and gender. For informative and astute arguments about this history, see Lipsitz (1994b).

2. See also Gitlin (1994). In a context similar to Philipson's discussion, Charles Taylor (1991) makes reference to a "contemporary culture of authenticity" (371).

3. For an impassioned and eloquent reconstruction and critique of the emergence of identity politics from the fragments of the New Left, see Gitlin (1995).

4. The literature on the evolution of popular culture and its commercialization

and politicization in the postwar era is extensive. For comments on consumerism and the rise of youth, see Lee (1993: 106–7). For treatments of youth culture and reviews of the literature, see Frith (1978, 1981). For overviews of popular culture, see Denisoff and Peterson (1972) and Lewis (1972). For a recent study of the formation of female identity and the mass media, see Douglas (1994).

5. For postwar discussions of the problems of identity, culture, and politics in a "mass society," see Bramson (1961), Jacobs (1961), Klapp (1969), Kornhauser (1959), Olson (1963), Rosenberg and White (1957), Stein, Vidich, and White (1960), and White (1961). For a dissenting view, see Swingewood (1977). For an earlier, prewar rendering of the inroads of mass society on traditional institutions, see the prophetic study of Middletown by Lynd and Lynd (1929).

6. Despite the visible and overwhelming tendencies toward paranoia, conformity, and apathy during the Cold War fifties, it is nonetheless misleading to think of this decade in wholly negative terms. Far from being a cultural and political void, as many critics have alleged, the fifties engendered innumerable innovations in music, art, literature, poetry, and politics, fertile developments that played a crucial role in the cultural and political passions and protests of the sixties. See Lhamon (1990). For more general treatments of the fifties, see Goldman (1956), May (1989), and Miller and Nowak (1975).

7. While sometimes displaying progressive impulses, the hegemonic overtones of identity politics are quite evident. Wendy Brown (1993) sees identity politics as a formation of bourgeois liberalism reflecting an abandonment of class politics and a "*renaturalization* of capitalism" serving to further the interests of particular groups within the existing system (394; emphasis in original).

8. For critical assessments of the idea and practice of multiculturalism, see Goldberg (1994), Gordon and Newfield (1996), and Taylor (1992).

9. Brown (1993) criticizes identity politics for failing to give up "investments in itself and especially in its own history of suffering," which it must do to pursue "an emancipatory democratic project" (390–91).

10. Linda Alcoff (1986) speaks of "relationality" as an aspect of her broader notion of "positionality" as a concept she proposes for addressing the subjectivity of women. See also Somers and Gibson (1994).

11. This is not to say that Freud was still not very much a modern thinker in his commitment to the goal of integration and self-unity. For him, instability meant internal discord and pathology, which was to be "cured" through the supposedly rational techniques of psychoanalysis. Many contemporary poststructuralist writings implicitly appropriate from Freud the image of disunity while ignoring that Freud himself held out hope for unity and wholeness.

12. Aspects of symbolic interactionism can also be traced to the pragmatist philosophies of William James and John Dewey. The seminal ideas, however, originated in George Herbert Mead's *Mind, Self, and Society* (1934) and to a lesser extent Charles Horton Cooley's *Human Nature and the Social Order* (1902) and the writings of W. I. Thomas. The term "symbolic interactionism" was coined by Herbert Blumer, who codified his own interpretation of Mead. See Blumer's *Symbolic Interactionism: Perspective and*

Method (1969). For general statements, see Denzin (1992), Hewitt (1984), Manis and Meltzer (1972), and Rose (1962). Also, see Berger and Luckmann (1966).

13. Mead appreciated the role of language in society, as have many of his followers. Blumer, his most prominent student, argued tirelessly for the importance of "interpretation" in social processes of action and interaction.

14. This seems to be Alcoff's reading (1986) of Foucault, a major source of contemporary poststructuralist and constructionist thinking, when in describing his position she refers to "social discourses" and "social practices" as the source of "subjective experiences." I would argue that feminist theorizing has for the most part given equal if not greater weight to the social dimensions of identity construction, despite the strong influences of discourse theory.

15. Concepts such as cultural relativism, role differentiation, role conflict, and social conflict, widely used in sociology, carry connotations of difference without explicitly engaging in any internal analysis of it. Efforts to consider the implications for the social sciences of various humanities-based theoretical developments emphasizing difference—poststructuralism, feminist theory, gay and lesbian theory, cultural studies—have been slow to emerge. See Dickens and Fontana (1994), Rosenau (1992), Seidman (1994), and Seidman and Wagner (1992). Examples of attempts to present, critically engage, and/or practice a sociology that incorporates some of these movements can be found in Collins (1990), Denzin (1992), Lembo (forthcoming), Seidman (1992), and Wiley (1994).

16. In a recent critique of postmodernism, Terry Eagleton (1996) exposes the contradictoriness of the postmodern repudiation of biology. As he puts it, postmodernism, which often rhetorically invokes a "materialist" stance (for instance, in its current fascination with the body), turns right around and, "understandably wary of racist or sexist biologisms, proceeds to suppress the most obviously materialist part of human beings, their biological makeup. . . . The oppression of women is a matter of gender, which is wholly a social construct; but women are oppressed *as women*, which involves the kind of body one happens to have" (58). Similarly, Donna Haraway (1991) has argued against those who dismiss biological thinking on the grounds of its essentialism. Not only should biology continue to be taken as important to feminist theory, she suggests, but it is also important to recognize that not all biological thinking is essentialist.

17. The issue of social and other forms of determinism has divided symbolic interactionists from conventional or "mainstream" sociologists, who are usually more committed to determinist notions of structure or system. Yet symbolic interactionists themselves have been divided over this problem. The Chicago school, led by Blumer, has remained close to the classic Meadian notion of the self while amplifying the indeterminate elements in Mead's thought. The Iowa school, headed by Manford Kuhn, took a more structuralist and empiricist direction, attempting to "operationalize" Meadian concepts by more conventional sociological methods, explicitly adopting a more determinist stance. See Meltzer and Petras (1972) and Turner (1962) for further discussions of the determinism-indeterminism debate.

18. The contemporary popularity of constructionist thinking can be seen as a reflection of the increasing awareness of the constructed nature of "reality" in the mass

media. In a society and culture dominated by processes of signification, where indeed the culture has acquired a "textual" quality, and where the power to define is now embedded in a massive system of representation and image making, one cannot escape the sense that what used to be naively taken for reality is now a cultural construction, a product of the mediating powers of technological means of representation.

19. For a discussion of these issues, see Berger and Luckmann (1966), Hewitt (1984), Rose (1962), and Yardley and Honess (1987).

20. A number of feminists have seen the dangers in a refusal to employ essentializing categories, proposing instead what has been called "strategic essentialism." For discussions of the problem, see Fuss (1989), Spivak (1987, 1992), and essays by Jane Flax, Christine Di Stefano, Susan Bordo, Nancy Hartsock, and Judith Butler in Nicholson (1990).

21. The tradition of British cultural studies is rich in examples of resistance to hegemonic cultural/class codes and opposition to dominant institutions. See Brake (1980), Fiske (1987, 1989a, 1989b), Hall and Jefferson (1976), Hebdige (1979), and Willis (1978, 1990).

22. Some of the most interesting contemporary writing about identity has stressed the creative potentialities inherent in "borderland" spaces where social and cultural contacts remake the meanings of marginality, producing composite, bricollage, multidimensional identities and cultures. This can include what George Lipsitz calls a "bifocality" that reflects the way in which marginals both see themselves and are seen by others (Lipsitz 1990a: 135). See also Clifford and Marcus (1986), Clifford (1988), hooks (1990), Rosaldo (1989), Spivak (1992), and Wellman (1996).

23. This has come to be known in feminism as standpoint theory. See Harding (1986, 1991) for discussions of the promises and problems of this epistemology.

24. Laclau warns that the assertion of mere particularity or difference sanctions the status quo by ignoring the power relations among groups.

25. For critical but variously unsympathetic accounts of the "linguistic turn" in philosophy and theory, and specifically the problems of poststructuralism, see Anderson (1984), Dews (1987), Jameson (1972, 1981), and Palmer (1990).

26. Patricia Hill Collins's discussion (1990) of black feminist thought exemplifies the importance of categories like consciousness and experience in understanding race and gender and their potential transformation: "This level of *individual consciousness* is a fundamental area where new knowledge can generate change" (227; emphasis added).

2. Modernity and Postmodernity: Transformations in Identity Formation

1. Heated debate has arisen around a cluster of issues raised by the term "postmodern." Does it exist? What is it? How does it differ from modernity? Is it possible to periodize? By what criteria are "modern" and "postmodern" distinguishable? How is it to be evaluated? For discussions of postmodernism and the problem of distinguishing the postmodern from the modern, see Arac (1986), Bauman (1992), Best and Kellner (1991), Calinescu (1987), Dunn (1991), Featherstone (1988, 1991), Foster (1983), Giddens (1990, 1991), Harvey (1989), Hebdige (1988), Hutcheon (1988, 1989), Huyssen

(1986), Jameson (1987, 1991), Jencks (1986), Kumar (1995), Lash (1990), Lash and Friedman (1992), Lyotard (1984), *New German Critique* (1984), Newman (1985), Rose (1991), Smart (1992), *Theory, Culture and Society* (1985, 1988), and Turner (1991). For negative critiques of postmodernism, see Callinicos (1990), Eagleton (1996), Norris (1990), and O'Neill (1995).

2. By *commodity* I mean any object that has acquired exchange value, that is, that can be bought and sold in a market. See Marx (1906), book 1, part 1, chapter 1, "Commodities."

3. For some representative discussions among the abundant studies of modernity, see Berman (1982), Calinescu (1987), Cascardi (1992), Frisby (1988), Giddens (1990, 1991), Habermas (1983, 1987b), Harvey (1989), Kern (1983), Lash (1990), Lash and Friedman (1992), Taylor (1989), *Theory, Culture and Society* (1985), and Touraine (1995).

4. In literature, a discourse of alienation first appeared in Balzac's classic treatment of modern capitalist civilization, *Lost Illusions* (1971).

5. Georg Simmel's writings on the metropolis, the money economy, and other aspects of modern life initiated a rich stream of thought within social theory on the impact of "urbanism as a way of life" (Wirth 1938). See also Simmel (1950) and *Theory, Culture and Society* (1991).

6. Historically, this has undoubtedly been truer for members of middle- and upper-income groups than for those in the working class. For the most part, we have only descriptive, indirect, and culturally mediated measures of how, when, and why the shift from a production to a consumption orientation occurred in the United States and other Western capitalist countries, and the extent of identification with this shift among members of different groups. For some accounts, see Erenberg (1981), Ewen (1976), Ewen and Ewen (1982), Fox and Lears (1983), Lowenthal (1961, chapter 4, "The Triumph of Mass Idols"), Susman (1973), and Veblen (1934).

7. The distinction between *modernity* and *modernism*, overlooked by many writers, helps to clarify numerous disputes about the nature of the modern and to reconcile conflicting interpretations of modernity. Berman (1982) speaks of the "experience" of modernity associated with the urban landscape and the myth of development and progress but then proceeds to conflate *modernity* with modernism. I use "modernity" to refer to a historical period, a condition, an outlook, and experience associated with urbanism, individualism, rapid change, Weberian rationalization, secularization, and social differentiation (Featherstone 1988). In contrast, "modernism" refers to an intellectual and aesthetic outlook and movement, based on experimentation in the fields of painting, sculpture, music, fiction, poetry, theater, and dance. Modernism in these fields has taken many complex forms, including an investigation into consciousness (Bradbury and McFarlane 1976) and the means of artistic representation. To a large extent, modernism is inseparable from the development of criticism (Frascina and Harrison 1982) and notions of an avant-garde (Bürger 1984; Crane 1987; Poggioli 1968; Russell 1985). A key role of modernism has been to give voice to the *antinomies* of modernity, to struggle with the opposition between the rational and irrational in search of reconciliation of these contrary tendencies of the modern mind on the plane of aesthetic realization. Far

from simply reflecting or endorsing modernity, modernism registered *disillusionment* with the consequences of modernity and modernization (Lunn 1982). On the one hand, modernism was a *protest* against the alienating conditions of modernity and on the other an attempt at *redemption* through aesthetic reconciliation. Harvey (1989) argues that the modern artist was searching for a means of representing the eternal and immutable amid the chaos of modernity. Modernism can thus be defined as the search for new forms of aesthetic consciousness and a new mythology. On the distinction between modernity and modernism, see also Calinescu (1987) and Kumar (1995).

8. The debate stirred in recent years by "communitarianism" is a case in point. See also Iris Young (1990), who disavows community as undemocratic and repressive of social difference.

9. See chapter 3 for a fuller discussion.

10. While ultimately seeking wholeness, modernism's main burden was always to articulate the multiplicity as well as divisiveness, atomization, and alienation of modern existence.

11. While not germane to my analysis, Mark Poster (1995) has recently drawn a systematic distinction between broadcast technologies on the one hand and informational technologies (computerized communication systems such as the Internet) on the other, proclaiming that the latter signify the arrival of "the second media age."

12. Within the larger constellation of postmodernist writings, we find an interesting valorization of notions of "performance" or "performativity." For example, Lyotard (1984) advances the "performativity criterion" as a strategy for combating "metaphysical discourse" (62), claiming that performativity "is what the postmodern world is all about" (41). In another context, Judith Butler (1990b) has written that "gender proves to be performative" (25). The invocation of performance by postmodernists is a revealing manifestation of the pragmatist proclivities of postmodern thought and offers insights into how postmodernists think about the problem of identity. The stress on performance, however, raises important questions about postmodernism's abandonment of substantialist norms (what Butler calls a "metaphysics of substance," 25) in favor of relativistic and instrumentalist conceptions of identity. (On Butler, see chapter 6.)

13. As some critics have argued, this abolition of the modern subject in recent postmodernist writings perhaps ought to be regarded as discourse theory's more extreme and disembodied version of an earlier theory of the decline of the individual in a rationalized and bureaucratic society as expounded in the writings of Max Weber and the Frankfurt School (Dews 1987).

14. The theory of the commodity form was first developed by Marx, who regarded it as the major structural feature of capitalist society. Later Marxists, most notably Georg Lukács (1971), Theodor Adorno (1941, 1945, 1957, 1978), and Herbert Marcuse (1964) critically developed the implications of the commodity form beyond the sphere of production, seeing commodification as a process extending to all realms of capitalist society, especially culture and subjectivity. For a more recent treatment that examines commodification in the context of everyday life, see Susan Willis (1991).

15. As Douglas Kellner has suggested, we can choose between a view of postmoder-

nity as destructive of identity entirely, which seems implausible, or a view that recognizes the shaping of identity by mass culture. However, Kellner's accurate statement that various forms of mass culture "play key roles in the structuring of contemporary identity" (1992: 148) overlooks the extent to which identity has *also* been destabilized and problematized by these cultural forms.

16. For wide-ranging and provocative readings of contemporary media culture and its relationship to identity, social relations, and politics, see Kellner (1995). Whereas Kellner attempts to ground cultural studies more thoroughly in material, political, and social contexts, focusing attention on the *contents* of the media at particular historical moments, my discussion is concerned with the impact of media *form* on identity. For an interesting treatment of the place of clothing fashion in the construction of contemporary identities, see Davis (1992).

17. As will become apparent in chapter 4, this transition corresponds to the changing needs of U.S. capitalism. Stuart Hall (1981) has provided much-needed historical perspective on how capital transforms "subjects" as its purposes require. See also Eagleton (1996).

18. See the mass society theorists cited in chapter 1, especially Kornhauser (1959) and Lynd and Lynd (1929).

19. I say "ironic" because the major thrust of critical academic theory of the mass media has been to presuppose simplistically that television could be nothing but an apparatus of hegemonic ideology. In contrast, postmodern characterizations of mass culture imply that media complicate and *disrupt* identity rather than fixing it in ideology. Considering the limitations of both perspectives, the *actual* ideological effects of television remain to be explored by theorists and researchers. Spectators would seem to stand in more complicated relationships to television than most scholars and critics have previously thought. See Dunn (1986a) and Lembo (forthcoming).

20. For an excellent summary and critique of trends in cultural studies, see Kellner (1995).

21. To some extent, television in this respect reflects a more general phenomenon of mass culture, a tendency to efface age structures and cultures toward a valorization of "youth," the cultural norm in fashion and a major market for the television and advertising industries. The dissolution of age structure on television, however, might also be considered from the standpoint of what members of the Frankfurt School regarded as a tendency within mass culture toward psychological regression. See Adorno (1957), Horkheimer and Adorno (1972), and Lowenthal (1957). Leo Lowenthal, for instance, wrote: "We wish to know whether the consummation of popular culture really presupposes a human being with preadult traits or whether modern man has a split personality: half mutilated child and half standardized adult" (57).

22. This is not to say that mass communications do not always operate in a field of social relations (Dunn 1986b) but only to reaffirm the isolating and privatizing positioning of the spectator *inherent* in mass media. As cultural studies has demonstrated, spectators are often active, bringing social meanings *with them* to the television viewing experi-

ence. My argument, rather, is simply that there is a fundamental difference between individuals as social actors and as spectators consuming images.

23. Of course, television is anything but realistic in the sense of being connected to "real life." Its power of believability consists of its realist ontology as a visual medium, especially its "live" aspects. For a discussion of realism in television, see Feuer (1983).

24. I am by no means suggesting that the decline of sociality is attributable exclusively to television or other mass media, as has been mistakenly implied in some versions of classic mass society theory. The disruption and attenuation of social relations is a consequence of numerous interconnected developments in the postwar era, including the automobile, freeways, suburbia, shopping malls, geographical mobility, and, more recently, urban renewal, runaway shops, and other instances of "creative destruction" (Berman 1982) associated with relentless economic development under capitalism. My argument is that as a consumption relation, television in important ways exemplifies how the commodity form undermines and displaces social relations, thus serving as both model and figure of the corrosive effects of consumption relations on associational and community life generally. For insightful and detailed historical studies of consumerism, suburbia, and other changes eroding public space in postwar U.S. society, see Lipsitz (1994b) and Spigel (1992).

25. This theoretical discussion only skims the surface of a potentially vast field of research, most of which has yet to be conducted. For instance, one of the obvious issues for research on identity formation and the mass media is the differential impact of television on spectators of different ages in different stages of the life cycle. For example, we should expect the influences of television to be more powerful among younger than among older people. We should expect social withdrawal to be less consequential for adults, whose identities and ego capacities are more fully developed than those of children.

26. Among the many who have commented on this trend, see, for example, Hechtman (1993).

27. How to account for structural and cultural change in whole societies is an enduring historical problem of the chicken-and-egg variety. The "puzzle" of consumption (Campbell 1987) is such a problem for our time. Does consumption weaken or destroy traditional forms of social interaction, or does it simply replace or substitute for a set of changes already under way, "filling a void," so to speak? For examples of the first position, see Baudrillard (1983a; 1983b; 1983c; 1988a, chapters 1 and 2) and Alt (1975, 1976). For the second position, see Kavolis (1970), who writes, "Consumption becomes psychologically important, the less content of a specifiable nature—or the less structure—one can sense within one's own self" (441). Besides regarding consumption as a *response* to social decay, Kavolis also implies that consumption might provide a means of "finding oneself" for those with weak or troubled identities. The more frequently discussed puzzle of consumption is the relative importance of its economic sources in the imperatives of capitalist development as opposed to its cultural origins and forms. For emphasis on the former, see Baran and Sweezy (1966), Bocock (1993), Ewen (1976), Ewen and Ewen (1982), Haug (1986), Jameson (1983, 1984a), Lee (1993), and Preteceille and Terrail (1985). For a focus on cultural sources, see Campbell (1987), Fox and Lears (1983),

McCracken (1990), Miller (1987), and Susman (1973). Also, see Leiss (1976), Rojek (1985), and *Theory, Culture and Society* (1983). For an overview of recent scholarly studies of consumption, see Miller (1995).

28. Although Miller's (1987) interesting reconstruction of Hegel's "positive" theory of objectification and the rather ambiguous legacy of Simmel's more tragic conception of objectification (chapter 3) opens the door to the possibility of transforming consumer culture into a means of self-development and fulfillment, he ignores the many structural obstacles in present-day corporate capitalism to such a future of self-directed reappropriation. While providing much-needed elaboration of the nature of consumption and correcting reductionist and one-sided critiques of mass culture, Miller is too sanguine about the destruction of social relations and community by the commodity form as well as the structured inequalities of consumption society.

3. On the Transition from Modernity to Postmodernity:
Transformations in Culture

1. I argue for a distinction between the terms *semiotic* and *symbolic,* although they are often used interchangeably. Here, I deliberately say "semiotic" as opposed to "symbolic" exchange to indicate that in postmodern culture "signs" tend to replace "symbols." This distinction follows Baudrillard's (1981) argument of a transition from symbolic value and exchange (marked by "ambivalence") to semiotic exchange, in which "the symbolic is transformed into the instrumental, either commodity or sign" (125). According to Baudrillard, "*This semiological reduction of the symbolic properly constitutes the ideological process*" (98; emphasis in original). From a less structuralist perspective, corporate mass culture has with deliberate intention appropriated signs—defined as conventional, largely mechanical relationships of signifiers, signifieds, and referents—as means of selling products. In Saussure's (1974) theory, a sign acquires its function and significance as a structural element in a larger *system* of relations characterizing language, serving to *signify* meaning according to the conventionalized rules of this system. In mass culture, signs have become instruments of signification operating in functionally predetermined systems of meaning (such as advertising). In contrast, a symbol is generally any image or object having the capacity to refer to something else by means of association, suggestion, and so on. Importantly, symbols arise through a process of the valuation and meaning construction of objects or images deemed subjectively significant. In other words, symbols are created by *subjects,* forming in the cognitive and emotional space between subjects and objects. Signs can *become* symbols (the advertisement as a symbol of capitalism), but symbols transcend signs, eliciting a *complex* of meanings rather than a single, instrumental response. Thus, whereas signs function through *denotation,* symbols are rich in *connotation,* characterized by deep, charged, and multiple meanings created by human subjects. Cultural theory could benefit from further clarification and elaboration of this distinction. Such a distinction is necessarily implicit in any critical perspective on contemporary mass culture, which according to some critics displays alarming symptoms of symbolic loss (Jaeger and Selznick 1964). The field of semiotics, I argue, is a theoretical consequence and reification of the gradual elimination of the referent in the system of

images characterizing the rise of mass communications and reproductive technologies in the nineteenth and twentieth centuries. In his early critiques of commodity society as a system of exchange among signifiers, Baudrillard (1993) advocates a return to the "symbolic exchange" of primitive society. See Kellner (1994: 6–7). For more general treatments of the symbol, see Durkheim (1961), Harris (1987), Langer (1951), Mead (1934), and White (1949).

2. We often hear that in politics, perception is reality. The statement "perception is reality," however, seems *generally* true in a society where more and more of experience is technologically and semiotically mediated. This might partially explain the increasing politicization of cultural space and the culturalization of politics. More mundanely, cases of imagined events and hysteria about statistically insignificant threats seem to abound in media-dominated society. While excessive anxieties over crime, missing children, child abuse, satanic cults, UFOs, and so on (generally unsupported by empirical evidence) are undoubtedly manifestations of social, psychological, and political forces at work in the culture, they are also clearly attributable to the power of the media to exaggerate and distort our sense of reality. For example, research has found that frequent television viewers have worse fears of crime than less frequent viewers. Some studies reported by Daniel Goleman of the *New York Times* (carried in the *San Francisco Chronicle*, November 1, 1994) found there was practically no corroborating evidence in support of thousands of accusations a year of satanic sexual abuse in the United States. Nina Eliasoph (1986) has demonstrated that wide media coverage and news construction of missing children in the United States has led to gross exaggerations of the problem. And the list could go on. Of course, years ago, many Europeans believed gypsies and Jews were stealing their children. Nonetheless, in contemporary culture, reality is increasingly what it is claimed to be by the media.

3. From "The Painter of Modern Life," published in 1863, quoted in Harvey (1989: 10).

4. Lash and Friedman (1992) refer to this distinction as one between a "low modernism" and a "high modernism."

5. Simmel is certainly worth more attention than I am allotting him here, indeed, having been "rediscovered" in recent years by a newly appreciative array of scholars. Bauman (1992) has referred to him as "the sole 'postmodern' thinker among the founding fathers of sociology" (31). For Simmel's little-known essays on culture and its tragedy, in which he expounds a more negative version of Hegel's principle of objectification, see Simmel (1968). For further discussion and interpretation, see Weingartner (1962) and Miller (1987). Also, see Simmel (1990). On Simmel in general, see *Theory, Culture and Society* (1991).

6. Poster, too, makes an important distinction between the *explosion* of information and the communicational *structures* of the new information technologies. See Poster (1990: 14).

7. Just as conceptions of time and space are not naturally given but socially and culturally constructed, Giddens's conceptions are not free of cultural biases. As David Harvey reminds us, ideas about time and space can vary radically from one culture to the

next and are largely a product of underlying material processes, as demonstrated, for example, in the arguments of Wilhelm Dilthey and Durkheim (Harvey 1989: 201–10).

8. One of the ironies of modernization has always been that in the very process of creating a historical consciousness of time it has ultimately destroyed a sense of the past, not to mention its actual remnants.

9. See chapter 4.

10. See also Jameson (1991) for discussions of the postmodern privileging of space.

11. See Weber (1958b), Whimster and Lash (1987), and Habermas (1984).

12. The following discussion closely follows Lash but attempts to clarify and elaborate the issues he raises.

13. This is one reason that the field of anthropology has been in the forefront of postmodern thinking in the social sciences and why ethnography has become the research method of choice.

14. Many suggestive observations are possible regarding the odd congruities between postmodern and preliterate culture. For example, William Dunning (1993) has commented on the shift from European constructs of linear time (and thus notions of history) to earlier, premodern conceptions of cyclical time, a turn of events, he argues, supported by recent scientific constructs, for example, those of quantum mechanics. He relates this observation to the reversal of the modern notion of an indivisible self to a postmodern divisible self that is comparable to tribal notions of "a split self that might exist in more than one place or body in cyclical time" (135).

15. Lash's treatment of the processes of de-differentiation provides an important model for understanding postmodernism and postmodernity as novel configurations of cultural phenomena, especially eclecticism. However, he offers only a weak account of why, when, and how processes of differentiation reverse themselves. For a critique, see Crook et al. (1992), who argue that the breakdown of the boundaries among cultural spheres results from "the proliferation of boundaries within them" (70). In their view, de-differentiation follows from "hyperdifferentiation," which produces fragments within and between cultural spheres that are then free to migrate and intermix with those of other spheres.

16. For definitions and discussions, see Aronowitz (1993); Blundell, Shepherd, and Taylor (1993); Hall et al. (1980); Grossberg et al. (1992); and McGuigan (1992).

17. This reconceptualization has provided a basis for the theory that readers and spectators can and do "resist" preferred codings of cultural products. See especially Fiske (1987, 1989a, 1989b) and Morley (1980, 1986).

18. The following discussion is taken from Dunn (1991: 117–18).

19. A major caveat to these participatory media, however, is that they still leave consumers dependent on corporate-shaped technology. Furthermore, existing interactive television technology has been mostly limited to only certain kinds of programs, primarily games and amusements.

20. Excerpt from news coverage of a concert by Genesis in Oakland, California, in June 1992, by Bruce Britt, *Los Angeles Daily News,* appearing in The *San Francisco Chronicle,* June 18, 1992.

21. See the cover story of *Time,* February 8, 1993, "Cyberpunk!," 58–65.

22. Compare the cyberpunk phenomenon to Donna Haraway's (1991) conception of the cyborg.

23. For a critique, see Kellner (1989: 73–76; 1994: 1–23).

24. For discussions of the concept of "public sphere," its alleged erosion, the role of informational and communications technologies, and the implications for democracy, see the volumes by Calhoun (1993) and Woodward (1980).

4. Explaining the Destabilization of Identity: Postmodernization, Commodification, and the Leveling of Cultural Hierarchy

1. Many of the problems associated with earlier histories and "colonial discourses" predicated on such divisions are undergoing rethinking and sometimes sweeping revision in what is referred to as postcolonial theory. For expositions and criticisms of the notion of the postcolonial, see Dirlik (1994), *Social Text* (1992), Williams and Chrisman (1994), and Young (1990).

2. Several of the themes I touch on in this chapter are voiced and developed in greater detail in the work of Jonathan Friedman (1994) and Mike Featherstone (1995). Friedman focuses on identity change through a theory of globalization concentrating on the massive economic, social, cultural, and political fragmentations and reconfigurations now occurring throughout the world.

3. Crook, Pakulski, and Waters (1992) argue that postmodernization is an extreme extension of the major processes driving modernization—differentiation and rationalization.

4. A broad and comprehensive discussion of the relationship between changing economic conditions and the emergence of postmodernity can be found in Lash and Urry (1987), who see the decline of modern social and cultural structures as a consequence of what they call "disorganized capitalism." In what follows, I focus attention on David Harvey's work because it specifically explains transformations in the nature and patterns of consumption.

5. Modern notions of development and progress have been largely absorbed into consumer culture, transformed into ideologies of the "new" and "improved." The "tradition of the new" (Rosenberg 1994) has been degraded to the "novelty of mass culture." For all practical purposes, most ideas about progressive social change have been abandoned for the endless recycling and pseudoprogress of consumerism as a way of life.

6. Interestingly, *Webster's Third New World International Dictionary* defines "consume" as to destroy, waste, or squander.

7. Despite the relative absence of class distinctions in the United States compared to other countries, especially in the postwar period, and without engaging all the possible definitions of class, a case could be made that classes in an objective sense, and to degrees in a subjective sense, still do exist in the United States and have consequences socially, politically, and in other ways. Arguments for the fragmentation of class notwithstanding, evidence supports the view that classes still have effects. For a recent debate, see Clark and Lipset (1991), Clark et al. (1993), Hout et al. (1993), and Pakulski (1993). On class

consciousness in the United States, see Jackman and Jackman (1983), Vanneman and Cannon (1987), and Fussell (1983). For an argument that class theory and class analysis are a thing of the past, see Pakulski and Waters (1996).

8. A virtue of the post-Fordist conception of consumption practices is that it refuses to separate consumption from production, a frequent mistake in studies of consumption and consumer culture. As Miller (1987) points out, Bourdieu's analysis suffers not only from a lack of historical perspective but in its detachment from the sphere of production, where, as Harvey recognizes, consumption patterns are shaped in a highly calculated way by experts in packaging, design, marketing, advertising, and distribution.

9. In a powerfully apt way of characterizing the condition of postmodernity, Charles Newman (1985) has appropriated the term "inflation" to describe the condition of the arts, ideas, discourse, the academy, and most other aspects of an excessively high-demand, commercialized culture that no longer recognizes modern cultural distinctions.

10. In fact, just as monetary inflation endangers the economy, threatening total devaluation of the currency, so an excess of goods and meanings can pose a threat to the commodity system by breeding consumer confusion and indifference.

11. This is not to deny that postmodernization involves changes in the class structure and is a manifestation of various kinds of class phenomena. In fact, a major class restructuring has been occurring in the United States, and throughout the world, as both cause and consequence of the economic regime of flexible accumulation, and new and deeper lines have been drawn between those economic and social groupings benefiting from innovative economic practices and those that are not. Also, the beneficiaries and aficionados of postmodern cultural tendencies are concentrated in the educated and affluent sectors of the population, and in this sense the contemporary professional-managerial class has emerged as an "agent" of postmodern consumption. It is also true that the term "postmodern" is seldom heard outside highly mobile middle-class circles in academia, media, and the arts. All of this is a way of saying that cultural experiences are class based and constructed discursively and intellectually by specific social groups. In fact, to my knowledge, no one has yet attempted to ascertain empirically whether anyone outside the immediate orbit of cultural intermediaries and rising academics in a predominantly white middle-class world finds any meaning in the term "postmodern" in terms of their own experiences or aspirations.

12. The actual extent to which it might be said that mass culture is comprised of "free-floating signifiers" is problematic since to do so implies that signifiers have lost all meaning and reference, which is strictly speaking implausible. In a given advertisement, for example, the signifiers must be loaded with meaning to have an effect. As discussed in chapter 3, however, the saturation of society in commodified images problematizes meaning by its very excess.

13. Reception theory, bolstered by some encouraging evidence from audience studies, suggests that spectators do "resist" at least the ideological content of images. See Fiske (1987), Hall (1980b), Lembo and Tucker (1990), Morley (1980, 1986), Press (1991), and Radway (1984).

14. The transition to a service-, information-, or knowledge-based economy has

often been captured in the notion of a postindustrial society (Bell 1973). Not surprisingly, many scholars have attempted to connect the concepts of the postmodern and the postindustrial (Kumar 1995; Lyotard 1984; Rose 1991; Smart 1992). For a thoughtful reformulation of postindustrial theory, see Block (1990).

15. Appadurai (1994) has proposed examining the relationship among five dimensions of "global cultural flow" that he terms *ethnoscapes, mediascapes, technoscapes, finanscapes,* and *ideoscapes* (328–31). He sees these landscapes as building blocks of what he calls "*imagined worlds,* that is, the multiple worlds which are constituted by the historically situated imaginations of persons and groups spread around the globe" (329; emphasis in original).

16. Bluestone and Harrison (1982) report that "between 1950 and 1980, direct foreign investment by U.S. businesses increased *sixteen times,* from about $12 billion to $192 billion" (42; emphasis in original).

17. For some provocative and celebratory essays on this phenomenon and its impact on our cultural experience, see the work of Ian Chambers (1986, 1990, 1994).

18. This is not to deny the reemergence of racism in places in the United States and parts of Europe where immigration has produced a reactionary backlash against newly arrived racial and ethnic minorities. These trends are evidenced in the interracial strife in the Los Angeles rebellion of 1992; the recent passage in California of Proposition 187 prohibiting the provision of health, education, and other services to illegal immigrants; and Proposition 209 banning affirmative action practices in government employment and higher education admissions. Nevertheless, despite such ominous trends, world migration has led to the formation of new kinds of interethnic communities and cultures in the metropolitan centers of the West that are not always hostilely divided.

19. Many critics have viewed "Westernization" as cultural imperialism and as inherently Anglo-American, on the grounds that cultural exports from core countries come predominantly from the United States and the United Kingdom. See Mattelart (1979), Schiller (1969), and Tunstall (1977). For a thoughtful reexamination of the cultural imperialism thesis that critically qualifies some of these claims, see Tomlinson (1991).

20. John Tomlinson (1991) has argued that while the concept of "cultural imperialism" implies coercion, understood as the spread of modernity, this is really less a process of cultural imposition than of cultural loss (173). He demonstrates that "native" recipients of Western technology and cultural goods often adapt them to their own purposes and expressive needs. What Tomlinson fails to address, however, is that much depends on the nature of the cultural technology introduced. The older media of film, television, and radio are essentially one-way communications systems that tend to homogenize culture for passive audiences. The newer media, however, are more participatory and decentralizing. Video, cassette, compact disk, computer, fax, and photocopying technologies contain more democratic potentials for the production and consumption of culture. Peter Manuel (1993) has shown how the massive spread of the cassette in North India resulted in the emergence of a popular music culture separate from the oligopolistic structures of the film or record industries, revitalizing local communities and subcultures.

21. Some studies have reported that during the 1970s and 1980s most job growth

occurred in the small-business sector of the economy. However, the topic is complicated and controversial. The definition of "small" remains vague, small businesses continue to suffer high rates of failure, and many are actually owned by corporations. See Bluestone and Harrison (1982).

22. This trend reflects the widely discussed erosion of the U.S. middle class beginning in the late 1970s. Whereas the upscale boutique of the eighties and nineties resonates a new affluence in the upper reaches of the middle class, the massive growth of the discount chain (K-Mart, Wal-Mart, Target) indicates a broad downward movement toward the lower-income levels of this same class. Both movements away from the middle have been blamed for displacing the older, more traditional locally owned small business. For discussions of the "shrinking middle class," see Currie, Dunn, and Fogarty (1980) and Phillips (1993).

23. While the growth of specialized cable channels and the advent of various other electronic information services could be seen as threatening a common national culture with fragmentation, this does not appear to be occurring. Recent research suggests that all the new media technologies are interconnected, implying integration, and that the economic costs of electronic media place natural constraints on the proliferation of programming for small, special-interest audiences. See Neuman (1991).

24. See the special issue of *Theory, Culture and Society* (1990), 7/2–3 devoted to "Global Culture."

25. The British cultural studies tradition has focused much of its attention on the relationships among popular culture, social groups, mass communications, audiences, and places. For examples of this kind of work having special relevance to the relationship between mass communications and the struggle over cultural meanings, see Angus and Jhally (1989), Chambers (1986), Hall et al. (1980), Hebdige (1979), Lipsitz (1990a, 1994a), and Willis (1990).

26. The possibilities for new kinds of popular cultural practices in these contexts have been examined extensively in the work of George Lipsitz (1990a, 1994a), especially his *Dangerous Crossroads,* which explores and documents a wide range of popular music fusions in the racial and ethnic interstices of immigrant populations.

27. Alberto Melucci (1989) has focused attention on the new social movements' concern for issues of individual need and experience, understanding them as "identity movements."

28. On the historical formation of the high culture-low culture division in U.S. life, see Levine (1988). On the destruction of this distinction, see Twitchell (1992).

5. Identity, Politics, and the Dual Logic of Postmodernity:
Fragmentation and Pluralization

1. The distinction is akin to Lash's distinction between mainstream and oppositional postmodernism. However, I find his dichotomization problematic for a number of reasons. First, it does not adequately articulate the difference between postmodernism as *reflective* of technology and the commodity form, and postmodernism as a *reaction* against these. Second, it posits too simple a distinction between a status quo identified

with consumerism and an opposition identified with progressive change, instead of seeing a complicated intermingling of commercial and political interests. Third, it fails to recognize the role of tradition in both postmodernisms.

2. This is another way of understanding the process of de-differentiation formulated by Lash (1990) and discussed in chapter 3, in which the breaking up of cultural spheres allows their fragments to migrate freely (Crook et al. 1992). The resulting cultural democratization is based on a particularistic recognition of different beliefs, values, interests, and styles throughout society. The latter authors, however, fail to distinguish between the commercial and political aspects of this process. The commodity form democratizes through an eclectic mixing of particular fragments of culture for the commercial marketplace, while in the realm of cultural politics particularism becomes a mode of fashioning new group-based meanings and identities. In the resurgence of "the particular" in postmodern discourse, these tendencies are usually conflated.

3. I use the term *reflexive* here to mean a self-consciousness of underpinnings—origins, contexts, sources, locations, and interests. In this regard, there seem to be two kinds of postmodernists: those who practice reflexivity as a prescribed but rather abstract ritual; and those who practice it to understand the objective bases of their own positions. Many postmodernists want to relativize in the name of particularity but refuse to apply this strategy to themselves (see chapter 1).

4. See Takagi (1993) and Zinn (1980) for comprehensive histories of the struggles of oppressed groups against the dominant social powers in the United States.

5. However, consistent with Ernesto Laclau's (1992) conception of the interdependencies of "the universal" and "the particular" discussed in chapter 1, group challenges to prevailing social power have necessarily mobilized universalistic principles, such as freedom and due process, on behalf of the oppressed. In this respect, the new pluralization has been in part dependent on a reassertion of universalistic notions, which have been recontextualized at the cultural margins of society.

6. It has become commonplace since the sixties, in advertising and consumer products, and throughout the media generally, for elements of oppositional culture to be appropriated and transformed in the context of consumption. Some examples include advertising's appropriation of rock music, rap, and black street culture and the fashion industry's absorption of threatening expressive styles such as the black militant afro, S and M, grunge, unisex, and various symbols of youth violence. In these and other ways, threatening political symbols are turned into images of consumer pleasure and excitement and marketed as consumables.

7. In this sense, the media will always remain a potentially contested site of identity and politics and a source of readings of the tendencies and contradictions of the larger political culture. Herman Gray (1995), for example, has explored changing representations of blackness in prime time television to demonstrate how "commercial culture operates as both a site of and a resource for black cultural politics" (5). Also, see Kellner (1995) for a collection of critical political readings of media culture. It is important also to note that the media have a curious way of creating their own dialectical oppositions. In a recent conference paper titled "Contesting Culture: Alcohol-Related Identity

Movements in Contemporary African American Communities," Denise Herd of the School of Public Health at the University of California at Berkeley demonstrated how corporate appropriation of cultural resistance can generate oppositional movements. She tells the story of how the appropriation of rap in an advertisement for St. Ides, a high-alcohol-content beer targeted to the black youth market, generated strong community opposition.

8. Does the commodification of oppositional cultural practices completely neutralize their politics? The answer is always by nature equivocal. Aside from controversy about the impact of the recording industry on the social and political messages of popular musical forms such as rock and rap, music video has become a frequent focal point of debates over the consequences of commercialization. The persistent issue is whether audiences respond to the video or to the music and its lyrics. Is the message in the visuals, or the sounds and words? For a convincing discussion of the political efficacy of commercialized reggae, see Lipsitz (1990b). In a different vein, Gray (1988) has examined the commercial and other kinds of pressures limiting the ability of an independent jazz recording company to produce vital and innovative music.

9. Attempts to use the media for political purposes have a long history and comprise one of the more treacherous aspects of popular resistance. The fate of commercial attempts to make critical statements is illustrated by the efforts of filmmakers like Oliver Stone, who has been accused of overindulgence in and celebration of violence in his movie *Natural Born Killers,* which he claims to have produced as a *critique* of the excessive violence in Hollywood entertainment. In another example of the power of the commercial system to reassert itself stubbornly, a party celebrating the world premiere of Robert Altman's movie *Ready to Wear,* a parody of the fashion industry, was described as ironically turning into a fashion event itself, "brimming with fashion and entertainment stars decked out in designers of their choice" (*San Francisco Chronicle,* December 14, 1994, E1).

10. The framing of events and construction of groups and movements in the mass media are not merely "ideological" but the effect of a complex and interacting set of professional, organizational, economic, and political factors. For a range of views on this problem, with examples, see Bagdikian (1990), Gans (1980), Gitlin (1980), Herman and Chomsky (1988), Manoff and Schudson (1986), Parenti (1986), and Schudson (1978).

11. The figures on cultural saturation from various media are staggering. The market in periodicals now numbers approximately ten thousand, and the book publishing industry puts out around forty thousand titles a year. A. C. Nielson reports the average household television is on 7 hours per day and watched by the average adult 4.5 hours per day. In combination with radio, newspapers, and magazines, this adds up to an average of 6 hours and 43 minutes of media exposure per day. For discussion of these and other figures, see Neuman (1991). Also, for a rare and provocative consideration of the problem of sensory overload, see Klapp (1986).

12. Terry Eagleton (1996) poses an argument that runs parallel to Harvey's. The resurgence of traditional values is a response to the subversion of stability threatened by the forces of the marketplace. Eagleton regards this situation as consistent with "the

political ambivalences of postmodernism" (see discussion below), suggesting that postmodernism is often "politically oppositional but economically complicit" (132).

13. Studies suggest that the United States, Europe, and other countries are undergoing a revival of religion in general, as illustrated by a poll reported by the Associated Press on May 18, 1993, and in a *Time* magazine cover story of April 5, 1993.

14. Measures of the conservative drift toward traditional moral values and beliefs in the United States are often difficult to evaluate and will produce widely varying results depending on the language used, the way questions are posed, and the particular case in question, for example, family values or school prayer. Nonetheless, in addition to the Republican electoral victory in Congress in the November 1994 election, there is accumulating evidence of a fairly massive shift to the right, or at least rising support for conservative views. For example, an August 1994 poll conducted by People for the American Way found the following: only one-third of the respondents viewed the growing role of religious groups in U.S. politics as worrisome; 51 percent blamed society's major problems on a decline in moral values, while only 34 percent blamed economic or financial pressures on the family; 74 percent expressed support for political candidates who "put top priority on returning to traditional moral values"; and 53 percent said they would support a candidate who backed school prayer (*San Francisco Chronicle*, September 15, 1994, A10).

Measures of changing religious attitudes and affiliations are also telling. Whereas in 1986 only a third of all adults polled in the United States described themselves as bornagain or evangelical Christians, by 1993 this figure had climbed to 45 percent (Henwood 1994: 73). In a January 1992 poll, the Bama Report found strong support for religion throughout the age structure. Among their findings, agreement with the statement "Religion is very important to me" was registered among 54 percent of those between the ages of eighteen and twenty-six, 65 percent between twenty-seven and forty-five, and 79 percent between ages forty-six and sixty-four (*Time,* April 5, 1993). Interestingly, the older, more established, and more liberal, white-dominated Protestant churches in the United States have been rapidly losing members while conservative evangelical churches and New Age, Eastern, and other unconventional religions have been on the rise. On these changes and other information on religion among the so-called baby-boomers, see Roof (1993). More recent evidence suggests that the shift to religious conservatism is difficult to read politically. For example, in a piece in the newsletter of the Sociology of Culture Section of the American Sociological Association (11:1), Chris Smith et al. report that in their recent research the religious conservatives they talked to blamed "economic pressures more than moral decline" (9) as the primary cause of social ills, sounding a liberal tone despite their avowed religiosity.

15. See chapter 4.

16. *San Francisco Chronicle*, "This World" section, January 10, 1993.

17. There is always room for interpreting why identity politics has manifested itself in particular ways in various regions of the political arena. For example, George Lipsitz (personal communication) has suggested that right-wing groups have launched revivalist appeals to family and religion precisely to occlude notions of class, a move designed to

protect against criticism of capitalist inequality. It is also true that for a host of historical, social, and other reasons, in the United States race, ethnicity, gender, and other identities are more susceptible to political organization than class, especially in the postwar era. However, I am more interested in why identity and cultural issues generally have become so politicized and have taken the specific forms that they have in contemporary political culture.

18. The commercial absorption or "co-optation" of subterranean/radical/oppositional/ subversive tendencies by an "establishment" that thrives and survives on them is an old story but one that continues to reveal unimagined levels of sophistication. A *Time* magazine cover story of August 8, 1994, ". . . IS ANYONE HIP?" tells all. The text of the article discusses the history of hip and its multifarious authentic and commercial incarnations since its alleged invention by urban blacks in the United States, while openly acknowledging the pervasive commercialization to which such cultural trends succumb with increasing velocity. However, the subtext the authors create is itself a remarkable specimen of co-optation. Numerous points are worth noting. First, this article illustrates how the media always stay ahead of the game. In this case, *Time* not only acknowledges the process of commercial absorption by the market but actually *explains* how it happens: "In its infinite pliancy, capitalism proved itself well suited to absorb whatever it was in hip that might fascinate consumers, while discarding the uncomfortable parts. For every counterculture, there emerged a corresponding sales counterculture" (51). Furthermore, the media seem unusually willing, now that the cat is out of the bag, to join the chorus of opposition to commercialization. By thus absorbing the *criticism* of co-optation, they simply repeat the process at a deeper and more impenetrable level, thoroughly preempting their enemies. Second, as this article serves to illustrate, in a seeming contradiction the media are hardly reluctant to *congratulate* themselves on their own successes at co-opting anticommercial culture, turning what might otherwise be cultural boredom and despair into a cause célèbre. In effect, *Time* says, "Isn't it wonderful that the sales pitch has made it possible for *everyone* to be hip!" Third, organizations like *Time* can pride themselves on their intellectual self-understanding of the cultural processes and effects of consumer capitalism (another co-optation), as if this provided the media some redemption. Thus, the article *laments* that once commercial mainstreaming enables everyone to be hip the phenomenon loses its life and meaning. Fourth, the article immediately takes this back, suggesting that knowledge of media absorption, based partly on its own willingly shared insights, might make it possible to save hip: "Such healthy cynicism about media manipulation may be a sign that hipness is still alive" (55). Finally, of course, the moment of truth in mass culture always comes at narration's end. Quoting a hip informant, the article's closing lines are: "'Hipness today is people not being hip.' Quick, get me my editors; I think I've spotted a trend here" (55). The pseudocomplexity and contortions of this "hip" article on hip not only evade the fundamental problem but illustrate the arrogance of self-appointed arbiters of cultural and political meaning.

19. The commercial packaging of "nature" or "the environment" has reached unseemly proportions and yet has become so commonplace as to hardly deserve mention. Examples abound of commercial attempts to meld the commodification of ethnic and

regional traditions with a celebration of nature and preservation of the environment. For example, a mail order catalogue titled *Aurora* and subtitled "Expressions of Alaska" (1994 Holiday Season) features on its cover a beautiful color photograph of pristine Alaskan wilderness (packaged nature) as a lead-in to a commodification of the customs and crafts of the Eskimos in the form of baskets, jewelry, dinnerware, clothing, foods, and assorted collectibles (packaged ethnic style). While appealing to a genuine hunger for cultural authenticity and soulful restoration of a relationship with nature, such commercial promotions not only commodify our experience of these things but invariably misrepresent the originals.

20. I consider this a variation on Stuart Hall's (1981) claim that "there is *no* whole, authentic, autonomous 'popular culture' which lies outside the field of force of the relations of cultural power and domination" (232). But I also agree with Hall's many remarks over the years that culture in all its forms necessarily remains a contested site, and, despite the incorporating powers of the commodity form, I regard the relations between what I am calling the commercial and political dimensions of postmodern culture as moments of "the dialectic of cultural struggle" (Hall 1981: 233).

21. For example, most of us have experienced the discomforts of striving to retain a sense of genuine spontaneity in relation to, say, intimate others or nature in the knowledge that replicas of our most precious experiences have often already been constructed for commercial purposes, usually through advertising and packaging.

22. Despite his perceptive observations and insights, Gergen's (1991) understanding of the postmodern condition is fundamentally flawed. He sees postmodernity as a "new self-consciousness" based on deep immersion in the social world through various "technologies of social saturation" that "populate" the self (49). For Gergen, the postmodern means that the self has become saturated through excessive contact with others. Yet he fails to make any significant distinctions between saturation through *social* as opposed to *technological* relationships, as if they were part of the same order of developments. For example, "Of course it is television that most dramatically increases the variety of relationships in which one participates—*even if vicariously*" (63, emphasis added). As if "vicariously" didn't change matters! Oddly enough, he verges on a reversal of the contrast I have drawn between modernity and postmodernity, associating greater social involvement with postmodernity rather than modernity, where it began, while utterly ignoring the contraction of social space caused by the new technologies. Gergen seems fundamentally ambivalent but wants to highlight the positive side of the new intensification of involvement with others and the proliferation of possibilities for self-construction. Gergen's interpretation invites comparison to Robert Jay Lifton's (1993) notion of "the protean self," which presupposes similar conditions of multiplicity and fluidity in identity formation, which Lifton sees in "sequential," "simultaneous," and "social" manifestations (8), but which he also associates with modernity. Both authors celebrate openness and change in their portrayal of the contemporary self but seem unable to respond adequately to its problematizations under postmodernity.

23. This is an ironic historical inversion of the view presented many years ago by the German sociologist Karl Mannheim (1956), who argued in an essay "The Democratiza-

tion of Culture" that democracy in modern politics was a manifestation of a more fundamental, underlying democratization of culture. Of course, Mannheim's concept refers to changes of an order different from the ones I have been considering. While hardly a postmodern thinker, Mannheim nonetheless provides important historical and philosophical insights into the impact of democracy on the organization and practices of culture in Western societies. Indeed, his analysis complements the views of Alexis de Tocqueville (1945) that a major cultural democratization was occurring in the United States. Regarding the contemporary context, one of the reasons for the frequent equation of "postmodern" and "American" culture is that the processes of cultural democratization, and commercialization, have gone furthest in the United States. As Gitlin (1989) has argued, echoing these earlier thinkers, postmodernism can be approached as "specifically, though not exclusively, *American*" (355; emphasis in original). Although he has allegedly dissociated himself from the concept, it is perhaps no accident that Baudrillard (1988b), in his fascination with postmodernity, has celebrated contemporary America as an expression of this condition.

24. For a history of populism in the United States, see Michael Kazin's (1995) more recent study *The Populist Persuasion: An American History.*

25. Folk and working-class cultural traditions have sometimes been effectively appropriated in protest politics in the United States over the past several decades. The invocation of ethnic tradition has become a familiar means of defending one's heritage and community politically against outside threats and is thus not uncommon in identity and cultural politics. The revitalization of ethnic tradition among oppressed peoples of color, for example, African Americans, is an especially provocative example of the retrieval of tradition for progressive political purposes. For an example of the turn to religious tradition in search of a progressive cultural politics, see the work of Michael Lerner (1994, 1996).

26. This partial and miscellaneous list typifying postmodern trends in artistic production runs the gamut between authentic and commercial forms and influences. The phenomenon of *cross-over*, a term used by John Walker (1987), is a distinctively British adaptation to the dilemma of reconciling art and commerce that in many ways exemplifies the possibility of a postmodern merging of commercial and serious forms into new kinds of artistic activity. Cross-over, described by Walker as "art into pop, pop into art," is the wedding of British art school influences with pop music. Simon Frith and Howard Horne (1987) construct this phenomenon as expressive of the new situation of postmodernity as illustrated by pop videos, which in their words constitute "an equation of art and commerce. . . . [The videos'] aesthetic effect can't be separated from their market effect; the desires they address can't be realized except in exchange" (168). These authors seem to endorse the fusing of commercial product and artistic creativity as a viable solution to the collapse of modern models of artistic production on the grounds that "the interplay of artifice and authenticity is central to *everyone's* lives in consumer capitalism" (180; emphasis in original). It is curious that many British scholars have shown considerable intellectual animosity to postmodernism while this country has led in the formation of quintessentially postmodern art forms, whereas the United States seems to be the

country where postmodernity is most fully developed and postmodernism most welcome, and yet where there is the least coherence in the formation of postmodern art, in theory or practice. Britain is a source of critical condemnation of postmodern theory while at the same time of optimism toward the popular media. The United States has cultivated postmodern theory but also pessimism toward mass culture. Perhaps the difference results from the relative strengths of the Marxist tradition in Britain and the lack of commercial development there compared to the United States and the lack of Marxism and the greater saturation of life in the United States with media and consumerism.

27. This variety of deconstruction might be seen as an academic displacement of the earlier radical impulses and strategies of sixties and seventies political activism, for which it might be seen as a substitute.

28. Politically inflected poststructuralist and deconstructionist influences can be found in the work of such writers as Judith Butler (1990b, 1993), Rey Chow (1993), Thomas Dumm (1994), Nancy Fraser (1989), Michael Ryan (1982), and Gayatri Spivak (1987, 1990).

6. Redeeming the Subject: Poststructuralism, Meadian Social Pragmatism, and the Turn to Intersubjectivity

1. *Screen* magazine was a major site of this approach.

2. My interpretation of Mead will be based mainly on *Mind, Self, and Society* (1934) and *The Philosophy of the Present* (1932). Mead's other two major works are *Movements of Thought in the Nineteenth Century* (1936) and *The Philosophy of the Act* (1938).

3. In their attack on metaphysics, the French thinkers of the twentieth century have effectively repeated the nineteenth-century move of Auguste Comte, who rejected metaphysical thought for positive knowledge.

4. The French assault on the metaphysical subject also found a strong ally in the work of Jacques Lacan, who radically reinterpreted Freud in the context of language. In denouncing the autonomous ego of psychoanalysis in favor of a theory of symbolic self-construction, Lacan returned to the unconscious, attempting to demonstrate how its laws and those of language were the same, how in fact the "unconscious is structured as language" (Turkle 1978: 55). Adopting an antibiological stance by emphasizing the "meaningful" dimensions of self-development, Lacan argued that self-formation depended on entry into what he called the imaginary and (subsequently) symbolic orders. It was in the latter that desire was structured linguistically. For Lacan, the unconscious was the terrain on which the subject was structured by the Other and on which desire was shaped by socially and symbolically based significations.

5. As many have noted (Dews 1987), the poststructuralist abandonment of the historical subject and Enlightenment notions of progress invites comparison to the classical Frankfurt School's critique of instrumental reason. Disillusionment with the failure of Marxism in the West led the early Frankfurt thinkers to reflect on the fate of historical reason years before the emergence of poststructuralism. In *Dialectic of Enlightenment* (1972), Max Horkheimer and Theodor Adorno described the process by which totalizing reason acquired an instrumental character, turning the subject's drive to control the exter-

nal world into the domination of the subject's own inner nature. The withering of individual subjectivity in the reifying structures of modern science and bureaucracy was the unintended outcome of a "unifying, objectifying, controlling and disciplining reason" (Wellmer 1985: 348). Foucault's account of the rise of disciplinary structures parallels in striking ways both Max Weber's earlier formulations of the new forms of power embedded in the productivity and efficiency of rational-purposive organization accompanying the rise of bureaucracy and the early Frankfurt School's critique of the demise of the autonomous ego under conditions of organized capitalism and mass culture (Dews 1987: 151). In a remarkable interview with Duccio Trombadori (Foucault 1991), Foucault addresses his relationship to the Frankfurt School, admitting that, presumably in his formative years, he "knew little about the Frankfurt School" (116). In an intriguing confession, he admits, "When I recognize all these merits of the Frankfurt School, I do so with the bad conscience of one who should have known them and studied them much earlier than was the case. Perhaps if I had read those works earlier on, I would have saved useful time, surely: I wouldn't have needed to write some things and I would have avoided certain errors. At any rate, if I had encountered the Frankfurt School while young, I would have been seduced to the point of doing nothing else in life but the job of commenting on them" (120–21). This lends ample support to Dews's (1987) claims that the novelty of poststructuralism has often been exaggerated and that "there are striking convergences between the Frankfurt interpretation of Marxism and post-structuralist thought" (xvii). On the relationship between critical theory and postmodern theory, see also Best and Kellner (1991), chapter 7.

6. For another reading of this Nietzschean problem of the "subject as multiplicity," see Booth (1985).

7. This problem resembles another dilemma emerging from Nietzsche's thought and reappears in a split in the claims of postmodernism more generally. Whereas some postmodernists like to proclaim, following Nietzsche, that "everything is interpretation" (paralleling the Apollonian dimension that imposes "being" on "existence"), other postmodernists want to reduce reality to appearance, sense, or sensation, in a celebration of Nietzsche's other, Dionysian moment of perpetual flux. The denial of sovereign consciousness thus results in both a new subjectivism in which the subject is entirely detached from an empirically validated world and a crude and undifferentiated objectivism that reduces reality to mere sense perception and pure heterogeneity.

8. Mead's work has been poorly understood and received, except in some quarters of sociology and social psychology, where his writings on mind, self, and society have been rather influential. Mead's lack of impact can be attributed in part to both the vagueness and complexity of his ideas and the irregular trajectory of his intellectual project. In addition, his major writings remained in the form of notes and manuscripts until after his premature death, hindering systematic and reliable presentation of his theories.

9. See Huyssen (1986).

10. As mentioned in chapter 2 (note 12), the idea of performativity was Lyotard's way of characterizing the postmodern condition. While forming a connection to prag-

matism, however, performativity also connotes the reduction of identity as an aspect of self to its social and discursive enactments.

11. Butler offers a strong critique of foundational approaches to identity. Focusing on gender, her claims about the performative character of identity seem to threaten the very distinctions of male and female, heterosexual and homosexual. Indeed, Butler's intent is to thoroughly disrupt the categories of sex, gender, and desire, which she sees as the foundations of a masculinist and heterosexual order or "signifying economy." She calls attention to "the gender discontinuities that run rampant within heterosexual, bisexual, and gay and lesbian contexts" (1990a: 336). According to one observer, her "subversion of identity is an attack simultaneously on masculinism, gender, compulsory heterosexuality, and the metaphysics of presence" (Warner 1992: 19). This reflects a radical shift in our conception of politics toward a politics of subversion based on discursive practices that could undermine the dominant order of signification. In her words, "The subject is not *determined* by the rules through which it is generated because signification is *not a founding act, but rather a regulated process of repetition* that both conceals itself and enforces its rules precisely through the production of substantializing effects. In a sense, all signification takes place within the orbit of the compulsion to repeat: 'agency,' then, is to be located within the possibility of a variation on that repetition" (Butler 1990b: 145; emphasis in original). Here again Butler's notion of agency is unacceptably vague, seeming to refer simply to empty spaces in the repetitiveness of signifying practice. But her intent is to redefine politics as the deconstruction of identity and to postulate signifying practices as the terrain of political struggle. This strategy reflects the movement toward a politics of cultural struggle in which discursive practices are taken as the arena in which oppositional forces might operate. The danger in Butler's position, nonetheless, would seem to be that it threatens the destruction of any kind of identity whatsoever. It is unclear how such a political strategy would manifest itself and what it might look like in terms of organized political action. Furthermore, Butler's rather doctrinaire antiessentialism re-creates many of the original problems of French poststructuralism. Reminiscent of Foucault, her analysis fails ultimately to distinguish between descriptive and normative accounts of subjectivity (Warner 1992) by reducing the grounds of opposition to the terms of the established discursive system, thereby begging the question of where to locate actual points of resistance. Finally, it is not clear whether what Butler says about sex and gender could be extended to class, race, ethnic, and other identities, which arguably manifest themselves in different forms and degrees of unity and stability.

12. The passive grammatical constructions characterizing Butler's mode of argumentation betray a strong unwillingness to enter into any kind of subjective theoretical stance. Although, along with sustained abstraction, this might serve her theoretical goals, it creates a tendency toward circularity as her discourse keeps weaving back on itself in search of an active subject. At worst, some of Butler's arguments tend to be rhetorically self-validating.

13. See Aboulafia (1986), Habermas (1987a, 1992), and Joas (1985) for critiques of Mead.

14. See Joas (1985) and Mead (1936).

15. One of Mead's more prominent students, Herbert Blumer, remarked to me when I was his student, in response to my query as to why Mead sounded at times so much like Hegel, that all serious scholars in Mead's generation studied Hegel prodigiously.

16. That Mead more fully appropriated Darwin than did the other pragmatists can be seen in his special preoccupation with the naturalistic and evolutionary bases of mind and the disciplinary development of science as a strategic mode of discovery and cognition in the adaptation of the human organism to its environment. See Joas (1985).

17. Since evolution involves sequential change in nature—and society—Mead rejects mechanistic or idealistic worldviews that hold that the passage of events is subjective. The perception of change is *objective* in the sense that it is rooted in an actual order of events in the real world. This leads to Mead's notion of the "objective reality of perspectives" (Miller 1973: 209). While new perspectives have their source in the individual, these perspectives are for that reason no less "real" or "objective" since they are part of what Mead calls "the act," understood as the basic unit of existence: "It is then such a coincidence of the perspective of the individual organism with the pattern of the whole act in which it is so involved that the organism can act within it, that constitutes the objectivity of the perspective" (Mead 1932: 174–75). Based in the social process of adjustment, perspectives originate with individuals but come to be shared by other members of the community, constituting a "common praxis as a common world" (Joas 1985: 181) in the completion of acts.

18. The principle of emergence was also a cornerstone of Emile Durkheim's conception of the social, especially his theory of collective representations. For Durkheim, the collective forms and forces of social life were a product of the interactions of separate individuals, resulting from the combinatory effects of their separate actions. However, Durkheim had a rather rudimentary and mechanistic conception of this process. He saw smaller units or entities simply combining to create larger ones with different properties, much as the molecules of hydrogen and oxygen combine to produce the molecules of water. While advancing sociology as a mode of scientific analysis, his reliance on models of explanation taken from the physical sciences, and his particular use of biological models, ultimately impeded his progress toward a properly social psychological understanding of the origins and workings of social or institutional life. See Durkheim (1961, 1964, 1982). In other respects, one finds suggestive and fruitful parallels between Durkheim and Mead. While rejecting the subjective pragmatism of William James, and the idea of pragmatism more generally (on the widely shared European misconception that it was no different from utilitarianism), Durkheim was nonetheless searching for an objective social theory of mind, the tools for which were (unlike for Mead) unavailable to him. Durkheim also converged with Mead in his estimation of the social importance of symbols as collective objectifications of human experience and their functions in mobilizing social responses. See Durkheim (1983), Habermas (1987a), Joas (1993), and Stone and Farberman (1967).

19. My discussion barely skims the surface of the extensive intellectual currents shaping Mead's thought and the range of his theoretical and philosophical concerns. For a detailed scholarly treatment, see Joas (1985).

20. According to Joas (1985), "The concept of 'intersubjectivity' designates a structure of communicative relations between subjects, a structure that is suited for transcending, on the theoretical plane, the opposition between the individualistic bias in the theory of action and a structural theory that does not recognize subjects or human agency. The political correlate of this concept is a social order in which the atomization of individuals is eliminated, not through their subordination to a collectivity, but instead through the participation of all in reasoning discussion to determine their common future" (13).

21. Mead (1934) sees the self as essentially cognitive, referring to "the internalized conversation of gestures which constitutes thinking" (220). He thus tends to equate the social, the cognitive, and the rational, seeing the self as the functional core of all three characteristics of action. Accordingly, Mead could be faulted for constructing an overly "intellectual" self. Yet, he seemed to be quite aware that he was conceptualizing the self in this particular way and was prepared to defend it on the grounds of his larger pragmatist agenda of developing the social character and relevance of the experimental sciences as a model of all human thought and action.

22. Mead's choice of the familiar pronouns "I" and "Me" to capture the subjective and objective phases of the self was both propitious and unfortunate. These terms are commonly used, immediately recognizable and understood, and highly connotative on a personal, experiential level. They thus lend his account of the self a descriptive and explanatory power that might otherwise be lacking. But for the very same reasons, these words are imprecise and ambiguous. Worse, in his hands they paradoxically become abstract and vague. Further, by constructing these concepts as referring both to temporal and functional processes, Mead introduces some confusion as to how the self is to be understood. Part of the problem stems from the fact that *Mind, Self, and Society*, where he explicates these concepts, was compiled from student lecture notes and therefore assumes a rather fragmentary form. For convincing expositions and critiques of the "I" and the "Me," see Aboulafia (1986) and Cronk (1973).

23. When first translated into English and published in 1973, both *Marxism and the Philosophy of Language* and its author were virtually unknown. However, the work originally had a close association with the name of Mikhail M. Bakhtin, leaving room for speculation that he was the actual author. See the translator's preface (dated 1986) in Voloshinov (1973).

24. One could identify several points of convergence between Meadian thought and the Marxist philosophy of praxis. Yet Mead and symbolic interactionism more generally are susceptible to serious criticisms from a left standpoint. On the one hand, Mead has been seen as complementary to Marx on such topics as alienation, reification, and ideology critique. On the other hand, the Meadian perspective has been criticized for lacking an adequate conception of the self, ignoring the alienation of labor, having an astructural bias, and neglecting questions of power. See Becker (1968), Berger and Luckman (1966), Israel (1971), Lichtman (1970), Mills (1967), and *Catalyst* (1973). For a sympathetic left attempt to defend Mead against some of these criticisms, see Cronk (1973).

25. Mead (1934) explicitly situated language as a social psychological phenomenon: "The study of the process of language or speech—its origins and development—is a

branch of social psychology, because it can be understood only in terms of the social processes of behavior within a group of interacting organisms" (120, n. 6).

26. In his critical reconstruction of Mead, Habermas attempts to demonstrate that Mead fails to explain how normatively binding social structures arise from the socially shared symbolic use of language, what Habermas calls "signal language." The missing links, he claims, can be partially found in Wittgenstein's concept of the rule but more so in Durkheim's theory of the authority of the sacred, which allegedly accounts for normatively structured social processes of institutionalization. Habermas seems to be vaguely proposing a "synthesis" of Mead and Durkheim (who he argues did not pay sufficient attention to "communicative action") with his notion of the "linguistification of the sacred," by which he means "the transfer of cultural reproduction, social integration, and socialization from sacred foundations over to linguistic communication and action oriented to mutual understanding" (Habermas 1987a: 107).

27. This appears to be Voloshinov's strategy for addressing what was later to become an obligatory move among Western Marxists, namely, the overcoming of the base-superstructure dichotomy. Voloshinov's subtext seems to be that language should not be consigned exclusively to the "secondary" realm of cultural superstructure but grounded in the practical context of the concrete actions and struggles of classes and other social groups.

28. In this respect, Voloshinov (1973) calls into question Saussure's distinction between *la langue* and *la parole* (59–60; 146) as well as his separation of synchrony from diachrony (66).

29. In chapter 3, I drew a distinction between "signs" and "symbols." I characterized *signs* as more instrumental in nature, limited to narrowly functional relationships of predetermined meaning. *Symbols*, in contrast, are rich in meaning, multidimensionally complex. *Sign* reflects the Saussurean bias that language is to be regarded as a highly structured formal system of relations that predetermines linguistic meanings in a relatively fixed way. *Symbol* carries both Durkheimian connotations of sacred and authoritative meanings, richly textured and embedded in ritual, and Meadian implications of the generation and transformation of meaning through socially shared, interactive experiences.

30. This term was invented by Mead's student Herbert Blumer, who notes, "The term 'symbolic interactionism' is a somewhat barbaric neologism that I coined in an off-hand way in an article written in *Man and Society* (Emerson P. Schmidt, ed. New York: Prentice-Hall, 1937). The term somehow caught on and is now in general use" (1969: 1).

31. While building on Mead's basic conceptualizations, Habermas seems most critical of him at the point at which he discontinues the discussion of language and pursues the notion of normatively regulated action within the larger problem of the relationship between the I and the Me. According to Habermas (1987a), Mead develops a model of socially controlled action "and neglects the path that leads to propositionally differentiated *communication* in language" (23). Habermas regards Mead as a primary source for the creation of a theory of "communicative action" but distinguishes between Mead's view of language as a medium for "coordinating action and socializing individuals" and his own concerns for "language as a medium for reaching understanding" (23). Here,

Habermas neglects to mention that Mead actually understood the process of symbolization as facilitating "communication," which he saw as the basis of universal knowledge among social actors. Contained in symbolization, then, were inherently universalizing tendencies. See Joas (1985) and Miller (1973). Although I therefore think that Habermas underestimates Mead's basic agreement with his project of pursuing "communicative competence" or the "ideal speech situation," in contrast to Habermas's more linguistic reading of Mead, my own reading is more social. The importance I attach to Mead's work lies in his comprehensive social theorization of language and meaning, specifically his position, however abstractly formulated, that these can only be studied and understood through their social contextualization. While both Mead and Habermas have neglected the problems of social interests and power that impede universalization, I believe Mead's and Voloshinov's social theories of language are inherently more indicative of the kinds of social analysis required prior to the development of universalizing models of social action than the direction taken by Habermas.

32. See Habermas (1987a: 108–10).

33. As Antonio and Kellner (1994) point out, "Mead's decentered conception of subjectivity . . . still presumed a 'complete self' (reflecting the 'unity and structure of the social process' [Mead]) that mediated its underlying multiplicities" (136).

Bibliography

Aboulafia, Mitchell. 1986. *The Mediating Self: Mead, Sartre, and Self-Determination.* New Haven, Conn., Yale University Press.

———. 1995. "Habermas and Mead: On Universality and Individuality," *Constellations* 2/1: 94–113.

Adorno, T. W. 1941. "On Popular Music," *Studies in Philosophy and Social Science* 1: 17–48.

———. 1945. "A Social Critique of Radio Music," *Kenyon Review* 7/2: 208–17.

———. 1957. "Television and the Patterns of Mass Culture." In *Mass Culture: The Popular Arts in America,* ed. Bernard Rosenberg and David Manning White, 474–88. Glencoe, Ill., Free Press.

———. 1978. "On the Fetish-Character in Music and the Regression of Listening." In *The Essential Frankfurt School Reader,* ed. Andrew Arato and Eike Gebhardt, 270–99. New York, Urizen Books.

Alcoff, Linda. 1986. "Cultural Feminism vs. Post-Structuralism: The Identity Crisis in Feminist Theory." In *Feminist Theory in Practice and Process,* ed. Micheline R. Malson, Jean F. O'Barr, Sarah Westphal-Wihl, and Mary Wyer, 295–326. Chicago, University of Chicago Press.

Alt, John. 1975. "Work, Culture, and Crisis," *Telos* 23: 168–82.

———. 1976. "Beyond Class: The Decline of Industrial Labor and Leisure," *Telos* 28: 55–80.

Amin, Samir. 1974. *Accumulation on a World Scale: A Critique of the Theory of Underdevelopment,* Vols. 1 and 2. New York, Monthly Review Press.

Anderson, Benedict. 1991. *Imagined Communities: Reflections on the Origins and Spread of Nationalism.* London, Verso.

Anderson, Perry. 1984. *In the Tracks of Historical Materialism*. Chicago, University of Chicago Press.

Angus, Ian, and Sut Jhally, eds. 1989. *Cultural Politics in Contemporary America*. New York, Routledge.

Antonio, Robert J., and Douglas Kellner. 1994. "The Future of Social Theory and the Limits of Postmodern Critique." In *Postmodernism and Social Inquiry*, ed. David R. Dickens and Andrea Fontana, 127–52. New York, Guilford.

Anzaldúa, Gloria, ed. 1990. *Making Face, Making Soul: Creative and Critical Perspectives by Feminists of Color*. San Francisco, Aunt Lute Books.

Appadurai, Arjun. 1994. "Disjuncture and Difference in the Global Cultural Economy." In *Colonial Discourse and Post-Colonial Theory*, ed. Patrick Williams and Laura Chrisman, 324–39. New York, Columbia University Press.

Arac, Jonathan, ed. 1986. *Postmodernism and Politics*. Minneapolis, University of Minnesota Press.

Aronowitz, Stanley. 1979. "Film—The Art Form of Late Capitalism," *Social Text* 1: 110–29.

———. 1992. "Reflections on Identity," *October* 61: 91–103.

———. 1993. *Roll over Beethoven: The Return of Cultural Strife*. Hanover, Conn., Wesleyan University Press.

———. 1994. *Dead Artists, Live Theories*. New York, Routledge.

Bagdikian, Ben H. 1990. *The Media Monopoly*. 3d ed. Boston, Beacon Press.

Balzac, Honoré de. 1971. *Lost Illusions*. Harmondsworth, Penguin Books.

Baran, Paul, and Paul Sweezy. 1966. *Monopoly Capital*. New York, Monthly Review.

Barnet, Richard J., and John Cavanagh. 1994. *Global Dreams: Imperial Corporations and the New World Order*. New York, Simon and Schuster.

Barrett, William. 1958. *Irrational Man: A Study in Existential Philosophy*. Garden City, N.J., Doubleday Anchor.

Barthes, Roland. 1977. *Image, Music, Text*. New York, Hill and Wang.

Baudrillard, Jean. 1981. *For a Critique of the Political Economy of the Sign*. St. Louis, Telos Press.

———. 1983a. *Simulations*. New York, Semiotext(e).

———. 1983b. *In the Shadow of Silent Majorities*. New York, Semiotext(e).

———. 1983c. "The Ecstasy of Communication." In *The Anti-Aesthetic: Essays on Postmodern Culture*, ed. Hal Foster, 126–34. Port Townsend, Wash., Bay Press.

———. 1988a. *Jean Baudrillard: Selected Writings*, ed. Mark Poster. Stanford, Calif., Stanford University Press.

———. 1988b. *America*. London, Verso.

———. 1993. *Symbolic Exchange and Death*. London, Sage.

Bauman, Zygmunt. 1992. *Intimations of Postmodernity*. London, Routledge.

Baumeister, Roy. 1986. *Identity: Cultural Change and the Struggle for Self*. New York, Oxford University Press.

Becker, Ernest. 1968. *The Structure of Evil: An Essay on the Unification of the Science of Man*. New York, Braziller.

Becker, Howard S. 1963. *Outsiders: Studies in the Sociology of Deviance*. New York, Free Press.

———, ed. 1964. *The Other Side: Perspectives on Deviance*. New York, Free Press.

Bell, Daniel. 1973. *The Coming of Post-Industrial Society: A Venture in Social Forecasting*. New York, Basic Books.

———. 1977. *The Cultural Contradictions of Capitalism*. New York, Basic Books.

Bellah, Robert N., Richard Madsen, William M. Sullivan, Ann Swidler, and Steven Tipton.1985. *Habits of the Heart: Individualism and Commitment in American Life*. Berkeley and Los Angeles, University of California Press.

Berger, John. 1972. *Ways of Seeing*. London, BBC and Penguin Books.

Berger, Peter L., and Thomas Luckmann. 1966. *The Social Construction of Reality: A Treatise in the Sociology of Knowledge*. Garden City, N.J., Doubleday.

Berman, Marshall. 1982. *All That Is Solid Melts into Air*. New York, Simon and Schuster.

Best, Steven. 1989. "Jameson, Totality, and the Poststructuralist Critique." In *Postmodernism/Jameson/Critique*, ed. Douglas Kellner, 333–68. Washington, D.C., Maisonneuve Press.

———. 1994. "The Commodification of Reality and the Reality of Commodification: Baudrillard, Debord, and Postmodern Theory." In *Baudrillard: A Critical Reader*, ed. Douglas Kellner, 41–67. Oxford, Blackwell.

Best, Steven, and Douglas Kellner. 1991. *Postmodern Theory: Critical Interrogations*. New York, Guilford.

Blau, Judith R. 1992. *The Shape of Culture: A Study of Contemporary Cultural Patterns in the United States*. Cambridge, Cambridge University Press.

Block, Fred. 1990. *Postindustrial Possibilities: A Critique of Economic Discourse*. Berkeley and Los Angeles, University of California Press.

Bluestone, Barry, and Bennett Harrison. 1982. *The Deindustrialization of America*. New York, Basic Books.

Blumer, Herbert. 1969. *Symbolic Interactionism: Perspective and Method*. Englewood Cliffs, N.J., Prentice Hall.

Blundell, Valda, John Shepherd, and Ian Taylor, eds. 1993. *Relocating Cultural Studies: Developments in Theory and Research*. London, Routledge.

Bocock, Robert. 1993. *Consumption*. London, Routledge.

Boggs, Carl. 1986. *Social Movements and Political Power*. Philadelphia, Temple University Press.

Booth, David. 1985. "Nietzsche on 'The Subject as Multiplicity,'" *International Philosophical Review* 18: 121–46.

Bourdieu, Pierre. 1984. *Distinction: A Social Critique of the Judgement of Taste*. Cambridge, Mass., Harvard University Press.

Bradbury, Malcolm, and James McFarlane, eds. 1976. *Modernism: A Guide to European Literature, 1890–1930*. London, Penguin Books.

Brake, Mike. 1980. *The Sociology of Youth Culture and Youth Subcultures*. London, Routledge and Kegan Paul.

Bramson, Leon. 1961. *The Political Context of Sociology*. Princeton, N.J., Princeton University Press.

Brenkman, John. 1979. "Mass Media: From Collective Experience to the Culture of Privatization," *Social Text* 1: 94–109.

Brown, Wendy. 1993. "Wounded Attachments," *Political Theory* 21/3: 390–410.

Bürger, Peter. 1984. *The Theory of the Avant-Garde*. Minneapolis, University of Minnesota Press.

Burgin, Victor. 1986. *The End of Art Theory: Criticism and Postmodernity*. Atlantic Highlands, N.J., Humanities Press International.

Butler, Judith. 1987. *Subjects of Desire: Hegelian Reflections in Twentieth-Century France*. New York, Columbia University Press.

———. 1990a. "Gender Trouble, Feminist Theory, and Psychoanalytic Discourse." In *Feminism/Postmodernism*, ed. Linda Nicholson, 324–40. New York, Routledge.

———. 1990b. *Gender Trouble: Feminism and the Subversion of Identity*. New York, Routledge.

———. 1993. *Bodies That Matter: On the Discursive Limits of 'Sex.'* New York, Routledge.

Calhoun, Craig, ed. 1993. *Habermas and the Public Sphere*. Cambridge, Mass., MIT Press.

———. 1994. "Social Theory and the Politics of Identity." In *Social Theory and the Politics of Identity*, ed. Craig Calhoun, 1–36. Oxford, Blackwell.

Calinescu, Matei. 1987. *Five Faces of Modernity: Modernism, Avant-Garde, Decadence, Kitsch, Postmodernism*. Durham, N.C., Duke University Press.

Callinicos, Alex. 1990. *Against Postmodernism: A Marxist Critique*. New York, St. Martin's.

Campbell, Colin. 1987. *The Romantic Ethic and the Spirit of Modern Consumerism*. Oxford, Basil Blackwell.

Cascardi, Anthony J. 1992. *The Subject of Modernity*. Cambridge, Cambridge University Press.

Catalyst. 1973. Issue on "Symbolic Interactionism." 7.

Chambers, Ian. 1986. *Popular Culture: The Metropolitan Experience*. London, Methuen.

———. 1990. *Border Dialogues: Journeys in Postmodernity*. London, Routledge.

———. 1994. *Migrancy, Culture, Identity*. London, Routledge.

Chen, Kuan-Hsing. 1987. "The Masses and the Media: Baudrillard's Implosive Postmodernism," *Theory, Culture and Society* 4/1: 71–88.

Chow, Rey. 1993. *Writing Diaspora: Tactics of Intervention in Contemporary Cultural Studies*. Bloomington, Indiana University Press.

Clark, T. J. 1984. *The Painting of Modern Life: Paris in the Art of Manet and His Followers*. Princeton, N.J., Princeton University Press.

Clark, Terry Nichols, and Seymour Martin Lipset. 1991. "Are Social Classes Dying?" *International Sociology* 6/4: 397–410.

Clark, Terry Nichols, Seymour Martin Lipset, and Michael Rempel. 1993. "The Declining Political Significance of Class," *International Sociology* 8/3: 293–316.

Clarke, John. 1991. *New Times and Old Enemies: Essays on Cultural Studies and America*. London, Harper Collins.

Clifford, James. 1988. *The Predicament of Culture: Twentieth Century Ethnography, Literature, and Art.* Cambridge, Mass., Harvard University Press.

Clifford, James, and George Marcus, eds. 1986. *Writing Culture: The Poetics and Politics of Ethnography.* Berkeley and Los Angeles, University of California Press.

Collins, James. 1952. *The Existentialists: A Critical Study.* Chicago, Henry Regnery.

Collins, Jim. 1989. *Uncommon Cultures: Popular Culture and Post-Modernism.* New York, Routledge.

———. 1992. "Postmodernism and Television." In *Channels of Discourse, Reassembled,* ed. Robert C. Allen, 327–53. Chapel Hill, University of North Carolina Press.

Collins, Patricia Hill. 1990. *Black Feminist Thought: Knowledge, Consciousness, and the Politics of Empowerment.* New York, Routledge.

Connolly, William. 1991. *Identity/Difference: Democratic Negotiations of Political Paradox.* Ithaca, N.Y., Cornell University Press.

Cooley, Charles Horton. 1902. *Human Nature and the Social Order.* New York, Scribner's.

Crane, Diana. 1987. *The Transformation of the Avant-Garde.* Chicago, University of Chicago Press.

Cronk, George. 1973. "Symbolic Interactionism: A 'Left-Median' Interpretation," *Social Theory and Practice* 2/3: 313–33.

Crook, Stephen, Jan Pakulski, and Malcolm Waters. 1992. *Postmodernization: Change in Advanced Society.* London, Sage.

Crosby, Christina. 1992. "Dealing with Differences." In *Feminists Theorize the Political,* ed. Judith Butler and Joan W. Scott, 130–43. New York, Routledge.

Culler, Jonathan. 1982. *On Deconstruction: Theory and Criticism after Structuralism.* Ithaca, N.Y., Cornell University Press.

Currie, Elliott, Robert Dunn, and David Fogarty. 1980. "The New Immiseration: Stagflation, Inequality, and the Working Class," *Socialist Review* 54: 7–31.

Darnovsky, Marcy, Barbara Epstein, and Richard Flacks, eds. 1995. *Cultural Politics and Social Movements.* Philadelphia, Temple University Press.

Davis, Fred. 1992. *Fashion, Culture, and Identity.* Chicago, University of Chicago Press.

Debord, Guy. 1977. *Society of the Spectacle.* Detroit, Black and Red.

de Lauretis, Teresa, ed. 1986. *Feminist Studies/Critical Studies.* Bloomington, Indiana University Press.

Deleuze, Gilles, and Félix Guattari. 1983. *Anti-Oedipus: Capitalism and Schizophrenia.* Minneapolis, University of Minnesota Press.

———. 1987. *A Thousand Plateaus: Capitalism and Schizophrenia.* Minneapolis, University of Minnesota Press.

Denisoff, R. Serge, and Richard A. Peterson. 1972. *The Sounds of Social Change.* Chicago, Rand McNally.

Denzin, Norman K. 1988. "Act, Language, and Self in Symbolic Interactionist Thought," *Studies in Symbolic Interaction* 9: 51–80.

———. 1992. *Symbolic Interactionism and Cultural Studies: The Politics of Interpretation.* Oxford, Basil Blackwell.

Derrida, Jacques. 1976. *Of Grammatology*. Baltimore, Johns Hopkins University Press.

———. 1978. *Writing and Difference*. London, Routledge and Kegan Paul.

Descombes, Vincent. 1980. *Modern French Philosophy*. Cambridge, Cambridge University Press.

Dews, Peter. 1987. *Logics of Disintegration: Poststructuralist Thought and the Claims of Critical Theory*. London, Verso.

Dickens, David R., and Andrea Fontana, eds. 1994. *Postmodernism and Social Inquiry*. New York, Guilford.

Diggens, John Patrick. 1994. *The Promise of Pragmatism: Modernism and the Crisis of Knowledge and Authority*. Chicago, University of Chicago Press.

DiMaggio, Paul. 1987. "Classification in Art," *American Sociological Review* 52/4: 440–55.

———. 1991. "Social Structure, Institutions, and Cultural Goods: The Case of the United States." In *Social Theory for a Changing Society*, ed. Pierre Bourdieu and James S. Coleman, 133–66. New York, Russell Sage Foundation.

Dirlik, Arif. 1994. "The Postcolonial Aura: Third World Criticism in the Age of Global Capitalism," *Critical Inquiry* 20/2: 328–56.

Douglas, Susan J. 1994. *Where the Girls Are: Growing Up Female with the Mass Media*. New York, Random House.

Dumm, Thomas. 1994. *united states*. Ithaca, N.Y., Cornell University Press.

Dunn, Robert G. 1986a. "Television, Consumption and the Commodity Form," *Theory, Culture and Society* 3/1: 49–64.

———. 1986b. "Mass Media and Society: The Legacy of T. W. Adorno and the Frankfurt School," *California Sociologist* 9/2: 109–43.

———. 1991. "Postmodernism: Populism, Mass Culture, and Avant-Garde," *Theory, Culture and Society* 8/1: 111–35.

Dunning, William V. 1993. "Post-Modernism and the Construct of the Divisible Self," *British Journal of Aesthetics* 33/2: 132–41.

Durkheim, Emile. 1961. *The Elementary Forms of the Religious Life*. New York, Collier.

———. 1964. *The Division of Labor in Society*. New York, Free Press.

———. 1982. *The Rules of Sociological Method and Selected Texts on Sociology and Its Method*, ed. Steven Lukes. New York, Free Press.

———. 1983. *Pragmatism and Sociology*, ed. John B. Allcock. Cambridge, Cambridge University Press.

Eagleton, Terry. 1983. *Literary Theory: An Introduction*. Minneapolis, University of Minnesota Press.

———. 1996. *The Illusions of Postmodernism*. Oxford, Blackwell Publishers.

Eliasoph, Nina. 1986. "Drive-In Morality, Child Abuse, and the Media," *Socialist Review* 90: 7–31.

Epstein, Barbara. 1991a. *Political Protest and Cultural Revolution: Nonviolent Direct Action in the 1970s and 1980s*. Berkeley and Los Angeles, University of California Press.

———. 1991b. "'Political Correctness' and Collective Powerlessness," *Socialist Review* 91/34: 13–35.

Epstein, Steven. 1987. "Gay Politics, Ethnic Identity: The Limits of Social Construction-ism," *Socialist Review* 93/94: 9–54.

———. 1991. "Sexuality and Identity: The Contribution of Object Relations Theory to a Constructionist Sociology," *Theory and Society* 20: 825–73.

Erenberg, Lewis A. 1981. *Steppin' Out: New York Night Life and the Transformation of American Culture, 1890–1930.* Chicago, University of Chicago Press.

Erikson, Erik. 1980. *Identity and the Life Cycle.* New York, W.W. Norton.

Erikson, Kai. 1966. *Wayward Puritans: A Study in the Sociology of Deviance.* New York, John Wiley & Sons.

Etzioni, Amitai. 1994. *The Spirit of Community: The Reinvention of American Society.* New York, Touchstone.

Evans, Sara, and Harry C. Boyte. 1986. *Free Spaces: The Sources of Democratic Change in America.* New York, Harper and Row.

Ewen, Stuart. 1976. *Captains of Consciousness: Advertising and the Social Roots of the Consumer Culture.* New York, McGraw-Hill.

Ewen, Stuart, and Elizabeth Ewen. 1982. *Channels of Desire: Mass Images and the Shaping of American Consciousness.* New York, McGraw-Hill.

Faludi, Susan. 1991. *Backlash: The Undeclared War against American Women.* New York, Crown Publishers.

Featherstone, Mike. 1988. "In Pursuit of the Postmodern: An Introduction," *Theory, Culture and Society* 5/2: 195–215.

———. 1991. *Consumer Culture and Postmodernism.* London, Sage.

———. 1995. *Undoing Culture: Globalization, Postmodernism and Identity.* London, Sage.

Ferrandino, Joe. 1972. "Rock Culture and the Development of Social Consciousness." In *Side-Saddle on the Golden Calf: Social Structure and Popular Culture in America,* ed. George H. Lewis, 263–90. Pacific Palisades, Calif., Goodyear.

Ferry, Luc, and Alain Renaut. 1990. *French Philosophy of the Sixties: An Essay on Anti-humanism.* Amherst, University of Massachusetts Press.

Feuer, Jane. 1983. "The Concept of Live Television: Ontology as Ideology." In *Regarding Television: Critical Approaches—An Anthology,* ed. E. Ann Kaplan, 12–22. Frederick, Md., University Publications of America.

Feuer, Lewis S., ed. 1959. *Marx and Engels: Basic Writings on Politics and Philosophy.* Garden City, N.J., Doubleday Anchor.

Fiske, John. 1987. *Television Culture.* London, Methuen.

———. 1989a. *Reading the Popular.* London, Routledge.

———. 1989b. *Understanding the Popular.* London, Routledge.

———. 1992. "British Cultural Studies and Television." In *Channels of Discourse, Reassembled,* ed. Robert C. Allen, 284–326. Chapel Hill, University of North Carolina Press.

Foster, Hal, ed. 1983. *The Anti-Aesthetic: Essays on Postmodern Culture.* Port Townsend, Wash., Bay Press.

———. 1984. "(Post)Modern Polemics," *New German Critique* 33: 67–78.

Foucault, Michel. 1965. *Madness and Civilization: A History of Insanity in the Age of Reason.* New York, Mentor.

——. 1977. *Language, Counter-Memory, Practice: Selected Essays and Interviews.* Ithaca, N.Y., Cornell University Press.

——. 1979. *Discipline and Punish: The Birth of the Prison.* New York, Vintage.

——. 1980. *Power/Knowledge: Selected Interviews and Other Writings.* New York, Pantheon.

——. 1991. *Remarks on Marx: Conversations with Duccio Trombadori.* New York, Semiotext(e).

Fox, Richard Wightman, and T. J. Jackson Lears, eds. 1983. *The Culture of Consumption.* New York, Pantheon.

Frampton, Kenneth. 1983. "Towards a Critical Regionalism: Six Points for an Architecture of Resistance." In *The Anti-Aesthetic: Essays on Postmodern Culture,* ed. Hal Foster, 16–30. Port Townsend, Wash., Bay Press.

Frankenberg, Ruth. 1993. *The Social Construction of Whiteness: White Women, Race Matters.* Minneapolis, University of Minnesota Press.

Frascina, Francis, and Charles Harrison, eds. 1982. *Modern Art and Modernism: A Critical Anthology.* New York, Harper and Row.

Fraser, Nancy. 1989. *Unruly Practices: Power, Discourse, and Gender in Contemporary Social Theory.* Minneapolis, University of Minnesota Press.

Freeman, Jo. 1983. *Social Movements of the Sixties and Seventies.* New York, Longman.

Freud, Sigmund. 1961. *Civilization and Its Discontents.* New York, W.W. Norton.

Fried, Michael. 1968. "Art and Objecthood." In *Minimal Art: A Critical Anthology,* ed. Gregory Battcock, 116–47. New York, E.P. Dutton.

Friedman, Jonathan. 1994. *Cultural Identity and Global Process.* London, Sage.

Frisby, David. 1988. *Fragments of Modernity.* Cambridge, Mass., MIT Press.

Frith, Simon. 1978. *The Sociology of Rock.* London, Constable.

——. 1981. *Sound Effects: Youth, Leisure, and the Politics of Rock 'n' Roll.* New York, Pantheon Books.

Frith, Simon, and Howard Horne. 1987. *Art into Pop.* London, Methuen.

Fuss, Diana. 1989. *Essentially Speaking: Feminism, Nature, and Difference.* New York, Routledge.

——. 1995. *Identification Papers.* New York, Routledge.

Fussell, Paul. 1983. *Class.* New York, Ballantine.

Gablik, Suzi. 1984. *Has Modernism Failed?* New York, Thames and Hudson.

Gans, Herbert J. 1974. *Popular Culture and High Culture: An Analysis and Evaluation of Taste.* New York, Basic Books.

——. 1980. *Deciding What's News.* New York, Vintage.

——. 1986. "American Popular Culture and High Culture in a Changing Class Structure," *Prospects: An Annual of American Cultural Studies* 10: 17–37.

Gergen, Kenneth J. 1991. *The Saturated Self.* New York, Basic Books.

Giddens, Anthony. 1979. *Central Problems in Social Theory: Action, Structure and Contradiction in Social Analysis.* Berkeley and Los Angeles, University of California Press.

————. 1984. *The Constitution of Society: Outline of a Theory of Structuration*. Berkeley and Los Angeles, University of California Press.

————. 1990. *The Consequences of Modernity*. Stanford, Calif., Stanford University Press.

————. 1991. *Modernity and Self-Identity: Self and Society in the Late Modern Age*. Stanford, Calif., Stanford University Press.

Gitlin, Todd. 1979. "Prime Time Ideology: The Hegemonic Process in Television Entertainment," *Social Problems* 26/3: 251–66.

————. 1980. *The Whole World Is Watching: Mass Media and the Making and Unmaking of the New Left*. Berkeley and Los Angeles, University of California Press.

————. 1983. *Inside Prime Time*. New York, Pantheon.

————. 1989. "Postmodernism: Roots and Politics." In *Cultural Politics in Contemporary America*, ed. Ian Angus and Sut Jhally, 347–60. New York, Routledge.

————. 1994. "From Universality to Difference: Notes on the Fragmentation of the Idea of the Left." In *Social Theory and the Politics of Identity*, ed. Craig Calhoun, 150–74. Oxford, Blackwell.

————. 1995. *The Twilight of Common Dreams: Why America is Wracked by Culture Wars*. New York, Metropolitan Books.

Gleason, Philip. 1983. "Identifying Identity: A Semantic History," *The Journal of American History* 69/4: 910–31.

Goffman, Erving. 1959. *The Presentation of Self in Everyday Life*. New York, Doubleday.

————. 1967. *Interaction Ritual: Essays on Face-to-Face Behavior*. Garden City, N.J., Doubleday Anchor.

Goldberg, David Theo, ed. 1994. *Multiculturalism: A Critical Reader*. Oxford, Blackwell.

Goldman, Eric F. 1956. *The Crucial Decade—and After: America, 1945–1960*. New York, Vintage Books.

Gordon, Avery, and Christopher Newfield, eds. 1996. *Mapping Multiculturalism*. Minneapolis, University of Minnesota Press.

Gramsci, Antonio. 1973. *Prison Notebooks*. New York, International Publishers.

Gray, Herman. 1988. *Producing Jazz: The Experience of an Independent Record Company*. Philadelphia, Temple University Press.

————. 1995. *Watching Race: Television and the Struggle for "Blackness."* Minneapolis, University of Minnesota Press.

Greenberg, Jay R., and Stephen A. Mitchell. 1983. *Object Relations in Psychoanalytic Theory*. Cambridge, Mass., Harvard University Press.

Grossberg, Lawrence, Cary Nelson, and Paula Treichler, eds. 1992. *Cultural Studies*. New York, Routledge.

Guntrip, Harry. 1971. *Psychoanalytic Theory, Therapy and the Self*. New York, Basic Books.

Gusfield, Joseph R. 1975. *Community: A Critical Response*. New York, Harper and Row.

Habermas, Jürgen. 1971. *Knowledge and Human Interests*. Boston, Beacon Press.

————. 1975. *Legitimation Crisis*. Boston, Beacon Press.

————. 1983. "Modernity—An Incomplete Project." In *The Anti-Aesthetic: Essays on Postmodern Culture*, ed. Hal Foster, 3–15. Port Townsend, Wash., Bay Press.

————. 1984. *The Theory of Communicative Action.* Vol. 1. *Reason and the Rationalization of Society.* Boston, Beacon Press.

————. 1987a. *The Theory of Communicative Action.* Vol. II. *Lifeworld and System: A Critique of Functionalist Reason.* Boston, Beacon Press.

————. 1987b. *The Philosophical Discourse of Modernity.* Cambridge, Mass., MIT Press.

————. 1992. *Postmetaphysical Thinking: Philosophical Essays.* Cambridge, Mass., MIT Press.

Hall, Stuart. 1980a. "Cultural Studies: Two Paradigms," *Media, Culture, and Society* 2: 57–72.

————. 1980b. "Encoding/Decoding." In *Culture, Media, Language,* ed. Stuart Hall, Dorothy Hobson, Andrew Lowe, and Paul Willis, 128–38. London, Hutchinson.

————. 1981. "Notes on Deconstructing the Popular." In *People's History and Socialist Theory,* ed. Raphael Samuel, 227–40. London, Routledge and Kegan Paul.

————. 1991. "Ethnicity: Identity and Difference," *Radical America* 23: 9–20.

Hall, Stuart, Dorothy Hobson, Andrew Lowe, and Paul Willis, eds. 1980. *Culture, Media, Language.* London, Hutchinson.

Hall, Stuart, and Tony Jefferson, eds. 1976. *Resistance through Rituals: Youth Subcultures in Post-War Britain.* London, Unwin Hyman.

Haraway, Donna. 1991. *Simians, Cyborgs, and Women.* New York, Routledge.

Harding, Sandra. 1986. *The Science Question in Feminism.* Ithaca, N.Y., Cornell University Press.

————. 1991. *Whose Science? Whose Knowledge? Thinking from Women's Lives.* Ithaca, N.Y., Cornell University Press.

Harris, Helena. 1987. "Subjectivity and Symbolization," *Psychoanalytic Review* 74/1: 1–17.

Harvey, David. 1989. *The Condition of Postmodernity.* Oxford, Basil Blackwell.

Haug, W. F. 1986. *Critique of Commodity Aesthetics: Appearance, Sexuality, and Advertising in Capitalist Society.* Minneapolis, University of Minnesota Press.

Hebdige, Dick. 1979. *Subculture: The Meaning of Style.* London, Methuen.

————.1988. *Hiding in the Light.* London, Routledge.

Hechtman, Todd. 1993. "The Self-Help Paradox: A Cultural Analysis of a Social Movement for the Self." Presented at the American Sociological Association Meetings, Miami Beach, Florida, August 13–17.

Heller, Thomas C., Morton Sosna, and David E. Wellbery, eds. 1986. *Reconstructing Individualism: Autonomy, Individuality, and the Self in Western Thought.* Stanford, Calif., Stanford University Press.

Henwood, Doug. 1994. *The State of the U.S.A. Atlas.* New York, Simon and Schuster.

Herd, Denise. 1994. "Contesting Culture: Alcohol-Related Identity Movements in Contemporary African American Communities." Presented at a conference on Consumer Culture and Resistance: Historical Perspectives, University of California, Santa Cruz, November 4–5.

Herman, Edward S., and Noam Chomsky. 1988. *Manufacturing Consent: The Political Economy of the Mass Media.* New York, Pantheon.

Hewitt, John P. 1984. *Self and Society: A Symbolic Interactionist Social Psychology*. Boston, Allyn and Bacon.

———. 1989. *Dilemmas of the American Self*. Philadelphia, Temple University Press.

Honneth, Axel. 1992. "Pluralization and Recognition: On the Self-Misunderstanding of Postmodern Social Theorists." In *Between Totalitarianism and Postmodernity*, ed. Peter Beilharz, Gillian Robinson, and John Rundell, 163–72. Cambridge, Mass., MIT Press.

hooks, bell. 1990. *Yearning: Race, Gender, and Cultural Politics*. Boston, South End Press.

———. 1992. *Black Looks*. Boston, South End Press.

Horkheimer, Max, and T. W. Adorno. 1972. *Dialectic of Enlightenment*. New York, Seabury Press.

Hout, Mike, Clem Brooks, and Jeff Manza. 1993. "The Persistence of Classes in Post-Industrial Societies," *International Sociology* 8: 259–77.

Hutcheon, Linda. 1988. *A Poetics of Postmodernism: History, Theory, Fiction*. New York, Routledge.

———. 1989. *The Politics of Postmodernism*. New York, Routledge.

Huyssen, Andreas. 1986. *After the Great Divide: Modernism, Mass Culture, Postmodernism*. Bloomington, Indiana University Press.

Israel, Joachim. 1971. *Alienation: From Marx to Modern Sociology*. Boston, Allyn and Bacon.

Jackman, Mary R., and Robert W. Jackman. 1983. *Class Awareness in the United States*. Berkeley and Los Angeles, University of California Press.

Jacobs, Norman, ed. 1961. *Culture for the Millions? Mass Media in Modern Society*. Princeton, N.J., D. Van Nostrand Company.

Jaeger, Gertrude, and Philip Selznick. 1964. "A Normative Theory of Culture," *American Sociological Review* 29: 653–69.

Jameson, Fredric. 1972. *The Prison-House of Language: A Critical Account of Structuralism and Russian Formalism*. Princeton, N.J., Princeton University Press.

———. 1979. "Reification and Utopia in Mass Culture," *Social Text* 1: 130–48.

———. 1981. *The Political Unconscious: Narrative as a Socially Symbolic Act*. Ithaca, N.Y., Cornell University Press.

———. 1983. "Postmodernism and Consumer Society." In *The Anti-Aesthetic: Essays on Postmodern Culture*, ed. Hal Foster, 111–25. Port Townsend, Wash., Bay Press.

———. 1984a. "Postmodernism, or the Cultural Logic of Late Capitalism," *New Left Review* 146: 53–92.

———. 1984b. "The Politics of Theory: Ideological Positions in the Postmodernism Debate," *New German Critique* 33: 53–65.

———. 1987. "Regarding Postmodernism—A Conversation with Fredric Jameson" (by Anders Stephanson), *Social Text* 17: 29–54.

———. 1991. *Postmodernism; or, The Cultural Logic of Late Capitalism*. Durham, N.C., Duke University Press.

Jeffords, Susan. 1989. *The Remasculinization of America: Gender and the Vietnam War*. Bloomington, Indiana University Press.

Jencks, Charles. 1984. *The Language of Postmodern Architecture.* 4th ed. New York, Rizzoli.

———. 1986. *What Is Post-Modernism?* 3d ed. London, Academy Editions.

Joas, Hans. 1985. *G. H. Mead: A Contemporary Re-examination of His Thought.* Cambridge, Mass., MIT Press.

———. 1993. *Pragmatism and Social Theory.* Chicago, University of Chicago Press.

Kavolis, Vytautas. 1970. "Post-Modern Man: Psychocultural Responses to Social Trends," *Social Problems* 17/4: 435–48.

Kazin, Michael. 1986. "Populism: The Perilous Promise," *Socialist Review* 89: 99–106.

———. 1995. *The Populist Persuasion: An American History.* New York, Basic Books.

Kellner, Douglas. 1983. "Critical Theory, Commodities, and the Consumer Society," *Theory, Culture and Society* 1/3: 66–83.

———. 1989. *Jean Baudrillard: From Marxism to Postmodernism and Beyond.* Stanford, Calif., Stanford University Press.

———. 1992. "Popular Culture and the Construction of Postmodern Identities." In *Modernity and Identity,* ed. Scott Lash and Jonathan Friedman, 141–77. Oxford, Blackwell.

———. 1995. *Media Culture: Cultural Studies, Identity and Politics between the Modern and the Postmodern.* London, Routledge.

———, ed. 1994. *Baudrillard: A Critical Reader.* Oxford, Blackwell.

Kern, Stephen. 1983. *The Culture of Time and Space: 1880–1918.* Cambridge, Mass., Harvard University Press.

Klapp, Orrin E. 1969. *Collective Search for Identity.* New York, Holt, Rinehart and Winston.

———. 1986. *Overload and Boredom: Essays on the Quality of Life in the Informational Society.* New York, Greenwood.

Kornhauser, William. 1959. *The Politics of Mass Society.* Glencoe, Ill., Free Press.

Kumar, Krishan. 1995. *From Post-Industrial to Post-Modern Society: New Theories of the Contemporary World.* Oxford, Blackwell.

Kurzweil, Edith. 1980. *The Age of Structuralism: Lévi-Strauss to Foucault.* New York, Columbia University Press.

Laclau, Ernesto. 1992. "Universalism, Particularism, and the Question of Identity," *October* 61: 83–90.

———. 1994. "Introduction." In *The Making of Political Identities,* ed. Ernesto Laclau, 1–8. London, Verso.

Lane, Michael, ed. 1970. *Introduction to Structuralism.* New York, Basic Books.

Langer, Susanne. 1951. *Philosophy in a New Key: A Study in the Symbolism of Reason, Rite, and Art.* New York, Mentor.

Lasch, Christopher. 1979. *The Culture of Narcissism: American Life in an Age of Diminishing Expectations.* New York, W.W. Norton.

———. 1984. *The Minimal Self: Psychic Survival in Troubled Times.* New York, W.W. Norton.

Lash, Scott. 1990. *The Sociology of Postmodernism*. London, Routledge.

Lash, Scott, and Jonathan Friedman, eds. 1992. *Modernity and Identity*. Oxford, Basil Blackwell.

Lash, Scott, and John Urry. 1987. *The End of Organized Capitalism*. Oxford, Basil Blackwell.

Lee, Grace Chin. 1945. *George Herbert Mead: Philosopher of the Social Individual*. New York, King's Crown Press.

Lee, Martyn J. 1993. *Consumer Culture Reborn: The Cultural Politics of Consumption*. London, Routledge.

Leiss, William. 1976. *The Limits to Satisfaction: An Essay on the Problem of Needs and Commodities*. Toronto, University of Toronto Press.

Lembo, Ronald. forthcoming. *Thinking through Television: Viewing Practices and the Social Limits to Power*. New York, Cambridge University Press.

Lembo, Ronald, and Kenneth H. Tucker. 1990. "Culture, Television, and Opposition: Rethinking Cultural Studies," *Critical Studies in Mass Communication* 7: 97–116.

Lerner, Michael. 1994. *Jewish Renewal: A Path to Healing and Transformation*. New York, G. P. Putnam's Sons.

———. 1996. *The Politics of Meaning: Restoring Hope and Possibility in an Age of Cynicism*. Reading, Mass., Addison-Wesley.

Levin, Jerome D. 1992. *Theories of the Self*. Washington, D.C., Hemisphere Publishing.

Levin, Kim. 1988. *Beyond Modernism*. New York, Harper and Row.

Levine, Lawrence W. 1988. *Highbrow/Lowbrow: The Emergence of Cultural Hierarchy in America*. Cambridge, Mass., Harvard University Press.

Lewis, George, ed. 1972. *Side-Saddle on the Golden Calf: Social Structure and Popular Culture in America*. Pacific Palisades, Calif., Goodyear Publishing.

Lhamon, W. T., Jr. 1990. *Deliberate Speed: The Origins of a Cultural Style in the American 1950s*. Washington, D.C., Smithsonian Institution.

Lichterman, Paul. 1992. "Self-Help Reading as a Thin Culture," *Media, Culture and Society* 14: 421–47.

Lichtman, Richard. 1970. "Symbolic Interactionism and Social Reality: Some Marxist Queries," *Berkeley Journal of Sociology* 15: 75–94.

Lifton, Robert Jay. 1993. *The Protean Self: Human Resilience in an Age of Fragmentation*. New York, Basic Books.

Lindlof, Thomas R. 1988. "Media Audiences as Interpretive Communities," *Communication Yearbook* 11: 81–107.

Lipsitz, George. 1990a. *Time Passages: Collective Memory and American Popular Culture*. Minneapolis, University of Minnesota Press.

———. 1990b. "How Does It Feel When You've Got No Food? The Past as Present in Popular Music." In *For Fun and Profit*, ed. Richard Butsch, 195–214. Philadelphia, Temple University Press.

———. 1994a. *Dangerous Crossroads: Popular Music, Postmodernism and the Poetics of Place*. London, Verso.

————.1994b. *Rainbow at Midnight: Labor and Culture in the 1940s.* Urbana, University of Illinois Press.

Lowenthal, Leo. 1957. "Historical Perspectives of Popular Culture." In *Mass Culture: The Popular Arts in America,* ed. Bernard Rosenberg and David Manning White, 46–58. Glencoe, Ill., Free Press.

————. 1961. *Literature, Popular Culture, and Society.* Englewood Cliffs, N.J., Prentice Hall.

Lukács, Georg. 1971. *History and Class Consciousness: Studies in Marxist Dialectics,* trans. Rodney Livingstone. Cambridge, Mass., MIT Press.

Lunn, Eugene. 1982. *Marxism and Modernism: An Historical Study of Lukács, Brecht, Benjamin, and Adorno.* Berkeley and Los Angeles, University of California Press.

Lynd, Robert S., and Helen Merrell Lynd. 1929. *Middletown: A Study in American Culture.* San Diego, Harcourt Brace Jovanovich.

Lyotard, Jean-François. 1984. *The Postmodern Condition: A Report on Knowledge.* Minneapolis, University of Minnesota Press.

Macpherson, C. B. 1962. *The Political Theory of Possessive Individualism: From Locke to Hobbes.* London, Oxford University Press.

————. 1973. *Democratic Theory: Essays in Retrieval.* Oxford, Clarendon Press.

Malson, Micheline R., Jean F. O'Barr, Sarah Westphal-Wihl, and Mary Wyer, eds. 1986. *Feminist Theory in Practice and Process.* Chicago, University of Chicago Press.

Manis, Jerome G., and Bernard N. Meltzer, eds. 1972. *Symbolic Interaction: A Reader in Social Psychology.* 2d ed. Boston, Allyn and Bacon.

Mannheim, Karl. 1956. *Essays on the Sociology of Culture.* London, Routledge and Kegan Paul.

Manoff, Robert Karl, and Michael Schudson, eds. 1986. *Reading the News.* New York, Pantheon.

Manuel, Peter. 1993. *Cassette Culture: Popular Music and Technology in North India.* Chicago, University of Chicago Press.

Marcuse, Herbert. 1964. *One-Dimensional Man: Studies in the Ideology of Advanced Industrial Society.* Boston, Beacon Press.

————. 1965. "Repressive Tolerance." In *A Critique of Pure Tolerance,* ed. Robert Paul Wolff, Barrington Moore Jr., and Herbert Marcuse. Boston, Beacon Press.

Marx, Karl. 1906. *Capital: A Critique of Political Economy.* New York, Modern Library.

————. 1978. "Economic and Philosophical Manuscripts of 1844." In *The Marx-Engels Reader.* 2d ed., ed. Robert C. Tucker, 66–125. New York, W.W. Norton.

Marx, Karl, and Friedrich Engels. 1978. "Manifesto of the Communist Party." In *The Marx-Engels Reader.* 2d ed., ed. Robert C. Tucker, 469–500. New York, W. W. Norton.

Mattelart, Armand. 1979. *Multinational Corporations and the Control of Culture: The Ideological Apparatuses of Imperialism.* Sussex, Harvester Press.

Matza, David. 1969. *Becoming Deviant.* Englewood Cliffs, N.J., Prentice Hall.

May, Larry. 1989. *Recasting America: Culture and Politics in the Age of Cold War.* Chicago, University of Chicago Press.

McCracken, Grant. 1990. *Culture and Consumption: New Approaches to the Symbolic Character of Consumer Goods and Activities.* Bloomington, Indiana University Press.

McGuigan, Jim. 1992. *Cultural Populism.* London, Routledge.

Mead, George Herbert. 1932. *The Philosophy of the Present.* Chicago, University of Chicago Press.

———. 1934. *Mind, Self and Society.* Chicago, University of Chicago Press.

———. 1936. *Movements of Thought in the Nineteenth Century,* ed. Merritt H. Moore. Chicago, University of Chicago Press.

———. 1938. *The Philosophy of the Act.* Chicago, University of Chicago Press.

Megill, Allan. 1985. *Prophets of Extremity: Nietzsche, Heidegger, Foucault, Derrida.* Berkeley and Los Angeles, University of California Press.

Meltzer, Bernard N., and John W. Petras. 1972. "The Chicago and Iowa Schools of Symbolic Interactionism." In *Symbolic Interaction: A Reader in Social Psychology.* 2d ed., ed. Jerome G. Manis and Bernard N. Meltzer, 43–57. Boston, Allyn and Bacon.

Melucci, Alberto. 1989. *Nomads of the Present: Social Movements and Individual Needs in Contemporary Society.* Philadelphia, Temple University Press.

———. 1996. *The Playing Self: Person and Meaning in the Planetary Society.* Cambridge, Cambridge University Press.

Messner, Michael. 1996. "Studying Up on Sex," *Sociology of Sport Journal* 13: 221–37.

Meyrowitz, Joshua. 1981. "Television and the Obliteration of Childhood: The Restructuring of Adult/Child Information Systems." In *Studies in Communication.* Vol. 1, ed. Sari Thomas, 151–67. Norwood, N.J., Ablex.

———. 1985. *No Sense of Place: The Impact of Electronic Media on Social Behavior.* New York, Oxford University Press.

Miller, Daniel. 1987. *Material Culture and Mass Consumption.* Oxford, Basil Blackwell.

———. 1995. *Acknowledging Consumption: A Review of New Studies.* London, Routledge.

Miller, David L. 1973. *George Herbert Mead: Language, Self and the World.* Austin, University of Texas Press.

Miller, Douglas T., and Marion Nowak. 1975. *The Fifties: The Way We Really Were.* Garden City, N.J., Doubleday.

Mills, C. Wright. 1956. *The Power Elite.* New York, Oxford University Press.

———. 1967. *Power, Politics, and People.* New York, Oxford University Press.

Morley, David. 1980. *The 'Nationwide' Audience.* London, British Film Institute.

———. 1986. *Family Television: Cultural Power and Domestic Leisure.* London, Comedia.

Mowitt, John. 1992. *Text: The Genealogy of an Antidisciplinary Object.* Durham, N.C., Duke University Press.

Neuman, W. Russell. 1991. *The Future of the Mass Audience.* Cambridge, Cambridge University Press.

New German Critique. 1984. Issue on "Modernity and Postmodernity." 33.

Newman, Charles. 1985. *The Post-Modern Aura: The Act of Fiction in an Age of Inflation.* Evanston, Ill., Northwestern University Press.

Nicholson, Linda, ed. 1990. *Feminism/Postmodernism.* New York, Routledge.

Norris, Christopher. 1990. *What's Wrong with Postmodernism?* Baltimore, Johns Hopkins University Press.

October. 1992. "The Identity in Question: A Special Issue." 61.

Olson, Philip, ed. 1963. *America as a Mass Society: Changing Community and Identity.* Glencoe, Ill., Free Press.

O'Neill, John. 1995. *The Poverty of Postmodernism.* London, Routledge.

O'Sullivan, Tim, John Hartley, Danny Saunders, Martin Montgomery, and John Fiske. 1994. *Key Concepts in Communication and Cultural Studies.* 2d ed. London, Routledge.

Pakulski, Jan. 1993. "The Dying of Class or Marxist Class Theory?" *International Sociology* 8/3: 279–92.

Pakulski, Jan, and Malcolm Waters. 1996. *The Death of Class.* London, Sage.

Palmer, Bryan D. 1990. *Descent into Discourse: The Reification of Language and the Writing of Social History.* Philadelphia, Temple University Press.

Parenti, Michael. 1986. *Inventing Reality: The Politics of the Mass Media.* New York, St. Martin's Press.

Pfeil, Fred. 1985. "Makin' Flippy Floppy: Postmodernism and the Baby-Boom PMC." In *The Year Left,* ed. Mike Davis, Fred Pfeil, and Michael Sprinker, 263–95. London, Verso.

Pheby, Keith C. 1988. *Interventions: Displacing the Metaphysical Subject.* Washington, D.C., Maisonneuve Press.

Philipson, Ilene. 1991. "What's the Big I.D.? The Politics of the Authentic Self," *Tikkun* 6/6: 51–55.

Phillips, Kevin. 1993. *Boiling Point: Democrats, Republicans, and the Decline of Middle Class Prosperity.* New York, Random House.

Poggioli, Renato. 1968. *The Theory of the Avant-Garde.* Cambridge, Mass., Belknap/ Harvard University Press.

Poster, Mark. 1975. *Existential Marxism in Postwar France: From Sartre to Althusser.* Princeton, N.J., Princeton University Press.

———. 1990. *The Mode of Information: Poststructuralism and Social Context.* Chicago, University of Chicago Press.

———. 1995. *The Second Media Age.* Cambridge, Polity Press.

Postman, Neil. 1982. *The Disappearance of Childhood.* New York, Dell.

Press, Andrea L. 1991. *Women Watching Television: Gender, Class, and Generation in the American Television Experience.* Philadelphia, University of Pennsylvania Press.

Preteceille, Edmond, and Jean-Pierre Terrail. 1985. *Capitalism, Consumption and Needs,* trans. Sarah Matthews. Oxford, Basil Blackwell.

Radway, Janice. 1984. *Reading the Romance: Women, Patriarchy, and Popular Literature.* Chapel Hill, University of North Carolina Press.

Rauschenberg, Robert. 1987. *Rauschenberg,* interview with Barbara Rose. New York, Vintage.

Reich, Robert B. 1992. *The Work of Nations.* New York, Vintage.

Riesman, David, with Nathan Glazer and Ruel Denney. 1950. *The Lonely Crowd: A Study of the Changing American Character*. New Haven, Conn., Yale University Press.

Ritchin, Fred. 1990. *In Our Own Image: The Coming Revolution in Photography*. New York, Aperture.

Rojek, Chris. 1985. *Capitalism and Leisure Theory*. London, Tavistock.

Rojek, Chris, and Bryan S. Turner, eds. 1993. *Forget Baudrillard?* London, Routledge.

Roof, Wade Clark. 1993. *A Generation of Seekers: The Spiritual Journeys of the Baby Boom Generation*. New York, Harper Collins.

Rorty, Richard. 1979. *Philosophy and the Mirror of Nature*. Princeton, N.J., Princeton University Press.

———. 1989. *Contingency, Irony, and Solidarity*. Cambridge, Cambridge University Press.

Rosaldo, Renato. 1989. *Culture and Truth: The Remaking of Social Analysis*. Boston, Beacon Press.

Rose, Arnold, ed. 1962. *Human Behavior and Social Processes: An Interactionist Approach*. Boston, Houghton Mifflin.

Rose, Margaret. 1991. *The Post-Modern and the Post-Industrial*. Cambridge, Cambridge University Press.

Rosenau, Pauline Marie. 1992. *Post-Modernism and the Social Sciences: Insights, Inroads, and Intrusions*. Princeton, N.J., Princeton University Press.

Rosenberg, Bernard, and David Manning White, eds. 1957. *Mass Culture: The Popular Arts in America*. Glencoe, Ill., Free Press.

Rosenberg, Harold. 1994. *The Tradition of the New*. New York, Da Capo.

Rosenthal, Michael. 1992. "What Was Postmodernism?" *Socialist Review* 92/3: 84–105.

Rubington, Earl, and Martin S. Weinberg, eds. 1978. *Deviance: The Interactionist Perspective*. New York, Macmillan.

Russell, Charles. 1985. *Poets, Prophets, and Revolutionaries: The Literary Avant-Garde from Rimbaud through Postmodernism*. New York, Oxford University Press.

Ryan, Michael. 1982. *Marxism and Deconstruction*. Baltimore, Johns Hopkins University Press.

Said, Edward. 1978. *Orientalism*. London, Routledge and Kegan Paul.

Sarbin, Theodore R., and John I. Kitsuse, eds. 1994. *Constructing the Social*. London, Sage Publications.

Saussure, Ferdinand de. 1974. *Course in General Linguistics*. London, Fontana.

Schiller, Herbert I. 1969. *Mass Communications and American Empire*. Boston, Beacon Press.

———. 1981. *Who Knows: Information in the Age of the Fortune 500*. Norwood, N.J., Ablex.

Schudson, Michael. 1978. *Discovering the News: A Social History of American Newspapers*. New York, Basic Books.

Schur, Edwin. 1976. *The Awareness Trap: Self-Absorption Instead of Social Change*. New York, Quadrangle.

Scott, Joan. 1992. "Multiculturalism and the Politics of Identity," *October* 61: 12–19.

Seidman, Steven. 1992. *Embattled Eros: Sexual Politics and Ethics in Contemporary America.* New York, Routledge.

————. 1994. *Contested Knowledge: Social Theory in the Postmodern Era.* Cambridge, Blackwell.

Seidman, Steven, and David G. Wagner, eds. 1992. *Postmodernism and Social Theory.* Cambridge, Blackwell.

Shibutani, Tamotsu. 1955. "Reference Groups as Perspectives," *American Journal of Sociology* 60: 562–69.

Shields, Rob, ed. 1992. *Lifestyle Shopping: The Subject of Consumption.* London, Routledge.

Simmel, Georg. 1950. *The Sociology of Georg Simmel,* ed. Kurt Wolff. Glencoe, Ill., Free Press.

————. 1968. *Georg Simmel: The Conflict in Modern Culture and Other Essays,* trans. K. Peter Etzkorn. New York, Teachers College Press.

————. 1990. *The Philosophy of Money.* London, Routledge.

Smart, Barry. 1992. *Modern Conditions, Postmodern Controversies.* London, Routledge.

————. 1993. *Postmodernity.* London, Routledge.

Smith, Paul. 1988. *Discerning the Subject.* Minneapolis, University of Minnesota Press.

Social Text. 1992. Issue on "Postcolonialism and the Third World." 31/32.

Soja, Edward. 1989. *Postmodern Geographies: The Reassertion of Space in Critical Social Theory.* London, Verso.

Somers, Margaret R., and Gloria D. Gibson. 1994. "Reclaiming the Epistemological 'Other': Narrative and the Social Constitution of Identity." In *Social Theory and the Politics of Identity,* ed. Craig Calhoun, 37–99. Oxford, Blackwell.

Sontag, Susan. 1966. *Against Interpretation.* New York, Farrar Straus Giroux.

Spigel, Lynn. 1992. *Make Room for TV: Television and the Family Ideal in Postwar America.* Chicago, University of Chicago Press.

Spivak, Gayatri Chakravorty. 1987. *In Other Worlds: Essays in Cultural Politics.* London, Methuen.

————. 1990. *The Post-Colonial Critic: Interviews, Strategies, Dialogues.* New York, Routledge.

Stein, Maurice R., Arthur J. Vidich, and David Manning White, eds. 1960. *Identity and Anxiety: Survival of the Person in Mass Society.* Glencoe, Ill., Free Press.

Stone, Gregory P., and Harvey A. Farberman. 1967. "On the Edge of Rapprochement: Was Durkheim Moving toward the Perspective of Symbolic Interaction?" *Sociological Quarterly* 8: 149–64.

Susman, Warren I. 1973. *Culture as History: The Transformation of American Society in the Twentieth Century.* New York, Pantheon.

Swingewood, Alan. 1977. *The Myth of Mass Culture.* London, Macmillan.

Takagi, Ronald. 1993. *A Different Mirror: A History of Multicultural America.* Boston, Little, Brown.

Taylor, Charles. 1989. *Sources of the Self: The Making of Modern Identity.* Cambridge, Mass., Harvard University Press.

———. 1991. *The Ethics of Authenticity*. Cambridge, Mass., Harvard University Press.

———. 1992. *Multiculturalism and "the Politics of Recognition."* Princeton, N.J., Princeton University Press.

Telos. 1988. "Roundtable on Communitarianism." 76: 2–32.

Theory, Culture and Society. 1983. Issue on "Consumer Culture." 1/3.

Theory, Culture and Society. 1985. Issue on "The Fate of Modernity." 2/3.

Theory, Culture and Society. 1988. Issue on "Postmodernism." 5/2–3.

Theory, Culture and Society. 1990. Issue on "Global Culture." 7/2–3.

Theory, Culture and Society. 1991. Issue on "Georg Simmel." 8/3.

Tocqueville, Alexis de. 1945. *Democracy in America*, Vol. 2. New York, Vintage.

Tomlinson, John. 1991. *Cultural Imperialism*. Baltimore, Johns Hopkins University Press.

Tompkins, Calvin. 1976. *The Bride and the Bachelors: Five Masters of the Avant-Garde: Duchamp, Tinguely, Cage, Rauschenberg, Cunningham*. New York, Penguin.

———. 1980. *Off the Wall: Robert Rauschenberg and the Art World of Our Time*. New York, Penguin.

———. 1988. *Post- to Neo-: The Art World of the 1980s*. New York, Henry Holt.

Tönnies, Ferdinand. 1957. *Community and Society*. New York, Harper and Row.

Touraine, Alain. 1985. "An Introduction to the Study of Social Movements," *Social Research* 52: 747–87.

———. 1995. *Critique of Modernity*. Oxford, Blackwell.

Tucker, Kenneth H. 1991. "How New Are the New Social Movements?" *Theory, Culture and Society* 8/2: 75–98.

Tunstall, Jeremy. 1977. *The Media Are American*. New York, Columbia University Press.

Turkle, Sherry. 1978. *Psychoanalytic Politics: Freud's French Revolution*. Cambridge, Mass., MIT Press.

———. 1995. *Life on the Screen: Identity in the Age of the Internet*. New York, Simon and Schuster.

Turner, Brian, ed. 1991. *Theories of Modernity and Postmodernity*. London, Sage.

Turner, Ralph H. 1956. "Role-Taking, Role-Standpoint and Reference Group Behavior," *American Journal of Sociology* 61: 316–28.

———. 1962. "Role-Taking: Process versus Conformity." In *Human Behavior and Social Processes,* ed. Arnold Rose, 20–40. Boston, Houghton Mifflin.

———. 1976. "The Real Self: From Institution to Impulse." *American Journal of Sociology* 81/5: 989–1016.

Twitchell, James B. 1992. *Carnival Culture: The Trashing of Taste in America*. New York, Columbia University Press.

Vanneman, Reeve, and Lynn Weber Cannon. 1987. *The American Perception of Class*. Philadelphia, Temple University Press.

Veblen, Thorstein. 1934. *The Theory of the Leisure Class*. New York, Modern Library.

Venturi, Robert, Denise Scott Brown, and Steven Izenour. 1977. *Learning from Las Vegas*. Cambridge, Mass., MIT Press.

Voloshinov, V. N. 1973. *Marxism and the Philosophy of Language*. Cambridge, Mass., Harvard University Press.

Wakefield, Neville. 1990. *Postmodernism: The Twilight of the Real.* London, Pluto.

Walker, John A. 1987. *Cross-Overs: Art into Pop / Pop into Art.* London, Methuen.

Wallerstein, Immanuel. 1974. *The Modern World System.* New York, Academic Press.

Warner, Michael. 1992. "From Queer to Eternity: An Army of Theorists Cannot Fail," *Voice Literary Supplement* 106: 18–19.

Weber, Max. 1958a. "Bureaucracy." In *From Max Weber: Essays in Sociology,* ed. Hans Gerth and C. Wright Mills, 196–244. New York, Oxford University Press.

———. 1958b. "Religious Rejections of the World and Their Directions." In *From Max Weber: Essays in Sociology,* ed. Hans Gerth and C. Wright Mills, 323–59. New York, Oxford University Press.

———. 1958c. *The Protestant Ethic and the Spirit of Capitalism.* New York, Charles Scribner's Sons.

Weingartner, Rudolph H. 1962. *Experience and Culture: The Philosophy of Georg Simmel.* Middletown, Conn., Wesleyan University Press.

Wellman, David. 1996. "Red and Black in White America: Discovering Cross-Border Identities and Other Subversive Activities." In *Names We Call Home: Autobiography on Racial Identity,* ed. Becky Thompson and Sangeeta Tyagi, 29–41. New York, Routledge.

Wellmer, Albrecht. 1985. "On the Dialectic of Modernism and Postmodernism," *Praxis International* 4/4: 337–62.

West, Cornel. 1992. "A Matter of Life and Death." *October* 61: 20–23.

Wexler, Philip. 1996. *Holy Sparks: Social Theory, Education, and Religion.* New York, St. Martin's Press.

Whimster, M. S., and Scott Lash, eds. 1987. "Introduction," *Max Weber: Rationality and Modernity.* London, Allen and Unwin.

White, Leslie. 1949. *The Science of Culture.* Farrar, Straus and Giroux.

White, Winston. 1961. *Beyond Conformity.* Glencoe, Ill., Free Press.

Wiley, Norbert. 1994. *The Semiotic Self.* Chicago, University of Chicago Press.

Williams, Patrick, and Laura Chrisman, eds. 1994. *Colonial Discourse and Post-Colonial Theory.* New York, Columbia University Press.

Williams, Raymond. 1975. *Television: Technology and Cultural Form.* New York, Schocken.

———. 1977. *Marxism and Literature.* Oxford, Oxford University Press.

———. 1980. *Problems in Materialism and Culture.* London, Verso.

Willis, Ellen. 1991. "Multiple Identities," *Tikkun* 6/6: 58–60.

Willis, Paul. 1978. *Profane Culture.* London, Routledge and Kegan Paul.

———. 1990. *Common Culture: Symbolic Work at Play in the Everyday Cultures of the Young.* Boulder, Colo., Westview Press.

Willis, Susan. 1991. *A Primer for Daily Life.* London, Routledge.

Wilmsen, Edwin N., and Patrick McAllister, eds. 1996. *The Politics of Difference: Ethnic Premises in a World of Power.* Chicago, University of Chicago Press.

Wirth, Louis. 1938. "Urbanism as a Way of Life," *American Journal of Sociology* 44: 1–24.

Wolfe, Tom. 1981. *From Bauhaus to Our House.* New York, Washington Square Press.

Wood, Peter H. 1982. "Television as Dream." In *Television: The Critical View*. 3d ed., ed. Horace Newcomb, 510–28. New York, Oxford University Press.

Woodward, Kathleen, ed. 1980. *The Myths of Information: Technology and Postindustrial Culture*. Madison, Wis., Coda.

Yankelovich, Daniel. 1981. *New Rules*. New York, Random House.

Yardley, Krysia, and Terry Honess, eds. 1987. *Self and Identity: Psychosocial Perspectives*. New York, John Wiley and Sons.

Young, Iris. 1990. *Justice and the Politics of Difference*. Princeton, N.J., Princeton University Press.

Young, Robert. 1990. *White Mythologies: Writing History and the West*. London, Routledge.

Zaretsky, Eli. 1994. "Identity Theory, Identity Politics: Psychoanalysis, Marxism, Post-Structuralism." In *Social Theory and Identity Politics*, ed. Craig Calhoun, 198–215. Oxford, Blackwell.

Zinn, Howard. 1980. *A People's History of the United States*. New York, Harper and Row.

Index

Compiled by Eileen Quam and Theresa Wolner

Adorno, Theodor, 28, 227, 228–29, 236n14, 237n21; *Dialectic of Enlightenment,* 252n5
Aesthetic populism, 164
Affirmative action, 24
African Americans: lifestyle of collective group, 68
Age: and marketing, 112–13
Alcoff, Linda, 232n10, 233n14
Alienation, 55, 59
Altman, Robert, 247n9
Americanism, 22
Anthropology, 241n13
Antihumanism, 176
Appadurai, Arjun, 245n14
Attitudes: change in, 110
Authenticity, 54–55, 69
Avant-garde: collapse of, 165

Balzac, Honoré de: *Lost Illusions,* 235n4
Baudelaire, Charles, 83–84, 86, 91, 153

Baudrillard, Jean: on class culture, 122; on commodity as sign form, 93, 126; on consumption, 113–14, 115, 120, 143, 222; on loss of real, 12, 161; on manipulated society, 171; on mass media, 72; on modern/postmodern, 83, 85; on simulations, 99–104; on subject in commodity society, 65
Bauman, Zygmunt, 83, 85
Bell, Daniel, 121
Bellah, Robert, 78–79
Berman, Marshall, 85, 109
Best, Steven, 174
Biology: and identity, 35; postmodern repudiation of, 233n16
Blau, Judith, 117–18
Blumer, Herbert, 201, 218, 232–33n12, 232–33n13, 255n15
Bourdieu, Pierre: *Distinction,* 116–17, 124
Bourgeoisie. *See* Petite bourgeoisie
Brown, Wendy, 232n7

Butler, Judith, 15, 39, 179, 191–202, 227–28, 236n12; *Bodies That Matter,* 198; *Gender Trouble,* 191, 193, 199

Calhoun, Craig, 40–41
Capitalism: and culture, 91–96, 143, 145, 170; and difference, 147, 148–49; disorganized, 242n4; and Fordism, 111; and globalization, 108; and identity formation, 56, 58; and liberalism, 149; and realism, 56; and technology, 124–25
Cascardi, Anthony, 53
Change: in culture, 107
Civil rights movement: and inequality, 149, 150; and politics of exclusion, 21
Class: decline of class cultures, 117–18; disintegration of status, 121, 122–23; distinctions, 242n7; and commodity, 118–19; identities, 22; and marketing, 112–13; postmodernism bases in, 122
Cold War, 17, 155, 232n6
Collective identities, 2, 22, 25–26, 153
Collins, Patricia Hill, 234n26
Commodification/commodities, 236n14; and cultural experience, 144, 146; defined, 235n2; displacement by, 67; hypercommodification, 115; and incorporation, 159; and mass media, 125–29; and modernity, 86; as object, 125; as pervasive, 151; production, 110; and search for truth, 159, 161; as sign form, 115–16, 126; susceptibility to, 160. *See also* Consumerism/consumption; Mass media; Television

Communities/community: artificial/virtual, 76–77, 79; and consumption/mass culture, 76–80; disembedding process of, 61–62, 90; and identity, 76–80, 156; and individual, 59–64; interpretive, 77; vs. lifestyle, 78; and mass media/culture, 76–80; and modernity, 59–64; organic, 59–60, 76; search for, 156; and society, 60
Conformity: trends in, 149
Connolly, William, 41–42
Conservatism: resurgence of, 154
Constructionism: and determinism, 48–49; and essentialism, 37–43; and identity, 3, 8–9, 19, 34, 37–43; and interactionism, 37; and social relationality, 37–43
Consumer credit: and consumption, 119
Consumer culture: character of, 112
Consumerism/consumption, 64–70, 96–99; and capitalism, 145; and community, 76–80; and consumer credit, 119; critique of, 113–14; of culture, 2, 67; defined, 242n6; as deauthorization, 96–99; democracy of, 13–14; as depoliticizing, 69; and destabilization of identity, 2–3; and displacement of social relations, 70–76; as dominant, 11; expansion of, 143; and flexible accumulation, 110–24; and identity, 24, 66–67; and identity politics, 23–24; imperatives of, 64–70; as liberating, 68; and lifestyle, 12, 67, 69; and overproduction of culture, 143; and pluralized style, 68; and postmodernity, 64–70; practices, 243n8; privatized, 69,

111, 114, 144; and production, 143, 164; ritualized, 160; as self-reinforcing, 115; and social interaction, 238–39n27, 238–39n28. *See also* Commodification/commodities; Mass media
Cooley, Charles Horton: *Human Nature and the Social Order*, 232n12
Counter-Enlightenment tradition, 82–83, 176
Creation: change to decentering, 109
Crosby, Christina, 29
Cross-over, 251n26
Cubism, 56, 132
Cultural democracy, 13, 163. *See also* Populism
Cultural identities. *See* Ethnic identities
Cultural politics, 13–14; and commodification, 146; vs. cultural commercialism, 162; vs. cultural eclecticism, 150; of marginalized groups, 138; oppositional, 168–69, 246n6; and pluralism, 148, 151; rise of, 158. *See also* Populism
Cultural populism, 107; and tradition, 162–74
Cultural production: elitist models, 140; overproduction, 143; taste in goods, 116, 143
Cultural transformation, 7–16, 81–106; and fragmentation, 11
Culture: boundary erosion, 121; commercial vs. political in, 162; commodification of, 107, 147; consumer, 112; decentering of, 143; destabilization of, 120–21, 143, 150, 153, 227; elitist conception, 145; export of Western, 131–32, 244n19, 244n20;

fragmentation of, 144; and globalization, 129–36; and identity movements, 146–47; as image-constituted discourse, 127; patterns of, 107–8; and pluralism, 144, 151; and power, 36–37; as psychological idiom, 128; recombinant, 128; and tradition, 168; transformation and postmodernization, 139–41, 226. *See also* Popular culture
Cyberpunk, 102–3

Darwin, Charles, 190, 203–4
Debord, Guy, 92, 99, 105–6
Decentering, 109, 143, 176
Deconstruction, 181–82; cultural, 173
Deleuze, Gilles, 28, 182, 185, 187
Democracy: democratization of culture, 13, 163; and identity politics, 19. *See also* Populism
Derrida, Jacques, 5–6, 15; on cultural difference, 28, 124, 182, 185; on deconstruction, 172–73, 181–82; and poststructuralism, 45, 172
Desegregation, 24
Desire: and subject, 182, 185, 187
Destabilization: and cultural consumption, 2–3, 106; and globalization, 13, 25; of identity, 2–3, 6, 7, 8, 13, 18, 25, 26, 46, 51, 73, 106, 107–41, 222–23; and identity politics, 26; and poststructuralism, 6, 34, 227; of subject, 89
Destruction: change to destructuration, 109
Determinism: and constructionism, 48–49; and identity, 48–49, 63; and symbolic interactionism, 233n17

Development patterns, 108–9
Dewey, John, 189, 232n12
Dews, Peter, 184–86, 227, 228–29
Difference/differentiation, 94–96, 143, 241n15; and capitalism, 147, 148–49; and deconstruction, 182, 185; de-differentiation, 246; hyperdifferentiation, 153; and identity, 3–4, 7–8, 29–37, 215–20; and identity politics, 5, 8, 27–30; and modernity, 151; and modernization, 242n2; as novelty, 148; as otherness, 3; and particularity, 13; politics of, 36; and postmodernism, 5; in postmodernity, 147–53; and post-structuralism, 227; social relations of, 8–10, 17–49; and sociology, 233n15; as style, 145; and subordination, 29
DiMaggio, Paul, 117, 118, 120–21
Discrimination, 24, 34
Discursive structure. See Language
Disjunction, 108
Dispersal, 143
Duchamp, Marcel, 97
Dunning, William, 241n14
Durkheim, Emile, 55, 59, 87, 90

Eagleton, Terry, 48, 82, 146, 173–74, 233n16, 247n12
Eclecticism: and democratization, 13; and differentiation, 241n15; of television, 72
Economic transitions, 243–44n14
Economy: globalization in, 130; mass-market, 119
Electronic media. See Mass media
Emergence, philosophy of, 193, 205, 217, 255n18
Engels, Friedrich, 84
Enlightenment: counter-Enlightenment tradition, 82–83, 176; and postmodernism, 2, 5, 6, 28, 43, 82–83, 177; subject in, 180–81
Environment: commercial packaging of, 249–50n19
Epstein, Barbara, 25
Erikson, Erik, 20, 31–32
Ersatz being, 153, 160–61
Essentialisms: and constructionism, 37–43; and identity, 3, 8–9, 27, 34, 37, 38–39, 40; and identity politics, 5; strategic, 234n20
Ethnic identities, 9, 26, 131, 155, 156, 241n13, 251n25
Eurocentrism, 4–5, 138
Evolution, Theory of. See Darwin, Charles
Exclusion: consumption and, 24; and identity politics, 21–22, 24, 28
Existentialism, 55
Exploitation, 22

Featherstone, Mike, 121, 242n2
Feminism, 5, 29
First world: and change, 108
Flexible accumulation: and consumption, 110–24; defined, 111, 114; and strategic marketing, 112–13
Fordism: and capitalism, 111; and flexible accumulation, 120, 134; and marketing down, 119. See also Mass production
Foster, Hal, 167–68, 170
Foucault, Michel, 5–6, 15; on disciplinary practices, 149; on power, 36–37, 42, 182, 183, 187, 190, 199, 230; and poststructuralism, 45, 233n14; on resistance, 227–28
Fragmentation: and commodification of culture, 11, 13; countermovement to, 153–62; difference

as, 147–53; and modernity/
postmodern, 85–91; and pluralization, 13, 143–74; and politicization of culture, 148; postmodern, 153; processes of, 144
Frampton, Kenneth, 170
Frankfurt School, 236n13, 237n21;
on consumption, 113–14, 115;
on manipulated society, 171; and
poststructuralism, 228
Freud, Sigmund, 3, 25, 28, 31–32,
33, 54, 65, 181, 232n11
Fried, Michael, 98
Friedman, Jonathan, 242n2
Fuss, Diana, 216; *Identification
Papers,* 3, 7, 30, 37, 38–39

GATT. *See* General Agreement on
Tariffs and Trade
Gender: identities, 24, 39, 150,
191–92, 195, 198, 231n1; and
marketing, 112–13. *See also*
Women
General Agreement on Tariffs and
Trade (GATT), 133
Gesture, 210–13
Giddens, Anthony, 61–62, 83, 85,
89–90
Gitlin, Todd, 128
Globalization: and capitalism, 108;
and cultural geographies, 129–36,
244n15; defined, 129; and
destabilization, 13, 25; global
village, 82; and homogeneity/
heterogeneity, 132, 135; and
identity politics, 25–26; vs. localization, 134; scale of, 133; technological basis of, 135
Goffman, Erving, 192
Gray, Herman, 246n7
Group-based identities, 4–5, 13–14,
19, 21, 26; of African Americans,
68; and identity politics, 21. *See*

also Marginalization; Reference
group theory
Guattari, Félix, 182, 185, 187

Habermas, Jürgen, 82–83, 94, 150,
176, 180, 184, 186, 188, 207,
210, 228
Habitus, 116
Hall, Stuart, 25–26, 28, 168,
237n17, 250n20
Harvey, David: *Condition of Postmodernity,* 111; on cultural
commodification, 143, 222; on
flexible accumulation, 12, 114;
on modern/postmodern, 83; on
modernism as aesthetic, 84; on
oppositional groups, 151–52;
on representation, 95; on space
and time, 90, 240–41n7; on tradition, 159; on U.S. economy,
130
Hedonism, 68
Hegel, Georg Wilhelm Friedrich, 55,
57, 58, 60, 202–3, 239n28
Heidegger, Martin, 5–6, 65, 82–83
Herd, Denise, 246–47n7
Heterogeneity: of culture, 147;
and democratization, 13;
and modernity/postmodern,
85–91; and postmodernism/
postmodernity, 6, 143, 175;
of television, 72
Hewitt, John P., 58–59, 60, 61, 75
Hipness, 249n18
History: living in, 169; representa-
tion of, 159–60
Honneth, Axel, 67, 68, 174
Horkheimer, Max, 237n21; *Dialectic
of Enlightenment,* 252n5
Humanities: and postmodernism, 6
Hypercommodification, 115
Hyperdifferentiation, 153
Hyperreality, 12, 100

Idealism: and materialism, 46
Identification: externalization of, 3,
    10–11; and identity, 3, 58–59; as
    identity construction, 3; and mass
    media, 10; as originary, 3, 63;
    processes of, 4, 30–34; and social
    relations, 3. *See also* Identity
    formation
Identity: and continuity, 58; decen-
    terings of, 25, 28; defined, 1–2;
    and differentiation, 59; ego-
    centered, 176; and freedom, 63;
    and integration, 58; movements,
    146–47; in postwar Western soci-
    ety, 2, 25; production/marketing
    of, 160–61; as sameness, 3; social
    relations of, 8–10, 14, 17–49, 55,
    57; substantialist notions of, 3–4.
    See also specific types of identi-
    ties, e.g., Collective identities
Identity crises, 3, 9; and politics,
    4–7; as postmodern, 5; as socio-
    historical, 17–18
Identity formation, 2; and capital-
    ism, 56, 58; cultural change and,
    104–5; and difference, 33, 35; of
    individual, 53; as sociohistorical,
    18; transformations in, 10–11,
    51–80. *See also* Identification
Identity politics, 19–30; and com-
    modity society, 23–24; and com-
    munity and chaos, 25; as contra-
    dictory, 20; and counterculture,
    22, 150; vs. cultural eclecticism,
    150; defined, 18, 20; and desta-
    bilization, 26; and difference, 8,
    27–30; and essentialism, 5; and
    fragmentation/pluralization,
    143–74; and legitimation crisis,
    150; and liberalism, 232n7; of
    marginalized groups, 22, 25,
    138; origins and significance of,
    19–27; and pluralism, 27; as post-

modernism, 5, 14; of postwar so-
    ciety, 8, 17, 20, 21, 27, 46; and
    relativism, 28; and sameness, 28;
    and search for truth, 153–62;
    social origins of, 19; and subject,
    184; as tradition, 19
Images: commodification of,
    124–29; as democratizing, 128;
    of history, 159–60, 169
Incorporation: and commodification,
    159
Individualism, 114; authenticity of,
    69; and community, 59–64; and
    identity politics, 19; and interde-
    pendencies, 57; and modernity,
    59–64; social analysis of, 45–49;
    and society, 9, 10, 45–49
Inequality: models of, 116; and so-
    cial movements, 149, 150
Inflation: defined, 243n9; as threat,
    243n10
Interactionism, symbolic, 19,
    232–33n12; and determinism,
    233n17
Interdependency, 108, 228
Internalization, 194
Intersubjectivity, 206–9, 230,
    256n20

James, William, 189, 232n12
Jameson, Fredric, 65, 83, 90–91,
    143, 163–64, 171, 222

Kant, Immanuel, 55, 58, 176, 180
Kellner, Douglas, 145, 236–37n15
Kennedy, Robert, 165
King, Martin Luther, Jr., 165

Labeling theory, 218
Labor: commodification of, 147;
    movement, 149
Lacan, Jacques, 45, 187, 252n4
Laclau, Ernesto: *Making of Political*

Identities, 3, 234n24; on particularism, 44, 246n5
Language: social nature of, 192, 210–15; and object, 189, 191; and subject, 181, 187, 194–202, 228–29
Lash, Scott, 83, 93, 95, 98, 143, 222
Left: and identity, 1–2, 17, 18, 27
Legitimation crisis, 150
Lévi-Strauss, Claude: on desire, 185; structuralist theory of, 128, 181
Liberalism: and pluralism, 149
Lichterman, Paul, 78
Lindlof, Thomas, 77, 78
Lipsitz, George, 234n22, 248n17
Localization: vs. globalization, 134
Lowenthal, Leo, 237n21
Lukács, Georg, 236n14
Lyotard, Jean-François, 5–6, 83, 84, 85, 183, 236n12

McGuigan, Jim, 164
McLuhan, Marshall, 82, 99
Mannheim, Karl, 250–51n23
Manuel, Peter, 244n20
Marcuse, Herbert, 236n14
Marginalization, 234n22; and identity politics, 22, 25; of protest movements, 22; self-definitions of, 36
Marketing: and capitalism, 143; of identity, 160–61; marketing down process, 119; target, 112–13, 122–23, 148
Marx, Karl, 45–46; on absorption of individual, 55; on alienation of labor, 25; on commodity form, 236n14; on constraint, 40; on division of labor, 87; on identification, 32, 33; on modernity, 84, 90; on social relations of class, 32; on social relations of individual, 57; on subject, 54

Mass culture. *See* Culture
Mass media: and commodification of images, 124–29; and community, 76–80; and consumption, 12–13; and culture, 107; and fictionalization of reality, 67, 161; and identification, 10; and identity, 237n16; and politics, 247n9; and representation, 94–95; and simulation, 99–103; as spectacle, 92, 103–6; spectators, 237–38n22. *See also* Television
Mass production: and capitalism, 143; and commodity, 119; and flexible accumulation, 120. *See also* Fordism
Master narratives, 84
Materialism: and idealism, 46
Mead, George Herbert: and Judith Butler, 191–202; *Mind, Self, and Society,* 15, 204, 232n12; *Philosophy of the Present,* 15, 204, social pragmatism, 8, 14–16, 19, 32–33, 35, 57, 59, 179, 188–220, 223, 225–26
Mediascape, 88
Medieval culture, 155–56
Melucci, Alberto, 42, 244n27
Merleau-Ponty, Maurice, 186–87
Meyrowitz, Joshua: *No Sense of Place,* 73
Middle class: and consumption culture, 23–24, 92
Miller, Daniel, 69
Miller, David, 204, 210
Mills, C. Wright, 230
Modern: vs. traditional, 109
Modernism: aesthetic, 56, 58, 84; vs. modernity, 235–36n7; vs. postmodern, 177; theoretical, 58
Modernity: and community, 59–64; counter-Enlightenment tradition within, 82–83, 176; decline of,

12, 163; on difference, 151; disillusionment with, 153–54; and economic development, 84; and identity, 10, 52–59; and individual, 59–64; as interdisciplinary, 53–54; vs. modernism, 235–36n7; and postmodernity, 10–12, 51–80, 81–106; and search for truth, 153
Modernization: and colonialisms, 54; and contrast, 132; defined, 108–9; dynamic, 84; and imperialisms, 54; major processes in, 242n2; and nationalisms, 54; vs. past, 241n8; and patterns of development, 108; and postmodernization, 242n2
Morality: and identities, 157–58
Mowitt, John, 15
Multiculturalism, 20, 29

NAFTA. *See* North American Free Trade Agreement
Narcissism, 10, 68
Natural Born Killers (film), 247n9
Newman, Charles, 243n9
Nietzsche, Friedrich, 5–6, 44–45, 54, 65, 68, 82–83, 184–87, 228
North American Free Trade Agreement (NAFTA), 133
Nostalgia, 153, 156

Objective relativism, 204
Oppression, 5, 21, 29
Order: models of, 149
Otherness: and difference, 3, 41–42; and identity politics, 5; as postmodern, 4, 28; and self-identity, 41–42. *See also* Self-other relationship

Particularism: and universalism, 43–45, 246n5

Peirce, Charles Sanders, 189, 201
Perception: and reality, 240n2
Performativity, 191–93, 199
Personal choice, 114
Perspectivism, 186
Petite bourgeoisie: rise of, 116–17
Philipson, Ilene, 21, 22–23, 24
Philosophy: linguistic turn in, 127
Pleasure: and consumption, 114
Pluralization: and cultural politics, 148; difference as, 147–53; and fragmentation, 13, 143–74; and identity politics, 27, 143–74
Politics: and identity crises, 4–7. *See also* Conservatism; Cultural politics; Democracy; Liberalism
Popular culture: authentic, 250n22; and elite, 107. *See also* Culture
Populism: aesthetic, 164; definition and usage, 163–64; impulses of, 165–66; postmodernity as, 163–67
Positivism, 186
Poster, Mark, 89, 236n11
Postmodern: crisis of the real, 99–103; as cyclical moment, 83; definition and usage, 1, 13, 162; intellectual currency of, 1; vs. modern, 177; and otherness, 4; populism of, 12; and simulation, 99–103; and social change, 1; as sociohistorical, 16; and Western subjectivity, 4
Postmodernism: commercial, 13; and cultural conditions, 2; definition and usage, 1, 2, 243n11; political, 13, 172; as refraction, 175; as response to postmodernity, 2, 222; as sociohistorical, 6; themes in, 143
Postmodernity: commercial, 144–45, 147, 171; as cultural condition, 7; definition and

usage, 2; and identity, 64–70; and identity politics, 14; and modernity, 10–12, 51–80, 81–106; political, 144–45, 172; political ambiguities of, 162–74; postmodernism as response to, 2, 222; in revivalist culture, 14; and sociohistorical developments, 2, 7; themes in, 143; theoretical consequences, 221–30

Postmodernization: and decline of cultural hierarchy, 12; defined, 109–10; and modernization, 242n2

Poststructuralism: critique of, 14–16; and destabilization, 6, 34, 227; and difference, 227; and identity, 33, 34, 45; and language, 191, 193, 197, 228–29; and postmodernism, 5, 6, 7, 8; and representation, 34, 96; vs. social pragmatism, 189–91, 223, 225–26; and subject, 180–88, 200

Power: and consumption, 114; cultural, 36–37, 190; vs. knowledge, 175; and language, 230; and repression, 199; and subject, 182, 183, 187

Pragmatism, social. See Mead, George Herbert; Social pragmatism

Public sphere, 10, 105, 242n24

Race, 24, 231n1; and marketing, 112–13; reemergence of racism, 244n18. See also Civil rights movement

Rationalization: and modernization, 242n2

Rauschenberg, Robert, 97

Ready to Wear (film), 247n9

Realism: and capitalism, 56; hyperreality, 12, 100

Reception theory, 243n13

Reference group theory, 62

Reflexive, 207, 246n3

Relationality, social, 30, 31, 34; and constructionism, 37–43

Religions: evangelical, 154; rightwing, 157–58

Reproduction: and experience, 159–60

Resacralization, 153, 157

Revivalism, 156, 157

Riesman, David, 56, 57

Right: and identity, 2, 17

Roots (television miniseries), 155

Rorty, Richard, 5–6

Rousseau, Jean-Jacques: New Eloise, 85, 86

Russell, Charles, 172

Saussure, Ferdinand de, 25, 28, 128, 182

Scott, Joan, 33 34

Second world: and change, 108

Self. See Subject/subjectivity

Self-consciousness, 250n22

Self-creation, 68, 173

Self-definition, 9, 41–42, 48, 75–76, 80

Self-determination, 48, 63

Self-fulfillment, 68

Self-identity: and mass culture, 11, 70; and otherness, 41–42

Self-other relationship, 31–33, 35

Self-unity, 52, 58

Semiology, 177; semiotic vs. symbolic, 239–40n1

Sense of place, 158

Sherman, Cindy, 97

Sign form: commodity as, 115–16, 126

Simmel, Georg, 57, 85–86, 235n5, 239n28, 240n5

Simulation: and identity, 103–6; and

mass media, 99–103; and post-modern, 99–103

Slave rebellions, 149

Smith, Paul: *Discerning the Subject*, 187

Social class. *See* Class

Social contract: collapse of, 172

Social identities, 9, 10, 15, 19, 26, 32–33, 35, 47, 57, 59, 60, 202–9, 215–20, 223–25

Social movements: fate of, 151–53; and inequality, 149, 150; of 1960s and 1970s, 136–39, 150, 244n27

Social pragmatism, Meadian, 175–220; on difference and identity, 215–20; on language, 210–15; on meaning, 214; vs. poststructuralism, 189–202, 223, 225–26; on self/subject, 191–209, 225

Social roles: change in, 110

Sociality, 205–6, 216–17

Society: aestheticization of, 11–12, 91–96; and community, 60; and individual, 9, 10, 45–49; primitive, 81. *See also* Community

Society for Creative Anachronism, 155

Sociology: and difference, 233n15

Space: and time, 89–91

Status distinction. *See* Class

Stone, Oliver, 247n9

Structuralism: and language, 181, 189; and subject, 180–88

Structure of feeling, 158

Subject/subjectivity, 175–220; and antihumanism, 176; depth models of, 65; as desiring machine, 182; exaggerated, 86; Freudian theory on, 181; historical, 183; and identity, 7, 51, 54, 65–66; intersubjectivity, 206–9; and

language, 181, 187, 191, 194–202; meanings of, 177–79; and postmodern, 7, 176; and power, 182; social pragmatism on, 191–209, 225; and social relations, 10, 19; and structuralism/poststructuralism, 180–88, 200, 226

Subjektphilosophie, 228

Symbolism: and language, 212–14; semiotic, 239–40n1; vs. signs, 256n29

Technology: and capitalism, 124–25; horrors of, 154

Television: aesthetics of, 127; and age, 237n21, 238n25; as commodity form, 70–76; docudrama genre, 161; eclecticism of, 72; escapist character of, 74; heterogeneity of, 72; homogenization in, 73; ideological effects of, 237n19; and image–based identities, 75; and mass consumption, 11, 101–2; multiple images of, 72; nonsocial relational character of, 52, 75, 238n24; vs. real world, 73; realism in, 238n23; as storytelling, 101; use, 247n11

Third world: and change, 108; U.S. manufacturing operations in, 130

Thomas, W. I., 232n12

Time: and space, 89–91

Tomlinson, John, 244n20

Tonnies, Ferdinand, 60

Tradition: in architecture, 170; and cultural populism, 162–74; defined, 168; vs. modernism, 109; search for, 154–62, 169, 247–48n12

Universalism: and particularism, 43–45, 246n5

Values: change in, 110; traditional, 154–55
Voloshinov, V. N., 14, 16, 179, 210–12; *Marxism and the Philosophy of Language,* 210

Walker, John, 251n26
Wallace, George, 165
Warhol, Andy, 132
WASP culture, 155
Weber, Max, 55, 90, 94, 236n13

Wellmer, Albrecht, 186, 229–30
West, Cornel, 41
Wexler, Philip, 153, 157
Wiley, Norbert, 197
Williams, Raymond, 152, 158–59
Willis, Ellen, 22
Willis, Susan, 236n14
Wittgenstein, Ludwig, 210
Women: and inequality, 149, 150
Wundt, Wilhelm, 210

Robert G. Dunn has been teaching in the Department of Sociology and Social Services at California State University, Hayward, since 1969. His main teaching areas have been theory, social inequality, culture, identity, and postmodernity. His publications include articles on media theory, postmodernism, social inequality, and social theory in the journals *Media, Culture, and Society; Theory, Culture and Society; Socialist Review; California Sociologist;* and *The Sociological Quarterly.*